STRATEGIC
MARKET
MANAGEMENT

STRATEGIC MARKET MANAGEMENT

Third Edition

David A. Aaker
University of California, Berkeley

John Wiley & Sons, Inc.
New York ● *Chichester* ● *Brisbane* ● *Toronto* ● *Singapore*

ACQUISITIONS EDITOR / Timothy Kent
PRODUCTION MANAGER / Joe Ford
DESIGNER / Kevin Murphy
PRODUCTION SUPERVISOR / Charlotte Hyland
MANUFACTURING MANAGER / Lorraine Fumoso
COPY EDITING MANAGER / Deborah Herbert
COPY EDITOR / Patricia Brecht
ILLUSTRATION / Ishaya Monokoff

Recognizing the importance of preserving what has been written, it is a policy of John Wiley & Sons, Inc. to have books of enduring value published in the United States printed on acid-free paper, and we exert our best efforts to that end.

Library of Congress Cataloging in Publication Data:
Aaker, David A.
    Strategic market management / David A. Aaker.—3rd ed.
      p.   cm.
    Includes index.
    ISBN 0-471-53253-3 (paper)
    1. Marketing—Management. I. Title.
HF5415.13.A23   1992
658.8—dc20   91-37942
                    CIP

Printed in the United States of America

10 9 8 7 6 5 4 3 2

Printed and bound by Courier Companies, Inc.

PREFACE

The development, evaluation, and implementation of business strategies are the heart of successful management. The key is a management system that will help managers:

- Provide vision for their businesses.
- Monitor and understand dynamic environments.
- Generate strategic options that will be responsive to changes.
- Develop strategies based on competitive advantages that are sustainable.

THREE THRUSTS

The first of the book's three key thrusts is toward a structure and methodology for analyzing the external environment. The belief that strategic planning represents an automatic extension of what was done last year and is dominated by financial objectives and spreadsheets is inadequate and may even inhibit or prevent strategic change and innovation. Rather, strategy development should look outside the business to changes, trends, threats, and opportunities and to create strategies that are responsive. This book describes and illustrates a structured approach to external analysis, an approach that any business manager should find helpful in generating strategic options. This approach is supported by a summary flow diagram, a set of agendas to help start the process, and a set of planning forms.

The second thrust is toward sustainable competitive advantages (SCA). Having SCAs is crucial to long-term success. Without SCAs, a business will eventually be treading water if it survives at all. SCAs need to be based on organizational assets and skills. Thus, this book presents methods and concepts that will help readers to identify and select relevant assets and skills and to develop strategies in branding, advertising, distribution, manufacturing, and finance with which to exploit them.

The third thrust involves the investment decision. The need is to select investment or disinvestment levels for the existing product-market business areas and to chart growth directions. Among the alternative growth directions are market penetration, product expansion, market expansion, diversification, and vertical integration. By using a variety of concepts and methods, such as strategic questions, portfolio models, and scenario analysis, this book helps managers to introduce and to evaluate numerous strategic investment alternatives.

THE THIRD EDITION

A popular feature of this book has been that it is compact—the third edition retains this quality, even though approximately one-third of the book is comprised of revised or new material. Besides the numerous new illustrative examples that appear in the text and in boxed inserts, the most visible changes are the following:

- **A new SCA chapter.** A new chapter on sustainable competitive advantage discusses what an SCA is and related concepts, such as strategic vision, strategic opportunism, strategic drift, synergy, strategic flexibility, strategic intent, and strategic stubbornness.
- **An expanded introduction to external analysis.** The external analysis chapters now include an expanded introduction to the objectives of such an analysis and the basic constructs such as strategic questions.
- **Strategy-development discussion agendas.** Each of the four expanded external analysis chapters now includes a set of questions that can act as a discussion agenda for an external analysis task force, retreat, or assignment. They are supplemented with another agenda, presented in the final chapter, which addresses strategic options as well.
- **Shareholder value analysis.** This analysis approach and its limitations are now discussed in the self-analysis chapter.
- **The value chain.** This concept has been added to competitor analysis.
- **A revised differentiation chapter.** This substantially improved chapter now has material on the role of brand equity in creating advantage.
- **A revised global strategy chapter.** This chapter now includes a discussion of standardization versus customization and strategic alliances.

OBJECTIVES OF THE BOOK

This book has a number of objectives that influence its approach and style. The book attempts to:

- Promote management with a long-term perspective—to avoid creating weaknesses or problems because of the dominance of short-term goals or operational problems. The focus on assets and skills and away from short-term financials provides one approach.

- Provide methods and structures to create entrepreneurial thrusts. In many organizations, the key problem is how to maintain an organizational environment that will support both efficiency and an entrepreneurial spirit.

- Encourage management with a global perspective. Increasingly, effective strategies must consider—and be responsive to—both international competitors and markets.

- Present a proactive approach to strategic market management. The premise is that merely detecting change and reacting to it may be inadequate. Rather, the payoff can come from anticipating or creating change. The need is then for the strategy-development process to be driven by a dynamically oriented analysis of the market and the environment. The inclusion of the term market into the phrase "strategic market management" emphasizes this external orientation and a proactive approach.

- Encourage "on-line" strategy development by gathering information, analyzing the strategic context, precipitating strategic decisions, and developing strategic implementation plans outside the annual planning cycle.

- Draw on multiple disciplines. During the past decade, a variety of disciplines has made relevant and important contributions to strategic market management. An effort was made to draw on and integrate developments in marketing, economics, organizational behavior, finance, accounting, management science, and the field of strategy itself.

- Incorporate several important empirical research streams that have helped strategic market management become more professional and scientific.

- Introduce concepts, models, and methods that are or have promise of being useful to the strategy-development process. Among the concepts covered are strategic groups; exit, entry, and mobility barriers; industry structure; segmentation; unmet needs; positioning; strategic problems; strategic questions; strengths; weaknesses; strategic skills

and assets; mission; brand equity and flexibility; sustainable competitive advantage; synergy; preemptive strategies; key success factors;
usage gap; corporate culture; organizational structure; strategic types;
vision, strategic opportunism, strategic intent, and global strategies.
The models and methods covered include researching lead customers,
scenario analysis, impact analysis, the competitor strength grid, technological forecasting, experience curve, value chain analysis, portfolio
models, customer-based competitor identification, and shareholder
value analysis.

AN OVERVIEW

The book is divided into five parts. The first presents an introduction to
many of the concepts, methods, and strategy alternatives developed in
the book and provides an overview of strategic market management
based on a comprehensive flow model, which serves to structure the
book. The second part, drawing heavily from marketing and economics,
covers external analysis, which includes analyses of the customer, competitors, market, and environment.

The third part, internal analysis, includes performance analysis, the
analysis of strategically important organizational characteristics, and
portfolio analysis. The fourth part discusses and illustrates the SCA
concept, differentiation strategies, strategies based on low cost, focus, or
a preemptive move, alternative growth strategies, competing globally,
and competing in mature and stagnant industries. The final part contains
a chapter on how the organizational components interact with strategy
and a chapter on developing a formal planning system, which includes a
sample set of planning forms.

THE AUDIENCE

This book is suitable for any course in a school of management or business that focuses on the management of strategies. In particular, it is
aimed at:

● The marketing strategy course, which could be titled strategic market
  management, strategic market planning, strategic marketing, or marketing strategy.

● The policy or entrepreneur course, which could be titled strategic
  management, strategic planning, business policy, entrepreneurship,
  or policy administration.

The book is also designed to be used by managers who need to
develop strategies—those who have recently moved into general man-

agement positions or who run a small business and want to improve their strategy development and planning processes. Another intended audience are those general managers, top executives, and planning specialists who would like an overview of recent issues and methods in strategic market management.

ACKNOWLEDGMENTS

This book could not have been created without assistance from my friends and colleagues. This third edition benefited from the helpful comments of the following reviewers: John I. Coppett, University of Houston-Clear Lake; Susan P. Douglas, New York University; Ed Fern, Virginia Tech; Robert A. Swerdlow, Lamar University; Gloria P. Thomas, City University of New York; Peter F. Kaminski, Northern Illinois University; Stephen W. McDaniel, Texas A & M University. In addition, I would like to thank the many students who attended my course in strategic market management and my resourceful colleague and research assistant, Ziv Carmon.

Among the people who read large portions of the first or second edition were Lois Brown, Dan Dias, Ken Hardy, Reed Moyer, Carol Penskar, Alan Shocker, Robert Shoemaker, Norm Smothers, John Wagle, Bart Weitz and, again, MBA students in my strategy course and executive programs. In addition, I imposed on a host of specialists to help with individual segments of all editions, including Pete Bucklin, Greg Carpenter, George Day, David Downes, John Freeman, Carl Jacobson, Kevin Keller, Gene Laczniak, Don Leemon, Baruch Lev, Dick Holton, Ray Miles, Charles O'Reilly, Adrian Ryans, Jeff Skelton, David Teese and Oliver Williamson. I am substantially indebted to all of these people.

I am pleased to be associated with Wiley, a "class" organization, and two superb editors, Rich Esposito and John Woods. It is reassuring to be supported by competent professionals. I also thank Serena Joe for her competence, support, and good humor.

This book is dedicated to the women in my life: my mother, Ida, my wife, Kay, and my children, Jennifer, Jan, and Jolyn. They all have contributed understanding, support and, sometimes, patience.

September 1991 **David A. Aaker**

CONTENTS

10
DIFFERENTIATION STRATEGIES /201

11
OBTAINING AN SCA—LOW COST, FOCUS, AND THE PREEMPTIVE MOVE /223

12
GROWTH STRATEGIES: PENETRATION, PRODUCT-MARKET EXPANSION, AND VERTICAL INTEGRATION /243

13
DIVERSIFICATION /267

PART ONE

INTRODUCTION AND OVERVIEW

1

BUSINESS STRATEGY: THE CONCEPT AND TRENDS IN ITS MANAGEMENT

Plans are nothing, planning is everything.

Dwight D. Eisenhower

Where absolute superiority is not attainable, you must produce a relative one at the decisive point by making skillful use of what you have.

Karl von Clausewitz, On War, 1832

In the period from 1962 to 1972, the W. T. Grant Company nearly doubled its size in square footage and increased its profits from $9 million to $37 million. Four years later, the company went into bankruptcy and its assets were liquidated.[1] In the 1930s, Sears and Montgomery Ward were approximately equal in sales, profits, capability, and potential. Two decades later, Sears was roughly three times bigger than Ward. In 1991, Wal-Mart, a discount store upstart that began as a discounter to small towns in the rural South, surpassed Sears and Kmart to become the largest U.S. retailer. Clearly, some strategy choices caused these outcomes. Although these examples are dramatic, nearly every organization is affected by strategic decisions or, sometimes, nondecisions.

This book is concerned with helping managers identify, select, and implement strategies. The intent is to provide decision makers with concepts, methods, and procedures by which they can improve the quality of their strategic decision making. The chapter begins by defining a business strategy and discussing its components, particularly the concepts of sustainable competitive advantage (SCA) and strategic business unit. The process of developing and implementing strategies, strategic market management, is then discussed, first from a historical perspective, and then in terms of its thrusts and trends. The final section considers why it is useful to attempt to manage strategically.

This and the following chapter have several functions to perform. First, they identify the approach toward strategy and its management that is taken in this book. Second, they introduce and position most of the concepts and methods that will be covered in the book. Third, they position and structure the other parts and chapters. Fourth, they provide a general overview and summary. Thus, the reader can productively reread these two chapters as a way to review.

WHAT IS A BUSINESS STRATEGY?

A business strategy, sometimes termed a competitive strategy or simply strategy, is here defined by six elements or dimensions. The first four apply to any business, even if it exists by itself. The remaining two are introduced when the business exists in an organization with other business units. A business strategy specification includes a determination of:

1. **The product market in which the business is to compete.** The scope of a business is defined by the products it offers and chooses not to offer, by the markets it seeks to serve and not serve, by the competitors with whom it chooses to compete and to avoid, and by its level of vertical integration.

2. **Level of investment.** Although there are obvious variations and refinements, it is useful to conceptualize the alternatives in terms of:

- Invest to grow (or enter the product market)
- Invest only to maintain the existing position
- Milk the business by minimizing investment
- Recover as much of the assets as possible by liquidating or divesting the business

3. **The functional area strategies needed to compete in the selected product market.** The specific way to compete will usually be characterized by one or more functional area strategies such as a:

- Product line strategy
- Positioning strategy
- Pricing strategy
- Distribution strategy
- Manufacturing strategy
- Logistical strategy

4. **The strategic assets or skills that underlie the strategy providing the sustainable competitive advantage (SCA).** A strategic skill or, simply, skill, is something a business unit does exceptionally well, such as manufacturing or promotion, which has strategic importance to that business. A strategic asset or, simply, asset, is a resource, such as a brand name or installed customer base, that is strong relative to competitors. Strategy formulation must consider the cost and feasibility of generating or maintaining assets or skills that will provide the basis for a sustainable competitive advantage.

Multiple Businesses.   Except for the rare focused enterprise, most modern business units share an organizational framework with other business units. At the highest level, it may mean a group of diverse divisions—each involving many businesses. At the lowest level, it could mean a single product being delivered to a sharply segmented set of markets, or a set of product variations being delivered to a common market. In either situation, the concept of a business strategy for a group of business units is introduced and two additional components of strategy are needed:

5. **The allocation of resources over the business units.** Financial resources, generated either internally or externally, plus nonfinancial resources such as plant, equipment, and people all need to be allocated. Even for a small organization, the allocation decision can become a key strategic decision.

6. **The development of synergistic effects across the businesses—the creation of value by having business units that support and comple-

FIGURE 1.1   A Business Strategy

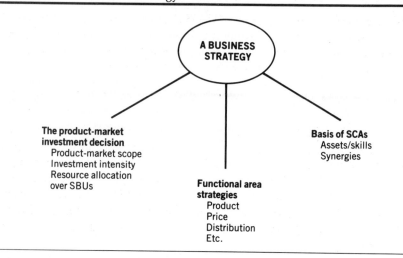

ment each other. It is only logical that multiple business organizations that can achieve synergistic effects will have an advantage over those that ignore or fail to achieve synergy.

All six elements of the strategy concept can be capsuled into three core elements as shown in Figure 1.1.

- The product-market investment decision that encompasses the product-market scope of the business strategy, its investment intensity, and the resource allocation over multiple businesses.
- The functional area strategies—what you do.
- The basis of a sustainable competitive advantage to compete in those markets; this core concept encompasses assets, skills, and/or synergies matched with functional area strategies.

STRATEGIC THRUSTS—THE SEARCH FOR SCARS

In any context, there is an infinite variety of potential strategies and many routes to achieving SCAs. It is useful to identify types of strategies that have similar strategic thrusts. Two stand out as particularly encompassing—differentiation and low cost. Harvard's Michael Porter, an economist and influential strategy researcher, has suggested that low cost and differentiation represent the two basic strategies available to firms—that all successful strategies will involve one or both of these thrusts.[2]

Differentiation Versus Low-Cost Strategies

A differentiation strategy is one in which the product offering is differentiated from the competition by providing value to the customer, perhaps by enhancing the performance, the quality, the prestige, the features, the service backup, the reliability, or the convenience of the product. It is often but not always associated with higher price, because the result of a differentiation strategy is usually to make price less critical to the customer.

In contrast, a low-cost strategy is one based on achieving a sustainable cost advantage in some important element of the product or service. The overall cost leadership position can be achieved through a high market share or through other advantages such as favorable access to raw materials or state-of-the-art manufacturing equipment. A low-cost strategy need not always be associated with low prices, because lower cost could lead to enhanced profits or increased advertising or promotion instead of reduced prices.

An in-depth study of 64 companies from eight major, mature, domestic industries all facing relatively hostile environments shows the importance of the differentiation and low-cost thrusts.[3] Although each industry had below-average profitability and growth, each contained several very profitable firms. The two (nondiversified) top performing companies in each of the eight industries had pursued either a differentiation strategy involving a high product/service/quality position or a low-cost strategy (two—Caterpillar and Philip Morris—employed both).

Focus, Preemptive Moves, and Synergy

Although most strategies will involve either or both differentiation or low cost, many other strategic thrusts or strategy types could also be identified such as being innovative, thinking globally, having an entrepreneurial style, or exploiting information technology. We will consider three that are frequently strategically important and are not easily covered by the umbrella of differentiation and low cost—namely, focus, preemptive moves, and synergy.

The Focus Strategy.   A focus strategy, which involves focusing the business on either a relatively small buyer group or a restricted portion of the product line, is also explicitly discussed by Michael Porter. Such a focus can be central to the creation of an SCA and therefore is the driving force even though differentiation or low cost will also be associated with the strategy. Thus, a retailer could focus on smaller women with hard-to-fit sizes or on a relatively narrow line such as fashion accessories.

A Preemptive Move.   A preemptive strategic move is the first implementation of a strategy into a business area that, because it was first, generates an asset or skill forming the basis of an SCA. For a first strategy implementation to create "first mover advantages," competitors must be inhibited or prevented from duplicating or countering it. Coca-Cola achieved an SCA in Japan by securing the best distributors in each area. Pepsi and other competitors were at a substantial disadvantage because they had been preempted.

Synergy.   Synergy occurs when a business has an advantage because it is linked to another business within the same firm or division. The two businesses, for example, may be able to share a sales force, office, or warehouse, and thus reduce costs or investment. They may be able jointly to offer a customer a combination of products such as tennis shoes and tennis apparel that are coordinated. The combination thus creates a value that would not exist if the two businesses were distinct.

Synergy is introduced in Chapter 9 where the concept of a sustainable competitive advantage is discussed in more depth. Differentiation strategies are discussed in Chapter 10. In Chapter 11, low cost, focus, and preemptive moves are detailed.

A STRATEGIC BUSINESS UNIT

A strategic business unit or SBU is any organizational unit that has (or should have) a defined business strategy and has a manager with sales and profit responsibility. The concept was formulated by firms such as General Electric as a way to help develop an entrepreneurial thrust in a diversified firm by creating business units that were more autonomous and by making strategy development more decentralized.

Often a selection of the most appropriate level of aggregation for an SBU will involve some judgment. For example, an SBU could be formed at the brand level—for instance, Tide, Drift, Ivory, and the like—or at the category level—for example, laundry products. In fact, there is a sharp movement toward managing and developing strategies at a broader level than brands, that is, at the level of product categories or brand families. The driving force is the power of the retailer supported by a wealth of detailed information. To deal with that force, manufacturers need to manage with a perspective that involves more scope. Retailers want to think in terms of the Minute Maid line and not just in terms of Minute Maid frozen orange juice.

When strategies and competitors have a high degree of commonality across businesses, it makes sense to combine those businesses into a single SBU. When they differ in meaningful ways, however, it will probably be more useful to use separate SBUs. Another consideration is the size of the business. If two businesses are extremely large in terms of sales and organizational needs, then it might be best to have two SBUs even if the involved business strategies are similar. Conversely, if the involved businesses are very small, then it might not be practical organizationally to structure each as an SBU.

Ideally, an SBU should have its own dedicated operations, including manufacturing, sales, distribution, engineering, and accounting. In practice, however, efficiency dictates that SBUs share some of these facilities and operations.

Often the conceptualization of a strategy is best done at an SBU level—the Sony Walkman, for example. However, a given SBU may well contain different product lines and be involved in very different markets. It will often be useful to develop strategies or at least strategy refinements for subunits with an SBU based on the specific product marketings involved—for instance, the European market for the Sony Walkman. In addition, strategies are also useful at the level of divisions or firms (Sony) that contain a host of SBUs.

STRATEGIC MARKET MANAGEMENT: A HISTORICAL PERSPECTIVE

The process of developing and implementing strategies has been described over the years by numerous terms, including budgeting and control, long-range planning, strategic planning, strategic management, and strategic market management. All these terms have similar meanings and are often used interchangeably. However, when they are placed in a historical perspective, some useful distinctions emerge.[4]

Budgeting/Control

The development of budgeting/control management systems can be roughly associated with the early 1900s. The emphasis is on controlling deviations and managing complexity. An annual budget is set for the various departments, and deviations from that budget are carefully scrutinized to find explanations and see whether remedial action is appropriate. The basic assumption is that the past will repeat itself. Figure 1.2 summarizes this approach.

Long-Range Planning

The second management system shown in Figure 1.2 is long-range planning, the development of which Igor Ansoff, long a leading strategy

FIGURE 1.2   Evolution of Management Systems

	Budgeting/ Control	Long-Range Planning	Strategic Planning	Strategic Market Management
Management emphasis	Control deviations and manage complexity	Anticipate growth and manage complexity	Change strategic thrust and capability	Cope with strategic surprises and fast-developing threats/ opportunities
Assumptions	The past repeats	Past trends will continue	New trends and discontinuities are predictable	Planning cycles inadequate to deal with rapid changes
The process	◄———————— Periodic ————————►			Real time
Time period associated with system	From 1900s	From 1950s	From 1960s	From mid–1970s

theorist, has associated with the 1950s. Its focus is on anticipating growth and managing complexity. The basic assumption is that past trends will continue into the future. The planning process typically involves projecting sales, costs, technology, and so on, into the future using data and experience from the past. The planning task is then to develop human resources and facilities to accommodate the anticipated growth or contraction. The time frame is not necessarily as limited as in the budgeting/control system and can anticipate two, five, or ten years, depending on the context.

Included under long-range planning is gap analysis. A gap occurs if the projected sales and profits do not meet the organizational goals. Changes in operations such as increasing the sales forces and/or plant capacity are then considered to remove the gap.

Strategic Planning

Strategic planning, the emergence of which Ansoff associates with the 1960s, is concerned with changing strategic thrusts and capabilities. The basic assumption is that past extrapolations are inadequate. There will be discontinuities from past projections and new trends, both of which will require strategic adjustments. An adjustment in strategic thrust or direction could involve moving into a new product market. The enhancement of research and development competence could represent an adjustment in strategic capability.

Strategic planning, also termed strategic market planning, focuses on the market environment facing the firm. Thus, the emphasis is not only on projections but also on an in-depth understanding of the market environment, particularly the competitors and customers. The hope is not only to gain insight into current conditions, but also to be able to anticipate changes that have strategic implications.

One characteristic that strategic planning shares with budgeting/ control and long-range planning management systems is that it is largely based on a periodic planning system, usually an annual system. Typically, an organization will develop a strategic plan in the spring and summer and then, during the fall, will use that plan as a base for developing the annual operating plans and budgets for the next year. The periodic planning cycle does provide a time in which managers must address strategic questions. Without such a device, artificial though it may be, even managers who realize the importance of strategic thinking might find their time absorbed by day-to-day operations and crises.

The difficulty with the periodic planning process is that the need for strategic analysis and decision making does not always occur on an annual basis. The environment and technology may change so rapidly and environmental shocks occur so unexpectedly that being tied to a planning cycle can be disadvantageous or even disastrous. If the planning process is allowed to suppress strategic response outside the planning cycle, performance can suffer, particularly in dynamic industries.

A study of managers making strategy decisions in a simulated business focused on the impact of planning. The study found that when the environment was made more turbulent (by reduced product life cycles and increasing product change), those businesses that were asked to plan formally (by projecting performance using planning forms) had performances inferior to those who did not plan.[5] Planning enhanced those in a less turbulent environment, however.

Strategic Market Management

Strategic market management or, simply, strategic management is motivated by the assumption that the planning cycle is inadequate to deal with the rapid rate of change that can occur in the environment facing the firm. To cope with strategic surprises and fast-developing threats and opportunities, strategic decisions need to be precipitated and made outside the planning cycle.

Recognition of the demands of a rapidly changing environment has stimulated the development or increased use of methods, systems, and options that are responsive. In particular, it suggests a need for continuous, real-time information systems rather than, or in addition to, periodic analysis. More sensitive environmental scanning, the identification and continuous monitoring of information-need areas, efforts to develop strategic flexibility, and the enhancement of the entrepreneurial thrust of the organization may be helpful. An information-need area is an area of uncertainty that will affect strategy such as an emerging consumer-interest area. Strategic flexibility involves strategic options that allow quick and appropriate responses to sudden changes in the environment.

Another characteristic of strategic market management is that it doesn't necessarily accept the environment as given, with the strategic role confined to adaptation and reaction. Rather, the possibility exists for strategy to be proactive with the possibility of affecting environmental change. Thus, governmental policies, customer needs, and technological developments can be influenced—and perhaps even controlled—by creative, active strategies.

The evolving systems shown in Figure 1.2 build on, rather than replace, earlier systems. In that spirit, strategic market management actually includes all four management systems: the budgeting/control system, the projection-based approach of long-range planning, the elements of strategic planning, and the refinements needed to adapt strategic decision making to real time. In strategic market management, there would normally be a periodic planning process supplemented by techniques to allow the organization to be strategically responsive outside the planning process.

The inclusion of the term "market" into the phrase "strategic management" serves to emphasize that strategy development needs to be driven by the market and its environment rather than being internally oriented. It also serves to underline the fact that the process should be proactive rather than reactive, and the task should be to try to influence the environment in addition to simply responding to it.

STRATEGIC MARKET MANAGEMENT: CHARACTERISTICS AND TRENDS

Several distinct characteristics or trends have emerged in the strategy field, some of which have already been mentioned. A review of these thrusts or trends will provide additional insight into strategic market management and into the perspective and orientation of the balance of the book.

External, Market Orientation

As already noted, organizations need to be oriented externally--toward the customer, competitors, the market, and the market's environment. In sharp contrast to the projection-based, internally oriented long-range planning systems, the goal is to develop market-driven strategies that are sensitive to the customer.

Proactive Strategies

A proactive strategy attempts to influence events in the environment rather than simply reacting to environmental forces as they occur. A proactive strategy is important for at least two reasons. First, one way to be sure of detecting and quickly reacting to major environmental changes is to participate in their creation. Second, such environmental changes can be so significant that it is important to influence them when possible. For example, an insurance firm may need to be involved in tort reform legislation because the legal environment is vitally important to its strategy.

Concern About Input to the Information System

An external orientation puts demands on the supporting information system. The determination of what information is needed, how it can be obtained efficiently and effectively, and how it should best be analyzed, processed, and stored can be the key to making the strategy development process effective.

On-Line Analysis and Decision Making

There is also a trend (previously mentioned) away from using only the annual planning cycle and toward more of a continuous, "on-line" system of information gathering, analysis, and strategic decision making. The design of such systems is demanding and will require new methods and concepts. The system must be structured enough to provide assistance in an inherently complex decision context, sensitive enough to detect the need to precipitate a strategic choice, and flexible enough to be applied in a variety of situations.

Entrepreneurial Thrust

The importance of developing and maintaining an entrepreneurial thrust is increasingly being recognized. The need is for the development of organizational forms and strategic market management support systems that allow the firm to be responsive to opportunities. The entrepreneurial skill is particularly important to the large diversified firm and to the firm involved in extremely fast-moving industries. Consider the high-tech firms or "hit industries" like video games, records, or movies. The strategy in such contexts must include providing an environment where entrepreneurs can function and flourish.

Considering Multiple Strategies

A tendency often exists to focus on a single strategy and its financial projections rather than on creatively attempting to develop the most effective strategy. The need is to focus on strategy development rather than on financial projections and to consider multiple strategies.

Implementation

There is a growing recognition that implementation of strategy is critical. There needs to be concern about whether the strategy fits the organization—its structure, systems, people, and culture—or whether the organization can be changed to make the strategy fit. Links also need to be made to the functional area policies and the operating plan. Chapter 16 is devoted to implementation issues.

Understanding Growth Markets and Market-Share Strategies

The nominal wisdom that it is always healthy to seek growth markets and to obtain a large market share has been exposed to close scrutiny in the past decade. As a result, a much more balanced and sophisticated understanding is emerging. Under some conditions, a business entering a growth market risks being caught in a damaging shakeout phase. Similarly, there are risks in attempting to gain a dominant market share, and situations under which the maintenance of a low market share is highly profitable.

International Realities

Increasingly, the international dimension is affecting strategy. Global markets are extremely relevant to many businesses from Boeing to McDonald's. Conversely, it is a rare firm that is not affected by competitors either based in or with operations in other countries. The international element represents both direct and indirect opportunities and threats. The financial difficulty of a major country or a worldwide shortage of some raw material may have a dramatic impact on an organization's strategy. Chapter 15 focuses on global strategies.

Longer Time Horizon

A major strategic problem for many businesses is to develop effective objectives and strategies with long-term horizons. Many observers have suggested that the visible success of Japanese firms is due, in part, to their ability to operate strategically with long time horizons. Furthermore, some of the competitive problems of industries, such as automobiles, consumer electronics, and steel, have been attributed by management theorists to a short-term orientation. Managing with respect to a longer time horizon is more difficult and places heavier demands on the strategic decision-making process. As a result, there is an increased need for better constructs and methods that reflect a long-term perspective.

Empirical Research

Historically, the field of strategy has been dominated by conceptual contributions based on personal experience and insights. The writings of Alfred Sloan, the architect of General Motors, and Peter Drucker, the author of the classic book, *The Practice of Management*, illustrate.[6] More recently, an empirical research tradition has begun to materialize. The qualitative case-study approach, associated with Harvard researchers, has provided useful hypotheses and insights. In addition, a host of quantitative research streams exists in which the performance and characteristics of samples of business units are compared and studied through time. These research streams can now be found in nearly all of the basic disciplines and in the field of strategy itself. They are an important indication that the strategy field is finally reaching a maturity in which theories can be, and are being, subjected to scientific test.

Methodological Developments

Another sign that the strategy area is maturing is the fact that a set of methods and concepts now exists or is emerging that has the potential to provide structured, analytical approaches to strategy development. Examples include portfolio models, experience curves, scenario analysis, market structure analysis, and technological forecasting.

Interdisciplinary Developments

One purpose of this book is to draw on and integrate a variety of disciplines now making important conceptual and methodological contributions to strategic market management. Among these disciplines, which have been remarkably isolated from strategic market management and each other, are the following:

Marketing. Marketing is by its very nature concerned with the interaction between the firm and the marketplace. During the last decade, strategic decisions have received increasing attention. Tools and concepts such as product positioning, the product life cycle, brand equity, brand loyalty, and customer-need analysis all have the potential to improve strategic decision making.

Organizational Behavior. Organizational behavior theorists have built on the classic works of the early 1960s on strategy and organizational structure. They have also considered the link between strategy and other elements of the organization such as systems and the management of people. Of particular relevance is the concept of corporate culture and its impact on strategy.

Finance and Accounting. One major contribution of the finance and accounting disciplines to strategy is shareholder value analysis (covered in Chapter 7)—the concept that strategic valuations should be concerned with the impact on the value of the firm. Another is a rich research tradition relating to diversification efforts, acquisitions, and mergers. Finance has, of course, also contributed to an understanding of the concept of risk and its management.

Economics. The economics subarea of industrial organizational theory has been applied to strategy using concepts and methods such as industry structure, exit barriers, entry barriers, and strategic groups. Furthermore, the concept of transaction costs has been developed and applied to the issue of vertical integration. Finally, economists have contributed to the experience curve concept, which has considerable strategic implications.

Strategy. The discipline of strategy is not only increasingly overlapping with other disciplines, but also is itself maturing. One sign of this maturity is the quantitative research streams that are emerging. Another is the maturity of some of the tools and techniques. Still another is the fact that the premier strategy journal, *Strategic Management Journal*, has given exposure for over a decade to the top academic efforts providing theoretical and empirical insights into strategy.

WHY STRATEGIC MARKET MANAGEMENT?

Strategic market management is often frustrating, in part, because the environment is so difficult to understand and predict. It requires communication and choices within the organization that can create strains and internal resistance. The most valuable organization resource, management time, is absorbed. The alternative of simply waiting for and reacting to the exceptional opportunities often seems efficient and adequate.

Despite these costs and problems, however, strategic market management offers many compelling benefits:

- **It precipitates the consideration of strategic choices.** What is happening externally that is creating opportunities and threats to which a timely and appropriate reaction should be generated? What strategic issues face the firm? What strategic options should be considered? The alternative to strategic market management usually is to drift strategically, becoming absorbed in day-to-day problems. Nothing is more tragic than an organization that fails because a strategic decision was not even addressed until it was too late.

- **It forces a long-range view.** The pressures to manage with a short-term focus are strong and frequently lead to strategic errors.

- **It raises the resource allocation decision.** Allowing resource allocation to be dictated by the accounting system, political strengths, or inertia (the same as last year) is only too easy. One result is that the small but promising business with "no problems" or the unborn business may suffer from a lack of resources, whereas the larger business areas with "problems" absorb an excessive amount.

- **It provides methods to help strategic analysis and decision making.** Concepts, models, and methodologies are now available to help a business collect and analyze information and address difficult strategic decisions.

- **It provides a strategic management and control system.** The focus on assets and skills and the development of objectives and programs associated with strategic thrusts will provide the basis for managing a business strategically.

- **It provides a communication and coordination system both horizontally and vertically.** Strategic market management provides a way to communicate problems and proposed strategies within an organization. In particular, the vocabulary adds precision.

- **It helps a business cope with change.** If a particular environment is extremely stable and the sales patterns are satisfactory, there may be little need for meaningful strategic change—either in direction or intensity. In that case, strategic market management is much less crucial. However, most organizations now exist in rapidly changing and increasingly unpredictable environments and therefore need approaches for coping strategically.

George Yip studied strategy development in 13 firms and concluded that strategic market management approaches have particular value for businesses that:[7]

● Need multifunctional strategies; one marketing-oriented firm used it to provide a strategic role for functions other than marketing.

● Need to achieve synergy among multiple markets.

● Need to coordinate the strategies of multiple brands.

● Are involved in complex markets where multiple or layered channels, regional variation, or multiple elements of the marketing mix are involved.

SUMMARY

A business strategy includes the determination of the product-market scope, the intensity of the business investment, the functional area strategy, and the assets or skills to be employed. When multiple businesses are involved, the strategy includes the allocation of resources over the business units and the creation of synergy.

Strategies that have similar strategic thrusts share characteristics that drive the strategy and are linked to the SCAs. Nearly all strategies have either a differentiation or low-cost strategic thrust or both. Other strategic thrusts that are isolated in this book are focus, preemptive moves, and synergy.

A budgeting/control management system focuses on an annual budget and deviations from it. Long-range planning relies on projections of past trends. Strategic planning involves the prediction and detection of discontinuities from past projections. Strategic market management breaks away from the annual planning cycle, recognizing the need for on-line decision making in a rapidly changing environment. It also includes the concept of proactive as opposed to reactive strategy development.

Among the thrusts in strategic market management is to develop strategies that are externally oriented, proactive, timely, entrepreneurial, global, implementable, and appropriate for a long time horizon. Strategic market management provides an approach to raising and addressing strategic choices and to managing complex organizations in a context of changing external pressures and threats.

FOOTNOTES

[1] These examples are discussed in detail in Robert F. Hartley, *Marketing Mistakes*, 4th ed., Columbus, Ohio: Grid Publishing, 1989.

[2] Michael E. Porter, *Competitive Strategy*, New York: The Free Press, 1980, Chapter 2.

[3] William K. Hall, "Survival Strategies in a Hostile Environment," *Harvard Business Review*, September–October 1980, pp. 75–85.

[4] This section and Figure 1.2 draw on the work of H. Igor Ansoff. Typical examples are his articles: "Strategic Issue Management," *Strategic Management Journal*, April–June 1980, pp. 131–148, and "The State of Practice in Planning Systems," *Sloan Management Review*, Winter 1977, pp. 61–69.

[5] Rashi Glazier and Alan Weiss, "Planning in a Turbulent Environment," Working Paper, University of California at Berkeley, April 1991.

[6] Alfred P. Sloan, Jr., *My Years with General Motors*, New York: Doubleday, 1963, and Peter F. Drucker, *The Practice of Management*, New York: Harper & Row, 1954.

[7] George S. Yip, "Who Needs Strategic Planning?", *The Journal of Business Strategy* 6, Fall 1985, pp. 30–41.

2

STRATEGIC MARKET MANAGEMENT: AN OVERVIEW

Chance favors the prepared mind.

Louis Pasteur

Far better an approximate answer to the right question, which is often vague, than an exact answer to the wrong question, which can always be made precise.

John Tukey, Statistician

If you don't know where you're going, you might end up somewhere else.

Casey Stengel

Strategic market management is a system designed to help management both precipitate and make strategic decisions, as well as create strategic visions. A strategic decision involves the creation, change, or retention of a strategy. In contrast to a tactical decision, a strategic decision is usually costly in terms of the resources and time required to reverse or change it. Sometimes a wrong decision is so costly to alter that it can threaten the very existence of an organization. Normally, a strategic decision will have a time frame greater than one year; sometimes decades are involved.

A strategic vision is a vision of a future strategy or sets of strategies. The realization of an optimal strategy for a firm may involve a delay because the firm is not ready or the emerging conditions are not yet in place. A vision will provide direction and purpose for interim strategies and strategic activities.

An important role of the system is to precipitate as well as make strategic decisions. In fact, the identification of the need for a strategic response is frequently a critical step. Strategic blunders have often occurred because a strategic decision process was never activated, not because an incorrect decision was made. Furthermore, the role of strategic market management is not limited to selecting among decision alternatives, but includes the identification of alternatives as well. Much of the analysis will therefore be concerned with identifying alternatives.

Figure 2.1 shows an overview of the external analysis and self-analysis that provide the input to strategy development and the set of strategic decisions that is the ultimate output. It provides a structure for strategic market management and for this book. A brief overview of its three principal elements and an introduction to the key concepts will be provided in this chapter.

EXTERNAL ANALYSIS

External analysis involves an examination of the relevant elements external to an organization. The analysis should be purposeful, focusing on the identification of threats, opportunities, strategic questions, and strategic choices. The danger of being excessively descriptive is always present. Because there is literally no limit to the scope of a descriptive study, the result can be a considerable expenditure of resources with little impact on strategy.

One output of external analysis is an identification and understanding of opportunities and threats facing the organization, both present and potential. An opportunity is a trend or event that could lead to a significant upward change in sales and profit patterns—given the appropriate strategic response. A threat is a trend or event that will result, in

FIGURE 2.1   Overview of Strategic Market Management

EXTERNAL ANALYSIS

- Customer analysis:
  Segments, motivations, unmet needs.
- Competitive analysis:
  Identity, strategic groups, performance, objectives, strategies, culture, cost structure, strengths, weaknesses.
- Market analysis:
  Size, projected growth, profitability, entry barriers, cost structure, distribution system, trends, key success factors.

- Environmental analysis:
  Technological, governmental, economic, cultural, demographic, scenarios, information need areas.

  ↓

Opportunities, threats, and strategic questions

SELF-ANALYSIS

- Performance analysis:
  Profitability, sales, shareholder value, value analysis, customer satisfaction, product quality, brand associations, relative cost, new products, employee attitude and performance, product portfolio analysis.

- Determinants of strategic options:
  Past and current strategies, strategic problems, organizational capabilities and constraints, financial resources and constraints, strengths, weaknesses.

  ↓

- **Strategic strengths, weaknesses, problems, constraints, and questions**

STRATEGY IDENTIFICATION AND SELECTION

- Review mission alternatives.
- Identify strategic alternatives.
  - Product market investment strategies.
  - Functional area strategies.
  - Assets, skills, and synergies.
- Select strategy.
- Implementation—the operating plan.
- Review of strategies.

the absence of a strategic response, in a significant downward departure from current sales and profit patterns. For example, consumers' concern with calories and cholesterol represents a threat to the dairy industry.

Another output is the identification of strategic questions or issues. A strategic question is an area of uncertainty about a business or its environment that has the potential to affect strategy. Its importance and urgency will depend on whether an in-depth analysis leading to a strategy decision will be needed or whether it should be monitored over time.

The frame of reference for an external analysis is usually a defined SBU. However, it is usually useful to conduct the external analysis at several levels. External analyses of submarkets provide insight sometimes critical to developing strategy. Thus, an external analysis of the mature beer industry might contain analyses of the import and nonalcohol submarkets, which are growing and have important differences. It is also possible to conduct external analyses for groups of SBUs, such as divisions, when there is sufficient commonality with respect to such characteristics as the segments served, the competitors faced, and environmental trends.

External analysis is divided into four sections or components: customer analysis, competitive analysis, industry analysis, and environmental analysis.

Customer Analysis

Customer analysis, the first step of external analysis and the subject of Chapter 3, involves identifying the organization's customer segments and each segment's motivations and unmet needs. Segment identification defines alternative product markets and thus structures the strategic investment decision (what investment levels to assign to each market). The analysis of customer motivations provides information needed to decide whether the firm can and should attempt to gain or maintain a sustainable competitive advantage. An unmet need, a need not currently being met by existing products, can be strategically important because it may represent a way that entrenched competitors can be dislodged.

For example, consider the luxury hotel industry. One segmentation scheme would distinguish between tourists, convention attendees, and business travelers. Each has a very different set of motivations. The tourist is more concerned with price, the conventioneer with convention facilities, and the business traveler with comfort. An unmet need for the tourist could be obtaining tickets for events such as plays or concerts.

The frozen-novelty industry includes individually packaged, single servings of a frozen snack or desserts such as chocolate-covered ice cream, Popsicles, juice bars, pudding bars, and ice cream-cookie combinations. One way to segment this industry is to distinguish between retail purchases and the food service segment; food service includes schools, hospitals, and recreational facilities that could be attracted by the ease of storing and serving the product. The market might also be segmented by motivation. Groups can be identified according to whether they are primarily concerned with calories, fat, taste, refreshment, price, or convenience. An unmet need for a nutritious snack in this industry in the early 1980s provided an opening for the frozen fruit bar.

Competitive Analysis

Competitive analysis, covered in Chapter 4, starts with the identification of competitors, current and potential. Some competitors will compete more intensely than others. Jell-O's pudding pop competes more vigorously with yogurt bars and juice bars than with ice cream, frozen cakes, cake mixes, and packaged cookies. Although the intense competitors should be examined in more detail, all competitors are usually relevant to strategy development.

Especially when there are many competitors, it is helpful to group them into strategic groups, groups that have similar characteristics (e.g., size and resources), strengths (e.g., brand name, distribution), and strategies (e.g., high quality). The luxury hotel industry might be grouped into those hotels that offer businessperson-oriented amenities and those that are ultraplush and prestigious. These two groups might be further divided into those that are members of chains with reservation systems and those that are autonomous. Regional dairies with strong ice cream brands are one strategic group in the frozen-novelty industry, a group that is declining in the face of competitors with national advertising and promotion support.

To develop a strategy, it is important to understand the competitor's:

- **Performance.** A healthy competitor is more formidable.
- **Objectives.** Is this competitor committed to the business and aiming for high growth?
- **Current and past strategy.** What are the implications for future strategic moves?
- **Culture.** What is important to the organization—cost control, entrepreneurship, or the customer?
- **Strengths and weaknesses.** Is it a brand name, distribution, or R&D?

Of special interest are the competitor's strengths and weaknesses. Strategy development often focuses on exploiting a competitor's weakness, or neutralizing or bypassing a competitor's strength.

Market Analysis

Market analysis, the subject of Chapter 5, has two primary objectives. The first is to determine the attractiveness of the market and of the individual submarkets. Will competitors, on the average, earn attractive profits or will they lose money? If the market is so difficult that everyone is losing money, it is not a place in which to invest. The second objective is to understand the dynamics of the market so that threats and opportunities can be detected and strategies adapted. The analysis should include an examination of the market size, growth, profitability, cost structure, channels, trends, and key success factors.

Size. A basic characteristic of a market and its submarkets is its size. Of interest in addition to current sales is its potential, the additional sales that could be obtained if new users were attracted, new uses were found, and existing buyers were enticed to use the product or service more frequently.

Growth Prospects. An assessment of the growth trend and product life-cycle stage for the industry and its submarkets needs to be made. An investment in a declining industry is not always unwise, but it usually would be if the erroneous impression were held that it was, in fact, a growth situation. Conversely, it is important to recognize growth contexts even though they will not always be attractive investments for a given firm.

Market Profitability. The competitive intensity of the market depends on five factors—the number and vigor of existing competitors, the threat of new competitors, the threat of substitute products, the profit impact of powerful suppliers, and the power of customers to force price concessions. For example, a luxury hotel could be faced with conventions or organizers with the power to negotiate low room prices, thus affecting the profitability of the market. An important structural component is the barriers to entry that must be overcome by potential competitors entering the industry. A barrier to entry for the luxury hotel business in Chicago is the availability of desirable sites.

Cost Structures. One issue is what value-added stage represents the most important cost component. In the parcel delivery system there is local pickup and delivery versus the sorting and combining function versus between-city transportation versus the customer service function. Achieving a cost advantage in an important value-added stage can be important. Another cost issue is whether the industry is appropriate for a low-cost strategy based on the experience curve model, discussed in Chapter 11.

Distribution Channels. An understanding of the alternative distribution channels and the trends in their relative importance can be of strategic importance. The growth in the importance of self-service retail gasoline stations and companion growth in the importance of convenience stores such as AM/PM in gasoline retailing has strategic significance both to oil companies and distributors as well as food retailing firms.

A significant factor in the frozen-novelty business is the distribution squeeze caused by product proliferation. There are more than 2000 products and only space for about 100 of them in the frozen food area of a grocery store. Clearly, the products without substantial backing and the ability to generate sales will be in trouble. Being a comfortable number three in a category will be risky.

Market Trends. Trends within the market can affect current or future strategies and assessments of market profitability. For example, an important trend in luxury hotels is toward businessperson suites that include a host of amenities, such as a living room/den with a library of books and VCR movies, a stereo system, a well-stocked refrigerator, and elegant furnishings.[1] Several chains are aggressively building and promoting all-suite hotels. Particularly popular among businesswomen, the occupancy rate of such hotels is 70 percent, about 6 percent higher than that of all hotels.

Trends in the frozen-novelty industry include the demand for "healthy" snacks, the exploitation of strong brand names such as Dole and Jell-O, the consolidation of competitors, product proliferation, and increased promotion and advertising.

Key Success Factors. A key success factor is a competitive skill or asset that is needed to compete successfully. Successful firms are usually strong in several key success factors and are not weak in any. In the luxury hotel business, a key success factor might be those characteristics that contribute to image, such as atmosphere or ambience. You simply cannot compete successfully in the business traveler, luxury hotel business without creating the "right" atmosphere.

Strategy development, however, needs to be based on difficult judgments about what the key success factors will be in the future.[2] Popsicle Industries, makers of Popsicles, Fudgsicles, and Creamsicles, recognized that control over product quality and the ability to engage in national advertising and promotion were emerging key success factors. Thus, it changed from a system using local dairies to one in which production was centralized using 25 manufacturers under tight supervision, with distribution and marketing still controlled by Popsicle.

In the catalogue business, a key success factor of the future will be the ability to deal with automated mailing lists. Employees of Williams-Sonoma, for example, track up to 150 different pieces of information per customer.[3] They know what a person has bought from each of its five catalogues and use this information to refine mailing lists and even to locate retail stores. As a result of this technology, a new Williams-Sonoma catalogue, The Chambers, which features bed and bath products, turned a profit on its first mailing.

Environmental Analysis

Important forces outside an organization and its immediate markets and competitors will shape its operation and thrust. Environmental analysis, the subject of Chapter 6, will attempt to identify and understand emerging opportunities and threats created by these forces. It is important to limit environmental analysis to the manageable and relevant, because it can easily get bogged down with excessive scope and volume. It is helpful to divide environmental analysis into five components: technological, governmental, economic, cultural, and demographic.

A technological development can dramatically change an industry and create difficult decisions for those who are committed to profitable "old" technologies. For example, digital watches, transistors, and nylon all revolutionized industries. Technology can also make less dramatic but strategically important changes. The hotel business might be able to exploit visual as well as audio communication, allowing conferences to be held with participants in different cities. Many important new products in the frozen-novelty industry are based on recently developed technologies such as the ability to quickly process, package, and transport food—for example, frozen fruit bars.

The governmental environment can be especially important to multinationals that operate in politically sensitive countries. A luxury hotel chain may be interested in building codes and restrictions that might affect new hotels it is planning.

Strategic judgments in many contexts are affected by the cultural environment. For example, the key success factor for many clothing industries is the capability to be "right" with respect to fashion. Understanding the reasons behind the public's interest in nutrition and health is important to strategists in the frozen-novelty business.

Understanding the economic environment facing a country or an industry helps in projecting that industry's sales over time and in identifying special risks or threats. The hotel industry, for example, can see a link between the overall health of the economy in general and its primary customer segments in particular.

Demographic trends are important to many firms. Age patterns are crucial to those whose customers are in certain age groups, such as infants, students, or retirees. The frozen-novelty industry was fighting a losing demographic battle until it developed products that appealed to adults as well as children. Geographic patterns can affect the investment decisions of such service firms as hotels.

One way to understand a complex and changing environment is to create two or three future scenarios, relatively comprehensive views of the future environment. One scenario might be optimistic, another pessimistic, and a third in between. For example, a pessimistic scenario for the frozen-novelty business in five years might depict a high level of competition in terms of the number and intensity of competitors. Each scenario should have strategic implications.

A strategic question stimulated by any external analysis component can generate an information-need area, a strategically important area for which there is likely to be a continuing need for information. Special studies and ongoing information gathering might be justified.

SELF-ANALYSIS

Self-analysis, presented in Chapter 7 and summarized in Figure 2.1, aims to provide a detailed understanding of those aspects of the organization that are of strategic importance. In particular, it covers performance analysis and an examination of the key determinants of strategy such as strengths, weaknesses, and strategic problems. Self-analysis, like external analysis, usually has an SBU as a frame of reference but also can be productive at the level of aggregations of SBUs, such as divisions or firms.

Performance Analysis

Profitability and sales provide an evaluation of past strategies and an indication of the current market viability of a product line. Return on assets, the most commonly used measure of profitability, can be distorted by the limitations of accounting measures—in particular, it ignores intangible assets such as brand equity. A key issue is to determine an appropriate target rate of return that takes into account the fact that not all strategies have the same degree of risk. Another performance measure is sales, which can reflect changes in the customer base with long-term implications.

Shareholder value analysis is based on generating a discounted present value of the cash flow associated with a strategy. It is theoretically sound and appropriately forward-looking (as opposed to current financials that measure the results of past strategies). However, it focuses attention on financial measures rather than other indicators of strategic performance. Developing the needed estimates is most difficult and subject to a variety of biases.

Other, nonfinancial performance measures are available that often provide better measures of long-term business health:

- **Customer satisfaction/brand loyalty**—How are we doing relative to our competitors at attracting customers and building loyalty?

- **Associations**—What do our customers associate with our business in terms of perceived quality, innovativeness, product class expertise, customer orientation, and so on?

- **Product/service quality**—Is our product delivering value to the customer and is it performing as intended?

- **Relative cost**—Are we at a cost disadvantage with respect to materials, assembly, product design, or wages?

- **New product activity**—Have we a stream of new products or product improvements that have made an impact?

- **Manager/employee capability and performance**—Have we created the type, quantity, and depth of management that are needed to support projected strategies?

Product Portfolio Analysis.   This analysis considers the performance/strength of each business area, together with the attractiveness of the business area in which it competes. One goal is to generate a business mix with an appropriate balance between new and mature products. An organization that lacks a flow of new products faces stagnation or decline. A balance also must exist between products generating cash and those using cash. Product portfolio analysis is covered in detail in Chapter 8.

Determinants of Strategic Options

Self-analysis should also review characteristics of the business that will influence strategy choice. Five areas are noted in Figure 2.1: past and current strategy, strategic problems, organizational capabilities and constraints, financial resources and constraints, and organizational strengths and weaknesses.

Strategy Review.   The past and current strategy provides an important reference point and should be understood. Has the strategy been one of milking, maintenance, or growth? Has it involved differentiation or low cost? What are its target segments? What is the sustainable differential advantage?

Strategic Problems.   A strategic problem is one that, if uncorrected, could have damaging strategic implications. An airline needs to finance new equipment or an instrument firm has a quality problem. A weakness, on the other hand, is more of an inherent characteristic such as a bad hotel location with which the organization will probably live. Of course, any weakness can be corrected. A hotel's location can be changed. In general, however, problems are corrected and weaknesses are neutralized by a strategy or compensated by strengths.

Financial Resources and Constraints.   An analysis of the financial resources available for investment either from planned cash flow or from debt financing helps determine how much net investment should be considered. One result could be a financial constraint such as having only $20 million per year available for investment during the next few years.

Organizational Capabilities and Constraints.   Self-analysis needs to include an analysis of the internal organization, its structure, systems, workers, and culture. The internal organization can be important strategically when it is a source of:

● **A strength**—The culture in some firms can be so strong and positive that it provides the basis for a sustainable competitive advantage.

● **A weakness**—A firm may lack the marketing personnel to compete in a business in which a key success factor is marketing.

● **A constraint**—A proposed strategy must "fit" the internal organization. A realistic appraisal of an organization may preclude some strategies.

Strengths and Weaknesses.   Future strategies are often developed by building on strengths and attempting to neutralize weaknesses. Strengths are based on assets, such as a brand name, or skills, such as advertising or manufacturing.

THE ROLE OF THE BUSINESS MISSION

A business mission, which can take several forms, may be used to address some basic questions about a business. In what business are we? What type of an organization are we? What is our strategic vision?

A business mission can be a very general statement about the

Pudding Pops: A Case Study

General Foods' Jell-O line of packaged dessert products was declining in the 1970s, in part due to the changing environment.[4] The number of households with children was declining, fewer traditional meals were being eaten, people were snacking more, money was available to buy more exotic gourmet products, and there was a greater concern about diet and health. The Jell-O line was inconvenient, unexciting, and linked to the declining dessert occasion and child population. Efforts to reverse the fortunes of Jell-O by changing its advertising using a popular rock group, adding new tastes and flavors, and making serving suggestions were all unsuccessful.

Jell-O did have substantial strengths: the Jell-O name; the wholesomeness and taste of the pudding; and its already established national marketing, manufacturing, and distribution system. The question was how to exploit these strengths to provide a new growth direction. An analysis of potential growth markets focused on the huge snack area. Snacks, perceived as good-tasting, convenient, and fun but lacking nutrition, seemed like an ideal target for a new Jell-O product.

Initial efforts to make the existing Jell-O product seem more convenient were not enough, because the product was still linked to the dessert category. The development thrust then turned to the idea of a frozen pudding on a stick. Consumer tests of the basic concept were positive with a 24-percent definitely buy score. When the concept was refined with a taste plus nutrition positioning, however, the score climbed to 36 percent.

The final product was distributed to stores with two other General Foods' brands, Cool Whip frozen topping and Bird's Eye frozen vegetable products. The advertising stressed Jell-O pudding's pudding heritage, the creamy taste and natural wholesomeness that it had brought to the snack market. A phenomenal success, the product has been followed with Jell-O Gelatin Pops and Jell-O Fruit Bars.

---

strategy of a business. It thus could include a specification of:

- The business scope—the product markets in which it does and does not want to compete.
- The growth direction—the product markets and technologies of the future.
- The essence of the functional area strategies.
- The key assets and skills on which it is based.

The development of a business mission statement can then provide a vehicle for generating and screening a wide variety of strategic options. The analysis and screening of these options would not involve the same detailed appraisal of a strategy alternative as is needed when a final strategy choice has to be made. Thus, the widest possible range of strategy alternatives can be considered. In that spirit, it is often useful to consider generic customer needs (see insert below) such as gaining information rather than products such as managing databases.

A variety of dimensions and concepts can provide the basis for a strategy-defining mission statement, including product definition, market definition, technology, levels of production/distribution, and asset or skill. Although it is useful to consider each, the selection of which combination will be the most helpful depends on the context. Any effort to specify rigid formulas as to the desired form of a mission statement will be constraining and counterproductive.

Another role of the mission statement is to provide employees, customers, and other organization stakeholders with a business definition that captures the essence of the strategic vision of the business in order to establish a sense of purpose, identity, and commitment. In that spirit, it can be helpful to develop a metaphor or elegant, positive phrase like "desktop publishing." A focus on competitors can also provide such a definition. For example, Komatsu motivated its organization with an "encircle (beat) CAT" competitor focus.

A business mission can also be a vehicle for the values that are associated with an organization. For example, policies toward the environment, employees, and the community can help provide a direction for an organization that will influence strategy and provide stakeholders with a positive sense of identity.

Generic Customer Need

In his classic article, "Marketing Myopia," Theodore Levitt suggested that firms that myopically define their business in product terms can stagnate even though the basic customer need that they are serving is enjoying healthy growth.[5] Because of a myopic product focus, others gain the benefits of growth. Thus, if firms regard themselves as being in the transportation rather than the railroad business, the energy instead of petroleum business, or the communication rather than the telephone business, they are more likely to exploit opportunities.

The concept is simple. Define the business in terms of the basic customer need involved rather than the product. Xerox attempted to change its focus from copiers to the "document" company. Visa has defined itself as being in the business of enabling a customer to exchange value—to exchange any asset including cash on deposit, the cash value of life insurance, the equity in a home—for virtually anything, anywhere in the world. As the business is redefined, both the set of competitors and the range of opportunities are often radically expanded. After redefining its business, Visa estimated that it had reached only 5 percent of its potential given the new definition.

Defining a business in terms of generic need can be extremely useful in fostering creativity in generating strategic options and in avoiding an internally oriented, product/production focus.

STRATEGY IDENTIFICATION AND SELECTION

The purpose of external analysis and self-analysis is twofold: to help generate strategic alternatives and to provide criteria to select among them. The consideration of mission, just discussed, often provides a first cut at strategy development. The operating plan provides the implementation details and controls. Finally, it is necessary to monitor the strategies to detect the need for review and change.

Figure 2.2 highlights the three dimensions of strategic alternatives. The first is the selection of the product markets in which the firm will operate and how much investment should be allocated to each. The second is the development of the functional area strategies and the third is the determination of the bases of sustainable competitive advantages in those product markets.

FIGURE 2.2   Selecting Strategic Alternatives

IDENTIFICATION OF STRATEGIC ALTERNATIVES
- Product-market investment strategies:
  - product-market scope
  - growth directions
  - investment strategies.
- Functional area strategies.
- Bases of competitive advantage—assets, skills, synergies.

CRITERIA FOR STRATEGY SELECTION
- Consider scenarios suggested by strategic questions and environmental opportunities/threats.
- Involve a sustainable competitive advantage.
  - Exploit organizational strengths or competitive weaknesses.
  - Neutralize organizational weaknesses or competitive strengths.
- Be consistent with organizational vision/mission/objectives.
  - Achieve a long-term return on investment.
  - Be compatible with vision/mission/objectives.
- Be feasible.
  - Need only available resources.
  - Be compatible with the internal organization.
- Consider the relationship to other strategies within the firm.
  - Foster product portfolio balance.
  - Consider flexibility.
  - Exploit synergy.

Product-Market Investment Strategies

Product Definition.   As a practical matter, many strategic decisions involve products: which product lines to continue, which to add, and which to delete. Mother's Cookies is in the cookie business, but not in the cracker or bakery business. Several firms have found it useful to reduce the scope of their product lines. In the early 1980s, Transamerica decided to return to the concept of being a financial services company.[6] It sold United Artists, its film subsidiary, and used the proceeds to buy Fred S. James, the nation's fifth largest insurance broker.

Product position is sometimes so critical that it becomes much more than a tactical marketing effort—it represents the essence of a business. A product (or service) position involves a set of associations. Thus, Dior is positioned as being a French designer and Neiman-Marcus is a prestige retailer with expensive, unusual items.

Market Definition.   Markets need to be selected for which a competitive advantage will exist. A small California savings and loan firm defined its business as serving individual savers who lived near its office. Dean Witter has focused on individual investors, and moved away from mortgage banking. Gerber Products used age, defining its market as infants and young children. ServiceMaster has defined its business as servicing the maintenance needs of hospitals and other healthcare facilities. Such statements of focus can drive the operations of a firm.

Vertical Integration.   A strategic option, not covered by product-market scope, is that of vertical integration. Some publishing companies have integrated backward into paper and wood products. General Motors makes batteries, spark plugs, and a host of other components. Other firms, such as Xerox and IBM, have the option of integrating forward into retailing. The question is, at what vertical levels should the business operate? The trade-offs between increased control and potential return from vertical integration on the one hand, and increased risk and loss of flexibility caused by the associated investment on the other are discussed in detail in Chapter 12.

Growth Directions.   It is crucial in strategy development to have a dynamic rather than static focus. The concept of a product-market matrix shown in Figure 2.3 is helpful in identifying options and encouraging a dynamic perspective.[7]

In the product-market matrix, four growth vectors are shown. The first is to penetrate the existing product market—a firm may attempt to attract customers from competitors or increase usage by existing cus-

FIGURE 2.3   Product-Market Structured Growth Directions

	Present products	New products
Present markets	Market penetration	Product expansion
New markets	Market expansion	Diversification

Growth
directions based on
   New levels of production/distribution
   Building on a skill or asset

tomers. A second growth vector involves product expansion while remaining in the current market. Thus, a firm offering cleaning services to healthcare facilities might expand to supervise other healthcare functions such as purchasing and building maintenance. A third growth vector is to apply the same products in new markets. The cleaning firm could alternatively expand its cleaning services into other industries. These first three growth directions are explored in more detail in Chapter 12. The fourth growth vector, to diversify into new product markets, is discussed in detail in Chapter 13.

Figure 2.3 adds a third dimension to the product-market matrix. It represents a growth vector based on vertical integration or exploiting an asset such as a brand name or a skill such as marketing. Such a growth direction may involve any of the four quadrants of the product-market matrix. For example, a brand name could be exploited in a penetration, product expansion, market expansion, or diversification strategy.

Investment Strategies.   For each product market, four investment options are possible. The firm could reduce or control the investment in a business area by either a milk or a hold strategy. Alternatively, it could withdraw completely if prospects become extremely unattractive or if the business area becomes incompatible with the overall thrust of the firm. Finally, it could invest to enter or grow.

Functional Area Strategies

The development of a business strategy involves the specification of the strategies in functional areas such as sales, brand management, R&D, manufacturing, and finance. The coordination of various functional area strategies so that they don't work at cross-purposes can be difficult. The role of strategic objectives is to help in that task.

Five strategic thrusts representing different routes to achieving sustainable competitive advantages were introduced in Chapter 1 and are elaborated in Chapters 10 and 11. All can be achieved in a variety of ways. Differentiation, for example, can be based on product quality, product features, innovation, service, distribution, or a strong brand name. Low-cost strategies can be based on an "experience curve," which links cost reduction to cumulative production volume. However, it also can be based on other factors such as "no-frills" products or automated production processes.

The remaining strategic thrusts introduced in Chapter 1—focus, preemptive moves, and synergy—introduce characteristics of strategies that can accompany a differentiation or low-cost approach, a focus usually on a narrow part of either the product line or the market. A preemptive move attempts to generate a "first mover" advantage. For example, in the frozen-novelty industry, the first firm to introduce a new novelty into a market, thereby establishing an identity, usually has a substantital SCA. A strategy based on synergy will capitalize on links to other businesses in a firm. The ability to share the facilities of an R&D staff can reduce costs and improve effectiveness, for example.

Bases of Sustainable Competitive Advantage

A strategy, if it is to be effective over time, needs to involve assets and skills or synergies based on unique combinations of businesses. Thus, identifying which assets, skills, and synergies to develop or maintain becomes a key decision. Approaches to identifying candidate assets and skills are presented in Chapter 4.

SELECTING AMONG STRATEGIC ALTERNATIVES

Figure 2.2 provides a list of some of the criteria useful in selecting alternatives. These are grouped into five general criteria.

- **Consider scenarios.** A future scenario can be stimulated by strategic questions or environmental opportunities or threats. Thus, the strategic question, "will a breakthrough in storage batteries make a general-use electric automobile feasible?", could lead to both "yes" and "no" scenarios. The threat of extreme pollution laws could also serve to identify scenarios relevant to the strategies of automobile and energy firms. It can be useful and prudent to evaluate strategic options in the context of any major scenarios identified.

- **Involve a sustainable competitive advantage.** A useful operational criterion is whether or not a sustainable competitive advantage exists as part of the strategy. Unless the business unit has or can develop a real competitive advantage that is sustainable over time in the face of competitor reaction, an attractive long-term return will be unlikely. To achieve a sustainable competitive advantage, a strategy should exploit organizational assets and skills and neutralize weaknesses.

- **Be consistent with organizational vision and objectives.** A primary purpose of a vision—what a future strategy should be—and objectives is to help make strategic decisions. Thus, it is appropriate to look toward them for guidance. They can be changed, of course, if circumstances warrant. An explicit decision to change a strategy is very different from ignoring it in the face of a tempting alternative.

- **Be feasible.** A practical criterion is that the strategy be feasible. It should be within the resources of the organization. It also should be internally consistent with other organizational characteristics such as structure, systems, people, and culture. These organizational considerations will be covered in Chapter 16.

- **Consider the relationship to other firm strategies.** A strategy can relate to other business units by:

  - Balancing the sources and uses of cash flow. Some business units should generate cash and others should provide attractive places to invest that cash. Chapter 10 elaborates on this.

  - Enhancing flexibility. Flexibility, in general, is reduced when heavy commitments are made in the form of fixed investment, long-term contracts, and vertical integration.

  - Exploiting synergy. A strategy that does not exploit potential synergy may be missing an opportunity.

Implementation

The implementation stage involves converting strategic alternatives into an operating plan. If a new product market is to be entered, then a systematic program is required to develop or acquire products as an entry vehicle. If a strong R&D group is to be assembled, a program to hire people, organize them, and obtain facilities will be needed. The operating plan may span more than one year. It might be useful to provide a detailed plan for the upcoming year that contains specific short-term objectives.

Strategy Review

One of the key questions in a strategic market management system is to determine when a strategy requires review and change. It is usually necessary to monitor a limited number of key measures of strategy performance and the environment. Thus, sales, market share, margins, profit, and ROA may be regularly reported and analyzed. Externally, the process is more difficult, requiring an effective information-scanning system. The heart of such a system will be an identified set of strategic questions or issues that needs to be continuously considered.

THE PROCESS

Figure 2.1 implies a logical, sequential process. After external analysis and self-analysis are completed, the mission and strategic options are then detailed and the optimal ones selected. Finally, the operating plan and strategy review program are implemented. Later, perhaps in the next annual planning cycle, the process is repeated and the plan updated.

Although Figure 2.1 provides a useful structure, the process should be more iterative and circular than sequential. The identification and selection of strategies should occur during external analysis and self-analysis. Furthermore, the process of evaluating strategies often suggests the need for additional external analysis, thus making it necessary to cycle through the process several times. As suggested earlier, strategies and indicators of the need to change them should be continually monitored to avoid being tied to an annual planning cycle. The process supporting the development of business strategies is covered in detail in Chapter 17.

SUMMARY

External analysis includes an analysis of customers, competitors, industry, and the environment. The components of each are summarized in Figure 2.1. The role of these analyses is to identify existing or emerging opportunities, threats, trends, strategic questions, and, ultimately, strategic options.

Self-analysis begins with an appraisal of performance, which should include not only financial performance but also indicators of long-term health such as customer satisfaction and delivered and perceived product quality. It should also include an examination of determinants of strategic options such as strategic problems and organizational capabilities and constraints. One role of self-analysis is to identify organizational strengths, weaknesses, problems, and constraints. Successful strategies often attempt to build on organizational strengths or competitive weaknesses.

The mission statement can play several roles, one of which is to provide a way to consider different strategy options without becoming immersed in detailed analysis. Identification of strategic options involves considering the product-market scope and degree of vertical intergration. The concept of a product-market matrix and its associated growth directions can be useful in helping provide a dynamic perspective to strategy. A strategy choice includes specification of the investment decision involving alternatives such as withdraw, milk, hold, or enter/grow. In addition, a strategy will involve functional area strategies and the development or maintenance of assets and skills to serve as the bases of SCAs.

Strategies should be selected that are responsive to the external environment as indicated in strategic questions, reflect threats and opportunities; include an SCA; are consistent with vision/objectives; are feasible; and fit with the other firm strategies. The process should be more iterative than sequential.

FOOTNOTES

[1] "The Executive Suite Goes Traveling," *Time,* March 30, 1987, p. 55.

[2] Richard W. Stevenson, "The Popsicle's Rejuvenation," *The New York Times,* July 18, 1986, p. D1.

[3] Fleming Meeks, "Preserving the Magic," *Forbes,* February 18, 1991, pp. 60–62.

[4] Drawn from John Small, "Pudding Pops: The Story Behind Their Success," *Prepared Foods,* April 1985, pp. 130–133.

[5] Theodore Levitt, "Marketing Myopia," *Harvard Business Review,* July–August 1960, pp. 45–56.

[6] "Transamerica Builds on Its Old Identity," *Business Week,* November 15, 1982, p. 39.

[7] The product-market matrix concept is due to Ansoff, the strategy pioneer. See, for example, H. Igor Ansoff, *Corporate Strategy,* New York: McGraw-Hill, 1965, pp. 103–121.

[8] Peter Lorange and Richard F. Vancil, *Strategic Planning Systems,* Englewood Cliffs, N.J.: Prentice-Hall, 1977, Chapter 2.

PART TWO

EXTERNAL ANALYSIS

3

CUSTOMER ANALYSIS

The purpose of an enterprise is to create and keep a customer.

Theodore Levitt

Consumers are statistics. Customers are People.

Stanley Marcus

Strategy development or review logically starts with external analysis, an analysis of the factors external to a business that can affect strategy. The four chapters of Part Two present concepts and methods useful in conducting an external analysis.

EXTERNAL ANALYSIS

A successful external analysis needs to be directed and purposeful. There is always the danger that it will become an endless process resulting in an excessively descriptive report. In any business there is no end to the material that appears potentially relevant which could be assembled. Without discipline and direction, volumes of useless descriptive material can easily be generated.

Affecting Strategic Decisions

The external analysis process should not be an end in itself. Rather, it should be motivated throughout by a desire to affect strategy, to generate or evaluate strategic options. As Figure 3.1 shows, it can impact on strategy directly by suggesting strategic decision alternatives or influencing a choice among them. More specifically, it should contribute to the investment decision, the selection of functional area strategies, and the development of a sustainable competitive advantage.

The investment decision, where to compete, involves questions such as the following:

- Should existing business areas be liquidated, milked, maintained, or invested for growth?
- What growth directions should receive investment?
- Should there be market penetration, product expansion, or market expansion?
- Should new business areas be entered?

The selection of functional area strategies suggests questions like:

- What functional area strategies should be implemented?
- What should be the positioning strategy, segmentation strategy, distribution strategy, manufacturing strategy, and so on?

The development of a sustainable competitive advantage (SCA)—how to compete—includes questions like:

- What are the key success factors?
- What skills and assets should be created, enhanced, or maintained?

Additional Analysis Objectives

Figure 3.1 also suggests that an external analysis can contribute to strategy indirectly by identifying:

- Significant trends and future events.
- Threats and opportunities.
- Strategic questions, key areas of uncertainty that could affect strategy outcomes.

A significant trend or event, such as concern with saturated fat or the emergence of a new competitor, can dramatically affect the evaluation of strategy options. A new technology can represent both a threat to an established firm and an opportunity to a prospective competitor.

Strategic Questions

A strategic question, a particularly useful concept in conducting an external analysis, involves an area of uncertainty that has the potential to affect strategy. If you could know the answer to one question prior to making a strategic commitment, what would that question be? Important strategic questions for Dreyer's Ice Cream, a strong, West Coast premium ice cream firm, as it considers options with respect to the superpremium market might include:

- What are Pillsbury's plans for Häagen Dazs in the West?
- What will consumer response be to Dreyer's expansion into the super-premium category?

A strategic question is different from a strategic decision in that it

FIGURE 3.1   The Role of External Analysis

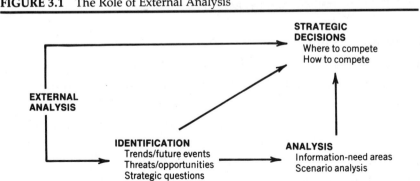

Strategic Questions	
Strategic Questions	Strategic Decisions
Will a major firm enter?	Investing in a product market
Will a tofu-based dessert product be accepted?	Investing in a tofu-based product
Will a technology be replaced?	Investment in a technology
Will the dollar strengthen against an off-shore currency?	Commitment to off-shore manufacturing
Will computer-based operations be feasible with current technology?	Investing in a new system
How sensitive is the market to price?	A strategy of maintaining price parity

focuses on uncertainties that will affect outcomes of strategic decisions. "Should Dreyer's extend its brand to the superpremium category?" is a strategic decision. "What will the consumer response be to Dreyer's expansion?" is a strategic question. Most strategic decisions will be driven by a set of strategic questions. Above are some examples of strategic questions and the strategic decisions to which they might relate.

Strategic questions often suggest subquestions. One common strategic question is, "What will be the future demand for a product?" such as ultrasound diagnostic equipment, for example. Asking "On what does that depend?" will usually generate useful subquestions. One subquestion might address uncertainty about technological improvements, whereas another might consider the technological development and cost/benefit levels achieved by competitive technologies. Still another might look into the financial capacity of the health-care industry to continue capital improvements. Each of these subquestions can, in turn, generate still another level of sub-subquestions.

Analysis

As Figure 3.1 suggests, the identification of events/trends, threats/opportunities, and strategic questions can lead to the identification of information-need areas and the potential need for scenario analysis.

Strategic Question	Strategic Subquestions
What will be the future demand?	Performance improvements? Competitive technological developments? Financial capacity of health-care industry?

An information-need area is an area of uncertainty that should be monitored and analyzed on a continuing basis. The priority of an information-need area will depend on its potential impact on strategy and its immediacy. A scenario is an alternative view of the future environment that is usually prompted by an alternative possible answer to a strategic question or by a prospective future event or trend. In Chapter 6, the last chapter in the external analysis section, information-need areas and scenario analysis will be covered in more detail.

A host of concepts and methods are introduced in this and the following three chapters. It would, of course, be unusual to employ all of them in any given context, and the strategist should resist any compulsion to do so. Rather, those that are most relevant to the situation at hand should be selected. Furthermore, some areas of analysis will be more fruitful than others and will merit more effort.

When Should an External Analysis Be Conducted?

There is often a tendency to relegate the external analysis to an annual exercise. Each year, of course, it may not require the same depth as the initial effort. It may be more productive to focus on a part of the analysis in the years immediately following major effort.

The annual planning cycle can provide a stimulus to review and change strategies that can be healthy. However, a substantial risk exists in maintaining external analysis as a once-a-year event. The need for strategic review and change is often continuous. Information-sensing and analysis therefore also need to be continuous. The framework and concepts of external analysis can still play a key role in providing structure even when the analysis is on-line and addresses only a portion of the whole.

Kathleen Eisenhardt studied 12 microcomputer firms in depth, focusing on the pace of strategic decision making.[1] One finding was that fast decision-making firms tended to obtain internal and external information on a real-time basis. The implications of significant new information are discussed at regular meetings and multiple strategic options are developed so that alternative fallback plans are usually in place. Of course, such firms are operating in a hyperactive industry, but still the lesson that on-line strategy development leads to faster decision making is instructive.

External analysis deliberately commences with customer and competitor analyses because they can serve in many contexts to define the relevant industry or industries. An industry can be defined in terms of the needs of a specific group of customers, those buying fresh cookies on the West Coast, for instance. Such a market definition then forms the basis for the identification of competitors and the balance of external analysis. An industry such as the cookie industry can also be defined in terms of all its competitors, Mrs. Fields, Otis Spunkmeyer, David's, and so on.

Because customers have such a direct relationship to a firm's operation, they are usually a rich source of relevant, operational opportunities, threats, and questions.

THE SCOPE OF CUSTOMER ANALYSIS

In most strategic market-planning contexts, the first logical step is to analyze the customers. Customer analysis consists of addressing the three sets of strategic questions that are shown in Figure 3.2.

FIGURE 3.2   Customer Analysis

SEGMENTATION

- Who are the biggest customers? The most profitable? The most attractive potential customers? Do the customers fall into any logical groups on the bases of needs, motivations, or characteristics?
- How should the market be segmented into groups that would require a unique business strategy? Consider variables such as:
  - Benefits sought
  - Usage
  - Organization type
  - Geographic location
  - Customer perceptions and attitudes
  - Price sensitivity

CUSTOMER MOTIVATION

- Why do customers select and use their favorite brands?
- What elements of the product/service do they value most?
- What are the customers' objectives? What are they really buying?
- What changes are occurring in customer motivation?

UNMET NEEDS

- Why are some customers dissatisfied? Why are some changing brands or suppliers?
- What are the severity and incidence of consumer problems?
- What are unmet needs that customers can identify? Are there some of which consumers are unaware?
- Do these unmet needs represent leverage points for competitors?

SEGMENTATION

Segmentation is often the key to developing a sustainable competitive advantage based on differentiation, low cost, or a focus strategy. Kenichi Ohmae, the longtime head of McKinsey in Japan, tells of a forklift firm that obtained an SCA, in part, by focusing on the retailing and construction industries. The firm left the more demanding segments in the heavy-duty harbor and logging applications to its competitors.[2] The focused product line developed a 20-percent cost advantage and still served the needs of more than 80 percent of the forklift truck market. The lower-priced, value-engineered product line soon swept to a dominant position.

In a strategic context, segmentation means the identification of customer groups that respond differently than other customer groups to competitive strategies. A segmentation strategy couples the identified segments with a program to deliver a competitive offering to those segments. Thus, the development of a successful segmentation strategy requires the conceptualization, development, and evaluation of a competitive offering.

How Should Segments Be Defined?

The task of identifying segments is difficult, in part, because in any given context there are literally millions of ways to divide up the market. Typically, the analysis will consider five, ten, or more segmentation variables. To avoid missing a useful way of defining segments, it is important to consider a wide range of variables. These variables need to be evaluated on the basis of their ability to identify segments for which different strategies are (or should be) pursued.

A segment justifying a unique strategy needs to be of worthwhile size to support a business strategy. Furthermore, that business strategy needs to be effective with respect to the target segment in order to be cost-effective. In general, it is costly to develop a strategy for a segment. The question usually is whether or not the effectiveness of the strategy will compensate for this added cost.

The selection of the most useful segment-defining variables is rarely obvious. Among the variables frequently used are those shown in Figure 3.3.

The first set of variables shown describe segments in terms of general characteristics unrelated to the product involved. Thus, a bakery might be concerned with geographic segments, focusing on one or more regions or even neighborhoods. It might also divide its market into organizational types such as at-home customers, restaurants, dining operations

FIGURE 3.3   Examples of Approaches to Defining Segments

CUSTOMER CHARACTERISTICS

Geographic	Small Southern communities as markets for discount stores
Type of organization	Computer needs of restaurants versus manufacturing firms versus banks versus retailers
Size of firm	Large hospital versus medium versus small
Life-style	Jaguar buyers tend to be more adventurous, less conservative than buyers of Mercedes-Benz and BMW
Sex	The Virginia Slims cigarettes for women
Age	Children versus adult cereals
Occupation	The paper copier needs of lawyers versus bankers versus dentists

PRODUCT-RELATED APPROACHES

User type	Appliance buyer—home builder, remodeler, homeowner
Usage	The heavy potato user—the fast-food outlets
Benefits sought	Dessert eaters—those who are calorie-conscious versus those who are more concerned with convenience
Price sensitivity	Price-sensitive Honda Civic buyer versus the luxury Mercedes-Benz buyer
Competitor	Those computer users now committed to IBM
Application	Professional users of chain saws versus the homeowner
Brand loyalty	Those committed to IBM versus others

in schools, hospitals, and so on. Demographics can define segments representing strategic opportunities such as single parents, professional women, and the elderly.

Marriott, for example, embarked on a $1 billion, 10-year strategy to build 200 nursing and "life-care" retirement communities for the elderly.[3] They capitalized on their proven skill in running hotels, restaurants, and a food service business as well as dramatic growth in the target segments. The number of people over 65, which stood at 32 million in 1990, will become 50 million in 2020, when more than 5 million will be 85 or older.

The second category of segment variables includes those that are related to the product. One of the most frequently employed is usage. A bakery may employ a very different strategy in serving a restaurant that is a heavy user of bakery products than restaurants that use fewer bakery products. Zenith has made a niche for itself in the very competitive personal computer industry by focusing on the government, the largest computer user.

Segmenting by competitor is also useful because it frequently leads to a well-defined strategy and a strong positioning statement. Thus, a target customer group for the Toyota Cressida consists of buyers of high-performance European cars such as the BMW. The Cressida is positioned against the BMW as the car that has a performance comparable to that of the BMW but at substantially less cost. Three other useful segment variables are benefits, price sensitivity, and applications.

Benefit Segmentation

If there is a "most useful" segmentation variable, it would be benefits sought from a product, because the selection of benefits can determine a total business strategy. In gourmet frozen dinners/entrées, for example, the market can be divided into buyers who are calorie-conscious and those who are not. People who are concerned about their weight want low-calorie meals that satisfy and a wide selection of products to compensate for the monotony of dieting. Another group might want entrées only instead of possibly more convenient full dinners because it wants to make its own side dishes, perhaps reducing the stigma traditionally attached to purchasing frozen dinners.

Price Sensitivity

One benefit dimension representing the trade-off between low price and high quality is so useful and pervasive that it is appropriate to consider it separately. In many product classes, there is a well-defined breakdown between those customers concerned first about price and others who are willing to pay for quality. As noted in Chapter 2, such a dimension drives the positioning of general merchandise stores where there is a well-defined hierarchy from the discounters to the prestige department stores.

The division of airline service into first class, business class, and economy class provides a good example of price/quality segmentation. The airline startups aimed at business travelers looking for luxury extend this segmentation scheme.[4] McClain Airlines offers leather four-abreast seating instead of the usual six-across seating, with telephones at every seat and seven-course dinners served with china and crystal at full-coach fares (as opposed to the discount fares enjoyed by most passengers on competing airlines). For first-class fares, MGM Grand Airlines plans to offer aircraft with just 33 seats instead of the usual 120, and include private staterooms.

Application Segmentation

Some products and services, particularly industrial products, can best be segmented by use or application. A portable computer may be needed by some for use while traveling, whereas others may need a computer at the office that can be conveniently stored when not in use. One segment may use a computer for word processing and another may be more interested in data processing. Some might use a four-wheel drive for light industrial hauling and others may be buying primarily for recreation.

The athletic shoe industry segments into the serious athletes, small in number but influential, the weekend warriors, and the casual wearers using athletic shoes for streetwear.[5] Recognizing that the casual wearer segment is 80 percent of the market and does not really need performance, Reebok and L.A. Gear have employed a style-focused strategy as an alternative to the performance strategy adopted by firms like Nike.

Multiple Segments Versus a Focus Strategy

Two distinct segmentation strategies are possible. The first focuses on a single segment, which can be much smaller than the market as a whole. Wal-Mart, a discounter who eventually surpassed Sears in sales, started by concentrating on cities with a population under 25,000 in 11 South Central states, a segment totally neglected by its competition, the large discount chains. This rural geographic focus strategy was directly responsible for several significant SCAs, including an efficient and responsive warehouse supply system, a low-cost, motivated work force, relatively inexpensive retail space, and a "lean and mean," hands-on management style. Union Bank, California's eighth largest bank, makes no effort to serve individuals and thus provides a service operation tailored to business accounts that is more committed and comprehensive than those of its competitors.

An alternative to a focusing strategy is to involve multiple segments. The case of General Motors mentioned in the previous chapter provides the classic example. In the 1920s the firm positioned the Chevrolet for price-conscious buyers, the Cadillac for the high end, and the Oldsmobile, Pontiac, and Buick for well-defined segments in between. A granulated potato company has developed different strategies for reaching fast-food chains, hospitals and nursing homes, and schools and colleges.

In many industries aggressive firms are moving toward multiple-segment strategies. Campbell Soup, for example, is refining its product and marketing programs for different regions.[6] It makes its nacho cheese soup spicier in Texas and California and introduced a Creole soup for Southern markets and a red-bean soup for Hispanic areas. In New York,

Campbell uses promotions linking Swanson frozen dinners with the New York Giants football team, and in the Sierra mountains, skiers are treated to hot soup samples. Developing multiple strategies is costly and often must be justified by an enhanced aggregate impact.

There can be important synergies between segment offerings. For example, in the alpine ski industry, the image developed by high-performance skis is important to sales at the recreational ski end of the business. Thus, a manufacturer that is weak at the high end will have difficulty at the low end. Conversely, a successful high-end firm will want to exploit that success by having entries in the other segments. A key success factor in the general aviation industry is to have a broad product line from fixed-gear, single-engine piston aircraft to turboprop planes, because customers tend to trade up and will switch to a different firm if the product line has major gaps.[7] Thus, the leading firms, Cessna, Piper, and Beech, have relatively broad product lines. An exception is Moody, which has carved out a small, profitable niche by focusing on the lowest end of the market, which is dominated by first-time buyers.

CUSTOMER MOTIVATIONS

After identifying customer segments, the next step is to consider their motivations: What lies behind their purchase decisions? For example, the business air traveler has a completely different set of needs and objectives than the vacationer. The business traveler is interested in easy-to-use airports, convenient schedules, and reliable and comfortable service, whereas the vacationer may be much more concerned with price. The small-business owner will have different objectives and requirements for copy machines than someone in a large company.

A knowledge of motivations can provide insight into relevant assets and skills. The absence of an asset or skill needed to satisfy a key motivation can be fatal to a strategy. The presence of a unique or particularly strong asset or skill responsive to a motivation can provide the basis for a sustainable competitive advantage (SCA). Because a key motivation of fast-food customers is convenience, strong locations can provide an SCA and weak locations can be a substantial weakness. If the prime motivation for buyers of gourmet frozen-food dinners is taste, a viable firm must be able to deliver at least acceptable taste, and a business capable of delivering superior taste will have an SCA. In terms of airlines, the business segment values convenience, schedule flexibility, and service and is relatively insensitive to price.

| customer motivations | — | key relevant assets and skills | — | sustainable competitive advantages |

The Campbell Soup "Hot Button" List

Campbell Soup identified a set of consumer motivations or "hot buttons," which they use to understand market dynamics and guide strategy development.[8] These "hot buttons" include:

- Flavor. Consumers are interested in both strong, perhaps ethnic tastes and light, delicate tastes. Responsive products have more spices, wines, and other flavorings and less salt, MSG, and bland sauces or gravies.
- Freshness and naturalness. There is a national love affair with salad and the more natural taste of refrigerated foods. As a result, supermarkets are finding growth in salad bars, the produce section, and the refrigerated case.
- Healthfulness. Consumers are more concerned with additives, salt, sugar, and fat. A host of "low-sodium" and "reduced-fat" products have emerged.
- Variety. Consumers are more willing to pay for "gourmet" foods; they want food to be more of an adventure. The explosion of restaurants offering ethnic and other interesting cuisines and the introduction of exotic foods into the supermarket are two such responses.
- Convenience. The increasingly busy and affluent consumer wants to minimize preparation or cleanup. Microwavability has thus become one of the most important considerations for food manufacturers.
- Portion control. Single servings or packaging is responsive to demands from singles who wish to avoid wasting both food and money.

It is sometimes useful to employ marketing research to more accurately and completely determine what attributes are important to various segments. The most direct approach—simply asking people what is important—often tends to be neither sensitive nor accurate. People will often say that all attributes are important and will attempt to appear more logical and objective than they actually are.

A second approach is to see which attribute judgments are associated with actual purchase decisions. Such an approach revealed that mothers often selected snack food based on what "the child likes" and what was "juicy" instead of qualities they had said were important (nourishing and easy to eat).[9]

A third approach is to ask trade-off questions.[10] If an engineer has to sacrifice either response time or accuracy in his or her oscilloscope, which would it be? Or how would an airline passenger trade off convenient departure time with price? The trade-off question asks customers to make difficult judgments about attributes.

Consumer motivations can be analyzed at two levels: the motivations that affect brand choice and those that affect whether a product class is purchased. A general motivation for healthfulness and reduced calorie

---

Stop N Go Looks to the Customer

In the mature convenience store industry, Stop N Go developed a spurt of growth by looking toward the changing customer.[11] Whereas the typical convenience store is a small, cramped store featuring cigarettes, beer, soda pop, fast food, and junk food, roomy new Stop N Go stores feature bright lights, decorative shelving, and trendy products such as fresh pasta, frozen yogurt, and deli items—a customer who shares an interest in health and nutrition will not be repelled. Stop N Go also has segmented the market into mainstream, upscale, and Hispanic components. Hispanic stores include a Mayan welcome sign as a logo and a host of Mexican-made products. A black-oriented segment was not developed when it was found that preferences simply did not differ significantly from those of mainstream white customers.

---

intake may lead to the purchase of a Lean Cuisine low-calorie entry. It can also affect food selection in general. An understanding of these more general motivations can be very helpful in charting growth directions. The Campbell Soup "hot button" list provides an excellent example.

UNMET NEEDS

An unmet need is a customer need that is not now being met by the existing product offerings. For example, ski areas have a need for snow-making equipment that can access steep, advanced trails. The chocolate industry could use a healthy candy category and also more variety. Sales of small portable computers were held back for years because the industry lacked flat displays with adequate quality and reasonable cost. The baby food industry has a need for packages that are unbreakable, microwavable, and environmentally sound.

Unmet needs are strategically important because they represent opportunities for firms that want to increase their market share or break into a market. They can also represent threats to established firms in that they can be a lever for competitors to disrupt an established position.

Foremost-McKesson in the mid–1970s came close to selling off its biggest business, drug wholesaling, because of very marginal profitability (2-percent return on equity) and profit growth (2 percent).[12] Only five years later the business was enjoying an annual 20-percent profit growth, a 10-percent return, and was poised for future growth. The key was its ability to identify unmet needs and respond to them.

Foremost-McKesson supplied drugstores with computer terminals for ordering inventories, which evolved into convenient devices used in store aisles. It also leased microcomputers to stores, thereby enabling them to do bookkeeping and marketing analyses. A pharmaceutical card system allowed Foremost to play the middleman role in servicing medical insurance claims. Foremost also provided drugstores with a massive "rack-jobbing" service and even became involved in designing drugstores. These innovations allowed drugstores to reduce labor costs and improve productivity. The net result was that Foremost was able to develop a differentiation strategy in only a few years by capitalizing on opportunities represented by unmet customer needs.

A major extension of the temporary-services industry has been created by firms responding to an unmet need for temporary lawyers, high-tech specialists, and doctors.[13] Users want to avoid the disruptions and inefficiency of hiring and firing staff.

Sometimes customers may not even be aware of their unmet needs because they are so accustomed to the implicit limitations of existing equipment. The same computer user who now views a hard disk as indispensable might not have viewed file storage as an unmet need prior to the availability of hard disks. The unmet needs that are not obvious may be more difficult to identify, but they can also represent a greater opportunity for an aggressive business, because there will be little pressure on established firms to be responsive.

User-Developed Products

For an internal application, IBM designed and built the first printed circuit card insertion machine of a particular type to be used in commercial production.[14] After building and testing the design in-house, IBM sent engineering drawings of its design to a local machine builder, along with an order for eight units. The machine builder completed this and subsequent orders and applied to IBM for permission to build essentially the same machine for sale on the open market. IBM agreed, and as a result, the machine builder became a major force in the component insertion equipment business.

In the early 1970s store owners and salesmen in Southern California began to notice that youngsters were fixing up their bikes to look like motorcycles, complete with imitation tailpipes and "chopper-type" handlebars.[15] Sporting crash helmets and Honda motorcycle T-shirts, the youngsters raced fancy 20-inchers on dirt tracks. Obviously onto a good thing, the manufacturers came out with a whole new line of "motocross" models. California users refined this concept into the mountain bike. Manufacturers were guided by the California-customer-developed components to further refine the concept, including the 21-speed gear shift that eliminates removing one's hand from the bars. In 1991 sales of mountain bikes are expected to exceed 21 million by firms that are still watching their West Coast customers.

Identifying Unmet Needs

Several structured market research approaches exist that can help identify opportunities or threats. One approach involves semistructured interviews with product users, in which their experience with the products is discussed. Such discussions can also be held with six to ten people in a focus group setting. This kind of research helped Dow come up with Spiffits, a line of premoistened, disposable cleaning towels that addressed the need for a towel that is already moistened with a cleaning compound.

A second approach, termed problem research, develops a list of potential problems with the product.[16] The problems are then prioritized by asking a group of 100 to 200 respondents to rate each problem as to whether (1) the problem is important, (2) the problem occurs frequently, and (3) a problem solution exists. A problem score is obtained by combining these ratings. A dog-food problem research study found that buyers felt dog food smelled bad, cost too much, and did not come in different sizes for different dogs. Subsequently, products responsive to these criticisms emerged. Another study led an airline to modify its cabins to provide more leg room.

A third approach, termed benefit structure analysis, has product users identify the benefits desired and the extent to which the product delivers those benefits for specific use applications.[17] The result is an identification of benefits sought that current products are not delivering.

A fourth approach uses customer satisfaction studies, perhaps repeated at regular intervals so that changes can be detected. The identification of events leading to dissatisfaction can lead to unmet needs.

From Unmet Needs to New Products.   One reaction to the identification of an unmet need is for a firm to develop a product or product modification that will be responsive. Sometimes customers will not only have identified problems but will have even developed products to solve them. An MIT professor, Eric von Hippel, has conducted studies to determine the source of new products, and he has concluded that in some industries most new products are actually developed by customers.[18] For example, users developed 80 percent of new scientific instruments studied by von Hippel and over 60 percent of semiconductor manufacturing equipment innovations. It might be worthwhile to identify those users who are so motivated and capable of developing useful products.

von Hippel also notes that some firms solicit customer-based new products. The Pillsbury Bake-Off Contest has contributed one of Pillsbury's cake products and several other product improvements. IBM has long had a department that acquires user-developed programs designed to run on its computers.

Using Lead Users

von Hippel suggests that "lead users" provide a particularly good source of unmet needs and new product concepts. Lead users are users that:[19]

- Face needs that will be general in the marketplace, but face them months or years before the bulk of the marketplace. A person that is very "into" health foods and nutrition would be a lead user with respect to health foods, if we assume that there is a trend toward health foods.

- Are positioned to benefit significantly by obtaining a solution to those needs. Lead users of office automation would be firms that today would benefit significantly from a particular type of office automation.

von Hippel suggests that lead users can be used to evaluate novel product concepts, as well as help identify them. Other potential users may find a novel concept too foreign to evaluate. Consider products such as minivans, microwave ovens, instant coffee, the personal computer, home rental movies, a Xerox machine, an office automation system, or a completely new food product before they were introduced. Lead users are often better suited to visualize the new product, its application and its benefits.

The challenge is to identify lead users. In a CAD (computer-aided design) application, the search for lead users involved identifying engineers who were considered experts in the use of existing CAD systems, who had developed and built their own CAD system and had devised applications involving the design of multiple layered boards with a high density of chips (which would thus benefit from CAD improvements). In another study, measures of dissatisfaction with current products provided an indicator of the extent to which a user might benefit from an innovation.

SUMMARY

The goal of external analysis is to influence strategy, in part, by identifying opportunities, threats, trends, and strategic questions. Its ultimate goal is to improve strategic choices—decisions as to where to compete and how to compete.

Customer analysis involves an examination of customer segmentation, motivation, and unmet needs. Segmentation means the identification of customer groups that can support different competitive strategies.

Segmentation approaches include benefits sought, the price/quality dimension, and application. A business can focus on a single segment or attempt to serve multiple segments, perhaps obtaining across-segment synergies.

A knowledge of motivation—what is important to customers and why they buy certain products and brands—can provide insights into what assets and skills are needed to compete and can form the bases of SCAs. Motivations can be identified through marketing research approaches such as asking attribute importance or trade-off questions.

An unmet need, a customer need that is not currently being met by the existing product offerings, can be strategically important because it may represent opportunities for those attempting to gain position and may pose threats to those attempting to maintain position. Problem research and benefit structure analysis can be used to identify unmet needs. "Lead users," users that face needs that will become more prevalent in the future and are thus positioned to benefit significantly, are particularly good sources of unmet needs and new product concepts.

FOOTNOTES

[1] Kathleen M. Eisenhardt, "Speed and Strategic Choice: How Managers Accelerate Decision Making," *California Management Review*, Spring 1990, pp. 39–54.

[2] Kenichi Ohmae, *The Mind of the Strategist*, New York: Penguin Books, 1982, pp. 43–46.

[3] Paul Farhl, "Marriott Corp. Gambles $1 Billion on Communities for Elderly," *Adweek's Marketing Week*, March 6, 1989, pp. 28–31.

[4] "Welcome Aboard. The Champagne Is on Ice," *Business Week*, January 19, 1987, p. 61.

[5] Daisuke Aihara, Werner Eschbach, Bridget Harper, and Hugues Ogier, "L.A. Gear," unpublished paper, 1991.

[6] "Marketing's New Look," *Business Week*, January 26, 1987, pp. 64–69.

[7] Mark Peters, Scott Johnson, Schalon Newton, and Jerry Weintraub, "General Aviation Industry Analysis," unpublished paper, 1981.

[8] R. Gordon McGovern, "The Consumer Revolution in the Supermarket," *The Journal of Business Strategy* 6, Fall 1984, pp. 93–95.

[9] James H. Myers and Edward W. Forgy, "Getting More Information from Customer Surveys," *California Management Review* 78, Winter 1975, pp. 66–72.

[10] See David A. Aaker and George S. Day, *Marketing Research*, 4th ed., New York: Wiley, 1990, Chapter 19.

[11] Kevin Helliker, "Stop N Go's Van Horn Wants to Reinvent the Convenience Store," *The Wall Street Journal*, February 6, 1991.

[12] "Foremost-McKesson: The Computer Moves Distribution to Center Stage," *Business Week*, December 7, 1981, pp. 115–122.

[13] "These 'Temps' Don't Just Answer the Phone," *Business Week*, June 2, 1986, p. 74.

[14] Eric von Hippel, "Leads Users: A Source of Novel Product Concepts," *Management Science*, July 1986, p. 802.

[15] Hiroko Katayama, "Three Men and a Derailleur," *Forbes*, January 21, 1991, p. 46.

[16] E. E. Norris, "Seek Out the Consumer's Problem," *Advertising Age*, March 17, 1975, pp. 43–44.

[17] James H. Myers, "Benefit Structure Analysis: A New Tool for Product Planning," *Journal of Marketing* 40, October 1976, pp. 23–32.

[18] Glen L. Urban and Eric von Hippel, "Lead User Analyses for the Development of New Industrial Products, "*Management Science*, May 1988, pp. 569–582; Eric von Hippel, "Get New Products from Customers," *Harvard Business Review*, March–April 1982, pp. 117–122.

[19] Eric von Hippel, "Leads Users: A Source of Novel Product Concepts," *Management Science*, July 1986, p. 802.

4

COMPETITOR ANALYSIS

Induce your competitors not to invest in those
products, markets and services where you expect to invest the most . . . that is the fundamental rule of strategy.

Bruce Henderson, Founder of BCG

There is nothing more exhilarating than to be
shot at without result.

Winston Churchill

There are numerous well-documented reasons why the Japanese automobile firms were able to penetrate the U.S. market successfully, especially during the 1970s. One important reason, however, is that they have been much better at doing competitor analysis than U.S. firms.[1]

Halberstam, in his account of the automobile industry, graphically described the Japanese efforts at competitor analysis in the 1960s. "They came in groups. . . . They measured, they photographed, they sketched, and they tape-recorded everything they could. Their questions were precise. They were surprised how open the Americans were."[2] The Japanese similarly studied European manufacturers, especially their design approaches. In contrast, according to Halberstam, the Americans were late in even recognizing the competitive threat from Japan and never did well at analyzing the competitive environment they represented.

Competitor analysis is the second phase of external analysis. Again, the goal should be on insights that will influence the product-market investment decision or the effort to obtain or maintain an SCA. The analysis should focus on the identification of threats, opportunities, or strategic questions created by emerging or potential competitor moves, weaknesses, or strengths.

Competitive analysis starts with identifying current and potential competitors. There are two very different ways of identifying current competitors. The first examines the perspective of the customer who must make choices among competitors. The result is grouping competitors according to the degree they compete for a buyer's choice. The second type of identification approach attempts to place competitors into strategic groups on the basis of their competitive strategy.

After competitors are identified, the focus shifts to attempting to understand them and their strategies. Of particular interest is an analysis of the strengths and weaknesses of each competitor or strategic group of competitors. Figure 4.1 summarizes with a set of questions that can provide a structure for competitor analysis.

IDENTIFYING COMPETITORS— CUSTOMER-BASED APPROACHES

In most instances, primary competitors are quite visible and easily identified. Thus, Calistoga competes with other sparkling mineral waters such as Perrier. However, it is usually worthwhile to look more closely at competitor identification. For example, Calistoga could also define its competitors by alternative criteria such as:

● Carbonated water drinks including Canada Dry soda.

● Bottled water including Evian and Arrowhead.

FIGURE 4.1   Questions to Structure Competitor Analysis

WHO ARE THE COMPETITORS?

- Against whom do we usually compete? Who are our most intense competitors? Less intense but still serious competitors? Makers of substitute products?
- Can these competitors be grouped into strategic groups on the basis of their assets, skills, and/or strategies?
- Who are the potential competitive entrants? What are their barriers to entry? Is there anything that can be done to discourage them?

EVALUATING THE COMPETITORS

- What are their strategies? Their level of commitment?
- Which are the most successful/unsuccessful competitors over time? Why?
- What are the strengths and weaknesses of each competitor or strategic group?
- What leverage points (our strategic weaknesses or customer problems/unmet needs) could competitors exploit to enter the market or become more serious competitors?
- Evaluate the competitors with respect to their assets and skills. Generate a competitor strength grid.

- Carbonated low-calorie drinks such as Diet 7UP.
- Carbonated nonalcoholic drinks.
- All nonalcoholic product substitutes like fruit drinks, canned fruit drinks, frozen-fruit drinks, packaged drinks (e.g., Kool-Aid), milk, coffee, and tea.
- All purchased beverages including product substitutes like beer and wine.

Note that substitute products such as fruit drinks can be relevant competitors.

Similarly, the makers of granulated potato buds used by institutions and restaurants for making mashed potatoes could usefully distinguish among the following types of competitors:

- Granulated potato buds.
- Other dehydrated potato products.
- Whole potatoes used to make mashed potatoes.
- Substitute potato products such as french fries, hash browns, boiled potatoes, potatoes au gratin, and so on.
- Substitute starch dishes such as rice and pasta.
- Substitute side dishes such as vegetables.

Actually, other potato products may be more intense competitors to granulated potato buds in the short run than whole potatoes, because institutions may not be set up to process whole potatoes. An institution may well substitute starch dishes if the price of mashed potatoes should increase. Furthermore, mashed potatoes have lost a share of side dishes over time to vegetables, because of changing attitudes toward health and nutrition.

These examples illustrate three principles:

- In most industries, competitors can be usefully portrayed in terms of how intensely they compete with the business that is motivating the analysis. There are usually several very direct competitors, others that compete less intensely, and still others that compete indirectly but are still relevant. A knowledge of this pattern can lead to a deeper understanding of the market structure. The competitor groups that compete most intensely may merit the most in-depth study, but other groups may still require analysis.

- The definition of the most competitive groups will depend on a few key variables, and it may be strategically important to know the relative importance of these variables. Thus, with respect to cola drinks, the most important variable could be either cola/noncola, diet/nondiet, or caffeine/noncaffeine. If noncaffeine is the most important attribute for a segment, the appropriate strategy will be different than if nondiet is the most important factor.

- Substitute products can be extremely relevant. For example, rice and pastas are very real competitors to granulated potato buds and have affected their sales level and price structure over time.

Customer Choices

A knowledge of how to identify such groupings will be of conceptual as well as practical value. One approach is to focus on customer choice. A Pepsi buyer could be asked what brand would have been purchased if Pepsi had been out of stock. A buyer for a nursing home meal service could be asked what would be substituted for granulated potato buds if they increased in price. A sample of sports car buyers could be asked what other cars they considered and perhaps what other showrooms they actually visited.

Product-Use Associations

Another approach that provides additional insights is the association of products with specific use contexts or applications.[3] Perhaps 20 or 30 product users would be asked to identify a list of use situations or applications. For each use context they would then be asked to name all the products that are appropriate. For each product so identified, appropriate use contexts would be identified so that the list of use contexts was more complete. Another group of respondents would then be asked to make judgments about how appropriate each product would be for each use context. Then products would be clustered, based on the similarity of their appropriate use contexts. Thus, if Pepsi was regarded as appropriate for snack occasions, it would compete primarily with products similarly perceived. The same approach will work with an industrial product that might be used in several distinct applications.

These two approaches suggest a conceptual basis for identifying competitors that can be employed by managers even when marketing research is not available. The concept of alternatives from which customers choose and the concept of appropriateness to a use context can be powerful tools in helping to understand the competitive environment.

IDENTIFYING COMPETITORS—STRATEGIC GROUPS

The concept of a strategic group provides a very different approach toward understanding the competitive structure of an industry. A strategic group is a group of firms that:

- Over time pursue similar competitive strategies (e.g., the use of the same distribution channel and heavy advertising).
- Have similar characteristics (e.g., size, aggressiveness).
- Have similar assets and skills (e.g., quality image).

A set of strategic groups includes a set of mobility barriers that inhibit or prevent businesses from moving from one strategic group to another.[4] For example, an industry like orange juice has national brands, price leaders, private label suppliers, and local fresh-squeezed entries. Each of those groups is protected from entry barriers such as low-cost production, brand names, low overhead, or a local customer base.

A member of a strategic group can have exit as well as entry barriers. For example, assets such as plant investment or a specialized labor force can represent a meaningful exit barrier.

The mobility barrier concept is crucial because one way to develop a sustainable competitive advantage is to pursue a strategy that is protected from competition by assets and skills that represent barriers to competitors. The existence of mobility barriers between strategic groups is supported by economic theory and by empirical studies. For example, Sharon Oster of Yale, in a study of 19 consumer products industries, defined strategic groups by the intensity of their advertising.[5] Mobility between groups over an eight-year period was found to be generally low—especially for industries in which high levels of advertising have likely created product differentiation barriers; industries like soap, drugs, and soft drinks as opposed to carpets, paint, and furniture. A study of the oil-well drilling industry in the 1970s classified 33 firms into three groups and found that only two movements occurred out of 109 possible opportunities.[6]

The strategy differences defining groups will depend on context, but could involve any of the elements of a business strategy introduced in Chapter 1. In particular, strategic groups could be defined by the following: the extent to which firms are engaged in milking versus growth strategies, which distribution channels they use, their position on the price/quality dimension, or the technology on which they rely. In any case, firms in different groups will have different bases on which they compete and different competitive advantages. They could also differ with respect to characteristics having possibly strategic importance such as firm size, diversification, and whether they are multinational.

Using the Strategic Group Concept

The conceptualization of strategic groups can make the process of competitor analysis more manageable. Numerous industries contain many more competitors than can be analyzed individually. Often it is simply not feasible to consider 30 competitors, to say nothing of hundreds. Reducing this set to a small number of strategic groups makes the analysis compact, feasible, and more usable. For example, in the wine industry, competitor analysis of an upscale wine maker such as Beringer or BV would probably consider the popular premium wine firms such as Gallo, Sebastiani, Sutter Home, and Glen Ellen as a strategic group because their strengths and strategies are similar. Furthermore, little strategic content and insight will be lost in most cases, because firms in a strategic group will be affected by and react to industry developments in similar ways. Thus, in projecting future strategies of competitors, the concept of strategic groups can be helpful.

Strategic groupings can refine the strategic investment decision. Instead of determining in which industries to invest, the decision can focus on what strategic group a firm should invest in. Thus, it will be necessary to determine the current profitability and future potential profitability of the strategic group. One strategic objective is to invest in those strategic groups that will tend to be profitable over time and to disinvest or avoid strategic groups that will not be profitable.

Ultimately the selection of a strategy and its supporting assets and skills will often mean selecting or creating a strategic group. Thus, a knowledge of the strategic group structure can be extremely useful.

Projecting Strategic Groups

The concept of strategic groups can also be helpful in projecting competitive strategies into the future. A McKinsey study of the effects of deregulation on five deregulated industries (summarized in Figure 4.2) forecasts with remarkable accuracy that successful firms will move toward one of three strategic groups.[7]

The evolution of the first group was expected to involve three phases. During the first phase, the medium and small firms attempt—usually unsuccessfully—to gain enough of a market share by merging to compete with the large firms. In the second phase, strong firms make acquisitions to fill in product lines or market gaps. During this phase, which occurs about three to five years following deregulation, the major firms try to develop broad product lines and distribution coverage. In the third phase, interindustry mergers occur. Strong firms merge with others outside their industry.

The second strategic group consists of low-cost producers entering the industry after deregulation by providing simple product lines with minimal service to the price-sensitive segment. The third group includes

FIGURE 4.2   Strategic Groups Emerging from Deregulation

Group	Industry	Examples
1. National distribution company with full line of differentiated products and emphasis on attractive service/price trade-offs	Brokerage Airlines Trucking Railroads Business terminals	Merrill Lynch Delta Consolidated Freightways Burlington Northern Western Electric
2. Low-cost producer—often a new entrant following deregulation	Brokerage Airlines Trucking Railroads Business terminals	Charles Schwab Midway Air Overnite Transportation Oki
3. Specialty firm with strong customer loyalty and specialized service targeted toward an attractive customer group	Brokerage Airlines Trucking Railroads Business terminals	Goldman Sachs Air Wisconsin Ryder Systems Sante Fe Northern Telecom

those pursuing a focus strategy, with a specialized service targeted toward a specific customer group.

POTENTIAL COMPETITORS

In addition to current competitors, it is important to consider potential market entrants. Among the sources of potential competitors are firms that might engage in:

1. **Market expansion.** Perhaps the most obvious source of potential competitors is firms operating in other geographic regions or in other countries. A cookie company may want to keep a close eye on a competing firm in an adjacent state, for example.

2. **Product expansion.** The leading ski firm, Rossignol, has expanded into ski clothing, thus exploiting a common market, and has moved into tennis equipment, which takes advantage of technological and distribution overlap.

3. **Backward integration.** Customers are another potential source of competition. General Motors bought dozens of manufacturers of components during its formative years. Major can users such as Campbell Soup have integrated backward, making their own containers.

4. **Forward integration.** Suppliers are also potential competitors. AST, a major computer manufacturer, started out as a maker of add-on boards for IBM computers. Suppliers, believing they have the critical ingredients to succeed in a market, may be attracted by the margins and control that come with integrating forward.

5. **The export of assets or skills.** A current small competitor with critical strategic weaknesses can turn into a major entrant if it is purchased by a firm that can reduce or eliminate those weaknesses. Predicting such moves can be difficult, but sometimes an analysis of competitor strengths and weaknesses will suggest some possible synergistic mergers to watch for. A competitor in an above-average growth industry that does not have the financial or managerial resources for the long haul might be a particularly attractive candidate for merger.

COMPETITOR ANALYSIS—
UNDERSTANDING COMPETITORS

Understanding competitors and their activities can provide several benefits. First, an understanding of the current strategy strengths and weaknesses of a competitor can suggest opportunities and threats that will merit a response. Second, insights into future competitive strategy may allow the prediction of emerging threats and opportunities. Third, a decision about strategic alternatives might easily hinge on the ability to forecast the likely reaction of key competitors. Finally, competitor analysis may result in the identification of some strategic questions, questions that will be worth monitoring closely over time. A strategic question, for example, might be, "Will Competitor A decide to move into the western U. S. market?"

As Figure 4.3 indicates, competitive actions are influenced by seven elements. The first of these reflects its financial performance, as measured by its size, growth, and profitability.

Size, Growth, and Profitability

The level and growth rates, sales, and market share provide indicators of the vitality of a business strategy. The maintenance of a strong market position or the achievement of rapid growth usually reflect a strong competitor (or strategic group) and a successful strategy. In contrast, a deteriorating market position can signal financial or organizational strains that might affect the interest and ability of the business to pursue certain strategies.

After size and growth comes profitability. A profitable business will generally have access to capital for investment unless it has been designated by the parent to be milked. A business that has lost money over an

FIGURE 4.3 Understanding the Competitors

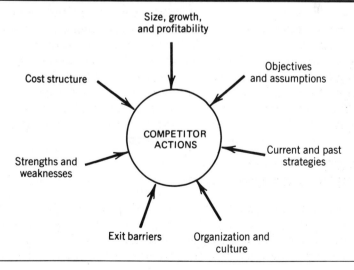

extended time period or has experienced a recent sharp decrease in profitability may find it difficult to gain access to capital either externally or internally.

Competitor's Objectives and Assumptions

A knowledge of competitor objectives provides the potential to predict whether or not a competitor's present performance is satisfactory or strategic changes are likely. The financial objectives of the business unit can indicate the competitor's willingness to invest in that business even if the payout is relatively long-term. In particular, what are the competitor's objectives with respect to market share, sales growth, and profitability? Nonfinancial objectives are also helpful. Does the competitor want to be a technological leader? Or to develop a service organization? Or to expand distribution? Such objectives provide a good indication of the competitor's possible future strategy.

The objectives of the competitor's parent company (if one exists) are also relevant. What are the current performance levels and financial objectives of the parent? If the business unit is not performing as well as the parent, pressure might be exerted either to improve or withdraw its investment. Of critical importance is the role attached to the business unit. Is it central to the parent's long-term plans, or is it peripheral? Is it seen as a growth area, or is it expected to supply cash to fund other areas? Does the business create synergy with other operations? Does the parent have an emotional attachment to the business unit for any reason?

The competitor may have assumptions about itself or its industry that may or may not be true, but which still can influence its strategy. For example, the competitor may perceive itself as having a high-quality premium product. Thus, it may believe that it should not or need not respond to a price cut or the use of discount stores by a competitor. Or it may be overly optimistic about the industry and make decisions accordingly.

Current and Past Strategies of Competitors

The competitor's current and past strategies should be reviewed. In particular, past strategies that have failed should be noted, because such experiences can inhibit the competitor from trying similar strategies again. Also, a knowledge of a competitor's pattern of new product or new market moves can help one anticipate its future growth directions. If a differentiation strategy is detected, to what extent does it rely on product-line breadth, product quality, service, distribution type, or brand identification? If a low-cost strategy is employed, is it based on economies of scale, the experience curve, manufacturing facilities and equipment, or access to raw material? What is its cost structure? If a focus strategy is evident, describe the business scope.

Competitor's Organization and Culture

Knowledge about the background and experience of the competitor's top management can provide insight into future actions. Are the managers drawn from marketing, engineering, or manufacturing? Are they largely from another industry or company? Clorox, for example, has a very heavy Procter & Gamble influence in its management, lingering from the years that Procter & Gamble operated Clorox before the courts ordered divestiture.

An organization's culture, supported by its structure, systems, and people, often has a pervasive influence on strategy. A cost-oriented, highly structured organization that relies on tight controls to achieve objectives and motivate employees may have difficulty innovating or shifting into an aggressive, marketing-oriented strategy. A loose, flat organization that emphasizes innovation and risk taking may similarly have difficulty pursuing a disciplined product-refinement and cost-reduction program. In general, as Chapter 16 will make clearer, organizational elements such as culture, structure, systems, and people limit the range of strategies that should be considered.

Cost Structure

Knowledge of a competitor's cost structure, especially a competitor that is relying on a low-cost strategy, can provide an indication of its likely future pricing strategy and its staying power. The goal should be to obtain a feel for both direct costs and fixed costs, which will determine break-even levels. The following information can usually be obtained and can provide insights into cost structures:

● The number of employees and a rough breakdown of direct labor (variable labor cost) and overhead (which will be part of fixed cost).

● The relative costs of raw materials and purchased components.

● The investment in inventory, plant, and equipment (also fixed cost).

● Sales levels and number of plants (on which the allocation of fixed costs is based).

Exit Barriers

Exit barriers can be crucial to a firm's ability to exercise an exit alternative. They include:[8]

- Specialized assets—plant, equipment, or other assets that are costly to transform to another application and that therefore have little salvage value.

- Fixed costs such as labor agreements, leases, and a need to maintain parts for existing equipment.

- Relationships to other business units in the firm due to the firm's image or to shared facilities, distribution channels, or sales force.

- Government and social barriers—governments may regulate whether a railroad, for example, can exit from a passenger service responsibility; firms may feel a sense of loyalty to workers, thereby inhibiting strategic moves.

- Managerial pride or an emotional attachment to a business or its employees that affects economic decisions.

Assessing Strengths and Weaknesses

Knowledge of a competitor's strengths and weaknesses provides insight that is key to the firm's ability to pursue various strategies. It also offers important input into the process of identifying and selecting strategic alternatives. One approach is to attempt to exploit a competitor's weakness in an area where the firm has an existing or developing strength. The desired pattern is to develop a strategy that will pit "our" strength against a competitor's weakness. Conversely, a knowledge of "their" strength is important so it can be bypassed or neutralized.

An example of a firm that developed a strategy to neutralize a strategic weakness was a small software firm that lacked a retail distribution capability or the resources to engage in retail advertising. It directed its efforts to value-added software systems firms, firms that sell total software and sometimes hardware systems to industries such as investment firms or hospitals. These value-added systems firms could understand and exploit the power of the product, integrate it into their systems, and use it in quantity. The absence of a distribution channel or resources to support an advertising effort was thus neutralized.

The assessment of a competitor's strengths and weaknesses starts with an identification of relevant assets and skills for the industry and then evaluates the competitor on the basis of those assets and skills. We now turn to these topics.

COMPETITOR STRENGTHS AND WEAKNESSES

What Are the Relevant Assets and Skills?

Competitive strengths and weaknesses are based on the existence or absence of assets or skills. Thus, an asset such as a well-known name or a prime location could represent a strength, as could a skill such as the ability to develop a strong promotional program. Conversely, the absence of an asset or skill can represent a weakness.

To analyze competitive strengths and weaknesses, it is thus necessary to identify the assets and skills that are relevant to the industry. As Figure 4.4 summarizes, a series of five questions can be helpful.

1. What businesses have been successful over time? What assets or skills have contributed to their success? What businesses have had chronically low performance? Why? What assets or skills do they lack?

By definition, assets and skills that provide SCAs should affect performance over time. Thus, businesses that differ with respect to performance over time should also differ with respect to their skills and assets. Analysis of the causes of the performance usually suggests sets of relevant skills and assets. Typically, the superior performers have developed and maintained key assets and skills that have been the basis for their performance. Conversely, weakness in several assets and skills relevant to the industry and its strategy should visibly contribute to the inferior performance of the weak competitors over time.

For example, in the CT scanner industry the best performer, General Electric, has superior product technology and R&D, has a systems capability due to its organization, a strong sales and service organization due, in part, to its X-ray product line, and an installed base. The largest competitor, Johnson & Johnson, has a CT scanner business that has been a chronic money loser for a decade, lacks the synergistic combination of businesses, the product technology and R&D, and the sales and service organization.[9]

FIGURE 4.4   Identifying Relevant Assets and Skills

1. Why are successful businesses successful?
   Why are unsuccessful businesses unsuccessful?
2. What are the key customer motivations?
3. What are the large cost components?
4. What are the industry mobility barriers?
5. Which components of the value chain can create competitive advantage?

---

2. What are the key customer motivations? What is really important to the customer?

Customer motivations usually drive buying decisions and thus can dictate what assets and skills potentially create meaningful advantages. In the heavy-equipment industry, customers value service and parts backup. Caterpillar's promise of "24-hour parts service anywhere in the world" has been a key asset because it is important to customers. Sometimes needs exist that are unmet by current offerings. As noted in the last chapter, unmet needs represent opportunities for the "outs" and threats for the "ins." For example, the successful Macintosh computer was developed in response to an unmet need for a user-friendly system. The technology surrounding the Macintosh has provided an enormous asset in an industry of IBM clones.

An analysis of customer motivations can also identify assets and skills that a business will need to deliver unless a strategy can be devised that will make them unimportant. If the prime buying criterion for a snack is freshness, a brand will have to develop the skills to deliver that attribute. A business that lacks competence in an area important to the customer segment can experience problems even if it has substantial other SCAs.

3. What are the large value-added parts of the product or service? What are the large cost components?

An analysis of the cost structure of an industry can reveal which value-added stage represents the largest percentage of total cost. Obtaining a cost advantage in a key value-added stage can represent a significant SCA whether that advantage is used to support a low price or a differentiation strategy. Cost advantages in lower value-added stages have less leverage. Thus in the metal can business, transportation costs are relatively high and a competitor that can locate plants near customers or on a customer's premises will have a significant cost advantage.

4. What are the mobility barriers in the industry?

The cost and difficulty of creating the assets and skills needed to support an SCA represent the mobility barriers in an industry. Mobility represents both entry barriers and barriers to the movement from one strategic group or competitive arena to another. For example, in the oil-well drilling industry of the 1970s and early 1980s, barriers prevented firms from moving from shallow on-shore drilling to deep on-shore drilling to off-shore to foreign drilling. Foreign, off-shore drilling requires specialized assets and skills in establishing and operating off-shore equipment, in dealing with foreign governments and firms, and in operating in different countries. The assets and skills that prevent entry into an industry or strategic group should be among those that are relevant to that industry.

5. Consider the components of the value chain. Do any provide the potential to generate competitive advantage?

Michael Porter conceptualized the value chain of competitors as one way to expose differences that determine competitive advantage.[10] A business' value chain (see Figure 4.5) consists of two types of value-creating activities:

Primary Value Activities

Inbound logistics—material handling and warehousing.
Operations—transforming inputs into the final product.
Outbound logistics—order processing and distribution.
Marketing and sales—communication, pricing, and channel management.
Service—installation, repair, and parts.

Secondary Value Activities

Procurement—procedures and information systems.
Technology development—improving the product and processes/systems.
Human resource management—hiring, training, and compensation.
Firm infrastructure—general management, finance, accounting, government relations, and quality management.

FIGURE 4.5   The Value Chain

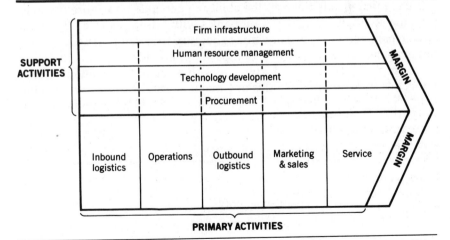

Reprinted with permission of The Free Press, a Division of Macmillan, Inc. from *Competitive Advantage: Creating and Sustaining Superior Performance* by Michael E. Porter. Copyright © 1985 by Michael E. Porter.

Each of the activities in the value chain is a potential source of competitive advantage and thus should be considered in assessing a competitor.

A Checklist of Assets and Skills

Figure 4.6 provides an overview checklist of the areas in which a competitor can have strengths and weaknesses. The first category is innovation. One of the strengths of Kao Corporation is its ability to develop innovative products in soaps, detergents, skin care, and even floppy disks. Its new products usually have a distinct technological advantage. In a highly technical industry the percentage spent on R&D and the emphasis along the basic/applied continuum can be one indicator of the cumulative ability to innovate. The outputs of the process in terms of product characteristics and performance capabilities, new products, product modifications, and patents provide more definitive measures of the company's ability to innovate.

The second area of competitor strengths and weaknesses is manufacturing. Perhaps the major area of strength of Texas Instruments' semiconductor and related businesses has been its manufacturing. One of the key potential strength areas in manufacturing involves sources of sustainable cost advantages. Is there anything about the nature of the plant or equipment, the raw material access, the level of vertical integration, or the type of work force that would support a sustainable cost advantage? Excess capacity can increase fixed costs, but it can also be a source of strength if the market is volatile or growing.

The third area is finance, the ability to generate or acquire funds in both the short and long run. Companies with "deep pockets" (financial resources) have a decisive advantage because they can pursue strategies not available to smaller firms. Compare General Motors with Chrysler, for example, or Miller and Budweiser with some of the smaller regional breweries. Operations provides one major source of funds. What is the nature of cash flow that is being generated and will be generated given

FIGURE 4.6   Analysis of Strengths and Weaknesses

INNOVATION

Technical product or service superiority
New product capability
R&D
Technologies
Patents

FIGURE 4.6   *(Continued)*

MANUFACTURING

Cost structure
Flexible production operations
Equipment
Access to raw material
Vertical integration
Work-force attitude and motivation
Capacity

FINANCE—ACCESS TO CAPITAL

From operations
From net short-term assets
Ability to use debt and equity financing
Parent's willingness to finance

MANAGEMENT

Quality of top and middle management
Knowledge of business
Culture
Strategic goals and plans
Entrepreneurial thrust
Planning/operation system
Loyalty—turnover
Quality of strategic decision making

MARKETING

Product quality reputation
Product characteristics/differentiation
Brand name recognition
Breadth of the product line—systems capability
Customer orientation
Segmentation/focus
Distribution
Retailer relationship
Advertising/promotion skills
Sales force
Customer service/product support

CUSTOMER BASE

Size and loyalty
Market share
Growth of segments served

the known uses for funds? Cash or other liquid assets provide other sources, as does a parent firm. The key is the ability of the business to justify the use of debt or equity and the will to access this source.

Management is the fourth area. ITT, during the era of Harold Geneen, prided itself on its strength in controlling and motivating a set of highly disparate business operations. One general dimension of analysis is simply the quality and depth of top and middle management and their loyalty as measured by turnover. Another is the culture. The values and norms that permeate an organization can energize some strategies and inhibit others. In particular, some organizations such as 3M possess both an entrepreneurial culture that allows them to initiate new directions and an organizational skill to nurture them. Strategic goals and plans can represent significant skills. To what extent does the business have a vision and the will and competence to pursue it?

The fifth area is marketing. Often the most important marketing strength, particularly in the high-tech fields, involves the product line, its quality reputation, the product-line breadth, and the features that serve to differentiate it from other products. Del Monte's brand name and its distribution were two areas of strength valued by Reynolds when it acquired Del Monte. The ability to develop a true customer orientation can be an important strength. Another strength can also be based on the ability and willingness to advertise effectively. The success of Perdue chickens was due, in part, to Perdue's ability to generate superior advertising. Other elements of the marketing mix such as sales force and service operation can also be sources of sustainable competitive advantage. One of Caterpillar's strengths is the quality of its dealer network. Still another possible strength, particularly in the high-tech field, is a competitor's ability to stay close to its customers.

The final area of interest is the customer base. How substantial is the customer base and how loyal is it? How are the competitor's offerings evaluated by its customers? What are the costs that customers will have to absorb if they switch to another supplier? Extremely loyal and happy customers are going to be difficult to dislodge. What are the size and growth potentials of the segments served?

The Competitive Strength Grid

With the relevant assets and skills identified, the next step is to scale your own firm and the major competitor or strategic groups of competitors on the relevant assets and skills. The result is termed a competitive strength grid and serves to summarize the posture of the competitors with respect to assets and skills.

A sustainable competitive advantage is almost always based on having a position superior to that of the target competitors on one or more assets or skill areas that are relevant both to the industry and to the strategy employed. Thus, information about each competitor's position with respect to relevant assets and skills is central to strategy development and evaluation.

If a superior position does not exist with respect to assets and skills important to the strategy, it probably will have to be created or the strategy may have to be modified or abandoned. Sometimes there simply is no point of difference with respect to the firms regarded as competitors. A skill that all competitors have will not be the basis for an SCA. For example, flight safety is important among airline passengers, but if airlines are perceived to be equal with respect to pilot quality and plane maintenance, it cannot be the basis for an SCA. Of course, if some airlines can convince passengers that they are superior with respect to antiterrorist security, then an SCA could indeed emerge.

The Gourmet Frozen-Food Industry.   A competitor strength grid is illustrated in Figure 4.7 for the gourmet frozen-food industry.[11] The relevant assets and skills are listed in order of their importance to the extent that an ordering can be obtained. The principal competitors are then positioned on each dimension according to their relative strengths and weaknesses. The process can generate insight into the nature of the assets and skills, competitor capabilities, and your own situation.

In Figure 4.7, eight assets and skills are listed and seven main competitors in the gourmet frozen-food industry in the mid–1980s are positioned. The grid suggests that Lean Cuisine is well positioned with the dominant market share, distribution, and advertising effort. Other firms have developed packaging advantages, however, and there may be an industry gap with respect to quality.

Analyzing Submarkets.   It is often desirable to conduct analysis for submarkets or strategic groups and perhaps for different products. A firm may not compete with all other firms in the industry but only those engaged in similar strategies and markets. For example, a competitor strength grid may look very different for the controlled-calorie portion of the gourmet frozen-food industry. In that context the weight-control dimension will be the most important and the Weight Watchers name will thus be a key advantage. In fact, during the late 1980s Weight Watchers invested heavily in product quality and packaging and, as a result, it narrowed the gap on both dimensions and surpassed Lean Cuisine as the leading brand.

FIGURE 4.7 Competitor Strength Grid

Assets and Skills	Weakness						Strength
Product quality	W	V B		A	L	M	L
Market share/share economies	V	B W		G V G	A L		L
Parent in related business	B	W	W	G	L	M	
Package		V B M	B	V	L	A A	W M
Low-calorie position	V	B M	B	A	L		M
Sales force/distribution	V	B W	G	A	A*	M	L
Advertising/promotion	V	B	A	L	W G	M	L
Ethnic position	W	A L	M	G		V	B

L   Stouffer's Lean Cuisine (Nestlé—also makes Stouffer's "Red Box" line)
M   Le Menu (Campbell Soup—also makes Swanson's, Mrs. Paul's)
W   Weight Watchers (Heinz)
A   Armour Dinner Classic/Classic Lite (ConAgra—also makes Banquet)
V   Van deKamp Mexican Classic and other ethnic lines
B   Benihana
G   Green Giant Stir Fry Entrées (Pillsbury)

The Analysis Process.   The process of developing a competitive strength grid can be extremely informative and useful. One approach is to have several managers create their own grids independently. The differences can usually illuminate different assumptions and information bases. A reconciliation stage can disseminate relevant information and identify and structure strategic questions. For example, different opinions about the quality reputation of a competitor may stimulate a strategic question that justifies marketing research. Another approach is to develop the grid in a group setting perhaps supported by preliminary staff work. When possible, objective information based on laboratory tests or customer perception studies should be used. The need for such information becomes clear when disagreements arise about where competitors should be scaled on the various dimensions.

OBTAINING INFORMATION ON COMPETITORS

Information on competitors is usually available from a variety of sources. Competitors usually communicate extensively to their suppliers, customers, and distributors; to security analysts and stockholders; and to government legislators and regulators. Contact with any of these can provide information. Monitoring of trade magazines, trade shows, advertising, speeches, annual reports, and the like can be informative. Technical meetings and journals can provide information about technical developments and activities. Thousands of databases accessible by computer are now available from which detailed information on competitors and facilities can be obtained.

One way to secure detailed information about a competitor's market standing with its customers is to use market research. For example, in a telephone survey of 1500 people from Los Angeles and Orange counties in California, respondents were asked a series of questions about supermarkets.[12] Which is closest to your home? Which do you shop at most often? Which has the lowest price? Best specials? Best customer service? Cleanest stores? Best-quality meat? Best-quality produce, and so on? The analysts allowed judgments to be made about the competitor's standing, the reasons behind it, and strategic implications.

The study showed that Ralph's had a strong image across the board and seemed to be in a good position to expand. On the other hand, Lucky used price leadership to compensate for a weak image and was thus vulnerable to competitive price moves. Two major chains, Alpha Beta and Safeway, were weak on many dimensions and seemed to need some significant strategy changes or infusions of capital to compete with Ralph's or Lucky. Three smaller chains all had extremely strong specialty department images, relatively high prices, and small market coverage. They were judged to be possible merger candidates.

SUMMARY

The first step in competitor analysis is to identify groups of competitors. One approach is customer-based and considers customer choice, the set of competitors from which the customer selects; another is based on product-use associations, the set of competitors whose products are used in the same use situation. In nearly all industries, competitors can be portrayed in terms of how intensely they compete with a reference business.

A second approach is to identify strategic groups, groups of competitive firms that pursue similar strategies and have similar assets, skills, and other characteristics. Mobility barriers between strategic groups are strategically important because they can protect a profitable strategy. It is also important to identify potential competitors—firms with the motivation and ability to enter an industry.

To gain an understanding of competitors, it is useful to analyze them on the basis of several dimensions. Their size, growth, and profitability provide a gross measure of their relative importance. An analysis of objectives and of past and current strategies can provide insights into intentions. Organizational factors such as culture and exit barriers can point out strategic constraints. Cost structures and exit barriers can be clues to likely price strategies and staying power.

The first step in analyzing competitor strengths and weaknesses is to identify the relevant assets and skills in an industry. Toward that end it is useful to consider the characteristics of successful and unsuccessful businesses, key customer motivations, large cost components, mobility barriers, and the value chain. The competitive strength grid, in which competitors or strategic groups are scaled on each of the relevant assets and skills, provides a compact summary of key strategic information.

Information on competitors can be obtained from market research and from a variety of other sources such as trade magazines, trade shows, customers, and suppliers.

FOOTNOTES

[1] David Halberstam, *The Reckoning*, New York: William Morrow, 1986, p. 310.

[2] Halberstam, *Reckoning*, p. 310.

[3] George S. Day, Allan D. Shocker, and Rajendra K. Srivastava, "Customer-Oriented Approaches to Identifying Product Markets," *Journal of Marketing* 43, Fall 1979, pp. 8–19.

[4] Briance Mascarenhas and David A. Aaker, "Mobility Barriers and Strategic Groups," *Strategic Management Journal*, September–October 1989, pp. 475–485.

[5] Sharon Oster, "Intraindustry Structure and the Ease of Strategic Change," *The Review of Economics and Statistics* 3, August 1982, pp. 376–383.

[6] Mascarenhas and Aaker, *op. cit.*

[7] Donald C. Waite III, "Deregulation and the Banking Industry," *Bankers Magazine* 163, January–February 1982, pp. 76–85.

[8] Michael E. Porter, *Competitive Strategy*, New York: The Free Press, 1980, pp. 20–21. The concept of exit barriers will be discussed again in Chapter 14.

[9] "Changing a Corporate Culture," *Business Week*, May 14, 1984, pp. 130–137.

[10] Michael E. Porter, *Competitive Advantage*, New York: The Free Press, 1985, Chapter 2.

[11] Material is drawn from papers prepared in 1984 by Alan Donald and Harvey Scodel and by David Barnes, Jacquelyn Boykin, Joe Jimenez, Barbara May, and Jill Stewart.

[12] Douglas J. Tigert, Sylvia Ma, and Terry Cotler, "Consumer Attitudes Towards and Shopping Habits at Major Supermarket Chains," Toronto, Canada: University of Toronto, December 1, 1976.

5

MARKET ANALYSIS

As the economy, led by the automobile industry, rose to a new high level in the twenties, a
complex of new elements came into existence
to transform the market: installment selling,
the used-car trade-in, the closed body, and
the annual model. (I would add improved
roads if I were to take into account the environment of the automobile.)

Alfred P. Sloan, Jr., General Motors

Market analysis builds on customer and competitor analyses to make some strategic judgments about the market (and submarkets) and its dynamics. One of the primary objectives of a market analysis is to determine the attractiveness of a market to current and potential participants. Market attractiveness, the market's profit potential as measured by the long-term return on investment achieved by its participants, will provide important input into the product-market investment decision. The frame of reference is all competitors. Whether or not a market is appropriate for a particular firm is a related but very different question. It will depend not only on the market attractiveness but also on how the firm's strengths and weaknesses match up against competitors'.

A second objective of market analysis is to understand the dynamics of the market. The need is to identify emerging key success factors, trends, threats, and opportunities and to develop strategic questions that can guide information gathering and analysis. A key success factor is an asset or skill that is needed to "play the game." If a firm has a strategic weakness in a key success factor that isn't neutralized by a well-conceived strategy, its ability to compete will be limited. The market trends can include those identified in customer or competitor analysis, but the perspective here is broader and others will usually emerge as well.

Defining the Market

To conduct a market or submarket analysis, the market boundaries need to be specified. The scope can involve an industry such as sporting goods or tennis rackets or a focused segment such as the market for recreational tennis rackets. Judgment about the most appropriate market scope can usually be based on competitor and customer analyses. The market frequently consists of the relevant products of the competitors identified in a competitor analysis.

The analysis usually needs to be conducted at several levels. The tennis racket industry might be the major focus of the analysis. However, an analysis of sporting goods might suggest and shed light on some substitute product pressures and market trends. Also, the analysis may be needed at the segment level because entry, investment, and strategy decisions are often made at the level of a segment. Furthermore, the key success factors could differ for different product markets within a market or industry. The result is a layered analysis, with the primary level obtaining the most depth of analysis. Ultimately, the decision on market boundaries will depend on the degree of cross-competition among the competitor groups and the likely strategic alternatives facing the firm.

DIMENSIONS OF A MARKET ANALYSIS

The nature and content of an analysis of a market and its relevant product markets will depend on context. However, it will often include the following dimensions:

● Actual and potential market size
● Market growth
● Market profitability
● Cost structure
● Distribution systems
● Trends and developments
● Key success factors

Figure 5.1 provides a set of questions structured around these dimen-

FIGURE 5.1   Questions to Structure a Market Analysis

SIZE AND GROWTH

What are the important and potentially important submarkets? What are their size and growth characteristics? What submarkets are or will soon decline? How fast? Will there be pockets of enduring demand?

PROFITABILITY

For each major submarket consider the following: Is this a business area in which the "average firm" will make money? How intense is the competition among existing firms? Evaluate the threats from potential entrants and substitute products. What is the bargaining power of suppliers and customers? How attractive/profitable are the market and its submarkets?

COST STRUCTURE

What are the major cost and value-added components for various types of competitors?

DISTRIBUTION SYSTEMS

What are the alternative channels of distribution? How are they changing?

TRENDS

What are the trends in the market?

KEY SUCCESS FACTORS

What are the key success factors, assets, and skills needed to compete successfully? How will these change in the future? How can the assets and skills of competitors be neutralized by strategies?

sions that can serve to stimulate a discussion identifying opportunities, threats, and strategic questions. Each of these dimensions will be addressed in turn, starting with an assessment of the market size. The chapter concludes with a section discussing the risks of growth markets.

ACTUAL AND POTENTIAL MARKET SIZE

A basic starting point for the analysis of a market or submarket is the total sales level. If it becomes reasonable to believe that a successful strategy can be developed that will gain a 15-percent share, it is important to know the total size. Knowledge of the submarkets is often critical. The value of the wine market may not be relevant when the competitive area is popular, premium or wine coolers.

Estimates of market size can be based on government sources or trade association findings. For example, such sources provide a breakdown of wine sales over time by type of wine, imported versus domestic, geographic markets, and even by competitor. Another approach is to obtain information on competitor sales from published financial sources, customers, or competitors. A more expensive approach would be to survey customers and project their usage to the total market.

Potential Market—The User Gap

In addition to the size of the current, relevant market, it is often useful to consider the potential market. A new use, new user group, or more frequent usage could change dramatically the size and prospects for the market.

There is unrealized potential for the cereal market in Europe and among institutional customers—restaurants and schools/day-care facilities.[1] All these segments have room for dramatic growth. In particular, Europeans buy only about 25 percent as much cereal as their U.S. counterparts. Furthermore, if technology allowed cereals to be used more conveniently away from home by providing shelf-stable milk products, usage could be further expanded. Of course, the key is not only to recognize the potential, but also to have the vision and program in place to exploit it. A host of strategists dismissed investment opportunities in industries because they lacked the insight to see the available potential and take advantage of it.

Ghost Potential

Sometimes the need for a product is so apparent that potential growth seems assured. However, this potential can have a ghostlike quality caused by factors inhibiting or preventing its realization.[2] For example, a huge demand for educational equipment exists in underdeveloped countries and in many sectors of developed countries, but a lack of funds inhibits buying.

Sometimes unanticipated political problems emerge, as happened to the atomic energy market in the mid–1970s.[3] Orders for reactors plummeted from 40 in 1973 to less than 5 in 1975 and fell to zero after the Three Mile Island accident in 1979. Pollution-control equipment is a market that grew much more slowly than had been anticipated. Potential participants failed to realize that purchases of unproductive equipment would be made only if required by legislation, and that legislation was not as forthcoming as public discussion implied.

Sometimes an area becomes so topical that its potential is easily exaggerated. As a Lewis Carroll character observed, "What I tell you three times is true." It is important to understand the assumptions and conditions underlying potential markets.

Small Can Be Beautiful

Some firms have investment criteria that prohibit them from investing in small markets. IBM and Procter & Gamble, for example, both look for large sales levels within a few years after launching a new product. The problem is that in an era of micromarketing, a lot of the action is in smaller niche segments. If a firm avoids them, it can lock itself out of much of the vitality and profitability of a business area. Furthermore, most substantial business areas were small at the outset, sometimes for many years. Avoiding the small market can thus often mean that a firm is always overcoming the first-mover advantage of others.

MARKET GROWTH

After the size of the market and its important submarkets has been estimated, the focus turns to growth rate. What will be the market's size in the future? If all else remains constant, growth means more sales and profits even without increasing market share. It can also mean less price pressure when demand increases faster than supply, and firms are not engaged in "experience curve" pricing, anticipating future lower costs. Conversely, declining market sales can mean reduced sales and often increased price pressure, as firms struggle to hold their shares of a diminishing pie.

The nominal strategy is thus to identify and invest in growth contexts and identify and avoid or disinvest in declining situations. Of course, the reality is not that simple. In particular, declining product markets can represent a real opportunity for a firm, in part because competitors may be exiting and disinvesting, instead of entering and investing for growth. The firm may attempt to become a profitable survivor by encouraging others to exit and by becoming dominant in the most viable segments. The pursuit of this strategy is considered in detail in Chapter 14.

The other half of conventional wisdom, that growth contexts are always attractive, can also fail to hold true. In fact, growth situations can involve substantial risks. Because of the importance of correctly assessing growth contexts, a discussion of these risks is presented at the end of the chapter.

Identifying Driving Forces

In many contexts, the most important strategic question involves the prediction of market sales. A key strategic decision, often an investment decision, can hinge on not only being correct but also understanding the driving forces behind market dynamics.

Addressing most key strategic questions starts with asking on what does the answer depend. In the case of projecting sales of a major market, the need is to determine what forces will drive those sales. It is often helpful to visualize several sales scenarios, like those shown in Figure 5.2. The following questions can then be posed. What has to happen if pattern C is to occur? What could cause pattern B? Answers usually provide the identity of strategic subquestions that may be pivotal in strategy development.

In the compact disk (CD) market of the mid–1980s, for example, the rate of growth could be driven by machine cost, the costs of the digital disks, the acceptance of the product in educational applications, government restrictions on recording digitally, and whether or not alternative technologies emerge. A key subquestion could then be what are the cost/price projections? A strategic subquestion can provide guidance for information search and analysis directions and can suggest scenario analyses. For example, low-cost versus high-cost scenarios could be explored.

In the wine market, the impact of anti-alcohol movements (like MADD), the tax policy, the relationship of wine to health, and the future demand for premium reds might be driving forces. One strategic subquestion might then focus on the likely strength of the anti-alcohol movements.

Forecasting Growth

Historical data can provide a useful perspective and help to separate hope from reality, but they need to be used with care. Apparent trends in

FIGURE 5.2   Sales Patterns

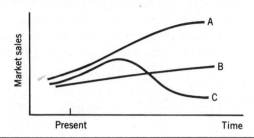

data can be caused by random fluctuations or by short-term economic conditions, and the urge to extrapolate should be resisted. Furthermore, the strategic interest is not on projections of history but rather the prediction of turning points, times when the rate and perhaps direction of growth change.

Sometimes leading indicators of market sales can be identified that may help forecasting and predicting turning points. Examples of leading indicators include:

- Demographic data. The number of births is a leading indicator for the demand for education, and the number of people reaching age 65 is a leading indicator of the demand for retirement facilities.
- Sales of related equipment. The sales of personal computers provide a leading indicator for the demand of supplies and service needs.

Market sales forecasts, especially of new markets, can be based on the experience of analogous industries. The trick is to identify a prior market with similar characteristics. The sales of color televisions might be expected to have a pattern similar to that of black-and-white televisions, for example. The sales of a new type of snack might look to the history of other previously introduced snack categories or of other consumer products, such as liquid diet products, granola cereal, or breakfast bars. The most value will be obtained if several analogous product classes can be examined and the differences in the product class experiences related to their characteristics.

Methods now exist to provide remarkably accurate forecasts of sales patterns for durable products such as appliances, cameras, and videotape machines. They are based, in part, on decomposing sales into first purchases and replacement sales.

Detecting Maturity and Decline

One particularly important set of turning points in market sales is when the growth phase of the product life cycle changes to a flat maturity phase, and when the maturity phase changes into a decline phase. These transitions are important to the health and nature of the market. Often they are accompanied by changes in key success factors. Historical sales and profit patterns of a market can help to identify the onset of maturity or decline, but the following often are more sensitive indicators:

- **Price pressure caused by overcapacity and the lack of product differentiation.** When growth slows or even reverses, capacity developed under a more optimistic scenario becomes excessive. Furthermore, the product-evolution process often results in most competitors matching product improvements. Thus, it becomes more difficult to maintain meaningful differentiation.

- **Buyer sophistication and knowledge.** Buyers tend to become more familiar and knowledgeable as the product matures and thus become less willing to apply a premium price to obtain the security of an established name. Computer buyers over the years have gained confidence in their ability to select computers—as a result, the value of big names like IBM recedes.

- **Substitute products or technologies.** The sales of CD players provide an indicator of the decline in tape players.

- **Saturation.** When the number of potential first-time buyers declines, market sales should mature or decline.

- **No growth sources.** The market is fully penetrated and there are no visible sources of growth from new uses or users.

- **Customer disinterest.** A reduction in the interest of customers in applications, new product announcements, and so on.

MARKET PROFITABILITY ANALYSIS

Economists have long studied why some industries or markets are profitable and others are not. Michael Porter, a Harvard economist, applied his theories and findings to the business strategy problem of evaluating the investment value of an industry or market.[4] The problem is to estimate how profitable the average firm will be. It is hoped, of course, that a firm will develop a strategy that will bring above-average profits. However, if the average profit level is low, the task of succeeding financially will be much more difficult than if the average profitability were high.

Porter's approach to estimate the profitability of a market is called industry structure analysis, but can be applied to a market or submarket within an industry. The basic idea is that the attractiveness of an industry or market as measured by the long-term return on investment of the average firm depends largely on five factors that influence profitability as shown in Figure 5.3.

● The intensity of competition.

● The existence of potential competitors who will enter if profits are high.

● Substitute products that will attract customers if prices become high.

● The bargaining power of customers.

● The bargaining power of suppliers.

Each plays a role in explaining why some industries are historically more profitable than others. An understanding of this structure can also suggest which key success factors are necessary to cope with the competitive forces.

Competitors

The intensity of competition from existing competitors will depend on several factors, including:

● The number of competitors.

● Their relative size.

● Whether or not their product offerings and strategies are similar.

FIGURE 5.3   Five-Factor Model of Market Profitability

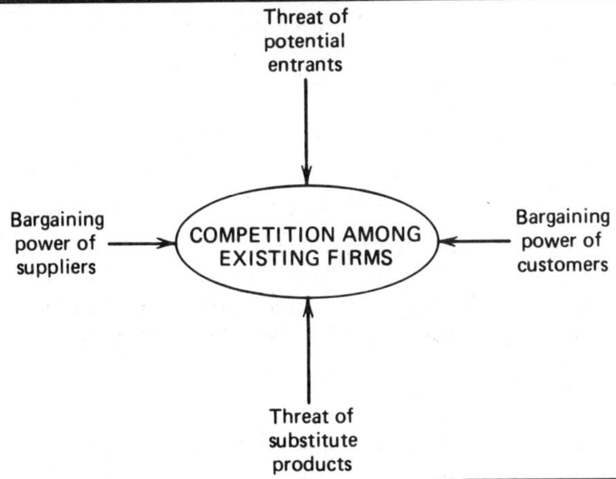

SOURCE: Adapted from Michael F. Porter, "Industry Structure and Competitive Strategy: Keys to Profitability," *Financial Analysis Journal,* July–August 1980, p. 33.

- The existence of high fixed costs.
- The commitment of competitors.
- The size and nature of exit barriers

As a first approximation, the more competitors, the more competitive intensity. However, the nature of the competitors will make a great deal of difference. The relative size of the competitors will affect competitive intensity, for example. If a ten-firm market is dominated by a few firms, the level of competition will usually be much less than if ten competitors of equal size are present. Furthermore, if the competitors have more highly differentiated products and employ different strategies, the pressure on prices will be less than in a commodity market such as steel. The existence of high fixed costs, as in the airline market, will stimulate price competition to improve capacity utilization.

Of particular importance in this analysis phase is to understand the commitment and exit barriers of the competitors. To what extent will they be motivated to spend whatever is needed to maintain position? In general, a firm that is undiversified and has made major commitments to facilities or sources of supply will be highly committed. Gallo, for example, has nearly all its sales tied to wine and has extensive vertical integration. It thus has a high level of commitment. A commitment to a business can also be created when that business supports other parts of a firm. A retailer may need to remain in several undesirable sites to maintain a critical mass regionally.

Another related consideration is the exit barriers such as specialized assets, long-term contracts, commitments to customers and distributors, and relationships to other parts of a firm. Exit barrier analysis (discussed further in Chapter 14) provides a tool for predicting the extent to which exiting will occur.

Potential Competitors

Chapter 4 discusses identifying potential competitors that might have an interest in entering an industry or market. Whether potential competitors, identified or not, actually do enter, however, depends in large part on the size and nature of barriers to entry. Thus, an analysis of barriers to entry is important in projecting the likely competitive intensity and profitability levels in the future. Entry barriers have helped the cereal market restrict entry for many decades so that Kellogg's, General Mills, Post (General Foods), and Quaker Oats control the market. Entry barriers include:

- **Capital investment required.** Industries like mining or automobiles require large investments that increase risk.

- **Economies of scale.** If scale economies exist in production, advertising, distribution, or other areas, it becomes necessary to obtain a large volume quickly. In the cereal market, for example, it has been estimated that production economies of scale occur at approximately 5 percent of U.S. sales. Since a successful brand may gain only a 1 percent share, a new firm would need to score five winners, which is virtually impossible.

- **Distribution channels.** Gaining distribution in some markets can be extremely difficult and costly. Even large established firms that sell products with substantial marketing budgets have trouble obtaining space on the supermarket shelf. The cereal firms have encouraged shelf space to be allocated according to historical share, making it hard for a newcomer to break in.

- **Product differentiation.** Established firms may have high levels of customer loyalty caused and maintained by protected product features, a brand name and image, advertising, and customer service. Markets in which product differentiation barriers are particularly high include cereal, soft drinks, beer, cosmetics, over-the-counter drugs, and banking.

Substitute Products

Substitute products are represented by those sets of competitors that are identified as competing with less intensity than the primary competitors. They are still relevant, however, and can influence the profitability of the market and, in fact, can be a major threat or problem. Thus, plastics, glass, and fiber-foil products exert pressure on the metal can market. Electronic alarm systems are substitutes for the security guard market. Fax machines and electronic mail provide a serious threat to the express delivery market pioneered by Federal Express. Substitutes that show a steady improvement in relative price/performance and for which the customer's cost of switching is minimal are of particular interest.

Customer Power

When customers have relatively more power than sellers, they can force prices down or demand more services, thereby affecting profitability. A customer's power will be greater when its purchase size is a large proportion of the seller's business, when alternative suppliers are available, and when the customer can integrate backward and make all or part of the product. Thus, tire manufacturers face powerful customers in the automobile firms. The customers of metal can manufacturers are large packaged-goods manufacturers who have over time demanded price and service concessions and who have engaged in backward integration.

Cereal firms face an increasingly strong and assertive supermarket industry. Supermarkets rather than cereal firms, for example, are now calling the shots on consumer promotions.

Supplier Power

When the supplier industry is concentrated and sells to a variety of customers in diverse markets, it will have relative power that can be used to influence prices. Power will also be enhanced when the costs to customers of switching suppliers are high. Thus, the highly concentrated oil industry is often powerful enough to influence profits in customer industries that find it expensive to convert from oil. However, the potential for regeneration whereby industries can create their own power, perhaps by recycling waste, may have changed the balance of power in some contexts.

COST STRUCTURE

An understanding of the cost structure of a market can provide insights into present and future key success factors. The first step is to conduct an analysis to determine where value is added to the product (or service). In most contexts, a series of value-added steps such as those shown in Figure 5.4 can be identified. The proportion of value added attributed to one production stage becomes so important an indicator that a key success factor is associated with that stage. It may be possible to develop control over a resource or technology as the OPEC cartel did. More likely, competitors will aim to be the lowest cost competitor in the highest value-added stage of production. Advantages in lower value-added stages will simply have less leverage. Thus, in the metal can business, transportation costs are relatively high and a competitor that can locate plants near customers will have a significant cost advantage.

Of course, it may not be possible to gain an advantage at high value-added stages. For example, a raw material such as flour for bakery firms may represent a high value added, but because the raw material is widely available at commodity prices, it will not be a key success factor. Nevertheless, it is often useful to look first at the highest value-added stages.

It is very important, especially in fast-moving growth markets, to be able to anticipate changes in key success factors. One approach is to examine the changes in the relative importance of the value-added stages. For example, the cement market was very regional when it was restricted to rail or truck transportation. With the development of specialized ships, however, waterborne transportation costs dropped dra-

FIGURE 5.4   Value Added by Production Stage

Production Stage	Markets That Have Key Success Factors Associated with the Production Stage
Raw material procurement	Gold mining, wine making
Raw material processing	Steel, paper
Production fabricating	Integrated circuits, tires
Assembly	Apparel, instrumentation
Physical distribution	Bottled water, metal cans
Marketing	Branded cosmetics, liquor

Source: Adapted from Management Analysis Center, Strategy Formulation, Cambridge, Mass.

matically. Key success factors changed from local ground transportation to access to the specialized ships and production scale. For many electronics goods, the largest value-added item changed from assembly to components, as more of the product was integrated into components.

Another market cost structure consideration is the extent to which experience curve strategies are feasible. Can firms develop sustainable cost advantages based on volume? Are there large, fixed costs that would generate economies of scale? The experience curve concept and approaches to determine whether the context is compatible with such a strategy are presented in Chapter 11.

DISTRIBUTION SYSTEMS

An analysis of distribution systems should include three types of questions:

● What are the alternative distribution channels?

● What are the trends? What channels are growing in importance? What new channels have emerged or are likely to?

● Who has the power in the channel and how is that likely to shift?

Access to an effective and efficient distribution channel is often a key success factor. Channel alternatives can vary in several ways. One is the degree of directness. Some companies—such as Avon, Tupperware, and many industrial businesses—sell directly through their own sales force. Others, such as Radio Shack and several shoe firms, sell through their own retail stores. Still other firms sell directly to retailers, sell through distributors or other middlemen, or use some combination of channels. The firms closest to the end user have the most control over marketing and usually assume the highest risk.

Sometimes the creation of a new channel form can lead to a sustainable competitive advantage. A dramatic example is the success that L'eggs hosiery achieved by its ability to market hosiery in supermarkets. L'eggs, of course, supported the idea of using supermarkets with a comprehensive program that addressed a host of issues. The L'eggs program involved performing in-store functions including ordering and stocking, selling on consignment a product relatively difficult to shoplift, using a space-efficient vertical display, and providing a high-quality, low-priced product supported by national advertising. Thus, it is useful to consider not only existing channels but potential ones.

An analysis of likely or emerging changes within distribution channels can be important in understanding a market and its key success factors. The increased sale of wine in supermarkets made it much more important for wine makers to focus on packaging and advertising. The decision by Levi Strauss to move beyond department and specialty stores and sell its products in Sears affects the channels for boys' and men's wear. The emergence of discount bookstores, the growth of convenience food stores in gas stations, the role of catalog discount stores, and the growth of specialty catalog retailing illustrate trends that have strategic importance to firms affected by the channels involved.

Related to customer power in market profitability analysis is channel power. In industries without strong brand names such as furniture, retailers usually have relatively high power and can hold down the price that manufacturers are paid. The enhanced power of supermarkets, caused in large part by the explosion of transaction information and the importance of promotions, has altered the way packaged goods are marketed. The influence that P&G and other packaged goods firms once had on promotions, stocking, and display decisions has been significantly reduced. The ability of pharmacists to substitute generic drugs has altered power in that industry.

MARKET TRENDS

Often one of the most useful elements of external analysis comes from addressing the question, what are the market trends? The question has two important attributes: it focuses on change and tends to identify what is important. As a result, strategically useful insights almost always result. A discussion of market trends can serve as a useful summary of customer, competitor, and market analyses. It is thus helpful to identify trends near the end of market analysis.

Rampant brand proliferation in the cereal market is a trend with substantial strategic implications.[5] During the last half-decade some 80 new brands have been introduced, in the face of increased introduction costs and constraints on shelf space. This trend suggests that a skill in new product activity as well as a strong base of established brands is a key success factor in the market.

A significant trend in the discount brokerage business is the growth in products and services being offered by discounters.[6] Once solely focused on stocks and bonds, discounters have added or are considering a host of products and services such as mutual funds, IRAs, access to software databases, and 24-hour trading. The primary motivation is to offer enhanced customer service. A strategic problem is how to expand services without undercutting their cost advantage and their positioning as a no-frills, low-cost option.

One trend in the early 1990s in the workstation market was a progressively blurring distinction between personal computers and workstations.[7] Personal computers were becoming more powerful and workstation manufacturers were moving into the office market. Workstation manufacturers were developing "server" computers that could provide data-sharing and networking capabilities with some of the graphics that were needed for advanced engineering applications. An implication for the personal computer market was that a major new strategic group had appeared.

KEY SUCCESS FACTORS—BASES OF COMPETITION

An important output of market analysis is the identification of key success factors for strategic groups in the market. They are a set of assets and skills that provide the bases for competing successfully. There are two types. First, there are the strategic necessities, which do not necessarily provide an advantage because others have them, but their absence will create a substantial weakness. Second, there are the strategic strengths, those at which a firm excels, the assets or skills that are superior to those of competitors and provide a base of advantage. The set of skills and assets developed in competitor analysis provides a base set from which key success factors can be identified. The questions to consider are which are the most critical skills and assets now and, more important, which will be most critical in the future.

One study of six mature product industries showed that the key success factors (KSF) differed by industry in predictable ways—a capital goods maker will have different KSFs than an operating supplies firm—and those firms that have strengths matching the KSFs perform substantially better than other firms.[8] The failure of firms such as Philip Morris and P&G to crack the soda market while lacking the KSF of "access to bottlers" provides an illustration of the concept in action.

In the recording market where hit records need to be created and managed, the key success factors include:[9]

- An inventory of artists with a balance of developing artists and established mainstream acts.

- The skill of managing an artist's career to maximize the attractiveness of the firm to the artist and to create successful labels.

- The ability to control fixed and marginal costs and to obtain scale economies by manufacturing other labels if necessary.

- Quick response systems to exploit a hit when it occurs.

An analysis of the wine market in the early 1990s identified seven key success factors:[10]

- Access to a quality grape supply (50 percent of the variable cost), especially for those in the premium segments.

- Access to technology both in the vineyard and winery so that costs can be controlled.

- The achievement of adequate scale, perhaps with a set of brands.

- Expertise in wine making.

- Name recognition—a sense of tradition and a "California connection" are very helpful.

- Strong relationships with distributors.

- The financial resources to compete in a capital-intensive business.

An analysis will be needed for each strategic group, because the required skills and assets for each will likely be different. For example, the bulk wineries such as JFJ Bronco Wine Company make and sell wine in bulk to other wineries and to private labelers such as the major supermarkets and liquor-store chains. Key success factors for bulk wine include the ability to make wine at acceptable quality using modern production facilities and scale economies so that sustainable cost advantages can be achieved. These key success factors are very different from those for the wine market in general.

It is important not only to identify KSFs, but also to project them into the future and, in particular, identify emerging KSFs. Many firms have faltered when KSFs changed and the skills and assets on which they were relying became less relevant. For example, for industrial firms, technology and innovation tend to be most important during the introduction and growth phases, whereas the roles of systems capability, marketing, and service backup become more dominant as the market matures. In consumer products, marketing and distribution skills are crucial during the introduction and growth phases, but operations and manufacturing become more crucial as the product settles into maturity and decline phases.

RISKS IN HIGH-GROWTH MARKETS

The conventional wisdom that the strategist should seek out growth areas often neglects a substantial set of associated risks. As shown in Figure 5.5, there is the risk that:[11]

- The number and commitment of competitors is greater than can be supported by the market.
- A competitor enters with a superior product or low-cost advantage.
- Key success factors change and the organization cannot adapt.
- Technology changes.
- The market growth fails to meet expectations.
- Resources are inadequate to maintain a high growth rate.
- Adequate distribution may not be available.

Competitive Overcrowding

Perhaps the most serious risk is that too many competitors will be attracted by a growth situation and enter with unrealistic market share expectations. The reality may be that sales volume is insufficient to support all of them. Consider, for example, the hundreds of participants in the personal computer market in the early 1990s. The Japanese damaged the value of many high-growth markets by rushing in at large numbers and building excessive capacity.

The following conditions are found in markets in which a surplus of competitors is likely to be attracted, and a subsequent shakeout is highly probable:

1. The market and its growth rate have high visibility; as a result, strategists in related firms are encouraged to consider the market seriously and, in fact, may fear the consequences of turning their backs on an obvious growth direction.

2. Very high forecast and actual growth in the early stages are pointed to as evidence confirming high market growth as a proven phenomenon.

3. Threats to the growth rate are not considered or are discounted—little exists to dampen the enthusiasm surrounding the market. In fact, the enthusiasm may be contagious when venture capitalists and stock analysts become advocates.

FIGURE 5.5   Risks of High-Growth Markets

4. Few initial barriers to entry exist to prevent firms from entering the market.

5. Products employ an existing technology rather than a risky or protected technology. Technology sometimes provides a more obvious and formidable barrier than, for example, a finance or marketing barrier. The true significance of a marketing barrier to entry, such as limited retail space, may be evident only after the market is overcrowded.

6. Some potential entrants have low visibility and their intentions are unknown or uncertain; thus, the quantity and commitment of competitors are likely to be underestimated.

The shakeout itself often occurs during a relatively short period of time. The trigger is likely to be a combination of (1) an unanticipated slowing of market growth, either because the market is close to saturation or a recession has intervened; (2) aggressive late entrants buying their way into the market by cutting prices; (3) the market leader attempting to stem the previous erosion of its market position with aggressive product and price retaliation; or (4) the key success factors in the market change as a consequence of technological development, perhaps raising the minimum scale of operations, or a shift in the value-added structure. Each of these possible triggering events introduces further sources of risk.

A Superior Competitive Entry

The ultimate risk is that a position will be established in a healthy growth market and a competitor will enter late with a product that is demonstrably superior or that has an inherent cost advantage. Thus, although IBM entered the personal computer market late, it established a strong if not dominant position by capitalizing on its name, its assurance of being a survivor, software availability, and service backup. The late entry of low-cost products from the Far East has occurred in countless industries, including radios, TVs, semiconductors, VCRs, and computer peripherals and components.

Changing Key Success Factors

A firm may be successful at establishing a strong position during the early stages of market development, only to lose ground later when key success factors change. One forecast is that the surviving personal computer makers will be those able to achieve low-cost production through vertical integration or exploitation of the experience curve, those able to obtain efficient, low-cost distribution, and those able to provide software for their customers—capabilities not necessarily critical during the early stages of market evolution. Many product markets have experienced a shift over time from a focus on product technology to process technology. A firm that might be capable of achieving product technology-based advantages may not have the resources, skills, and orientation/culture needed to develop the process technology-based advantages that the evolving market demands.

Changing Technology

Developing the first-generation technology can involve a commitment to a product line and production facilities that may become obsolete, and to a technology that may not survive. A safe strategy is to wait until it becomes clear which technology will dominate and then attempt to improve it with a compatible entry. When the principal competitors have committed themselves, the most promising avenues for the development of a sustainable competitive advantage become more visible. In contrast, the early entry has to navigate with a great deal of uncertainty. For these reasons, most large computer companies were slow to make significant commitments to advanced office systems. They were uncertain what interconnecting software and hardware would be the basis for the systems adopted.

Disappointing Market Growth

Many shakeouts and price wars occur when market growth falls below expectations. For example, the software market enjoyed substantial growth in the mid–1980s, but the fact that it was considerably less than forecast contributed to a shakeout. After the breakup of AT&T in 1984, sales of telephones rose 60 percent over 1983 to $1.6 billion, which was far less than what the 200-plus firms that entered the home phone business in the early 1980s had expected.[12] The disappointing sales levels plus some mistaken judgments that consumers would be attracted by phones that were gimmicky or cheap caused disastrous write-offs. Forecasting is difficult, especially when the product market involved is new and dynamic and glamorized by popular euphoria.

The difficulty in forecasting is graphically illustrated by an analysis of over 90 forecasts of significant new products, markets, and technologies that appeared in *Business Week, Fortune,* and the *Wall Street Journal* from 1960 to 1979.[13] Forecast growth failed to materialize in about 55 percent of the cases cited. Among the reasons were overevaluation of technologies (e.g., three-dimensional color TV and tooth-decay vaccines) or consumer demand (e.g., two-way cable TV, quadraphonic stereo, and dehydrated foods) or a failure to consider the cost barrier (e.g., the SST and moving sidewalks) or political problems (e.g., marine mining). The forecasts for "roll-your-own" cigarettes, small cigars, Scotch whiskey, and CB radios suffered from shifts in consumer needs and preferences.

Resource Constraints

The substantial financing requirements associated with a rapidly growing business are a major constraint for small firms. Royal Crown's Diet-Rite Cola lost its leadership position to Coca-Cola's Tab and Diet Pepsi in the mid–1960s when it could not match the advertising and distribution clout of its larger rivals. Even large, well-financed firms may have problems if they face heavy competing demands on available investment resources. Furthermore, financing requirements frequently are increased by higher than expected product development and market entry costs and by price erosion caused by aggressive or desperate competitors.

The organizational pressures and problems created by growth can be even more difficult to predict and deal with than financial strains. Many firms have failed to survive the rapid-growth phase because they were unable to obtain and train people to handle the expanded business or to adjust their systems and structures. Tandem Computers, which has justifiably prided itself on its ability to manage growth, believes its ability to grow is limited by its capacity to hire and train people. It is careful to avoid allowing growth to outstrip its personnel resources. Tandem has also attempted to have systems and structures in place in anticipation of future growth. In contrast, Korvette was an extremely successful pioneer discount chain until it failed to digest a growth spurt that saw sales and store size triple from 1962 to 1966. It simply was not able to develop the systems, structure, and personnel needed to cope with a much larger scale of operations.

Distribution Constraints

Most distribution channels can support only a small number of brands. For example, few retailers are willing to provide shelf space for more than four or five brands of a houseware appliance. As a consequence, some competitors, even those with attractive products and marketing programs, will not gain adequate distribution, which means their marketing programs will become less effective.

Distribution limitations fueled the shakeout already appearing in the software business in the mid–1980s. Over 120 firms were making financial spreadsheet programs, whereas the market and distribution channels could not support more than a handful. Ultimately, only a few may survive.

A corollary of the scarcity and selectivity of distributors, as market growth begins to slow, is a marked increase in their power. Their willingness to use this power to extract price and promotion concessions from manufacturers or to drop suppliers is often heightened by their own problems in maintaining margins in the face of extreme competition for their own customers. Many of the same factors that drew in an overabundance of manufacturers also contribute to overcrowding in subsequent stages of a distribution channel. The eventual shakeout at this level can have equally serious repercussions for suppliers.

SUMMARY

Market analysis is intended to help determine the attractiveness of a market to current and potential participants and to understand that market's structure and dynamics. A market analysis is often conducted along the following seven dimensions:

1. **Actual and potential market size.** The potential market includes the usage gap, which can be penetrated by creating increased use frequency, more variety of uses, new users, and new uses.

2. **Market growth.** To forecast growth patterns, it can be helpful to consider the forces driving sales, leading indicators, analogous industries, pressure on prices, and the existence of substitute products.

3. **Market profitability.** The competitive intensity of a market or any submarket will depend on five factors—existing competitors, the power of suppliers and customers, and the threat of substitute products and potential entrants. Barriers to entry include capital invest-

ment, economies of scale, access to distribution channels, and product differentiation.

4. **Cost structure.** One way to detect key success factors is to analyze the value added by the production stage and observe how it is changing. Another consideration is whether or not the market setting makes an experience curve strategy appropriate or even feasible.

5. **Distribution channels.** The need is to identify alternative channels and trends in their relative importance and to analyze the power relationships in each channel and how they might be changing.

6. **Market trends.** What market trends will affect future market profitability and its key success factors?

7. **Key success factors.** What skills and assets are needed to compete in a strategic group now and in the future?

Growth market contexts involve a set of risks, the prime one being the threat of more competitors than the market can support. Other risks include the failure to gain distribution, inadequate resources, changing key success factors, changing technologies, the entry of superior products, and a failure of the market to meet growth expectations.

FOOTNOTES

[1] Greg Stanger, Clark Newby, Todd Andrews, Rob Kramer, Presley Stokes, and Lisen Stromberg, "The Ready to Eat Cereal Market". unpublished paper, 1991.

[2] Aubrey Wilson and Bryan Atkin, "Exorcising the Ghosts in Marketing," *Harvard Business Review*, September–October 1976, pp. 117–127.

[3] "Soviet Accident's Impact," *San Francisco Chronicle*, May 1, 1986, p. 31.

[4] This section draws on Michael E. Porter, *Competitive Advantage*, New York: The Free Press, 1985, Chapter 1.

[5] Stanger et al., *op. cit.*

[6] Dirk Cussler, Angela Hawkins, Deborah MacDonald, Ken Phillips, and Oscar Urizar, "The Discount Brokerage Industry," unpublished paper, 1987.

[7] Anjali Grover, Per Lindberg, Paul Roberts, and Barbara Swales, "A Marketing Analysis of the Workstation Industry," unpublished paper, 1991.

[8] Jorge Alberto Sousa De Vasconcellos and Donald C. Hambrick, "Key Success Factors: Test of a General Theory in the Mature Industrial-Product Sector," *Strategic Management Journal,* July–August 1989, pp. 376–382.

[9] Joe Brand, Lavon Eldemir, Ellen Ablow, and Stephen Ramirez, "The Record Industry," unpublished paper, 1990.

[10] John Dougery, Tomas Fabregas, Christan Koch, Lars Kogstad, and Alexis Nasard, "The California Wine Industry Report," unpublished paper, 1991.

[11] Drawn from David A. Aaker and George S. Day, "Perils of High-Growth Markets," *Strategic Management Journal* 7, 1986, pp. 409–421.

[12] B. O'Reilly, "Lessons from the Home Phone Wars," *Fortune*, December 24, 1984, pp. 83–86.

[13] Steven P. Schnaars, "Growth Market Forecasting Revisited: A Look Back at a Look Forward," *California Management Review* 28(4), Summer 1986.

6

ENVIRONMENTAL ANALYSIS

There is something in the wind.

William Shakespeare,
The Comedy of Errors

A poorly observed fact is more treacherous than a faulty train of reasoning.

Paul Valéry, French philosopher

External analysis is concerned with identifying trends, opportunities, threats, and strategic questions that will affect and influence strategy and choice. In Chapters 3 through 5, the analysis is restricted to the market or industry and its participants. In this chapter, the focus changes to the environment surrounding the market. The interest is in environmental trends and events with the potential to affect strategy either directly or indirectly. Environmental analysis should identify such trends and events and estimate their likelihood and impact.

Although environmental analysis is one step removed from the market or industry, it is only one step. When conducting environmental analysis, it is very easy to get bogged down in an extensive, broad analysis that is heavily descriptive. For practical reasons alone, it is necessary to restrict the analysis to those areas relevant enough to have a significant impact on strategy.

Environmental analysis can be divided usefully, as shown in Figure 6.1, into five areas: technological, governmental, economic, cultural, and demographic. Each area is discussed and illustrated. Then, methods to forecast trends and events are presented. Clearly, an ability to anticipate important changes will be helpful. Scenario analysis—ways of creating and using future scenarios to help generate and evaluate strategies—follows. The question of identifying and prioritizing information-need areas is then addressed.

DIMENSIONS OF ENVIRONMENTAL ANALYSIS

Technology

One dimension of environmental analysis is technological trends or technological events occurring outside the market or industry that have the potential to impact strategies. They can represent opportunities to those in a position to capitalize. A new alternate technology could also pose a significant threat. For example, the cable TV industry, with its massive investment in the wiring of homes, is rightfully concerned with systems that allow customers to obtain signals directly from orbiting satellites. Express delivery services such as Federal Express have been affected by new forms of communication such as fax and e-mail.

Impact of New Technologies.   Certainly it can be important, even critical, to manage the transition to a new technology. The appearance of a new technology, however, even a successful one, does not necessarily mean that businesses based on the prior technology will suddenly become unhealthy.

FIGURE 6.1 Environmental Analysis

TECHNOLOGY
To what extent are existing technologies maturing?
What technological developments or trends are affecting or could affect the
  industry?

GOVERNMENT
What changes in regulation are possible? What will their impact be?
What tax or other incentives are being developed that might affect strategy?
What are the political risks of operating in a governmental jurisdiction?

ECONOMICS
What are economic prospects and inflation outlets for the countries in which the
  firm operates? How will they affect strategy?

CULTURE
What are the current or emerging trends in life-styles, fashions, and other components of culture? Why? What are their implications?

DEMOGRAPHICS
What demographic trends will affect the market size of the industry or its submarkets? What demographic trends represent opportunities or threats?

GENERAL EXTERNAL ANALYSIS QUESTIONS
What are the significant trends and future events?
What threats and opportunities do you see?
What are the key strategic questions—areas of uncertainty as to trends or events
  that have the potential to impact strategy? Evaluate these strategic questions in
  terms of their impact.

SCENARIOS
What scenarios are potentially worth being the basis of a scenario analysis?

A group of researchers at Purdue studied 15 companies in five industries in which a dramatic new technology had emerged:[1]

● Diesel-electric locomotives versus steam
● Transistors versus vacuum tubes
● Ballpoint pens versus fountain pens
● Nuclear power versus boilers for fossil-fuel plants
● Electric razors versus safety razors

Several interesting conclusions emerged that should give pause to anyone attempting to predict the impact of a dramatic new technology. First, the sales of the old technology continued for a substantial period, in part because the firms involved continued to improve it. Safety-razor sales have actually increased 800 percent since the advent of the electric razor. Thus, a new technology may not even signal the end of the growth phase of an existing technology. In all cases, firms involved with an old technology had a substantial amount of time to react to a new technology.

Second, it is relatively difficult to predict the outcome of a new technology. The new technologies studied tended to be expensive and crude at first. Furthermore, they started by invading submarkets. Transistors, for example, were first used in hearing aids and pocket radios. In addition, new technologies tended to create new markets instead of simply encroaching on existing ones. Throw-away ballpoint pens and many of the transistor applications were completely new-market application areas.

The Technology Life Cycle. Many technologies have life cycles. In the computer-printer industry, dot matrix printers and ink-jet systems are on the decline and laser printers are in the late growth stage, while other technologies are just getting started. The key to managing the transition from one technology to another is to detect when the original technology is in the decline phase.

Richard N. Foster of McKinsey suggests three signals that indicate a technology is entering a decline and is ready to be replaced by another.[2] First, performance levels are approaching physical barriers. For example, fiber strength is limited by intermolecular bonds and thus cannot be improved indefinitely. Second, R&D efforts are becoming less effective and more oriented to process improvements than new-product breakthroughs. Ineffective R&D is often blamed on the quality of the R&D staff and its management when it is caused simply by the inherent difficulty of improving a mature technology. Third, small competitors are experimenting with alternative technologies that seem risky and uneconomical.

Forecasting New Technologies. One study indicated that past efforts to forecast technology have been remarkably successful. Richard N. Farmer looked back at the efforts to forecast environmental trends and events as represented by 21 articles that appeared in *Fortune* magazine during the 1930s and 1940s.[3] He found articles written prior to 1940 that made predictions about synthetic vitamins, genetic breakthroughs, the decline of railroads, the likelihood of TVs in all homes, the house-trailer explo-

---

Information Technology

In nearly every industry, it is useful to ask what potential impact new information technology based on computer systems and new databases will have on strategies. How will it create SCAs and key success factors? Apparel manufacturers such as Levi Strauss, drug wholesalers such as McKesson-Robbins, and retailers such as The Limited all have developed systems of inventory control, ordering, and shipping that represent substantial SCAs with which competitors have had to deal. Federal Express has stayed ahead of competitors by investing heavily in information technology. It was the first to have the ability to track packages throughout its systems and the first to link its systems with customers' computers. Merrill Lynch's Cash Management Account provided substantial customer benefits.

In supermarket retailing the use of "smart cards," cards that customers would present during checkout to pay for purchases, has been tested. Their use provides a record of all purchases that would potentially allow:

- Stores to build loyalty by rewarding cumulative purchase volume.
- Promotions to target individual customers based on their brand preferences and household characteristics.
- The use of cents-off coupons without the customer or store having to handle pieces of paper; the purchase of a promoted product would be discounted automatically.
- The store to identify buyers of slow-moving items to predict the impact on the store's choice of dropping an item.
- Decisions as to shelf space allocation, special displays, and store layout to be refined based on detailed data of customer shopping.

---

sion, and the advent of superhighways. An article in 1946 accurately predicted the advent of the automated factory and the associated-systems-analysis technology. Although Farmer found positive evidence of success at forecasting the impact of individual technologies, the record was much less impressive when it involved the cross-impact of one technology on another. For example, the impact of television on movies or the impact of diesel locomotives on steam locomotives was not considered. One implication of this study is that it is necessary to be more sensitive to the impact of a possible technological development on other technologies. We will return to cross-impact analysis shortly.

Government

The addition or removal of legislative or regulatory constraints can pose major strategic threats and opportunities. For example, the ban of some ingredients in food products (e.g., cyclamates) or cosmetics has dramatically affected the strategies of numerous firms. The impact of governmental efforts to reduce piracy in industries such as software (over one-fourth of all software used is copied), audiocassettes, and movie videos is of crucial import to those affected. Deregulation in air travel, banking, railroads, and other industries has had enormous implications for the firms involved.

One study indicated that governmental issues tend to follow an eight-year cycle.[4] For the first five years, the issues are low-key but can be detected in the press and in some polls. In the fifth or sixth year, the national press becomes interested and, finally, government action results. Obviously, the earlier a firm becomes involved, the better. For example, Sears identified the flammable-nightwear controversy early on and was able to stock nonflammable goods well before government action occurred.

In the Farmer study mentioned earlier, forecasting in the 1930s and 1940s was extremely poor when international political events were involved. Thus, a mid–1930s article did not consider the possibility of American involvement in a European war. A 1945 article incorrectly forecast a huge growth in trade with Russia, not anticipating the advent of the Cold War. A Middle East scenario development failed to forecast the emergence of Israel. International political developments, which can be critical to multinational firms, are still extremely difficult to forecast.

Economics

The evaluation of some strategies will be affected by judgments made about the economy, particularly inflation and general economic health as measured by unemployment and economic growth. Heavy investment in a capital-intensive industry might need to be timed to coincide with a strong economy to avoid a possibly damaging period of losses. Usually it is necessary to look beyond the general economy to the health of individual industries. In the early 1980s, for example, the depression in the automobile market and related industries, such as steel, was much greater than in the economy as a whole.

A forecast of the relative valuations of currencies can be relevant for industries with multinational competitors. Thus, an analysis of the balance of payments and other factors affecting currency valuations might be needed. For example, in most developed countries the automobile industry is extremely sensitive to changes in currency valuation.

Culture

Cultural trends can present both threats and opportunities for a wide variety of firms as the following examples illustrate.

A dress retailer conducted a study that projected women's life-styles.[5] It predicted that a more varied life-style would prevail, that more

---

"Yesbuts"

Some trends such as the increase in the number of working women, interest in health, and single-person households are well known and their implications seem obvious. However, William Wells of the advertising agency DDB Needham suggests that when such trends are examined more closely, their character and implications can change.[6] By using an annual, large-sample national survey with hundreds of questions on diverse subjects such as shopping, nutrition, fashion, eating out, jogging, movies, products and services used, it was possible to qualify some of these trends with some "yesbut" statements. For example:

YES, the number of working women in the population is and has been increasing BUT

- It is more glacial and long-term than explosive as the percent of women in the work force has changed as follows:

1950	1960	1970	1980	1990
34	38	43	52	57

- Only about 4 percent of these women fit the image of a young MBA with a tailored suit and Coach briefcase; those in the top professional and managerial occupations.
- These women are not unusually convenience-oriented; they are not heavy users of cold cuts, packaged cookies, cake mix, frozen pizza, and other "convenience" items.

YES, there is an increased interest in exercise and harmful elements in food, BUT

- A relatively small percent of people engage in strenuous physical activities. On an average day, only about 8 percent participate in an active sport such as jogging or tennis.
- Those doing strenuous exercise are younger and not necessarily worried about harmful elements in food such as sugar, salt, or cholesterol.

YES, "single-person" households are increasing, BUT
- The "swinging singles" image is a bit deceptive. Only 25 percent of all singles are under 25, and 26 percent are over 65.

time would be spent outside the home, and that those who worked would be more career-oriented. There were several implications relevant to the dress designer's product line and pricing strategies. For example, a growing number and variety of activities would lead to a broader range of styles and larger wardrobes, with perhaps somewhat less spent on each garment. Furthermore, more independence financially and socially would probably reduce the number of "follow-the-leader" fashions and the perception that certain outfits are required for certain occasions.

The growing pressure for organic food has even hit the baby food industry.[7] Regional firms such as Earth's Best have carved out 1 percent of the nearly $1 billion U.S. market, thus stimulating the big players to come out with competing lines. This trend has implications throughout the value chain for competitors.

General Mills detected a set of consumer trends that influenced its expansion plans, including increased concern about the quality of food, diet, physical fitness, and "naturalness." Food-consumption patterns shifted to increased away-from-home eating and staggered meals, because of more active life-styles.[8] In response General Mills:

- Developed a chain of "Good Earth" restaurants specializing in natural foods.

- Entered the market for "healthy" eat-on-the-run products with Yoplait and Nature Valley Granola Bars.

- Developed a high-fiber cereal, "natural" cereals, and a series of vitamin-fortified cereals.

- Used more contemporary values in the advertising for threatened traditional brands like Cheerios and Wheaties.

Demographics

Demographic trends can be a powerful underlying force in a market. Demographic variables include age, income, education, and geographic location.

The baby boomers, 77 million strong or 31 percent of the U.S. population, have been making themselves felt as they move through their life cycle. A recent spurt in the birth rate, with nearly half the births involving first-time parents, means that there is a large market for baby products, without established brand loyalty.

Ethnic populations are rising rapidly and support whole firms and industries, as well as affecting the strategies of mainline companies. Hispanic populations, for example, are growing about five times faster than non–Hispanic populations and are gaining in income as well. The

---

Is the Yuppie Culture Fading?

Yuppie culture and life-style may be fading. The yuppie generation is aging and finding that its toys such as portable telephones, exercise machines, BMWs, and designer clothing have not brought the fulfillment that was promised. Some former yuppies are looking toward life-styles and values not based on possessions. Simplicity, naturalness, value, recycling, and relationships are among the new keywords.

Questions arise. How should this trend be monitored and analyzed? What strategic impact will it have on affected industries? How can it be exploited?

Asian-American population, currently five million in the United States, will increase 165 percent by the year 2000.

The movement of businesses and populations into different areas of the country has implications for many service organizations such as brokerage houses, real-estate ventures, and insurance companies. Furthermore, the revival of downtown urban areas has had considerable implications for retailers and real-estate developers, just as the earlier development of suburbia had.

One study has pointed out the strong and continuing trend toward the population growth of women between the ages of 50 and 70.[9] This group has a higher per capita income, more free time, and fewer home responsibilities than younger women. In addition, these women seem less reluctant to spend money than in the past. The study further indicated that such women were dissatisfied with available product selection, because relatively few products are positioned for their age group. This may suggest a real opportunity for products that focus on the mature woman.

FORECASTING ENVIRONMENTAL TRENDS AND EVENTS

There is obviously a large potential payoff in being able to detect current trends or events and, even better, to forecast future ones. But, how does one go about it?

Asking the Right Questions

The first basic step is simply to ask the right questions. What trends or events in the environment will affect either industry size, our strategies, or those of our competitors? Figure 6.1 illustrates some questions that can form the basis for environmental analysis. Usually, those involved in developing a strategy are capable of formulating substantially complete answers to these questions if they simply take the time to consider them.

Trend Extrapolation

A simple method of forecasting is trend extrapolation. Demographic trends that are slow-moving are usually projectable. Some technological developments, like the cost of a unit of computer memory, can simply be extrapolated. In strategic decision making, however, it is often departures from an extrapolated trend that are of interest. Even in these cases, trend extrapolation provides a baseline from which a judgment can be made about turning points.

Asking Experts

An effective and efficient way to gain information about environmental trends and events is to ask questions of those who are experts in the various areas involved. Thus, in the early 1980s, retail merchants in the gourmet cookware business determined that the trend was toward basics and value, away from gadgets and gimmicks. Those knowledgeable in personal computers or in key application areas can make informal judgments about software trends for emerging computers.

There are several ways to obtain information from experts, all of which can be implemented by a research firm. One is to survey systematically their judgments as reported in trade and professional magazines. Another is to interview, perhaps by telephone, a set of experts. The interviews would usually be guided by an agenda but not a formal questionnaire. Cooperation can be encouraged by sharing study results. A variant would be to conduct group discussions with six to ten experts; the resulting personal interchange can stimulate ideas.

Group discussions can be costly and difficult to organize. Furthermore, group dynamics can sometimes stifle views that depart from conventional wisdom, views that often are the most useful. The Delphi approach attempts to retain the advantages of group feedback without requiring group meetings. In a Delphi study, a structured questionnaire is sent to a group of experts; they might be asked to predict the size of the solar-energy market and the nature of its composition 20 years hence, for example. The results would be summarized and tabulated and returned to the respondents, who would then be given a chance to change their opinions or to provide the rationale for their judgments. A third iteration would provide a new summary of the results, as well as arguments and rationales provided by the respondents.

Decomposing the Task

Predictions can often improve dramatically if the task is decomposed. Thus, instead of attempting to learn about the size of the solar-energy market in the year 2000, it might actually be easier to predict the demand for solar-energy use in swimming pools, water heaters, home heating, municipal power, and so on. Similarly, the demand for a new-technology medical-diagnostic instrument might be decomposed into first-time buyers, those buying a second unit, and those buying a replacement unit.

Cross-Impact Analysis

Cross-impact analysis is a set of methodologies designed to forecast an interrelated group of events. For example, consider Event A, that wind becomes an important energy source in the year 2000. Experts could estimate the probability of this event occurring. Using cross-impact analysis, they would consider simultaneously other events such as:

- **Event B**—a breakthrough in solar-energy cells by 2000 to make them economical.
- **Event C**—the large-scale production of shale oil by 2000.
- **Event D**—the widespread use of solar energy for homes by 2000.
- **Event E**—the cost of oil will triple (in constant dollars) by 2000.

The most interesting aspect of cross-impact analysis is determining the impact of one event on the probability of another. Thus, estimates of the probability that Event A will occur are obtained both under the assumption that Event B occurs and under the assumption that it does not. Similarly, Event A probabilities are estimated by assuming Event C occurs and by assuming it does not. With probability theory, the probability of patterns of technologies (or other environmental events) can be determined even though those providing judgments consider only two events at a time.

Whether or not this methodology is accessed, it is often worthwhile to consider the possible indirect impact of an environmental trend or event on a market. For example, what could be the impact on the health-food market of a further increase in people eating outside the home?

SCENARIO ANALYSIS

The forecasting of individual events and trends can be too simplistic in a complex environment where many other relevant trends and events interact with and affect one another, and where some key area of uncertainty simply cannot be resolved. Scenario analysis, one way to deal with both complexity and uncertainty, involves the development of a set of total scenarios of what the future environment will contain. Each scenario will typically contain rich descriptions of the environment and will involve different assumptions about key trends and events.

For example, an appliance manufacturer might develop one scenario for the next three to five years that would envision a very strong appliance market fueled by a healthy economy and housing market. The alternative scenario would involve a high inflation holding back the economy and crippling the housing industry. The uncertainties driving these scenarios are the economic forces impacting the industry.

Scenario analysis as suggested by Figure 6.2 can be divided into four elements, the first of which is to identify the key dimension of uncertainty.

Identifying Scenarios

If you could know one fact about the business environment five years from now (or the most appropriate planning horizon), what would that be? A maker of CT scanner equipment might want to know whether or not a technological advance will allow its machine to be fast enough to diagnose heart trouble. A farm equipment manufacturer or ski area operator may believe that weather, whether or not a drought will continue, for example, is the most important area of uncertainty. A workstation firm may want to know whether or not a single software standard will emerge or multiple standards will co-exist. One key area of uncertainty could then drive the development of two or more scenarios.

When a set of scenarios is based largely on a single variable, the scenarios themselves can usually be enriched by related events and circumstances. Thus, an inflation-stimulated recession scenario would be expected to generate a host of conditions for the appliance industry.

Often, of course, several variables are relevant to the future period of interest. The combination can define a relatively large set of scenarios. For example, a large greeting card firm might consider three variables important: the success of small "boutique" card firms, the life of a certain card type, and the nature of future distribution channels. The combina-

FIGURE 6.2   Scenario Analysis

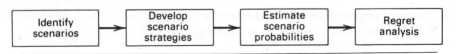

tion can result in a large set of possible scenarios. Experience has shown that two or three scenarios is the ideal number with which to work; any more and the process gets unwieldy and any value is largely lost.[10] Thus, it is important to reduce the number of scenarios by identifying a small set that ideally includes those that are plausible/credible, and those that represent departures from the present substantial enough to affect strategy development.

One common approach to scenario development that serves to combine multiple areas of uncertainty is to generate scenarios based on the health of the industry: optimistic, pessimistic, and most likely. The optimistic scenario would then have the preferred outcome with respect to a variety of variables.

Strategy Development

After scenarios have been developed, the next step is to relate them to strategies. An optimistic strategy might imply an aggressive effort to build capacity and to establish a strong market position. A pessimistic scenario could, conversely, suggest a strategy of avoiding investment and attempting to stabilize prices. The possibility of a technological breakthrough could mean that it will be critical to a participant in that technology.

The major purpose of scenario analysis is to create new strategic options. A natural tendency in strategic management is simply to continue past strategies. However, there are times when it is important to consider changes. Scenario analysis provides the stimulus to consider discontinuities from current trends and departures from current strategies.

Scenario Probabilities

To evaluate alternative strategies, it is usually useful to determine the scenario probabilities. The task is actually one of environmental forecasting, except that the total scenario may be a rich combination of several variables. Experts could be asked to assess probabilities directly. A deeper understanding will often emerge, however, if causal factors underlying each scenario can be determined. For example, the construction-equipment industry might develop scenarios based on three alternative levels of construction activity. These levels will have several contributing causes. One is the interest rate. Another could be the availability of funds to the home-building sector, which in turn will depend on the emerging structure of financial institutions and markets. A third cause might be the level of government spending on roads, energy, and other areas.

One of the leaders in the use of scenarios has been the Shell group of companies.[11] Their experience suggests that it is important to analyze completely the "predetermined elements," those driving forces of the environment that can be forecast.

For example, to understand future scenarios in an analysis of the future oil environment, Shell looked carefully at three principal issues. The analysis of the major oil-producing countries included a review of their reserves, production capacity, and capacity to use generated funds. The domestic demand and the development and use of alternative energy sources were forecast for each of the major consuming countries. The construction commitments to refining, drilling, and marine and market facilities by oil companies were determined. One result of this analysis was that a "three-miracle" scenario (new reserves would be found, all major producing countries would be happy to deplete their reserves as needed, and energy would be produced at capacity) was seen as being virtually impossible. Another was that a discontinuity scenario of a disruptive shortage was very plausible.

Regret Analysis

The final step is to compare the expected outcomes of each strategy if the wrong scenario emerges. How bad will it be if a strategy predicated on an optimistic scenario was pursued and the pessimistic scenario actually emerged? This exercise generates a feeling for and perhaps even a quantification of the risk associated with a strategy option. If such an evaluation can be quantified and we assume that the probability of each scenario is estimated, the expected value of each strategy could be determined—it would be simply the sum of the outcomes under each scenario multiplied by the scenario probability.

IMPACT ANALYSIS

Throughout the entire external analysis, the problem of information overload occurs. Literally thousands of directions are possible in information gathering and analysis, and most of these could absorb resources indefinitely. A publishing company may be concerned about cable TV, life-style patterns, educational trends, geographic population shifts, and printing technology. Any one of these issues involves a host of subfields and could easily spur limitless research. For example, cable TV might involve a variety of pay-TV concepts, suppliers, technologies, and viewer reactions.

In conducting an external analysis in general, and an environmental analysis in particular, it is necessary to decide which information-need areas to monitor and analyze and to determine the depth of information and analysis appropriate for each. An information-need area provides a logical focus for information gathering. It will include one or more current or potential trends or events that will provide either threats or opportunities for the organization. Unless distinct priorities are established, external analysis can become descriptive, ill-focused, and inefficient.

The extent to which an information-need area should be monitored and analyzed depends on its impact and immediacy.

1. The impact of an information-need area is related to the following:

   ● The extent to which it involves trends or events that will impact existing or potential SBUs (strategic business units).

   ● The importance of the involved SBUs.

   ● The number of involved SBUs.

2. The immediacy of an information-need area is related to:

   ● The probability that the involved trends or events will occur.

   ● The time frame of the trend or event.

   ● The reaction time likely to be available, compared with the time required to develop and implement appropriate strategy.

Impact of an Information-Need Area

Each information-need area contains potential trends or events that could have an impact on present, proposed, and even potential strategic business units (SBUs). For example, the super-premium beer market could define an information-need area for a beer firm. If we assume that the beer firm has both a proposed super-premium entry and an imported beer positioned in the same area, trends in the super-premium beer market could have a high impact on the firm. The trend toward "natural" foods may present opportunities for new beverages for the same firm. These new beverages might represent a potential SBU, and as such they may not be completely well-defined. Nevertheless, it would be risky to evaluate information-need areas and their underlying trends and events only in terms of existing and proposed SBUs.

The impact of an information-need area will depend on the importance of the impacted SBU to a firm. Some SBUs are more important than others. The importance of established SBUs may be indicated by their associated sales, profits, or costs. However, such measures might need to be supplemented for proposed or growth SBUs in which present sales, profits, or costs may not reflect their real value to a firm. Finally, an information-need area may affect several SBUs, so the number of involved SBUs can be relevant.

The Impact Matrix. To identify and evaluate the various information-need areas more systematically, and perhaps even to quantify their impact, the creation of an impact matrix as shown in Figure 6.3 can be useful.[12] The vertical axis lists potential information-need areas, areas in which information could be gathered and organized. Note that they can be drawn not only from an environmental analysis but also from analyses of the customer, competitor, and market. Thus, a manufacturer of personal computers could be concerned with product acceptance by certain segments, the entry of workstations, the growth of Unix, the future of

FIGURE 6.3 Impact Matrix

| Information-Need Areas | | Strategic Business Units (SBUs) | | | | | | Impact | |
| | | Present | | Proposed | | Potential | | | |
		B_1	B_2 B_3 . . .	B_{10}	B_{11} . . .	B_{20}	B_{21} . . .	+	−
Customer									
Segment A	S_1	0	3	0	4	−3	0	1	8 −3
Segment B	S_1	0	0	4	0	0	3	−3	7 −3
Competitor									
Competitor A	C_1	0	−2	0	−1	0	0	−2	0 −5
Potential competitor B	C_2	−4	−2	0	0	0	−4	−1	0 −11
Market									
Application A	M_1	4	−4	0	0	2	0	0	6 −4
Product line B	M_2	0	0	0	0	0	1	−3	1 −3
Environment									
Technology A	E_1	2	0	−3	0	1	4	0	7 −3
Regulation B	E_2	0	0	2	0	−3	0	−2	2 −5
Economic trend C	E_3	0	3	3	−1	0	−4	0	6 −5
Cultural trend D	E_4	−1	2	3	0	4	1	0	10 −1
Demographic trend E	E_5	0	0	2	0	−2	0	0	2 −2
TOTAL	+	6	8	14	4	7	9	1	
	−	−5	−8	−3	2	−8	−8	−11	
Importance of SBU		H	H	M	L	L	M	H	

Impact Scale

Threats						Opportunities		
−4	−3	−2	−1	0	+1	+2	+3	+4
High negative impact				No impact		High positive impact		

the Apple platform, and economic trends. The horizontal axis represents the present SBUs, plus proposed and potential SBUs. It will, of course, sometimes be difficult to identify potential SBUs, but such an exercise can still be helpful.

The entries in the matrix represent the relative impact that the trends or events associated with the information-need areas will have on the SBUs. The impact can be positive or negative, as the scale shown at the bottom of Figure 6.3 indicates. Thus, the entry of a particular workstation firm (C_2) into the personal computer market could have a negative (-4) impact on an SBU (B_1), and the development of a technology (E_1) could have a positive impact ($+4$) on a potential business area (B_{20}).

The exercise of listing information-need areas and assessing their impact on SBUs can help both identify and prioritize the information-need areas for a given SBU. The areas with greatest impact will be those with the highest scale values. Furthermore, the matrix makes visible those information-need areas that impact on several SBUs. The column at the right, which adds the positive and negative entries for each row, provides a summary measure of the impact associated with an information-need area.

The columns are also totaled and provide a rough indication of an SBU's sensitivity to trends and events in the environment. A large negative sum suggests substantial potential for adverse developments. Conversely, a large positive total indicates the possibility of up-side developments. Such judgments can help to provide an overview of the positive and negative risk factors. In Figure 6.3, the relative importance of each SBU is also shown. An explicit consideration of that dimension may also be useful in deciding which information-need area to monitor and analyze and in what depth.

Immediacy of an Information-Need Area

Events or trends associated with information-need areas may have a high impact but such a low probability of occurrence that it is not worth actively expending resources to gather or analyze information. Similarly, if occurrence is far in the future relative to the strategic-decision horizon, then it may be of little concern. Thus, the harnessing of tide energy may be so unlikely or may occur so far into the future that it is of no concern to a utility.

Finally, there is the reaction time available to a firm, compared with the reaction time likely to be needed. After a trend or event crystallizes, a firm needs to develop a reaction strategy. If the available reaction time is inadequate, it becomes important to better anticipate emerging trends and events so that a reaction strategy can be initiated sooner.

Figure 6.4 suggests a categorization of information-need areas for a

FIGURE 6.4   Information-Need Categories for an SBU

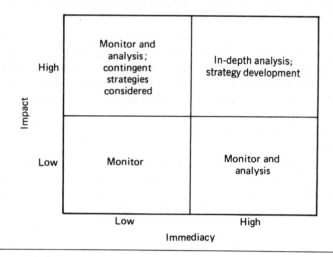

given SBU. If both the immediacy and impact are low, then a low level of monitoring may suffice. If the impact is thought to be low but the immediacy is high, the area may merit monitoring and analysis. If the immediacy is low and the impact high, then the area may require monitoring and analysis in more depth, and contingent strategies may be considered but not necessarily developed and implemented. When both the immediacy and potential impact of the underlying trends and events are high, then an in-depth analysis will be appropriate, as will be the development of reaction plans or strategies.

Issue Management

Issue management involves formally assigning people or groups within an organization the responsibility for the analysis of particular issues and the development of responsive strategies. Issues are specific trends and events within information-need areas that have a high level of immediacy and potential impact. For example, Arco has a group tracing 140 issues, including state taxes, the Clean Air Act review, natural-gas decontrol, and state legislation on hazardous wastes. Arco's intention is to supplement the numbers-oriented planning with more qualitative and perceptive analysis.[13]

SUMMARY

The role of environmental analysis is to detect, monitor, and analyze those current and potential trends and events that will create opportunities or threats to a firm. Environmental analysis can be divided, as shown in Figure 6.1, into five areas: technological, governmental, economic, cultural, and demographic.

Expert opinions often are helpful in environmental forecasting. It is usually worthwhile to consider the cross-impact of one environmental development on others. Scenario analysis provides rich descriptions of future environments and, as such, can be a useful forecasting device. Scenario analysis involves the creation of two to four plausible future scenarios, the development of strategies appropriate to each, the assessment of scenario probabilities, and the evaluation of the resulting strategies across the scenarios.

Impact analysis can help identify and prioritize information-need areas. The approach is systematically to assess the impact and immediacy of the trends and events that underlie each potential information-need area.

FOOTNOTES

[1] Arnold Cooper, Edward Demuzzio, Keneth Hatten, Elijah Hicks, and Donald Tock, "Strategic Responses to Technological Threats," *Academy of Management Proceedings*, 1976, pp. 54–60.

[2] Richard N. Foster, "A Call for Vision in Managing Technology," *Business Week*, May 24, 1982, pp. 24–33.

[3] Richard N. Farmer, "Looking Back at Looking Forward," *Business Horizons*, February 1973, pp. 21–28.

[4] Earl C. Gottschalk, Jr., "Firms Hiring New Type of Manager to Study Issues, Emerging Troubles," *Wall Street Journal*, June 10, 1982, p. 26.

[5] "New Woman's Wardrobe to Be Varied, Voluminous," *Mass Marketing News*, April 8, 1977.

[6] William D. Wells, "YESBUTS," Chicago: DDB Needham, unpublished paper, 1990.

[7] Ruta Duncia, Tod Dyksta, Carol Fitton, Dan Lew, and Jesse Treger, "Analysis of Beech-Nut & the Baby Food Industry," unpublished report, 1991.

[8] Sandra D. Kresch, "The Impact of Consumer Trends on Corporate Strategy," *Journal of Business Strategy* 3, Winter 1983, pp. 58–63.

[9] "Don't Neglect Women Over 50, DDB Advises," *Advertising Age*, February 26, 1979, p. 5.

[10] Robert E. Linneman and Harold E. Klein, "The Use of Multiple Scenarios by U.S. Industrial Companies," *Long-Range Planning* 12, February 1979, p. 84.

[11] Pierre Wack, "Scenarios: The Gentle Art of Re-Perceiving," Division of Research, Harvard Business School, working paper, 1984.

[12] A similar matrix is proposed in F. Friedrich Neubaven and Norman B. Solomon, "A Managerial Approach to Environmental Assessment," *Long-Range Planning* 10, April 1977, pp. 13–26.

[13] Gottschalk, "Firms Hiring," p. 84.

PART THREE

INTERNAL ANALYSIS

7

SELF-ANALYSIS

We have met the enemy and he is us.

Pogo

Self-conceit may lead to self-destruction.

"The Frog and the Ox," Aesop

The fish is the last to know if it swims in water.

Chinese Proverb

In addition to the threats and opportunities of external analysis, strategy development must also be based on the objectives, strengths, and capabilities of a business. Thus, Quaker Oats decided that its major assets were brands and their link with the consumers and its primary skill was marketing branded consumer products. As a result of this self-analysis, it sold several special retailing units and purchased firms with strong brands such as Kretschmer cereals.[1]

Understanding a business in depth is the goal of self-analysis. A business self-analysis is similar to a competitor analysis, but it has a greater focus on performance assessment and is much richer and deeper. It is more detailed because of its importance to strategy and because much more information is available. The analysis is based on detailed, current information on sales, profits, costs, organizational structure, management style, and so on.

Just as strategy can be developed at the level of a firm, a group of SBUs, an SBU, or a business area within an SBU, self-analysis can be conducted at each of these levels. Of course, such analyses will differ from each other in emphasis and content, but their structure and thrust will be the same. The common goal is to identify organizational strengths, weaknesses, constraints, and, ultimately, responsive strategies, either exploiting strengths or correcting or compensating for weaknesses.

Self-analysis begins by examining the financial performance of a business, its profitability and sales. Indications of unsatisfactory or deteriorating performance might stimulate strategy change. In contrast, the conclusion that current or future satisfactory performance is acceptable can suggest the old adage, "If it ain't broke, don't fix it." Of course, something that is not broken may still need some maintenance, refurbishing, or vitalization. Performance analysis is especially relevant to the strategic decision of how much to invest in or disinvest from a business.

The first section considers financial performance as measured by return on assets and sales. The next section discusses shareholder value analysis, a very different perspective. The third section covers other performance dimensions linked to future profitability, such as customer satisfaction, product quality, brand associations, cost, new products, and employee capability. Chapter 8, "Portfolio Analysis," extends the material of this chapter by focusing on the performance of business units relative to each other and on the attractiveness of the external context of each.

Another perspective on self-analysis considers those business characteristics that limit or drive strategy choice. The fourth section examines five issues: past and current strategy, strategic problems, organizational capabilities and constraints, financial resources and constraints, and organizational strengths and weaknesses.

FINANCIAL PERFORMANCE—PROFITABILITY AND SALES

Self-analysis often starts with an analysis of current financials, measures of profitability and sales. The ultimate "bottom-line" test of performance for a business as well as a corporation is profitability and sales. Changes in either can signal a change in the market viability of a product line and the ability to produce competitively. Furthermore, they provide an indicator of the success of past strategies and thus can often help in evaluating whether or not strategic changes are needed. In addition, profitability and sales objectives at least appear to be specific and easily measured. As a result, it is not surprising that they are so widely used as performance evaluation tools.

Shetty, a management professor and consultant, obtained a statement of corporate objectives from 82 large companies from four basic industrial groups.[2] The top objective types were:

Objective Category	*Percent of Firms Using*
Profitability	89
Growth	82
Market share	66
Social responsibility	65
Employee welfare	62
Product quality and service	60
Research and development	54
Efficiency	50

Note that profitability and growth were the two dominant objectives listed.

Profitability

Profits are certainly important indicators of business performance. They provide the basis for the internally or externally generated capital needed to pursue growth strategies, to replace obsolete plants and equipment, and to absorb market risk.

One basic profitability measure is return on assets, the profitability divided by the assets involved:

$$\text{ROA} = \frac{\text{profit}}{\text{assets}}$$

Equivalently, the following formula, developed by General Motors and DuPont in the 1920s, can be used to decompose ROA to return on sales and asset turnover:

$$\text{ROA} = \frac{\text{profits}}{\text{sales}} \times \frac{\text{sales}}{\text{assets}}$$

Thus, return on assets can be considered as having two causal factors. The first is the profit margin, which depends on the selling price and cost structure. The second is the asset turnover, which depends on inventory control and asset utilization.

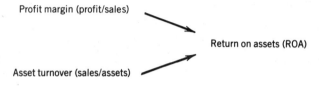

The determination of both the numerator and denominator of the ROA terms is not as straightforward as might be assumed. Substantial issues surround each, such as the distortions caused by depreciation and the fact that book assets do not reflect intangible assets like brand equity or the market value of tangible assets. These issues are discussed further in the appendix to this chapter.

What Is Good Performance?

What should the target-projected ROA be for existing businesses? What rate of return or hurdle rate should be expected from a proposed strategic move? The term hurdle rate is used because it is a hurdle that must be cleared before an investment is considered viable. The hurdle rate will also be the discount rate used to determine the net present value of a proposed investment, the present value of the net stream of cash that flows from the investment.

The answer is that each business should earn an ROA that meets or exceeds the cost of capital that is an average of the cost of equity and the cost of debt weighted by the relative size of the two.[3] The cost of equity is the cost of a risk-free investment (such as government bonds) plus an increment to account for the risk of the investment. The capital asset pricing model (CAPM) suggests that the only relevant risk is the "systematic" risk associated with the business area, that area of uncertainty caused by economy-wide fluctuations. The CAPM assumes that any other source of uncertainty, "unsystematic risk," will be unique to the business and can be controlled by an investor simply by buying a diversified portfolio of stocks. However, even a diversified portfolio will be subject to economy-wide fluctuations and therefore systematic risk. Thus, an investor needs only to be compensated for assuming systematic risk.

The CAPM risk increment is the average risk premium of all stocks, the difference between the average return of all stocks and that of a risk-free investment, times the level of systematic risk of the business, its "beta." The average risk premium will vary from year to year, but from 1926 to 1977 it averaged 8.8 percent.[4]

Setting Hurdle Rates Too High

In a provocative and influential article, Hayes and Garvin suggest that U.S. firms tend to set pretax hurdle rates artificially high, in the range of 25 to 40 percent, even when the ROI of their existing business might be much lower.[5] Furthermore, they cite a study showing that 25 percent of U.S. manufacturing firms demanded a three-year payoff from investments in modernization and replacement of equipment, a percentage that was up 10 percent from 10 years earlier.

The high hurdle rates seem to be "safe" in that they are appropriate for the riskiest investments. The problem is that they are not adjusted down for individual decisions, but tend to be fixed. Hayes and Garvin conclude that these high hurdle rates are one reason for the decline in reinvestment in the United States and the resulting decline in productivity. Reinvestment decisions have inherently less risk, but they also have less expected return and thus often fail to meet the hurdle rate. In contrast, investments into more unknown areas will often have higher projected rates of return and their increased risk is either neglected or underestimated.

Sales and Market Share

A sensitive measure of how customers regard your product or service can be sales or market share. After all, if the relative value to a customer changes, sales and share should be affected, although in some cases there may be a delay caused by market inertia and the difficulty of breaking customer habits. Thus, sales share provides a sensitive measure of marketplace performance.

Sales levels can be strategically important. Increased sales can mean that the customer base has grown, there are more customers using more. An enlarged customer base, if we assume that new customers will develop loyalty, will mean future sales and profits. Increased share can provide the potential to gain SCAs in the form of economies of scale and experience curve effects. Conversely, decreased sales can mean decreases in customer bases and a loss of scale economies.

A problem with sales as a measure is that it can be affected by short-term actions such as promotions by a brand and its competitors. Thus, it is important to disentangle changes in sales that are caused by tactical actions and those that represent fundamental changes in the value delivered to the customer. It is therefore important to couple an analysis of sales or share with that of customer satisfaction which will be discussed shortly.

SHAREHOLDER VALUE ANALYSIS

Perhaps the most visible and influential development in strategy during the 1980s was the concept of shareholder value analysis (SVA). This interest is reflected in the many books and articles devoted to it and the number of consulting firms basing their practice on it. A host of major companies have applied it not only to place value on firms to be divested or acquired, but also to evaluate business units and their strategy options within a firm.

SVA is simple and straightforward and is compatible with well-established concepts in finance.[6] A business should be evaluated with respect to the value it creates for shareholders. Attaching a value to a business involves:

1. The estimation of the annual after-tax cash flows for a planning horizon

   annual unit sales times gross margin

   less

   taxes, fixed costs (advertising, R&D, etc.)

   and investments in plant and working capital
2. Obtaining the discounted value of this profit stream by applying the cost of capital for the business.
3. Estimating the residual value of the business unit, its value after the planning horizon. One approach is to assume that the profit level achieved during the end of the planning horizon will continue indefinitely or will grow or contract at a known growth rate.
4. The total shareholder value is then the sum of the present values of future cash flows and residual value less the market value of any debt associated with the business. A positive value means that the business is creating shareholder value. A negative value means that shareholder value is being eroded.

Shareholder Value Analysis at Coca-Cola

An SVA at Coca-Cola led to the conclusion that its entertainment business was not contributing positively to shareholder value.[7] As a result, it was spun off into a new firm called Columbia Pictures Entertainment.

SVA applied to the existing SBUs revealed that Coca-Cola's soda fountain business was not contributing to shareholder value because the business was very capital-intensive. Its return was only 12.5 percent, whereas the company's cost of capital was estimated to be 16 percent. Switching from an expensive, five-gallon, stainless steel container to a disposable bag-in-a-box plus 50-gallon containers for large customers reduced the assets employed and increased return to 17 percent.

If a new strategy is to be considered, its value will be the difference between the value without the strategy option and the value with it.

SVA offers solutions to many of the problems associated with an analysis of business profitability using ROA as a standard. First, a focus on cash flow eliminates many accounting problems such as distortions caused by depreciation and asset book values. Second, and perhaps more important, SVA looks to future measures of profitability to evaluate a business. ROA considers current/past profits that are likely caused by investments years ago. The profits due to current investments and strategies are ignored unless there is a willingness to rely on the assumption that the present is a good predictor of the future.

SVA theoretically helps reduce the tendency of managers to be driven by the short-term pressures of the stock market because of its forward-looking thrust.[8] However, it does stress and reinforce the dominance of shareholder interest over that of other stakeholders such as employees, suppliers, customers, and communities. In that sense, it could, especially for those who do not employ it carefully, actually inhibit movements from the short-term financials that appear to influence investors.

SVA also focuses attention on financial analysis and a stream of numbers rather than on the development of creative, innovative strategic options and the underlying SCAs that must exist to generate future success. In general, strategy focuses on customers and competitors, whereas SVA focuses on shareholders. In the long run, of course, customer value and competitive advantage will generate shareholder value, but an undue emphasis on the shareholder and financial analysis may inhibit the convergence of the two.

Of course, SVA is fundamentally based on the ability of managers to provide good objective estimates of future profits, including residual value. Providing such estimates is extremely difficult. There is a pervasive tendency to be overly optimistic about market acceptance of new ventures and underestimate the time and investment required. In addition, there are numerous sources of uncertainty, including competitor reactions. In fact, as the uncertainty goes up, so does the potential to make the numbers match the managerial instinct that they are supposed to replace.

Of special concern is the ability to properly evaluate strategic options associated with a strategy. A move into a new market, for example, provides the possibility of developing new products for that market or of engaging in geographic expansion. When, for instance, Black & Decker bought GE's small appliance business, it really bought an option to develop other products for that market. Usually a tendency exists to underestimate or even ignore the value of such strategic options. Even when they are included, estimation problems are substantial.

PERFORMANCE MEASUREMENT—
BEYOND PROFITABILITY

One of the difficulties in strategic market management is developing performance indicators that convincingly represent long-term prospects. The temptation is to focus on short-term profitability measures and to

---

Japanese versus U.S. Managers

Japanese managers differ sharply from U.S. managers with respect to their priorities.[9] The following table illustrates this point by showing that Japanese managers place almost no value on stockholder capital gain in assessing objective priorities. Shown are the average objective importance ratings in which three points are assigned the objective considered most important (from a set of nine objectives), two points for the second-most important, and one point for the third-most important. The rank order is shown in parentheses.

| | Objective Importance | |
Objectives	U.S. Firms	Japanese Firms
ROI	2.43 (1)	1.24 (2)
Stockholder capital gain	1.14 (2)	0.02 (9)
Increase in market share	0.73 (3)	1.43 (1)
New product ratio	0.21 (7)	1.06 (3)
Number of firms responding	227	255

FIGURE 7.1   Performance Measures Reflecting Long-Term Profitability

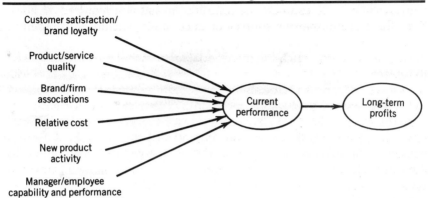

reduce investment in new products and brand image that have long-term payoffs.

The concept of net present value does represent long-term profit stream, but often it is simply not very operational. It often provides neither a criterion for decision making nor a useful performance measure. It is somewhat analogous to preferring $6 million to $4 million. The real question involves determining which strategic alternative will generate $6 million and which will generate $4 million.

Thus, it is necessary to develop performance measures that will reflect long-term viability and health. The focus should be on the assets and skills that underlie the current and future strategy and its SCAs. What are the key assets and skills for a business during the planning horizon? What strategic dimensions are most crucial: to become more competitive with respect to product offerings, to develop new products, or to become more productive? These types of questions can help identify performance areas that a business should examine. Answers will vary depending on the situation but, as suggested by Figure 7.1, they will often include customer satisfaction/brand loyalty, product/service quality, brand/firm associations, relative cost, new product activity, manager/employee capability, and performance.

Customer Satisfaction/Brand Loyalty

Perhaps the most important asset of many firms is the loyalty of the customer base. Measures of sales and market share are useful but crude indicators of how customers really feel about a firm. Such measures reflect market inertia and are noisy, in part, because of competitor actions and market fluctuations. Measures of customer satisfaction and brand loyalty are much more sensitive and provide diagnostic value as well.

Several Guidelines.   First, problems and causes of dissatisfaction that may motivate customers to change brands or firms should be identified. Second, often the most sensitive and insightful information comes from those who have decided to leave a brand or firm. Thus, "exit interviews" for customers who have "left" a brand can be very productive. Third, there is a big difference between a brand or firm being liked and the absence of dissatisfaction. The size and intensity of the customer group that truly "likes" a brand or firm should be known. Fourth, measures should be tracked over time and compared with those of competitors. It are relative comparisons and changes that are most important.

Product and Service Quality

A product (or service) and its components should be critically and objectively compared both with competition and with customer expectation and needs. How good a value is it? Can it really deliver superior performance? How does it compare with competitor offerings? How will it compare with competitor offerings in the future given competitive innovations? One common failing is to avoid tough comparisons with a realistic assessment of competitors' offerings now and those that will likely be soon announced.

Product and service quality usually are based on several critical dimensions that should be identified and measured over time. For example, an automobile firm can have measures concerning defects, ability to perform to specifications, durability, repairability, and features. A bank might be concerned with waiting time, accuracy of transactions, and making the customer experience friendly and positive. A computer manufacturer can examine relative performance specifications, and product reliability as reflected by repair data. A business that requires better marketing of a good product line is very different from one that has basic product deficiencies.

Brand/Firm Associations

An often overlooked asset of a brand or firm is what customers think of it—what are its associations? What is its perceived quality? Perceived quality, of course, can be very different from actual quality. It can be based on past experience with prior products or services and quality cues such as retailer types, pricing strategies, packaging, advertising, and a profile of the typical customer. Is a brand or firm regarded as expert in a product or technology area (such as designing and making sailboats)? Innovative? Expensive? For the country club set? Is it associated with a country, a user type, or an application area (like racing)? Such bases of positioning strategies can be key strategic assets for a brand or firm.

The word-processing software firm, WordPerfect, for example, is known for the helpful, efficient product support that uses a toll-free telephone back-up that it pioneered. Others can match this service but will find it hard to dislodge WordPerfect in the customers' minds on this dimension. The image of customer support is an enduring asset for WordPerfect.

Associations can be monitored in a gross but effective way by talking to groups of customers informally on a regular basis. The identification of changes in important associations will likely emerge from such efforts. More structured tools are also available. A brand or firm can be scaled on its key dimensions using a representative sample of customers. Key dimensions can then be tracked over time.

Relative Cost

A careful cost analysis of a product (or service) and its components, which can be critical when a strategy is dependent on achieving a cost advantage or cost parity, can involve tearing down competitors' products and a detailed analysis of their systems. The Japanese consultant, Ohmae, suggested that such an analysis, when coupled with performance analysis, can lead to one of the four situations shown in Figure 7.2.[10]

If a component such as the braking system in a car or a bank's teller operation is both more expensive and inferior to that of the competition, a strategic problem requiring change may exist. An analysis could show, however, that the component is such a small item both in terms of cost and customer impact that it should be ignored. If the component is competitively superior, however, a cost-reduction program may not be the only appropriate strategy. A value analysis, in which the component's value to the customer is quantified, may suggest that the point of superiority could support a price increase or promotion campaign.

If, on the other hand, a component is less expensive than that of the competition but inferior, a value analysis might suggest that it be de-emphasized. Thus, for a car with a cost advantage but handling disadvantage, a company might de-emphasize its driving performance and position it as an economy car. An alternative is to upgrade the relative rating with respect to this component. Conversely, if a component is both less expensive and superior, a value analysis may suggest that the component be emphasized, perhaps playing a key role in positioning and promotion strategies.

FIGURE 7.2   Relative Cost Versus Relative Performance—Strategic Implication

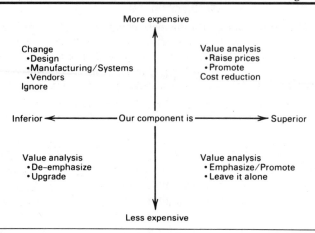

SOURCE: Adapted from ideas suggested by Kenichi Ohmae, *The Mind of the Strategist*, New York. Penguin Books, 1982, pp. 21–28.

Sources of Cost Advantage.   The many routes to cost advantage will be discussed in Chapter 11. They include economies of scale, the experience curve, product design innovations, and the use of a no-frills product offering. Each provides a different perspective to the concept of competing on the basis of a cost advantage.

Average Costing.   In average costing some elements of fixed or semi-variable costs are not carefully allocated but instead are averaged over total production. Thus, a plant may contain new machines and older machines that differ in the amount of support required to operate them. If support expenses are averaged over all output, the new machines will appear less profitable than they are and some inappropriate decisions could be precipitated.

Average costing can provide an opening for competitors to enter an otherwise secure market. For example, the J. B. Kunz Company, a maker of passbooks for banks, created a situation in which large-order customers were subsidizing small-order customers because of average costing.[11] The cost system inflated the costs of processing very large orders and thus provided an opportunity for competitors to underbid Kunz on the large orders that were very profitable. A product line that is subsidizing other lines is vulnerable, representing an opportunity to competitors and thus a potential threat to a business.

Benchmarking

Comparing the performance of a business component with others is called benchmarking. Xerox used benchmarking in the early 1980s to help correct a serious cost deficiency.[12] As part of the program, Xerox tore down the machines of its competitors. The finding that its costs were excessive led to ambitious cost goals and the elevation of cost as a prime design goal. To obtain cost-reduction ideas, Xerox attempted to identify organizations in other industries that were particularly good in functional areas similar to those at Xerox.

L. L. Bean, the outdoor sportswear retailer and mail-order house, became one of the models for the Xerox warehouse operations. Like the Xerox system, the L. L. Bean system involved products diverse in size, shape, and weight, which precluded the use of automation. The L. L. Bean warehouse system involved a computer system and included the following characteristics:

- Fast-moving items were stocked closest to the picking route. (An order is filled by "picking" the needed items from the warehouse inventory.)
- Incoming items were stored randomly to maximize space utilization and to minimize forklift travel distance.
- Orders were sorted to minimize picker travel distance.
- Incentive bonuses were based on picking productivity adjusted for errors.

Five other warehouse benchmark studies were also made. An electrical components manufacturer, for example, used bar-code labeling and a label scanner, and an appliance manufacturer developed an efficient way to maximize the forklift operation. These benchmark studies helped Xerox improve its annual productivity gains in the logistics and distribution area from 3 to 5 percent to around 10 percent. Company-wide efforts of this type helped Xerox to overcome a cost gap with respect to Japanese manufacturers that many felt was insurmountable.

New Product Activity

Does the R&D operation generate a stream of new product concepts? Is the product concept to new product introduction process managed well? Is there a track record of successful new products that have affected the product performance profile and market position?

The key self-analysis at Xerox that led to a remarkable turnaround in the 1980s showed that a critical problem was the company's inability to compete successfully in several major new product efforts.[13] The result was a product line that was at a growing performance disadvantage and increasingly vulnerable to competition. This assessment led to a restructuring of the organization to remove impediments to the new product process. For example, multifunctional new product teams were created and the approval process was streamlined.

Manager/Employee Capability and Performance

Another key asset is the people who must implement strategies. Are the human resources in place to support current and future strategies? Do those added to the organization match its needs in terms of types and quality? Or are there gaps that are not being filled? Tandem Computers sustained rapid growth by deliberately staffing and organizing for the next growth phase. In contrast, Osborne Computer, which enjoyed huge sales in the early 1980s with a low-cost system that included popular software programs, could not develop the systems, people, and structure to cope with growth and subsequently failed.

An organization should be evaluated on the basis of not only obtaining human resources but also nurturing them. A healthy organization will consist of individuals who are motivated, challenged, fulfilled, and growing in their professions. Each of these dimensions can be observed and measured perhaps through employee surveys and group discussions. Certainly the attitude of production workers represents a key factor in the quality and cost advantage that the Japanese automobile firms enjoyed throughout the 1970s. In service industries such as banking and fast foods, the ability to sustain positive employee performance and attitude is usually a key success factor.

DETERMINANTS OF STRATEGIC OPTIONS

Another perspective on self-analysis is to consider the determinants of strategic options. What characteristics of a business make some options nearly infeasible without a major organizational change? What characteristic will be pivotal in making a choice between strategic options? Again, the answers to these questions will depend on the situation, but as noted in Figure 7.3, five areas warrant close scrutiny.

Past and Current Strategies

In understanding the bases of past performance and attempting to sort out new options, it is important to be able to profile accurately past and current strategies. Sometimes the strategy has evolved into something very different than is assumed. For example, a firm positioned itself as an innovator spending heavily on R&D to repeat its early breakthrough innovation. However, an honest analysis of its operations over the past two decades indicated that its success was based on manufacturing

FIGURE 7.3   Determinants of Strategic Options and Choices

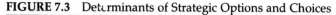

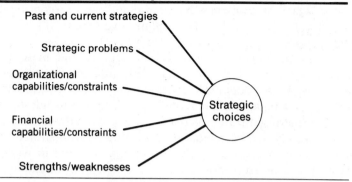

strengths and scale economies. In reality, others had introduced almost all the meaningful innovations in the industry during that period. A recognition that the R&D effort had been successful in improving product features, reliability, and cost but not in developing any technological breakthroughs was helpful in structuring strategic options.

Strategic Problems

Another relevant and helpful construct is the strategic problem, a problem with strategic implications such as the package tampering of Tylenol capsules or a delay in bringing a computer-based ordering system on-line. A strategic problem differs from a weakness or liability, the absence of an asset (e.g., good location) or skill (e.g., new product introduction skills). A business copes over time with liabilities by adjusting strategies. Strategic problems, in contrast, need to be addressed and corrected even if the fix is difficult and expensive.

For example, U.S. automobile firms in the late 1970s decided that they had a quality (or "fit and finish") problem with respect to their Japanese and German competitors. Such a problem could and did precipitate and drive some important strategic moves involving product design and production decisions. General Telephone's California operation was plagued by a deservedly bad service image.[14] As a result, needed rate increases were denied and the sales of communication systems faltered.

Organizational Capabilities/Constraints

The internal organization involving a company's structure, systems, people, and culture can be an important source of both strengths and weaknesses. The flexible, entrepreneurial organizational structure of 3M, in which new business teams and divisions are continually spun off, is a key to its growth. The systems of McDonald's and some other fast-food chains are important strengths. The background of Texas Instruments management, largely engineering and manufacturing, has been a source of strength in its semiconductor businesses, but was a weakness in its consumer products' efforts. The productivity, low-cost culture at Dana and White has allowed it to pursue a low-cost strategy.

Internal organization can affect the cost and even the feasibility of some strategies. There must be a "fit" between a strategy and the elements of an organization. If the strategy does not fit well, it might be expensive or even impossible to make it work. For example, an established centralized organization with a background oriented to one industry may have difficulty implementing a diversification strategy requiring a decentralized organization and an entrepreneurial thrust. Internal organization is considered in more detail in Chapter 16, which discusses strategy implementation and the concept of fit.

Financial Resources and Constraints

Ultimately, judgments need to be made about whether or not to invest in an SBU or withdraw cash from it. A similar decision needs to be made about the aggregate of SBUs. Should a firm increase its net investment or decrease it by holding liquid investments or returning cash to shareholders or debt holders? A basic consideration is the firm's ability to supply investment resources.

A financial analysis to determine probable, actual, and potential sources and uses of funds can help provide an estimate of this ability. A cash flow analysis projects the cash that will be available from operations and depreciation and other assets. In particular, a growth strategy, even if it simply involves greater penetration of the existing product market, usually requires working capital and other assets, which may exceed the funds available from operations. The appendix to this chapter provides a discussion of how to conduct a cash flow analysis.

In addition, funds may be obtained either by debt or equity financing. To determine the desirability and feasibility of either option, an analysis of the balance sheet may be needed. In particular, the current debt structure and a firm's ability to support it will be relevant. The appendix also reviews some financial ratios that are helpful in this regard.

A division or subsidiary may need to consider how much support it can anticipate from a parent organization. Involved will be its role in the total organization, as well as the prospects of its investment proposals. The scenario of multiple SBUs all planning investments that, in the aggregate, are far beyond a firm's willingness and ability to support is all too common. A realistic appraisal of a firm's resources can make strategy development more realistic and effective.

Organizational Strengths and Weaknesses

A key step in self-analysis is to identify the strengths and weaknesses of an organization that are based on its assets and skills. In fact, much of self-analysis is motivated by the need to detect strengths and weaknesses. There are, of course, many possible sources of strengths and weaknesses. In Chapter 4, methods to identify sources of strengths and weaknesses are presented and a list is discussed. In Chapter 9, we discuss how assets and skills become the bases of sustainable competitive advantages.

FROM ANALYSIS TO STRATEGY

In self-analysis, organizational strengths and weaknesses not only need to be identified but also related to competitors and the market. Strategic market management, as noted in Chapter 1, has three interrelated elements. The first is to determine areas in which to invest or disinvest. Investment could go to growth areas such as new product markets or programs designed to create new strength areas or to support existing ones. The second is the specification and implementation of functional area strategies involving product policy, manufacturing strategy, distribution choices, and so on. The third element of strategic market management is to develop bases of sustainable competitive advantages in the product markets where a firm competes.

In making strategic decisions, inputs from a variety of types are relevant, as the last several chapters have already made clear. However, the core of any strategic decision should be based on three types of assessments. The first concerns organizational strengths and weaknesses. The second evaluates competitor strengths, weaknesses, and strategies, because an organization's strength is of less value if it is neutralized by a competitor's strength or strategy. The third assesses the competitive context, the customers and their needs, the market and the market environment. These assessments focus on determining how attractive the selected market will be, given the strategy selected.

The goal is to develop a strategy that exploits business strengths and competitor weaknesses and neutralizes business weaknesses and competitor strengths. The ideal is to compete in a healthy growing industry with a strategy based on strengths that are unlikely to be acquired or neutralized by competitors. Figure 7.4 summarizes how these three assessments combine to influence strategy.

FIGURE 7.4   Structuring Strategic Decisions

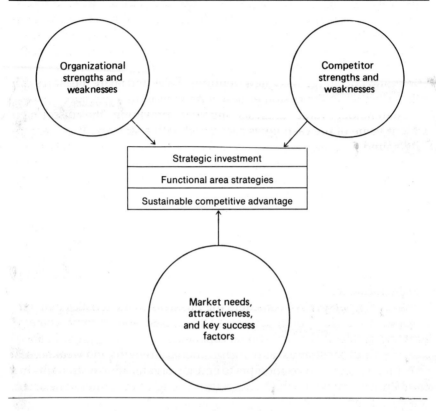

PRODUCT PORTFOLIO ANALYSIS

A very useful part of self-analysis is a product portfolio analysis in which the various business units are examined to determine the attractiveness of the market involved, the strength of a firm's position in that market, and whether or not that business has been generating or using cash. The analysis then suggests some baseline decisions as to how the various businesses should be treated—whether or not cash should be invested into or withdrawn from them. Product portfolio analysis uses several well-developed models and techniques. Chapter 8 is devoted to their description. Some of the product portfolio models are based on experience curve theories that are discussed in Chapter 11.

SUMMARY

Profitability and sales provide an evaluation of past strategies and an indication of the current market viability of a product line. Return on assets, a basic measure, can be distorted by the limitations of accounting measures. An appropriate target rate of return should reflect a return premium over the prevailing risk-free interest rate to reflect the systematic risk of the business, the variation in profits driven by economy-wide fluctuations. There is a danger that target rates set too high will discourage, the investment needed to maintain product lines and market positions and encourage risky new ventures. Sales and share measures can reflect changes in the customer base with long-term implications.

Shareholder value analysis involves providing the discounted present value of the cash flows associated with a strategy. It is theoretically sound and appropriately forward-looking (as opposed to current financials that measure the results of past strategies). However, it focuses attention on financial measures rather than other indicators of strategic performance, and developing the needed estimates is most difficult and subject to a variety of biases.

Performance should also be evaluated along other dimensions relevant to a business and its strategy. Included are customer satisfaction/ brand loyalty, product/service quality, brand/firm associations, relative cost, new product activity, productivity, manager/employee capability, and performance.

Another perspective considers the business characteristics that limit or drive strategic choice, factors such as past and current strategy, strategic problems, organizational capabilities and constraints, financial resources and constraints, and organizational strengths and weaknesses. The final strategy choice attempts to employ organizational strengths in a competitive context in which competitor strengths are either nonexistent or neutralized.

FOOTNOTES

[1] Julie Franz, "Quaker Adapts," *Advertising Age*, January 19, 1987, pp. 3, 86.

[2] Y. K. Shetty, "New Look at Corporate Goals," *California Management Review* 22, Winter 1979, pp. 71–79.

[3] The formula is

$$\text{Cost of capital} = r_D\,(1 - T)\,D/(D + E) + r_E\,E/(D + E)$$

where: r_D = the interest rate associated with the debt

r_E = the rate of return on an equity investment in the business

D = the size of the debt

E = the size of the equity in the business

T = the corporate tax rate

[4] Roger G. Ibbotson and Rex A. Sinquefield, *Stocks, Bonds, Bills and Inflation: The Past (1926–1976) and the Future (1979–2000)*, Charlottesville, Va.: Financial Analysts Research Foundation, 1977.

[5] Robert H. Hayes and David A Garvin, "Managing as if Tomorrow Mattered," *Harvard Business Review*, May–June 1982, pp. 70–79.

[6] For descriptions of SVA see Alfred Rappaport, *Creating Shareholder Value*, New York: The Free Press, 1986; David L. Wenner and Richard W. LeBer, "Managing for Shareholder Value—From Top to Bottom," *Harvard Business Review*, November–December, 1989, pp. 52–68; Roger A. Kerin, Vijay Mahajan, and P. Rajan Varadarajan, *Strategic Market Planning*, Boston: Allyn and Bacon, 1990; Chapter 9; Enrique R. Arzac, "Do Your Business Units Create Shareholder Value?" *Harvard Business Review*, January–February 1986, pp. 121–126.

[7] Bernard C. Reimann, "Managing for the Shareholders: An Overview of Value-Based Planning," *Planning Review*, January–February 1988, pp. 10–22.

[8] For an excellent discussion of the limitations of SVA and the problems of implementing the concept, see George S. Day and Liam Fahey, "Putting Strategy into Shareholder Value Analysis," *Harvard Business Review*, March–April 1990, pp. 156–162.

[9] Tadao Kagono, Ikujiro Nonaka, Kiyonori Sakakibara, and Akihiro Okumura, *Strategic vs. Evolutionary Management—A U.S.-Japan Comparison of Strategy and Organization*, New York: North-Holland, 1985, p. 28.

[10] Kenichi Ohmae, *The Mind of the Strategist*, New York: Penguin Books, 1982, p. 26.

[11] J. B. Kunz Company A, Case 9-577-115, Boston, Mass.: Intercollegiate Case Clearing House.

[12] Frances G. Tucker, Seymour M. Zivan, and Robert C. Camp, "How to Measure Yourself Against the Best," *Harvard Business Review*, January–February 1987, pp. 8–10.

[13] Gary Jacobson and John Hillkirk, *Xerox: An American Samurai*, New York: Macmillan, 1985.

[14] "General Telephone of California: Trying to Disconnect a Bad Image," *Business Week*, November 29, 1982, pp. 66–67.

APPENDIX: THE ANALYSIS OF FINANCIAL RESOURCES

This appendix is designed to discuss some basic accounting issues and methods that affect the self-analysis of a business. The first two sections detail the problems of two key accounting constructs: book assets and accounting profits. The third provides a description of how to conduct an analysis of the sources and uses of funds that is the basis for cash flow projections. In the fourth section, the concept of affordable growth is discussed, the idea being that there are limits to growth given a fixed debt-to-equity policy without raising equity capital.

Book Assets

The most accessible estimate of both existing and future asset values is usually the book value, the original cost less accumulated depreciation. Book value, however, is usually a distorted measure of assets employed. Sometimes a major business investment does not appear on a balance sheet as a book asset. For example, to enter a business area, a new product is developed requiring R&D effort, marketing research expenditures, and market introduction costs, all of which are expensed. Thus, the asset created, a new brand and most of what is associated with it, does not appear as a book asset. Advertising, which can create a strong brand name and associated image, is also expensed. The most important asset of many businesses, particularly services, is their people assets, but they are rarely reflected in book assets. Even when physical assets such as a building are a major asset component, their book value will depend on the depreciation schedules, which are driven by tax considerations. As a result, book asset value may bear little resemblance to either replacement cost or liquidation value.

Thus, book assets must be examined when interpreting ROA measures. It is sometimes possible to adjust book assets to reduce distortions. Book assets can be replaced with liquidation values or replacement costs. Investments in new products or advertising can be considered assets for the purposes of ROA analysis. Another approach is to supplement ROA with other profitability measures such as the profit margin, the profit per person (for a law firm), or profit per square foot of selling space (for a retailer).

Accounting Profits

There are several problems with accounting profits. One is allocated costs over which the business unit may have little control, costs such as corporate executives and corporate staff. In that context, it may be useful to use contribution margin, which is the gross profit prior to allocating costs, to represent profits in the numerator. Another issue arises when several SBUs share activities or assets such as sales forces, staff activities, production facilities, or distribution activities. It is important that these costs be properly and consistently divided among the SBUs so that what appear to be changes in performance are not simply based on changes in cost allocations.

Depreciation is another potential source of misinterpretation. It can, for example, understate the investment needed to maintain a business at its present level. A seemingly profitable business can be mortgaging its future, if investment necessary to maintain the business is not forthcoming. If depreciation is inadequate to fund this necessary investment level, the investment needs to be funded either from profits or other sources, or the business will decline. For example, Chrysler, by reducing investment in the late 1960s, provided short-term profits at the expense of long-term business health. The concept of the investment level needed to maintain a current business, if it differs markedly from the depreciation level, may be useful.

Sometimes cash flow is of interest in addition to, or even instead of, profitability because cash flow is not affected by depreciation.

Projecting Cash Flow—Sources and Uses of Funds

A projection of cash flow during the strategy horizon is usually essential to determine what base of cash resources is available and what cash needs will be required. At the outset a reasonable baseline assumption might be made that current strategies and trends will extend into the near future. It can be helpful also to project the flow of funds given both optimistic and pessimistic scenarios. The impact of changes in strategies and the introduction of new strategies can then be determined.

Figure 7A.1 shows a simplified balance sheet and the major categories of sources and uses of funds. It will provide a context in which to discuss the principal elements of a cash flow analysis. As the sources and uses of funds items are presented, some useful balance sheet ratios will be introduced. They provide measures of the financial health of a firm in terms of its assets and debt structure. As such, they are helpful in making judgments concerning the desirability and feasibility of raising money through debt or equity financing.

The first item under the source and use of funds in Figure 7A.1 is changes in net working capital. Working capital is defined as current assets less current liabilities (generally liabilities under one year). The current ratio is one way of measuring the adequacy of working capital:

$$\text{current ratio} = \frac{\text{current assets}}{\text{current liabilities}}$$

The most desirable ratio will depend, of course, on the nature of a business. In particular, firms with large amounts of assets in inventories may require a higher ratio. Another ratio that deletes inventories is called the quick or acid-test ratio:

$$\text{quick ratio} = \frac{\text{current assets less inventory}}{\text{current liabilities}}$$

As sales grow, of course, working capital will have to grow also so that it will continue to be adequate in supporting operations.

The second item concerning the sources and uses of funds in Figure 7A.1 is the sale or purchase of fixed assets. The acquisition of fixed assets might be divided into that necessary for maintaining current operation levels and that for more discretionary expenditures to generate growth.

FIGURE 7A.1   Balance Sheet and Sources and Uses of Funds Statement

Balance Sheet, December 31
(Millions)

Current Assets		6.0	Current Liabilities	3.0
Cash, receivables,	3.5		Accounts payable	2.0
investments			Other	1.0
Inventory	2.5			
			Long-term Liabilities	2.0
Fixed Assets		6.0		
Property, plant, and	10.0		Equity	7.0
equipment			Capital stock	4.0
Less accumulated	4.0		Retained earnings	3.0
depreciations			and other	
Total Assets		12.0	Total Liabilities	12.0

Projected Sources and Uses of Funds

Sources of Funds		Uses of Funds	
Decrease in net	0	Increase in	1.0
working capital		networking capital	
Sale of fixed assets	0	Purchase of fixed	2.5
		assets	
Issue L.T. liabilities	2.0	Retire L.T. liabilities	0
Sell capital stock	0	Buy back capital	0
		stock	
Operations: net	1.0	Operations: net	0
income		losses	
Depreciation	.5	Dividends	0
Total Sources of Funds	3.5	Total Uses of Funds	3.5

Again, the sources and uses of funds analysis should reflect the implications of any proposed growth strategy.

The third funds-flow category is the issue or retirement of long-term debt. In determining the appropriate debt level, useful ratios are

$$\text{debt-to-equity ratio} = \frac{\text{long-term liabilities}}{\text{equity}}$$

$$\text{total debt-to-equity ratio} = \frac{\text{total liabilities}}{\text{equity}}$$

Of course, the higher these ratios are, the larger the interest burden in a downturn and the lower the ability to obtain new debt in an emergency. The optimal level will depend on the ability of the earnings to carry added interest expense, the policy of a firm toward debt and its associated risk, the return expected on future investment, and the debt-to-equity ratio of competing firms. The use of funds obtained from debt financing will be relevant in determining how much debt to undertake. If the funds are to be used to buy a firm, the structure of the resulting combined balance sheet and funds flow must be considered.

The fourth category shown in Figure 7A.1 is changes in capital stock. To what extent is it feasible and desirable to raise capital through the sale of stock? Conversely, it may be beneficial to use funds to buy stock if the stock is undervalued, as compared with alternative investments.

Finally, there are the sources of funds from operations, which provide the base from which investment planning will begin. To net income, depreciation expense is added, and dividends to be paid are subtracted. Depreciation is an expense item that does not involve cash outflow. Thus, depreciation is actually a source of funds. Obviously, the net income from operations will interact with other sources. For example, increasing debt will increase interest expense, which will reduce the funds available from future operations. And, the ability to raise stock may depend on dividend policy. Furthermore, investment or disinvestment in assets will affect depreciation in future years.

In evaluating the balance sheet, considerable judgment and reservation may be appropriate. There may be bad debts among the reported receivables, the depreciation may not reflect plant deterioration, and assets and liabilities may have market values that differ substantially from their reported book value. Inflation effects contribute to the interpretation difficulties. Thus, it might be appropriate to interpret or adjust the ratios and cash flow projection accordingly.

Affordable Growth

Higgins observes that, given a policy of not selling new equity shares and of maintaining a fixed total debt-to-equity ratio and dividend payout rate, it's possible to determine the maximum sustainable growth rate for a business.[1] He assumes that depreciation will cover asset deterioration and that sales growth will require additional assets (working capital and other assets) such that the sales-to-asset ratio will remain constant. These new assets will be financed by the earnings not paid out in dividends and by the additional long- and short-term debt made possible by the existing sales increase in equity. Thus, without a reduction in the dividend payouts or a decrease in the target total debt-to-equity ratio, growth will be limited. He also notes that inflation adversely affects the real affordable growth achievable, because depreciation becomes inadequate to maintain assets.

FOOTNOTES

[1] Robert C. Higgins, "How Much Growth Can a Firm Afford?" *Financial Management*, Fall 1977, pp. 7–16. The formula for the sustainable growth rate in sales, given Higgins' assumptions, is

$$\frac{p(1 - d)(1 + L)}{t - p(1 - d)(1 + L)}$$

where: p = the after-tax profit margin

d = the proportion of earnings paid in dividends

L = the target total debt-to-equity ratio

t = the ratio of total assets-to-sales for new and existing sales

8

PORTFOLIO ANALYSIS

A little neglect may breed great mischief . . .
for want of a nail the shoe was lost; for want of
a shoe the horse was lost.

Benjamin Franklin

Dig a well before you are thirsty.

Chinese proverb

A key element of self-analysis is the assessment of the strength of a business position in the market. Portfolio analysis, which has had a rich and colorful history in strategy management, extends strength assessment in three directions.

First, portfolio analysis combines the assessment of business position with a market attractiveness evaluation, which emerges from external analysis in general and market analysis in particular. One output of portfolio analysis is thus a compact summary representation of the two most important assessments of any business.

Second, portfolio analysis includes multiple SBUs in the same analysis and addresses the SBU investment decision—which organizational units should receive resources, which should have resources withheld, and which should be resource generators. Such investment decisions can be especially difficult when a firm unit must manage multiple SBUs and make resource allocation decisions among them.

The basic resource allocation problem is created as follows. A firm has a variety of SBUs, each needing cash and each able to generate cash. In a decentralized organization, it is natural for the manager of a cash-generating SBU to control the available SBU cash. The basic incentive of an SBU manager, after all, is profitable growth, and any SBU manager will have ready investment opportunities that will stimulate growth for his or her SBU. However, the result is that a fast-growing SBU, which may have low profit or even losses but enormous potential, with a huge need for cash, will often be starved of needed cash. The culprit is the decentralization policy that requires or encourages SBUs to fund their own growth. The irony is that SBUs involving mature products may have inferior investment alternatives, but because cash flow is plentiful in these SBUs, their investments still get funded. The net effect is to channel available cash to low-potential areas and to withhold it from the most attractive areas. The portfolio models force the issue of which SBUs should receive the available cash.

Third, portfolio analysis offers baseline recommendations concerning the investment strategies for each SBU based on an assessment of business position and market attractiveness. These baseline recommendations can serve to introduce strategic options that might not otherwise be considered.

Of course, the strategic investment-allocation decision can occur at several levels. For example, at the corporate level it could be over divisions, groups of SBUs, or SBUs. At the SBU level, it could be over products when an SBU contains multiple products. At the product level, it could be over alternative markets. As will be seen, some of the portfolio models are more appropriate for certain levels than others and must be interpreted differently for various levels of analysis.

Portfolio analysis has had a colorful history in strategic management. It exploded on the scene in the mid–1960s with colorful labels such as dogs, stars, and cash cows, which have since become part of the strategy vocabulary. However, it was at first oversold as the model that provided strategy recommendations which should always be followed. In the 1970s, when it became clear that the model assumptions did not always hold, there was a tendency to discredit the models and dismiss them as being at best useless and at worst dangerous by leading to disastrous strategies. In the 1980s, a realization emerged that the models are useful but should be considered a part of internal analysis. Their role is thus to summarize information and to suggest strategy options, particularly with respect to the resource allocation decision, rather than to provide strategy choices.

In this chapter, three portfolio models are discussed: the BCG growth-share matrix, the industry attractiveness-business position matrix associated with General Electric, and the directional policy matrix developed by Shell Chemicals Ltd. The chapter concludes with a discussion of the experience of managers with portfolio analysis.

THE BCG GROWTH-SHARE MATRIX

The BCG concept of the experience curve evolved during the 1960s into a highly visible portfolio model termed the growth-share matrix. The BCG growth-share matrix, being both simple and easily quantifiable, is often a useful first step in portfolio analysis. It suggests that an analysis of the market can best be summarized by knowing its growth rate, and that the best summary indication of a firm's strength in a market is its relative market share. Thus, the growth-share matrix positions the various SBUs within a firm in terms of these two dimensions, as Figure 8.1 illustrates.

The Growth Dimension

Of all the characteristics of a market, why select growth as the single indicator of its desirability? The reasons include the following:

● Growth is perhaps the best measure of the product life cycle, a key strategic consideration.

● Market share is assumed to be more easily gained in a growth context when new users with no developed loyalties are attracted to the product class. Furthermore, competitors may react less aggressively to the loss of new customers than to the loss of their base of existing customers.

FIGURE 8.1   The Growth-Share Matrix

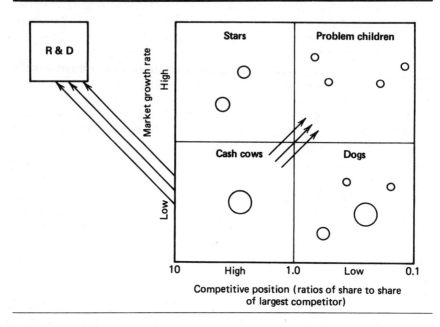

Share gain is important, in part, because of its link to the experience curve, a point that will be discussed in more detail when the second dimension of the growth-share matrix is introduced.

- A market position in a growth market will be worth more in the future as the market grows, if we assume the position can be retained. It is normally easier to retain market share than to gain it.

- In a growth market, demand often exceeds supply; excess demand will support premium prices and profit levels.

- By aggressively entering into a growth market and establishing a sustainable competitive advantage, a firm can discourage competitors from entering the market.

The midpoint of the growth dimension is somewhat arbitrary but is usually set at a 10-percent annual growth rate. Thus, markets growing in excess of 10 percent are considered to be high-growth markets, whereas those growing below 10 percent are low-growth markets.

The Market-Share Dimension

The second dimension of the growth-share matrix is market share. Actually, the horizontal axis in Figure 8.1 is a relative competitive position, as defined by the ratio of market share to the market of the largest competitor. The log scale is used so that the midpoint of the axis is 1.0, the point at which a firm's market share is exactly equal to that of its largest competitor. Anything to the left of the midpoint indicates that the firm has the leading market-share position.

Relative market share is selected for the single indicator of a firm's position for several reasons:

- The largest share firm will very likely enjoy advantages of size such as economies of scale, high brand recognition, channel dominance, and the strongest bargaining position with customers and suppliers.

- The market leader is in the best position to exploit the experience curve because it will accumulate experience faster than competitors. The experience curve model, to be discussed in detail in Chapter 11, suggests that cumulative production experience will result in lower unit costs because of learning effects, technology improvements in production/operations, and product redesign.

- Empirical evidence indicates that market share is related to profitability.

A host of empirical studies suggest that profitability is related to market share. One of the most relevant, because of the extensive database involved, is the PIMS (profit impact of market strategy) study. The PIMS database, its background, some empirical findings, and the ways in which firms can draw on it to help evaluate strategy are described in the boxed insert.

One of the dramatic PIMS findings is the relationship between ROI and market share. An analysis of the PIMS database generated the relationship shown in Figure 8.2. On the average, a difference of 10 percent in market share is accompanied by a difference of about 5 percent in pretax ROI.

The relationship shown in Figure 8.2 reflects differences among businesses. Clearly, high-market-share firms may differ from a low-share business on a host of dimensions besides market share. In particular, they may simply have better management and may be luckier. Having the good fortune or skill to be in the right market with the right product may have caused both market share and profits to increase. In fact, Jacobson and Aaker, also using the PIMS database, found that when an effort was made to control for management quality and luck, a 10-point change in market share by itself would result in only a 1-point improvement in ROI.[1] Thus, the relationship may not be as strong as is suggested by Figure 8.2.

The market share to ROI relationship will also depend on context.

THE PIMS PROGRAM[2]

In the early 1960s, General Electric embarked on an internal project to attempt to explain the differences in profitability among its various SBUs. This project was later expanded through a nonprofit research group to include SBUs from many diverse companies. The PIMS database now contains data from over 3000 SBUs representing over 450 firms. Some of these SBUs have been in the database since 1970. Each SBU supplies to the PIMS database detailed information such as

- ROI (return on investment)
- Market share
- Investment intensity, the ratio of investment to sales
- R&D expenditures
- Marketing expenditures
- Perceived product quality, the percent of offerings that were superior to competitors and the percent perceived by the SBU managers as inferior

Analysis of these data has revealed that highly capital-intensive businesses do not tend to have high ROI because of the high investment and because they tend to be capital-intensive industries characterized by vigorous price competition. Another finding, discussed in Chapter 10, is that high-quality producers can be more profitable than low-quality producers, regardless of whether or not a low or high price is charged.

In addition to general findings and observations, the PIMS project makes reports available to member firms that indicate what ROI an average SBU "should" be expected to make, given its characteristics in terms of the PIMS variables. These reports can be used to evaluate SBU performance.

Also available is a PIMS-based prediction of how the SBU's ROI would change if a policy change were made, such as increasing expenditures on R&D. Although such predictions are suggestive and provide an inexpensive way to explore policy changes, taking them too seriously is foolish. They are based largely on relationships between SBUs. The problem is that firms that spend more on R&D are different in many ways from firms that spend little on R&D—in particular, they have an R&D organization and a philosophy that are unique. It is unrealistic to think that if a firm increases its R&D expenditures, it will suddenly be similar to the firm with the large R&D expenditures and actually perform as well.

The PIMS input data and analysis are not without problems. The key market-share variable is sensitive to the product-market definition used by the SBU manager. Other variables such as perceived product quality depend on subjective judgments. In cross-section analysis, differences in ROI that appear to be caused by market share or other variables could actually instead be caused by differences among industries or among strategic groupings of firms. Also, the sample of firms in the PIMS database is likely to be biased toward larger firms that are industry leaders.

FIGURE 8.2   Relationship Between Market Share and Pretax ROI

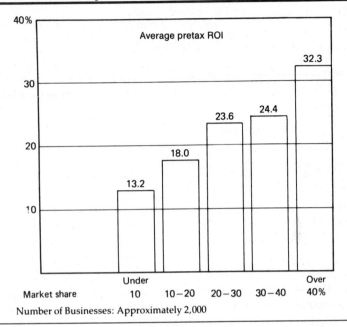

SOURCE: Robert D. Buzzell and Frederik D. Wiersema, "Successful Share-Building Strategies," *Harvard Business Review*, January–February 1981, p. 137.

Another PIMS study determined that high-market-share businesses with relatively low ROI tended to have low-quality reputations, charge higher prices, share marketing resources with other businesses, and be in regional and fragmented markets.[3]

The Matrix and Its Cast of Characters

The position of a set of SBUs is shown in Figure 8.1. The size of the circles represents the sales level of the SBU. The matrix is divided into four quadrants, and the products or SBUs in each have been given colorful labels. Each is associated with baseline policy implications.

Stars.   The upper left quadrant contains the high-share SBUs operating in high-growth markets. Because they are in growth contexts, the model predicts that they will have a heavy need for cash to support that growth. However, because they are in a strong competitive position (they are, in fact, the highest-share competitor), it is assumed they will be farthest down the experience curve, and should therefore have high margins and be generating large amounts of cash. Thus, they will be both users and providers of large cash flows. On balance they should generally be self-supporting with respect to their cash needs. If cash is required for a star to maintain its share position, however, then it should be provided. Any temptation to net out large amounts of cash, sacrificing position, should be resisted.

Cash Cows.   Cash cows are high-share SBUs operating in a low-growth market. Because of their market position, their cash generation should be high. Because the market is mature, the cash investment needs should be small and these businesses should therefore be a source of substantial amounts of cash that can be channeled to other areas.

Dogs.   Low-share SBUs that are in low-growth markets are called dogs. Because of their weak share, it is assumed that their progress on the experience curve is slow and thus their profits will be low or nonexistent. Furthermore, because growth is low, expansion of share is assumed to be very costly. Dogs are often cash users and possibly even "cash traps"— products that perpetually absorb cash, in part, because of the investment required to maintain position.

Problem Children.   Low-share businesses in high-growth markets, problem children (sometimes called question marks or wildcats), are assumed to have heavy cash needs because, although they need to fund growth, they generate little cash because they are not far down the experience curve. If a problem child's market share cannot be changed, it will continue to absorb cash. As its market matures, it will become a cash-absorbing dog, a cash-trap scenario. If market share can be adequately improved, however, a question mark can be converted into a star. Usually such a strategy will require heavy influxes of cash during the short run. Improved position should eventually enable it to generate cash, become a star and then, ultimately, a cash cow.

Strategy Implications

As Figure 8.1 indicates, the general strategy is to take cash from the cash cows to fund R&D, the source of future SBUs, and those problem children that have the potential to gain share to achieve star status. The cash cows should receive a maintenance investment level, but any tendency to automatically reinvest the cash they are generating should be avoided. Stars, on the other hand, should be managed to maintain share; current profitability should be of lesser concern. Given that the stars are adequately financed, a limited number of the most promising problem children are selected for investment to try to improve their shares. The other problem children should not receive investment. They should be sold, abandoned, or milked for whatever cash they can produce.

The dogs, usually the most prevalent category, present a challenge. Several alternatives are available. First, a dog can sometimes become very profitable through the pursuit of a "focus" segmentation strategy, in which the business specializes in a small niche where it can dominate. In effect, it would then be the star or cash cow of the redefined market. Second, investment can be withheld and the business milked or harvested of whatever cash is forthcoming until the business dies. Third, the business can be sold or simply liquidated. Managers should be wary of "turn-around" plans for dogs, particularly when there is no fundamental change in the market or environment.

One of the most dramatic examples of a strategy being driven by market share and related considerations is that of Jack Welch, the chairman of General Electric.[4] His policy is to compete only in those industries in which GE has a competitive advantage that will support its being either in the first or second position. During ten years as CEO, Welch focused the portfolio of major businesses from about 100 businesses to 14 with commanding market shares. GE is first in the United States and the world in aircraft engines, broadcasting (NBC), circuit breakers, electric motors, engineering plastics, industrial and power systems, lighting, locomotives, and medical diagnostic imaging. In major appliances and lighting, GE is second in the world market. Among the businesses that did not meet his criteria and were thus sold were computer chips, TV sets, small appliances, and coal mines.

In summary, the BCG growth-share portfolio model is a scheme for managing cash. It suggests that overt decisions need to be made regarding whether or not an SBU is to be a cash generator or cash user. It further suggests that the number of SBUs selected to be cash users should be limited so that enough resources will be available to improve each one's position. Similarly, some SBUs, namely, the cash cows and those dogs and problem children selected for milking, should generate cash and be allowed only minimal investment. It is also helpful to apply this analysis to competitors as a means of predicting what they might do, especially if the competitors are known to be using a portfolio model. The general strategies of divestment, milking, and holding position are discussed in more detail in Chapter 14. Chapters 12 and 13 cover growth strategies.

Assumptions and Limitations

The BCG growth-share matrix is usually easy to develop, because measures on the two dimensions are often readily available and the baseline conclusions usually clear. The fact that the model is so simple means also that its assumptions are both evident and vulnerable in many contexts.[5]

The Experience Curve Assumption.   The motivation for using relative share to describe competitive position is based on the experience curve. Thus, the growth-share-matrix logic applies only to those contexts in which the experience curve is relevant. In particular, it is unlikely to apply when a business consists of a variety of products, each with its own manufacturing operation and operating on its own experience curve. Thus, it is rarely helpful in allocating investment over divisions or groups of SBUs. Even an SBU can contain combinations of products that cannot be modeled by a single experience curve. Furthermore, an experience curve-based, low-cost strategy is only one of several ways to compete. Relative market share may not be relevant to a differentiation or to some focus strategies, for example.

Even if the experience curve is relevant for all the organizational units involved, there are difficulties in applying it. In particular, firms may not be operating on the same experience curve because one firm:

- Is better able to share experience with other SBUs.
- Has different overhead structures.
- Uses a different technology.
- Benefits from vendor experience or from knowledge of production method developments.
- Is less capable of reducing costs via product redesign, automation, or other approaches.

The Growth Dimension.   A basic premise of the growth-share matrix and, indeed, of much business strategy writing and practice is that growth markets are attractive investment areas. As the discussion in Chapter 5 makes clear, such a premise and its underlying assumptions should be carefully examined in each specific context.

Furthermore, it may not be easy to accurately forecast future growth. Past growth, which is usually available, may not be a good predictor of future growth.

The Product-Market Definition.   The whole analysis is highly sensitive to the definition of the product market. As noted in Chapter 5, there are almost always several levels of market definition that, although defensible, would each generate very different strategy implications. Is the appropriate market "laptop computers" or "all personal computers?" A firm like Toshiba might be strong in the laptop market but very weak in desktop computers. Should the market be only the market served? A California maker of beer or furniture, or a California seller of insurance could define its market as including only California, the West, or the whole United States. A refrigerator firm could define its market as apartment dwellers and ignore homeowners. An SBU manager can rather easily "change" his or her problem child into a star by suitably redefining its product market.

The Cash-Flow Focus. The growth-share matrix focuses on cash flow. However, the SBU is usually also interested in ROI, sales growth, and risk. It is not at all clear that the recommended investments in stars and selected question marks will maximize ROI. Furthermore, the recommendations could lead to investments clustered in a single technology, market, or production facility that would inherently involve relatively high risk. A consideration of risk, for example, could lead to investments in multiple technologies even if that meant investing in dogs.

Implementation. Increasing the market share of a problem child can involve unacceptable amounts of cash, especially if a competitor has a similar strategy or is protecting a star. Furthermore, the antitrust laws can inhibit growth. Xerox and IBM, for example, have both been restricted from combining service contracts with product sales by antitrust action. Others have been prevented from increasing share by acquisition. Government regulation or labor power, particularly in Europe, can make it difficult for a firm to withdraw from a market. Even the niche-strategy alternative for dogs and problem children can be difficult to implement. If a product line requires full-service backup, it might not be feasible to carve out a small product or market niche. These problems and others are discussed further in Chapter 14.

THE MARKET ATTRACTIVENESS-BUSINESS POSITION MATRIX

The BCG portfolio model is deliberately simplistic in that it focuses on cash flow and uses two variables, growth and share. General Electric planners, in reacting to the limitations of the BCG model, developed the market attractiveness-business position matrix, drawing on portfolio approaches used by the consulting firm, McKinsey.[6] The structure of this matrix is shown in Figure 8.3.

Consider first market attractiveness, the horizontal axis. Instead of just being based on market growth, it is based on as many relevant factors as are appropriate in a given context. Nine factors that could be used are shown in Figure 8.3. The managers involved need to select the most appropriate factors, weight them as to relative importance in terms of context, evaluate an industry on each factor, and then combine the evaluation into a summary measure. Thus, the analysis has the potential of being richer and more valid than one using only growth.

The evaluation of a market with respect to the factors selected is made on the basis of the prospective ROI. Thus, the focus is on ROI prospects rather than cash flow even though the analysis is usually more qualitative than quantitative.

Consider next the business-position assessment as shown on the vertical axis. Instead of using only market share as a criterion, as many factors as are appropriate for the given context are employed. A partial list of potentially useful factors is shown in Figure 8.3. Again, specific factors need to be selected, their relative appropriateness assessed, the SBU needs to be rated on each factor, and finally, the ratings need to be combined into an overall assessment of a firm's ability to compete in that market.

Applying the Matrix

The market attractiveness-business position matrix is a formal, structured way to attempt to match a firm's strengths with market opportunities. It is therefore similar to the ideas presented in Chapter 7 about developing strategy to reflect firm strengths and weaknesses, competitor strengths and weaknesses, and market attractiveness. In this context, the competitors' strengths and weaknesses are made a part of the market attractiveness assessment.

One implication is that when both firm position and market attractiveness are positive, as in the boxes marked 1 in Figure 8.3, then a firm should probably invest and attempt to grow. When the assessment is more negative, as in the boxes marked 3, however, the nominal recommendation would be to either harvest or divest. For the three boxes marked 2, an investment decision would be made only selectively, when there was a specific reason to believe the investment would be profitable.

A useful exercise is to attempt to predict whether either your position or the attractiveness of the market will change if we assume the current strategy is followed. A predicted movement to another cell can signal the need to consider a change in strategy.

In structuring alternative strategies, the following are among the logical alternatives:

- **Invest to hold.** Attempt to stop erosion in position by investing enough to compensate for environmental and competitive forces.
- **Invest to penetrate.** Aggressively attempt to move up the position, even at the sacrifice of earnings.
- **Invest to rebuild.** Attempt to regain a previously held position that

FIGURE 8.3   The Market Attractiveness-Business Position Matrix

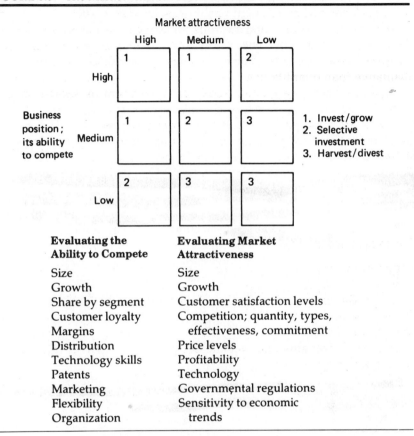

Evaluating the Ability to Compete

Size
Growth
Share by segment
Customer loyalty
Margins
Distribution
Technology skills
Patents
Marketing
Flexibility
Organization

Evaluating Market Attractiveness

Size
Growth
Customer satisfaction levels
Competition; quantity, types, effectiveness, commitment
Price levels
Profitability
Technology
Governmental regulations
Sensitivity to economic trends

has been lost by a milking strategy that, for whatever reason, is no longer appropriate.

● **Selective investment.** Attempt to strengthen position in some segments and let position weaken in other segments.

● **Low investment.** Attempt to harvest the business, drawing cash out and cutting investment to a minimum.

● **Divestiture.** Sell or liquidate the business.

The industry attractiveness-business position matrix is much richer than the growth-share matrix. As a result, it is not limited to "volume" industries, but can be applied in other competitive settings as well. Furthermore, its structure can be adapted more easily to higher-level investment-allocation decisions such as those across divisions. A business-position and a market-attractiveness rating may both represent averages of several component businesses. However, such average ratings can still have conceptual meaning for the purposes of structuring an allocation decision. It becomes a way to evaluate the extent to which an organizational unit has been able to match organizational strengths with competitive weaknesses in attractive markets. Recall the discussion at the end of Chapter 7 covering this underlying aim of strategy development.

Limitations

The market attractiveness-business position matrix is indeed much richer and more broadly applicable than the BCG growth-share matrix. Its measures can also be more subjective and ambiguous, however, especially across business units. The selection and weighting of factors and the subsequent development of both a firm's position and market attractiveness are highly subjective processes. They can be unduly influenced by historical perspectives and performance and by individual biases and backgrounds. The final evaluations are bound to be somewhat unreliable in that different people will obtain different evaluations. Furthermore, different business units will undoubtedly involve different factors, both in assessing business positions and in determining market attractiveness. The fact that two businesses have been evaluated with respect to different criteria adds ambiguity to the analysis.

As is true of the growth-share matrix, the results can be very sensitive to the definition of the product market. The analyses of market attractiveness and business position can both be dramatically affected if the market is luxury cars instead of all cars, stout instead of beer, or those greeting cards sold through drugstores instead of all greeting cards.

THE DIRECTIONAL POLICY MATRIX

A third portfolio model, developed by Shell Chemicals U.K., is the directional policy matrix (DPM).[7] As shown in Figure 8.4, its axes are labeled "business sector prospects" and "company's competitive capabilities." It offers three refinements or variations to the market attractiveness-business position matrix that warrant discussion.[8] First, it suggests a more structured and quantitative approach toward determining the position of the SBU in the matrix. Second, it offers more specific baseline strategy recommendations. Third, an extension provides an alternative way to analyze environmental risk.

FIGURE 8.4   The Directional Policy Matrix

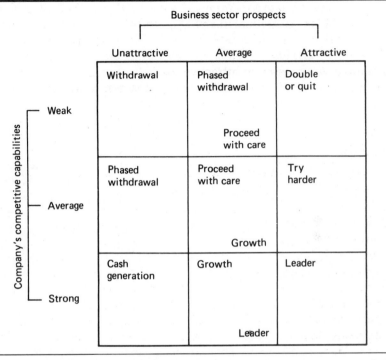

SOURCE: Adapted from D. E. Hussey, "Portfolio Analysis: Practical Experiences with the Direction Policy Matrix," *Long Range Planning*, August 1978, p. 3.

Quantifying the Position in the Matrix

The first step is to identify the main criteria by which the prospects of a business sector may be considered favorable or unfavorable. Such criteria usually include market growth and market quality. The other criteria will depend on the context. A scale value such as 0 to 4 is then assigned to each of the criterion areas for each business sector being evaluated. If appropriate, the criteria are weighted. If different weights are used for different business sectors, however, their comparison becomes somewhat ambiguous.

One study using DPM was done with Rolls-Royce, whose products include cars, diesel engines, and shunting locomotives. The business sector prospects criteria developed for Rolls-Royce were as follows:[9]

	Maximum Score
1. Market growth	4 points

2. Market quality   4 points
   Stable profitability
   Margins maintained in excess-capacity
      contexts
   Brand loyalty
   Customer/producer ratio
   Degree of substitutability (of the product)
   Restriction of technology
   Generation of after-sales business
3. Market supply (any major supply problems)   4 points

A single value was assessed for market quality. No effort was made in this case to push down the quantification to the level of subcriteria; however, an overall assessment was made taking the subcriteria into account.

The quantification of the competitive capabilities should proceed in a similar fashion. Criteria are identified by which the company's capability in a business sector can be judged strong or weak. In a chemical-industry study, the competitive capabilities criteria were

1. Market position
2. Production capability
3. Product research and development

Each SBU needs to be evaluated along each criterion. In the chemical-industry study, market position was scaled as follows:[10]

- **4   Leader.** Holds a pre-eminent market position, usually with acknowledged technical leadership.

- **3   Major producer.** One of two to four companies that jointly share the leadership role in an industry with no acknowledged leader.

- **2   Strong competitor.** A viable competitor that is a step below the top level of competitors.

- **1   Minor competitor.** Size is inadequate to support R&D and other services.

- **0   Negligible competitor.**

In the Rolls-Royce case, the following criteria were used to determine competitive capability:[11]

                                                           Maximum Score
1. Market position   4 points
   Market share
   Captive outlets

Dealer network
After-sales service network
2. Production capability   4 points
    Product economics
    Capacity in relation to market share
    Component availability
    Ability to handle product change
3. Engineering and support services   4 points
    Capability in relation to market position
    Production innovation ability
    Product quality

Again an overall assessment was made for each criterion, taking into consideration the subcriteria. Each criterion was weighted equally in the Rolls-Royce case study.

Baseline Strategy Recommendations

Like the BCG growth-share matrix, the DPM approach has associated with it some rather detailed and specific strategy recommendations. These are illustrated in Figure 8.4 and include:

● **Withdrawal.** These products will be losing money and their assets should be disposed of as rapidly as possible.

● **Phased withdrawal.** Profit prospects will be weak and efforts should be made to turn these assets to more profitable use; however, the withdrawal should be controlled and orderly.

● **Cash generation.** These products should be cash suppliers and should not require investment.

● **Proceed with care.** A product falling into this area of the matrix probably has a serious deficiency with respect to at least one of the competitive capability criteria. Major investments should be made with extreme caution and a milking strategy should be seriously considered. The problem is that many products fall between the "proceed with care" area of the matrix and the "growth" area.

● **Growth.** Investment should be made to allow the product to grow with the market. Generally the product should be profitable and the growth self-supporting.

● **Double or quit.** The best prospects in this group should be selected for investment to improve the company's position. Most of the products in this area should be abandoned.

● **Try harder.** This position in the matrix might be vulnerable over time.

Thus, consideration should be given to investment if it seems possible to improve the company's competitive position.

- **Leader.** The strategy is to give priority to maintaining this position even if investment is needed.

The Risk Matrix

The risk from environmental forces affecting a business area may not be easily integrated into the "business-sector-prospects" axis because it involves a very different type of analysis. Thus, it may be useful to consider environmental risk as a third axis in the model. Figure 8.5 shows an environmental-risk axis added to the business-sector-prospects-axis. In Figure 8.5, the third dimension, competitive capability, is suppressed.

The risk position will be based on the seriousness of environmental threats and the probability of their occurrence. The inclusion of the environmental-risk dimension will allow the baseline strategy recommendations to be adjusted for the risk factor.

Limitations

The DPM attempts to be more specific and quantitative than the industry attractiveness-business position matrix. As a result, its associated strategy choices may be regarded as more precise and valid than is appropriate. There is still much subjectivity in selecting criteria and in evaluating business units. Clearly, the baseline strategy recommendations need to be considered suggestive and not definitive. Each situation must be analyzed in depth to see whether the baseline strategy recommendations appear sound.

PORTFOLIO MODELS IN PRACTICE

Philippe Haspeslagh, a business policy professor at INSEAD in France, conducted a study of firms drawn from the Fortune "1000" industrial firms that had used portfolio models.[12] About one-third of the respondents in the study felt that the most important benefit of using portfolio models was achieving a better understanding of their businesses, which in turn, they felt, led to better strategic decision making. In part, the analysis contributes by providing a vocabulary and graphic tools that aid communication. Another one-third felt that the key benefits were improved resource allocation, strategic reorientation, and exit and entry decisions. The balance of firms had not developed an opinion or focused on the objectivity and commitment that emerged from the process.

FIGURE 8.5   The Risk Matrix

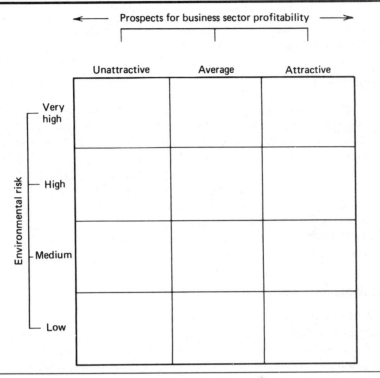

Source: Adapted from D. E. Hussey, "Portfolio Analysis: Practical Experiences with the Direction Policy Matrix," *Long Range Planning,* August 1978, p. 7.

The decision as to which portfolio model to use was not regarded as critical. In fact, the labels commonly used, such as dog, cash cow, and star, were often found to be irrelevant and even the source of problems. The implication is that the models tended to be used qualitatively and that the experience curve thrust of the growth-share matrix was not a dominant part of the use of the models. Considered fundamental to portfolio planning were

1. Defining the SBUs for purposes of strategic decisions.
2. Classifying those SBUs on a portfolio grid according to their competitive positions and the attractiveness of their markets.
3. Considering the implications of using this framework to assign growth and financial objectives to each SBU and to allocate resources accordingly.

SUMMARY

Portfolio models can help firms that are operating diverse businesses to understand their group of businesses and to allocate resources among them. The BCG growth-share matrix rates markets on the basis of their growth rate, the assumption being that growth markets are more attractive investments than mature markets (an assumption discussed in Chapter 5). Market position is indicated by relative market share, which is related to ROI in the PIMS studies, and is also crucial to an experience curve-based strategy. The resulting matrix has four quadrants that define an SBU as stars, cash cows, dogs, or problem children. The baseline strategy is to use cash generated by cash cows and selected dogs and problem children to fund embryonic businesses, promising problem children, and any stars requiring investment in excess of their own cash flow. Among the model's limitations are the fact that the experience curve is not always relevant or easy to work with, the inadequacy of the growth dimension to reflect market attractiveness, measurement issues, sensitivity to product-market definitions, the focus on cash flow, and the difficulty of implementing implied strategies.

The market attractiveness-business position matrix is richer and therefore potentially more valid but also more ambiguous and less reliable. Both market-attractiveness and business-position assessments are made on the basis of as many factors as appear relevant in a given context. The directional policy matrix (DPM) is similar in structure. It is associated with a more quantitative approach toward determining the position of the SBU in the matrix. A numerical value is generated for each SBU, reflecting its competitive capability and its market position. The DPM also offers more specific baseline strategy recommendations and is associated with a proposal to add environmental-risk assessment as a third dimension to portfolio models. Both are more suitable for use with groups of businesses within SBUs or divisions.

FOOTNOTES

[1] Robert Jacobson and David A. Aaker, "Is Market Share All That It's Cracked Up to Be?", *Journal of Marketing* 49, Fall 1985, pp. 11–22.

[2] Robert D. Buzzell and Bradley T. Gale, *The PIMS Principles*, New York: The Free Press, 1987.

[3] Carolyn R. Woo, "Market-Share Leadership—Not Always So Good," *Harvard Business Review*, January–February 1984, pp. 50–53.

[4] Stratford P. Sherman, "The Mind of Jack Welch," *Fortune*, March 27, 1989, pp. 39–50.

[5] George S. Day, "Diagnosing the Product Portfolio," *Journal of Marketing*, April 1977, pp. 29–38.

[6] One description emphasizing the determination of matrix positions is in William E. Rothschild, *Putting It All Together*, New York: AMACOM, 1976, Chapter 8; another is in Sidney Schoeffler, "In Defense of PIMS, GE and BCG," *Marketing News*, February 9, 1979, p. 8.

[7] This discussion of the DPM is based on S. J. Q. Robinson, R. E. Hichens, and P. P. Wade, "The Directional Policy Matrix Tool for Strategic Planning," *Long-Range Planning* 11, April 1978, pp. 8–15.

[8] D. E. Hussey, "Portfolio Analysis: Practical Experiences with the Direction Policy Matrix," *Long Range Planning*, August 1978, pp. 2–8.

[9] Hussey, "Portfolio Analysis," p. 4.

[10] Robinson, Hichens, and Wade, "The Directional Policy," p. 11.

[11] Hussey, "Portfolio Analysis," p. 5.

[12] Philippe Haspeslagh, "Portfolio Planning: Uses and Limits," *Harvard Business Review*, January–February 1982, pp. 58–73.

PART FOUR

ALTERNATIVE BUSINESS STRATEGIES

9

OBTAINING A SUSTAINABLE COMPETITIVE ADVANTAGE

Apple had become a value-added marketing company instead of a commodity marketing company. . . . Desktop publishing is really only the beginning of a new generation of knowledge tools that will help us rethink the way we perform work.

John Sculley, Apple Computers

Vision is the art of seeing things invisible.

Jonathan Swift

All men can see the tactics whereby I conquer, but what none can see is the strategy out of which great victory is evolved.

Sun-Tzu, Chinese Military Strategist

What are the strategic alternatives that should be considered? Which one is optimal? These questions have remained in the background but now become the focus—in this chapter and in Chapters 10 through 15. One goal is to increase the scope of available strategic alternatives to increase the likelihood that superior strategic choices are available. A good decision among inferior alternatives is much less desirable than a poor decision among superior alternatives.

Chapters 12 and 13 consider growth strategies involving the product-market investment decision. Chapter 12 discusses market penetration, product-market expansion, and vertical integration. Diversification, another growth option, is the subject of Chapter 13. Chapter 14 focuses on mature and declining markets and discusses industry revitalization, being the profitable survivor, and the hold, milk, and exit decisions. In Chapter 15, global strategies, of increasing importance to many firms, are analyzed.

This and the following two chapters focus on the development of an SCA, the key to a successful strategy, and how to understand and neutralize the SCAs of competitors. According to Stephen South, Corporate Planning Director of Clark Equipment, "The process of strategic management is coming to be defined, in fact, as the management of competitive advantage—that is, as a process of identifying, developing, and taking advantage of enclaves in which a tangible and preservable business advantage can be achieved."[1]

THE SUSTAINABLE COMPETITIVE ADVANTAGE

A strategy can involve a variety of functional area strategies such as positioning strategies, pricing strategies, distribution strategies, global strategies, and on and on. Infinite ways of competing exist. As illustrated by Figure 9.1, however, how you compete is not the only key to success. At least three other factors are requisite for the creation of an SCA and thus a strategy that will be successful over time.

Basis of Competition—Skills and Assets

The first factor is the basis of competition. The strategy needs to be based on a set of assets, skills, and capabilities. Without the support of skills or assets, it is unlikely that the SCA will be enduring. There is no point in pursuing a quality strategy without the design and manufacturing capability to deliver quality products. For instance, a department store premium service positioning strategy will not succeed unless the right people and culture are in place. It is who you are in addition to what you do.

FIGURE 9.1   The Sustainable Competitive Advantage

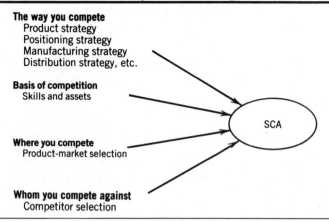

Furthermore, the activities of a business such as positioning its product line as one of high quality are usually easily imitated. What is less easy to imitate, however, is the actual delivery of high quality; that can require specialized skills and assets. Anyone can distribute cereal or detergent through supermarkets, but few have the assets and skills needed to do it effectively.

As discussed in Chapter 4, several questions can help to identify relevant skills, assets, and capabilities. What skills and assets are possessed by successful businesses and lacking in unsuccessful businesses? What are the key motivations of the major market segments? What are the large value-added components? What are the mobility barriers? What elements of the value chain can generate advantage?

Where You Compete

The second important determinant for an SCA is the choice of the target product market. A well-defined strategy supported by assets and skills can fail because it does not work in the marketplace. Thus, a strategy and its underlying assets and skills should involve something valued by the market. If distribution is to be an SCA for Heublein's wine operation, for example, distribution should be important to success in the industry. Procter & Gamble's Pringle's potato chips had a host of assets such as a consistent product, long shelf life, a crush-proof container, and national distribution and advertising, but these assets adversely affected taste perception, which was the most important attribute according to the market.

Whom You Compete Against

The third requirement for an SCA involves the identity of competitors. Sometimes an asset or skill will form an SCA only given the right set of competitors. Thus, it is vital to assess whether a competitor or strategic group is weak, adequate, or strong with respect to assets and skills. The goal is to engage in a strategy that will match up with that of competitors who lack strength in relevant assets and skills.

In general, for an asset or skill to be the basis of an SCA, it should help create either a cost advantage over competitors or a point of difference from competitors. For example, flight safety is important to airline passengers, but if airlines are perceived to be equal with respect to pilot quality and plane maintenance, it cannot be the basis for an SCA. Of course, if a strategic group such as the economy airlines is perceived to be weak on safety, or if some airlines are superior with respect to antiterrorist security, then an SCA could indeed exist.

Additional Characteristics of SCAs

Thus, an effective SCA will be created when a strategy has at least three characteristics. It should be supported by assets and skills. It should be employed in a competitive arena that contains segments that will value the strategy. Finally, it should be employed against competitors who cannot easily match or neutralize the SCA. In addition, an effective SCA should:

1. Be substantial enough to make a difference. A modest edge on competitive dimensions may not provide an advantage that will affect the marketplace. For example, an ability to produce marginally superior quality carpeting may not be valued adequately by the market.

2. Be sustainable in the face of environmental changes and competitor actions. A high-tech market such as that for personal computers can change over time to the point that the importance of technological advantage is reduced as the product becomes more of a commodity. Name recognition in some contexts may be easily countered with clever advertising or by the choice of distribution channels. A cost advantage enjoyed by Toyota in making automobiles may be compromised by Korean manufacturers that have developed cost advantages of their own. Some information technology innovations such as Merrill Lynch's Cash Management Account were replicated by followers and were not as much of an advantage as first perceived. If a strategy by design or accident confronts competitors that can neutralize or overcome the assets and skills, there will not be a sustainable advantage.

3. When possible, be leveraged into visible business attributes that will influence customers. The key is to link an SCA with the positioning of a business. Thus, skills and assets that relate to ensuring reliability in products may not be apparent to customers. If they can be made visible through advertising or a product design, however, then they can support a reliability positioning strategy. The key is to make this visible. Maytag is known as a reliability firm because its advertising is supported by product design and product performance that made the reliability claim believable.

In practice, an SCA can take a wide variety of forms. A study of SCAs identified by business managers illustrates.

What Business Managers Name as Their SCAs

Managers of 248 distinct businesses weighted toward service and high-tech industries were contacted and asked to name the SCA of their businesses.[2] The objectives were to learn the identity of frequently employed SCAs, to confirm that managers could articulate them, to determine whether or not different managers from the same SBU would identify the same SCAs, and to find how many SCAs would be identified for each SBU. The responses were coded into categories. The results, summarized in Figure 9.2, provide some suggestive insights into the SCA construct.

Figure 9.2 indicates the wide variety of SCAs mentioned, each representing distinct competitive approaches. The top few by no means dominated the list. Of course, the list did differ by industry. For high-tech firms, for example, name recognition was less important than technical superiority, product innovation, and installed customer base. The next two chapters discuss several SCAs in more detail.

Most of the SCAs in Figure 9.2 reflect assets or skills. Customer base, quality reputation, good management and engineering staff, for example, are business assets, whereas customer service and technical superiority usually involve sets of skills.

For a subset of 95 of the businesses involved, a second SBU manager was independently interviewed. The result suggests that managers can identify SCAs with a high degree of reliability. Of the 95 businesses, 76 of the manager pairs gave answers that were coded the same and most of the others had only a single difference in the SCA list.

Another finding is instructive—the average number of SCAs per business was 4.65, suggesting that it is usually not sufficient to base a strategy on a single SCA. Sometimes a business is described in terms of a single skill and asset, implying that being a "quality-oriented" business

FIGURE 9.2   Sustainable Competitive Advantages of 248 Businesses

	High-Tech	Service	Other	Total
1. Reputation for quality	26	50	29	105
2. Customer service/product support	23	40	15	78
3. Name recognition/high profile	8	42	21	71
4. Retain good management and engineering staff	17	43	5	65
5. Low-cost production	17	15	21	53
6. Financial resources	11	26	14	51
7. Customer orientation/feedback/market research	13	26	9	48
8. Product-line breadth	11	23	13	47
9. Technical superiority	30	7	9	46
10. Installed base of satisfied customers	19	22	4	45
11. Segmentation/focus	7	22	16	45
12. Product characteristics/differentiation	12	15	10	37
13. Continuing product innovation	12	17	6	35
14. Market share	12	14	9	35
15. Size/location of distribution	10	11	13	34
16. Low price/high-value offering	6	20	6	32
17. Knowledge of business	2	25	4	31
18. Pioneer/early entrant in industry	11	11	6	28
19. Efficient, flexible production/operations adaptable to customers	4	17	4	26
20. Effective sales force	10	9	4	23
21. Overall marketing skills	7	9	7	23
22. Shared vision/culture	5	13	4	22
23. Strategic goals	6	7	9	22
24. Powerful well-known parent	7	7	6	20
25. Location	0	10	10	20
26. Effective advertising/image	5	6	6	17
27. Enterprising/entrepreneurial	3	3	5	11
28. Good coordination	3	2	5	10
29. Engineering research and development	8	2	0	10
30. Short-term planning	2	1	5	8
31. Good distributor relations	2	4	1	7
32. Other	6	20	5	31
Total	315	539	281	1136
Number of businesses	68	113	67	248
Average number of SCAs	4.63	4.77	4.19	4.58

or a "service-focused" business explains success. This study indicates, however, that it may be necessary to have several skills and assets.

Strategic Thrusts—Routes to an SCA

There are a host of strategic thrusts that can underlie an SCA. Each SCA may be based on one or a combination of them. Five of the most notable, shown in Figure 9.3, are discussed explicitly in this chapter and the two that follow. Among others that could be important in some contexts include being innovative, thinking globally, having an entrepreneurial style, or exploiting information technology.

Two of the most important are differentiation or low cost. Michael Porter has suggested that all strategies will either provide a low cost or differentiation advantage.[3] Differentiation means that there is an element of uniqueness about a strategy that provides value to the customer. For example, firms differentiate their offerings by enhancing performance, quality, reliability, prestige, or convenience. In the following chapter, several differentiation strategies that appear in the Figure 9.2 SCA study are presented. A low-cost strategy can be based on a cost advantage that can be used to invest in the product, support lower prices, or provide high profits. Low-cost strategies are discussed in Chapter 11.

Strategies can have other strategic thrusts in addition to differentiation and low cost. Three appear in Figure 9.3. "Focus strategies" focus on a market segment or part of a product line. "Preemptive strategies" are strategies that employ first mover advantages to inhibit or prevent competitors from duplicating or countering. "Synergistic strategies" rely on the synergy between a business and other businesses in the same firm. In Chapter 11, focus and preemptive strategies are discussed in addition to low-cost strategies. We now consider the special role of synergy in the development of SCAs.

FIGURE 9.3   Strategic Thrusts

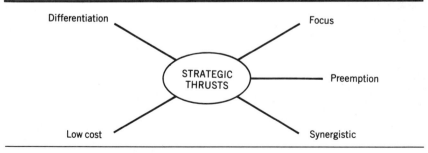

THE ROLE OF SYNERGY

Synergy between SBUs can provide an SCA that is truly sustainable because it is based on the characteristics of a firm that are probably unique. A competitor might have to duplicate an organization in order to capture the assets or skills involved. For example, the SCAs of General Electric in the CT scanner (an x-ray-based diagnostic system) business are in part based on its leadership in the x-ray business, where it has a huge installed base and a large service network, and in part based on the fact that it operates other businesses involving technologies used in CT scanners. The resulting system synergies are very difficult for competitors to duplicate or counter. In the following chapters a variety of strategies are discussed, most of which have the potential to involve synergy.

Synergy means that the whole is more than the sum of its parts. In this context, it means that two SBUs (or two product-market strategies) operating together will be superior to the same two SBUs operating independently. In terms of products, positive synergy means that offering a set of products will generate a higher return over time than would be possible if each of the products was operated autonomously. Similarly, in terms of markets, operating a set of markets within a business will be superior to operating them autonomously. Generally the synergy will be caused by some commonalty in the two operations such as:

- Distribution
- Image and its impact on the market
- Products combining to form a system
- Use or application
- Sales or advertising effort
- Plant usage
- R&D effort
- Operating costs

As a result of synergy, the combined SBUs will either have

1. Increased customer value and thus increased sales
2. Decreased operating costs
3. Reduced investment

Synergy is not difficult to understand conceptually, but it is slippery in practice, in part because it can be difficult to predict whether synergy will actually emerge. Often two businesses seem related, and sizable potential synergy exists but is never realized. Sometimes the perceived synergy is merely a mirage or wishful thinking, perhaps created in the haste to put together a merger. Other times, the potential synergy is real, but implementation problems prevent its realization. Perhaps there is a cultural mismatch between two organizations, or the incentives are inadequate. The material on implementation in Chapter 16 is directly relevant to the problem of predicting whether potential synergy will be realized.

Core Competences

A firm's asset or skill that is capable of being the competitive basis of many of its businesses is termed a core competence and can be a synergistic advantage. Prahalad and Hamel suggest a tree metaphor in which the root system is core competence, the trunk and major limbs are core products, the smaller branches are business units, and the leaves and flowers are end products.[4] You may not recognize the strength of a competitor by looking at its end products and failing to examine the strength of its root system. Core competence represents the consolidation of firm-wide technologies and skills into a coherent thrust. The key to strategic management can be the management of core competencies rather than business units because the SCAs of business units are, in fact, based on core competencies.

Consider, for example, the core competence of Sony in miniaturization, 3M in sticky tape technology, Black & Decker in small motors, Honda in vehicle motors and power trains, NEC in semiconductors (which underlie its attack on both the computer and communications businesses and their interface), and Canon in precision mechanics, fine optics, and microelectronics. Each of these competencies underlies a large set of businesses and has the potential to create more. Each of these firms invests in competence in a variety of different ways and contexts. Each would insist on keeping the primary thrust of its work related to the core competence in house. Outsourcing would not only risk weakening the asset, but also each firm would rightfully insist that there is no other firm that could match the state-of-the-art advances.

STRATEGIC VISION VERSUS STRATEGIC OPPORTUNISM

There are two very different approaches to the development of successful strategies and sustainable competitive advantages. Each can work but may require very different systems and even people and culture. In the first, there is a long-term perspective—the focus is on the future in both strategy development and the supporting analysis. In the second, the emphasis is on strategies that make sense today—the implicit belief is that the best way to have the right strategy in place tomorrow is to have it right today. The first leads to strategic vision and the second to strategic opportunism.

Strategic Vision

A strategic vision is based on a forward-looking, long-term perspective. The planning horizon extends into the future perhaps two, five, or more than ten years, depending on the business involved.

What trends will mature or emerge at that time? What will the driving forces of the market be? What will the key success factors in the market be? Who will the competitors be? What strategies will be viable? What assets and skills will be needed to underlie those strategies?

The goal of the supporting information system and analysis effort will thus be to understand the likely future environment, to address these questions. Experts who have insights into key future events and trends will be helpful. Scenario analysis, delphi techniques, technological forecasting, and trend analysis will likely be part of the analysis phase of strategy development. (See Figure 9.4).

The end result will be a vision of what strategy should be in place in the future—what product markets to serve and what synergies and assets and skills will be necessary to win—and a commitment to pursue that strategy. The organization, its people, and its culture, will provide a firm with the patience to develop and see through whatever investment in assets and skills needed is required. The firm will not be diverted by immediate problems or apparent opportunities, enticing though they may be, from the prime objective of achieving its vision.

Making the commitment visible can help make this happen. For example, the commitment might be strongly indicated to competitors to influence them away from the business area and to shareholders to gain their support for strategic investment at a sacrifice of current performance. In addition, a commitment to a clear vision can stimulate employees to pursue programs with dedication and energy.

A vision of a synergistic, technology-driven firm has helped Corning develop from a consumer products firm to a leader in such areas as fiber optics and liquid-crystal displays.[5] The strategy concept involves investing heavily in technology, sharing the technology across business units, and forming technology and marketing alliances. The goal is to lever technological developments to maximize the impact on the whole organization.

A strategic vision can take many forms. Jack Welch of GE had a vision of being the first or second competitor in each business area and dramatically changed GE as a result. Mercedes, Tiffany, and Nordstrom at one point were guided by a vision of being the best in their fields in terms of

FIGURE 9.4   Alternate Strategic Approaches

	Strategic approach	Strategic risk
Focus on future	Strategic vision	Strategic stubbornness
Focus on present	Strategic opportunism	Strategic drift

delivering quality products and services. Weight Watchers had a vision of building and exploiting its unique associations of dietary weight control and nutrition to gain a presence throughout the supermarket. The vision of Sharp is to succeed by being a technological innovator especially in eptoelectronic technologies.[6] The firm has already been the first to market flat screen TVs, double-cassette recorders, solid-state calculators, color desktop fax machines, HDTV projection systems and is the leading supplier of electroluminescent displays for computers.

Strategic Stubbornness

The risk of the strategic vision route is that the vision may be faulty and its pursuit may be a wasteful exercise in strategic stubbornness. There are a host of pitfalls that could prevent a vision from being realized. Three stand out.

First, the picture of the future may be substantially accurate, but the firm may not be able to implement the strategy required. That was, in part, the problem with the efforts of GE and others to crack the computer market in the 1960s and with the attempt of Sony to become the industry standard with its Beta VCR format.

Second, the vision might be faulty because it is based on faulty assumptions about the future. For example, the concept of a one-stop financial services firm that drove the vision of American Express, Sears, Merrill Lynch, and others was based, in part, on the erroneous assumption that customers would see value in a one-stop financial service—in fact, they preferred to deal with specialists.

A third problem occurs when a scenario changes meaningfully from that assumed, perhaps the market does not emerge as expected or new operators enter and change the game. For example, the environment envisioned by Businessland was affected by new forces that emerged. The Businessland founder built a dominant retail chain with a vision of attaining economies of scale while providing name computers (IBM, COMPAQ, and Apple) and valued-added service to large companies.[7] However, storefronts turned from assets to liabilities when personal contact or even mail order sales became the preferred method of interacting with vendors for large companies. These unanticipated distribution dynamics together with weak operations (especially computer control, ironically) and some product errors (attempting a private label brand and mismanaging the COMPAQ relationship) led the company into serious trouble in the early 1990s. The Businessland founder was quoted as saying, "You don't get to live on visions forever."

The power of a vision is based on the commitment that accompanies it. This commitment together with a focus on the future instead of the past can often result in pursuing a faulty vision beyond the point at which the probability of success or the likely return is unacceptably low. The trick, of course, is to maintain the commitment and patience in the face of adversity, while at the same time not allowing a failed vision to use up resources on a futile attempt at a miracle recovery.

Strategic Opportunism

Strategic opportunism, in contrast, is driven by a focus on the present. The premise is often that the environment is so dynamic and uncertain that it just is not feasible to aim at a fixed, known future target. The argument is that unless a business is structured to have strategic advantages at the present, it is unlikely to ever be strategically successful in the future.

The strategic questions posed are very different. What trends are most active and critical now? What are the current driving forces in the market? What are the strategic problems facing the business that need immediate correction? What technologies are ready to be employed? What are current strategic opportunities and threats? What are competitors doing in the area of marketing and in the lab? What strategy changes are occurring or are planned?

The supporting information system and analysis are also different. To support strategic opportunism, the effort is to monitor customers, competitors, and the trade to learn of trends, opportunities, and threats as they appear. The information gathering and analysis should be both sensitive and on-line. Frequent, regular meetings as a way of absorbing the most recent developments and news may be helpful. The organization should be quick to understand and act on changing fundamentals.

The hallmark of an organization that emphasizes strategic opportunism is strategic flexibility and the willingness to quickly respond to strategic opportunities as they emerge. The organization is adaptive in its ability to adjust its systems, structure, people, and culture to accommodate new ventures. The strategy is dynamic, change is the norm. New products are explored or initiated and others are deemphasized or dropped. New markets are entered and disinvestment is occurring in others. New synergies and assets are being created.

One example of strategic opportunism is the story of AM/PM. While other convenience stores were pursuing the original vision of a retailer that offered convenient locations, a limited selection of staples and snacks, and long hours, AM/PM was adapting, changing with conditions. Stores were developed that catered to new trends—for example, healthier snack food and yogurt. Roomier, brighter stores were constructed. Ethnic stores were developed to cater to the special tastes of ethnic groups—for instance, the Mexican American market. Opportunities were sought and exploited.

Otis Spunkmeyer is another example. A wholesale cookie company, the firm provides frozen dough and ovens to retailers who would like to compete with fresh cookie shops. It followed various opportunities to buy an oven company, to market muffins, to expand to the East Coast, to even buy a sightseeing airline and resort hotel that help promote its name.

James Brian Quinn, a Dartmouth policy professor, studied how ten companies made major strategy changes and found support for the strategic opportunism model.[8] Most of the strategic changes observed were precipitated by external or internal events (such as the dramatic development of a breakthrough product), over which management had little control. Typically, an organization reacted by making a set of incremental decisions, which Quinn termed "logical incrementalism," leading to a strategy. Sometimes, these decisions were formally part of a phased program planning system (not the annual formal planning system). With a new product, for example, sequential decisions could be made after concept testing, product refinement, and test marketing. However, they were rarely driven by the annual formal planning system.

Strategic Drift

The problem with the strategic opportunism model is that it can turn into strategic drift. Investment decisions are made incrementally in response to opportunities rather than being directed by a vision. As a result, a firm can wake up one morning and find that it is in a set of businesses for which it lacks the needed assets and skills and which provide few synergies.

At least two phenomena can turn strategic opportunism into

strategic drift. First, a short-lived transitory force is mistaken for one with enough staying power to make a strategic move worthwhile. If the force is so short-lived that a strategy does not pay off or perhaps does not even have a chance to get into place, the result will be a strategy that is not suitable for the business or the environment.

Second, opportunities to create immediate profits are rationalized as strategic when, in fact, they are not. For example, an instrumentation firm often receives offers to sell special-purpose instruments to customers; such equipment could conceivably be used by other customers but, in fact, has little strategic value. Most opportunities like this might result in a sizable initial order but divert R&D resources from more strategic activities.

Strategic drift not only creates a business without needed assets, it can also result in a failure to support a core business that does have a good vision. Without a vision and supporting commitment, it is tempting indeed to divert investment into seemingly sure things that are immediate—strategic opportunities. Thus, strategic opportunism can be an excuse to delay investment or divert resources from a core vision.

One example of strategic drift is a firm that designed, installed, and serviced custom equipment for steel firms. Over time, however, steel firms became more knowledgable and began buying standardized equipment mainly on the basis of price. Gradually, over the years, the firm edged into this commodity business to retain its share. The company finally woke up to find itself pursuing a dual strategy for which it was ill-suited—it had too much overhead to compete with the real commodity firms and its ability to provide upscale service had eroded and was now inferior to that of some niche players. Had there been a strategic vision, the firm would not have allowed itself to fall into such a trap.

Korvette, the first major successful discounter, started with a walk-up hard goods store in New York that offered name brands at $5 over wholesale cost.[9] Its low-cost image allowed it to expand into other locations and become a major retailing force—one industry spokesperson called its founder one of the most influential retailers of the century. However, the enticing opportunities to expand were its undoing. Over time it moved into soft goods, furniture, and food and aggressively expanded geographically. The firm's hands-on management style became ineffective in an organization with major coordination and communication problems. Worse, the basis of Korvette's low-cost image was undercut. It eventually drifted into a business requiring assets it did not have and its resulting decline, culminating in bankruptcy, was as spectacular as its prior rise.

Vision Plus Opportunism

Many businesses attempt to have the best of both worlds by engaging in strategic vision and strategic opportunism at the same time. Strategic opportunism can supplement strategic vision by managing diversification away from the core business and by managing the route to achievement of a firm's vision. Thus, if Weight Watchers has a vision to exploit brand associations by extending its name to other product categories, strategic opportunism could describe the process of selecting the identity of extensions and the order in which they are pursued.

The combination can and does work. However, there are obvious risks and problems. One is that strategic vision requires patience and investment and is vulnerable to the enticements represented by the more immediate return that is usually associated with strategic opportunism. It is difficult to maintain the persistence and discipline required by strategic vision in any case, even without distractions by alternative strategies that have been blessed as part of the thrust of the organization.

The organizational problems are worse. It is simply difficult for one organization to do both well because the systems, people, structure, and culture that are best for one approach are generally not going to be well suited for another. Strategic opportunism will thrive under an organization that is strategically flexible, has avoided commitment, and is involved in multiple-product markets and strategies. It will require a management style and supporting information system that are very sensitive to current developments affecting the business. Strategic vision, in contrast, will work best in an organization that is strategically focused and committed and that has a management style and information system oriented toward understanding the future. To create an organization that excels at or even tolerates both is not easy.

STRATEGIC INTENT

Hamel and Prahalad have suggested that some firms have strategic intent that couples strategic vision with a sustained obsession with winning at all levels of the organization.[10] They note that this model explains the successful rise to global leadership of companies such as Canon, Komatsu, Samsung (see insert), and Honda. Thus, Canon was out to "beat Xerox," Komatsu to "encircle Caterpillar," and Honda to become a "second Ford."

A strategic intent to achieve a successful strategy has several characteristics in addition to involving a strategic vision and an obsession with success. First, it should recognize the essence of winning. Coca-Cola's strategic intent has included the objective of putting a Coke within "arm's reach" of every consumer in the world because distribution and accompanied visibility are the keys to winning. NEC decided it needed to acquire the technologies that would allow it to exploit the convergence of computing and telecommunications. That became its guiding theme.

Second, strategic intent involves the stretching of an organization, a continuing effort to identify and develop new SCAs or to improve those that exist. Thus, it has a very dynamic forward-looking perspective. What will our advantage be next year and two years after that? Consider Matsushita, Toshiba, and the other Japanese television manufacturers. They first relied on low labor cost advantages. By servicing private label needs they added economies of scale. The next step was to obtain advantages in quality, reliability, features, brand name, and distribution. In contrast, an analysis of their strengths and weaknesses might have led to the conclusion that they should focus on a low-cost niche.

Third, strategic intent often requires real innovation, a willingness to do things very differently. Savin entered the U.S. copier market with a product that could be sold through dealers instead of being leased and that was simple, low-priced, and reliable. As a result, Xerox's huge advantage in sales and service and ability to finance leased equipment

---

Samsung and Microwave Ovens

In 1977, Samsung decided to make microwave ovens despite the fact that there were major established competitors with seemingly unbeatable SCAs who were making millions of ovens per year.[11] During the next four years it saw its first two prototypes melt down, redesigned its product again and again, bought the last magnetron factory from the United States, and received its first order for 240 ovens from Panama. In 1980, a J.C. Penny order requiring Samsung to build a unit 25% less expensive than existing ones necessitated still another redesign. In 1983, GE under pressure from Japanese firms turned to Samsung to source some of its products. Samsung's labor costs of $1.47 cost contrast to GE's $52.00. By the late 1980s Samsung was building over 4 million units per year and had cornered over one-third of the U.S. market.

It is clear that Samsung had a strategic intent to enter the microwave oven market. Its goals during the first decade were production and meeting whatever customer needs were required to gain sales. Financial return was of no consequence at all. An enormous investment was made in design and manufacturing engineering to make it happen—a large, competent staff was gathered who carefully analyzed how competitors had solved problems and what customers expected. The firm was very responsive to customer needs even when it met sizable losses. The firm capitalized on its cost advantage and the willingness of production and engineering personnel to work 68-hour weeks. The firm virtually willed its own remarkable success.

was neutralized. Honda made real advances in motor design in order to attack the large motorcycle market.

An obsession with winning can be created even without a competitor. Peter Johnson told how he created a phantom competitor when running Trus Joist, a maker of structural components for buildings that had a patent-based monopoly and then when running a legal power administration monopoly.[12] In each case, the phantom competitor would develop low-cost options and generate creative options for breaking into a business. As a result, Trus Joist was prompted to innovate in a companion market and the power agency shut down two partially completed atomic power plants.

A strategic intent provides a long-term drive for advantage that is sometimes essential to success. It provides a model that helps break the mold, getting away from doing the same as last year except doing it a bit better, working a bit harder. It has the capability to elevate and extend an organization, helping it reach levels it would not otherwise attain.

The focus on winning and sales volume that is a hallmark of strategic intent can be self-destructive as Kenichi Ohmae observes.[13] He criticizes the "winning by working harder" obsession of Japanese firms, claiming that it has made many industries less profitable than they might have otherwise been. For example, Japanese firms have created enormous overcapacity in shipbuilding, automobiles, and other industries and have engaged in destructive price competition in order to "win." Those in the whaling industry, for example, created an excess whale-killing capacity that resulted in negative public opinion that finally affected their business.

STRATEGIC FLEXIBILITY

Strategy intent usually represents a commitment to attaining an SCA. However, in some dynamic industries, attaining an SCA is a moving target. In those contexts, the answer is to attain strategic flexibility, so that a business will be ready when a window of opportunity arises. The concept is that there are too many uncertainties to proactively attempt to create an SCA because it is difficult to make the necessary predictions about customer needs, the technology, a competitive posture, and so on.

Strategic flexibility is the ability to adjust or develop strategies to respond to external or internal changes. As Aaker and Mascarenhas have noted, there are three ways to achieve strategic flexibility: by diversifying, investing in underused resources, and reducing commitment of resources to a specialized use.[14]

Diversification can involve participation in multiple-product markets, technologies, plant locations, or countries. It can also involve orga-

---

Lessons from U.S. Business Blunders

An analysis of some egregious blunders that have resulted in the loss of whole industries such as consumer electronics after a dominant position revealed four fatal misconceptions:[15]

1. Labor costs are killing us. In fact, the labor content is often a small percent of value added and the most efficient factories have more costly labor input but use and motivate it better.
2. You can't make money at the low end. Actually, too often last year's low end, from radios to semiconductors, forms the technological, manufacturing, and marketing basis for next year's high end.
3. We can't sell it. U.S. firms attempted to sell products, from microwave ovens (the major appliance firms) to fax machines (Xerox first introduced the fax), using marketing methods familiar to them, rather than approaches attuned to the innovation.
4. It's cheaper to buy it (a new business area) than grow it. Treating SBUs as stand-alone units to be bought or sold discourages unit synergy, diverts attention to external investment (the grass is always greener on the other side), and treats investments needed for survival as just another capital budgeting decision.

---

nizational forms like decentralized units, which are more responsive to the environment, and alliances. The concept is to reduce the impact of a localized undesirable event or trend and to increase the chances that a firm will participate in a desirable event or trend. An objective might, for example, be to participate in three technologies, including an important emerging one.

Flexibility can also be obtained by investing in underused assets. An obvious example is to maintain liquidity so that investment can be quickly funneled to opportunity or problem areas. Less obvious is the maintenance of excess capacity in manufacturing, in organization staffing, or in R&D in order to increase a firm's ability to react quickly. Thus, one objective could be to develop the capability to double production within three months' time.

Flexibility can be enhanced by reducing exit barriers to business areas. Reducing the commitment of resources to specialized uses can minimize the adverse impact of an undesirable event or trend. Thus, asset purchase (versus leasing), vertical integration, and technological leadership might be avoided. Conversely, entering foreign markets through exporting or licensing, subcontracting, and using temporary workers (an important part of the strategy of many Japanese firms) might be encouraged.

SUMMARY

For a strategy to involve a sustainable competitive advantage, it needs to have three characteristics. It must be supported by assets and skills. It should be employed in a competitive arena that contains segments which will value the strategy. Finally, it should face competitors who cannot easily match or neutralize the SCA. A wide variety of SCAs are available to a business. Over 30 are identified in the Figure 9.2 study, with perceived quality at the head of the list. Among the strategic thrusts are differentiation, low cost, focus, preemption, and synergy.

Synergy has the potential to provide an SCA that is truly sustainable because it is based on the unique characteristics of an organization. A concern is to make sure potential synergy actually exists and that any implementation problems can be overcome.

In developing strategies, it can be useful to consider the concepts of strategic vision, strategic stubbornness, strategic opportunism, strategic drift, strategic intent, and strategic flexibility. A strategic vision, based on a future focus, is a vision of what the strategy of the future should be. Strategic opportunism, a now focus, emphasizes current opportunities and strategy choices and allows a strategy to emerge from a set of incremental decisions. Strategic intent couples strategic vision with an obsession with winning in a particular product market even if innovation and an organizational stretch are involved. Strategic flexibility is the ability to adjust or develop strategies to respond to external or internal changes and can be achieved via diversification, maintaining underused assets, and avoiding commitment.

FOOTNOTES

[1] Stephen E. South, "Competitive Advantage: The Cornerstone of Strategic Thinking," *The Journal of Business Strategy* 4, Spring 1981, p. 16.

[2] David A. Aaker, "Managing Assets and Skills: The Key to a Sustainable Competitive Advantage," *California Management Review*, Winter, 1989, pp. 91–106.

[3] Michael E. Porter, *Competitive Advantage*, New York: The Free Press, 1985, Chapter 1.

[4] C. K. Prahalad and Gary Hamel, "The Core Competence of the Corporation," *Harvard Business Review*, May–June 1990, pp. 79–91.

[5] Keith H. Hammonds, "Corning's Class Act," *Business Week*, May 13, 1991, pp. 68–76.

[6] Neil Gross, "Sharp's Long-Range Gamble on Its Innovation Machine," *Business Week*, April 29, 1991, pp. 84–86.

[7] G. Pascal Zachary, "Businessland Teeters on the Edge," *San Francisco Chronicle*, March 24, 1991, p. D-1.

[8] James Brian Quinn, "Strategic Change: 'Logical Incrementalism,'" *Sloan Management Review*, Fall 1978, pp. 7–23.

[9] Robert F. Hartley, *Marketing Mistakes*, 4th ed., New York, John Wiley, 1989.

[10] Gary Hamel and C.K. Prahalad, "Strategic Intent," *Harvard Business Review*, May–June 1989, pp. 63–76.

[11] Ira C. Magaziner and Mark Patinkin, "Fast Heat: How Korea Won the Microwave War," *Harvard Business Review*, January–February 1989, pp. 83–92.

[12] Peter T. Johnson, "Why I Race Against Phantom Competitors," *Harvard Business Review*, September–October 1988, pp. 106–112.

[13] Kenichi Ohmae, "Companyism and Do More Better," *Harvard Business Review*, January–February 1989, pp. 125–132.

[14] David A. Aaker and Briance Mascarenhas, "Flexibility: A Strategic Option," *Journal of Business Strategy*, Fall 1984, pp. 74–82.

[15] Thomas A. Stewart, "Lessons from U.S. Business Blunders," *Fortune*, April 23, 1990, pp. 128–138.

10

DIFFERENTIATION STRATEGIES

Ever since Morton's put a little girl in a yellow slicker and declared, "When it rains, it pours," no advertising person worth his or her salt has had any excuse to think of a product as having parity with anything.

Malcolm MacDougal
Jordan Case McGrath

If you don't have a competitive advantage, don't compete.

Jack Welch, GE

The secret of success is constancy to purpose.

Benjamin Disraeli

A differentiation strategy is one in which a product offering is different from that of one or more competitors in a way that is valued by the customers or in some way affects customer choice. Most successful strategies that are not based entirely on a low-cost advantage will be differentiated in some way, perhaps by enhancing the performance, quality, prestige, features, service backup, reliability, or convenience of the product. A differentiation strategy is often but not always associated with higher price, because it usually makes price less critical to the customer.

This point of difference needs to provide value to the customer that is substantial enough to matter, customers must realize that the value exists, and the resulting advantage needs to be sustainable. If it appears modest in size or is easily matched or countered, then it is unlikely that an effective SCA will exist.

A common mistake is to provide a point of difference that is not valued by the customer, at least not valued enough to compensate for the attached price premium or to overcome the momentum of other brands. The business determines that an enhancement is feasible and implements it without really understanding the customer or sometimes even testing it. Or the enhancement is developed without consideration of the cost and only later it is learned that the cost is excessive. Thus, providing a convenience in ordering may not provide adequate value to compensate for the added cost.

A key is to develop the point of differentiation from the customer's perspective. The customer's use system should be examined in depth to understand what its components and objectives are. How does the point of differentiation increase buyer performance, satisfaction, or loyalty? The customer and competitor analyses should drive the development of value-enhancing points of differentiation to ensure that it has an external orientation. Finally, any proposed point of differentiation should be tested by determining the customer's reactions and perhaps by doing an economic analysis from the customer's perspective.

Another common mistake is to assume that a point of difference that adds value will be so perceived by the customer. The danger often is that the customer will be unaware of an improvement such as enhanced product reliability because he or she is unable to evaluate it. The customer will then look to signals such as a change in warranties. The task is then to manage signals. In other contexts, assets such as brand name awareness may not be recognized by the customer as having value. The need then is to understand the customer's decision-making process and the role of the brand name.

The resulting competitive advantage needs to be sustainable. A patent protection or an innovation stream fueled by a strong R&D capacity may provide the basis for sustainable advantages because either is hard to counter. Brand equity including strong name awareness and perceived attributes can be difficult for competitors to attain. However, many basic ideas can be copied especially in service businesses. One reason to identify two strategic thrusts—synergy from the last chapter and first mover advantage in the next—is that when they are involved with a differentiation thrust, sustainability is more likely.

It is instructive to recognize the wide variety of SCAs that are associated with differentiation strategies. The most explicit ones appear in the list of SCAs in Figure 9.2. Of course, most successful businesses will combine several of these approaches to differentiation into a single strategy. Next we will discuss the following as a basis for differentiating a business:

- The quality option
- Brand awareness
- Brand associations
- Customer orientation
- Brand loyalty (the brand that is liked)
- Customer base
- Product features
- Service features
- Technical superiority
- Distribution channels
- Product-line breadth

THE QUALITY OPTION

The prototype of a differentiation as opposed to a low-cost strategy is a "quality" strategy in which a business will deliver and be perceived to deliver a product or service superior to that of competitors with respect to its intended purpose. A reputation for quality was the most frequently mentioned SCA in Figure 9.2.

A quality strategy will usually mean that the brand, whether it is a hotel, car, or computer, will be a premium brand as opposed to a value or economy entry. Thus, Marriott Hotels, Mercedes automobiles, and IBM computers offer enhanced customer benefits, command a price premium, and are top of the line.

It is also possible, however, to develop a quality strategy within a group of brands positioned as value or economy brands by being the quality option within that strategic group. Thus, while Target does not

---

Redefining Quality in Automobiles[1]

Throughout the 1970s and 1980s the primary quality objective was to be defect-free—the J.D. Powers rating based on customer experience provided a credible measure. By this measure Japanese cars were far superior to those of competitors. However, in the late 1980s, U.S. cars began to catch up, to the point that the differences were of reduced consequence. The problem for U.S. car makers is that the Japanese car makers have now changed the quality game.

The new quality concept is called *miryokuteki hinshitsu* (literally meaning "things gone right")—it takes for granted defect-free manufacturing and changes the focus to making cars that fascinate and delight. The idea is to engineer extraordinary levels of look, sound, and feel into cars, the cumulative effect of which will alter the personality of a car. The whole concept is implemented with the *kaisen* (continuous improvement) philosophy, a research-based concern with customer desires and strong conceptualizations of what a car's personality should be.

Examples are not hard to find. Nissan developed the first computer-driven "active suspension" to smooth the ride of the Infinity without compromising handling and placed a counterbalanced lid on its Maxima to help people juggling groceries. Lexus developed its soft, comfortable interior based on extensive human engineering. The Miata was designed to have the look and feel of classic sports cars. Honda developed the same feel for all the buttons and a system to reduce vibration.

---

deliver the same level of personal service, the same quality merchandise, and the same store ambience as Nordstrom's, it could still have high quality with respect to those in its strategic group. It will simply be judged on a different set of criteria: perhaps ease of parking, waiting time at check-out, courtesy of the check-out person, and whether or not desired items are in stock.

Quality and Profitability

The PIMS database has been analyzed in hundreds of studies, most trying to find clues to strategic success. Perhaps the most definitive finding from this research is the role of product quality. Buzzell and Gale in their book, *The PIMS Principles*, conclude that:

> In the long run, the most important single factor affecting a business unit's performance is the (perceived) quality of its products and services, relative to those of competitors.[2]

In fact, businesses in the lowest 20 percentile (with respect to relative perceived quality) had around a 17 percent ROI, whereas those in the top 20 percentile earned nearly twice as much.

A detailed examination by Jacobson and Aaker of the relationship of perceived quality and other key strategic variables in addition to ROI provides insights into how perceived quality creates profitability:[3]

- **Perceived quality affects market share.** After controlling for other factors, products of higher quality are favored and will receive a higher share of the market. Thus, a "quality strategy" does not have to involve high costs and a focus on the small "Mercedes" segment.

- **Perceived quality affects price.** Higher perceived quality allows a business to charge a higher price. The higher price can directly improve profitability or allow the business to improve quality further to create even higher competitive barriers. Furthermore, a higher price tends to enhance perceived quality by acting as a quality cue.

- **Perceived quality has a direct impact on profitability in addition to its effect on market share and price.** Improved perceived quality will, on the average, increase profitability even when price and market share are not affected. Perhaps the cost of retaining existing customers becomes less with higher quality or competitive pressures are reduced when quality is improved. In any case, there is a direct link between quality and ROI.

- **Perceived quality does not affect cost negatively.** In fact, it doesn't affect costs at all. The conventional wisdom that there is a natural association between a quality/prestige niche strategy and high cost is not reflected in data. The concept that "quality is free" may be, in part, the reason—enhanced quality leads to reduced defects and lowered manufacturing costs. John Young of Hewlett-Packard noted that a focus on quality is one of the best ways to control costs and mentioned one study that demonstrated fully 25 percent of its manufacturing costs were involved in responding to bad quality.[4]

The Schlitz Story

The Schlitz story provides a dramatic illustration of the strategic power of perceived quality.[5] From a strong number 2 position in 1974 (selling 17.8 million barrels of beer annually) supported by a series of well-regarded "Gusto" ad campaigns, Schlitz fell steadily until the mid-1980s when it had all but disappeared (with sales of only $1.8 million). The stock market value of the brand fell over a billion dollars.

The collapse can be traced to a decision to reduce costs by converting to a fermentation process that took 4 days instead of 12, the substitution of corn syrup for barley malt, and a different shelf stabilizer. Word of these changes got into the marketplace. Then, in early 1976: "Flaky, cloudy" beer appeared on the shelves, a condition eventually traced to the new foam stabilizer. Worse still, in early summer of that same year, one attempted fix caused the beer to go flat after time on a shelf. In the fall of 1976, 10 million bottles and cans of Schlitz were "secretly" recalled and destroyed. Despite a return to its original process and agressive advertising, Schlitz never recovered.

Product Quality Dimensions

The pursuit of a quality standard involves understanding what dimensions underlie quality—which are relevant to customer satisfaction. With respect to product quality, Harvard's Garvin suggests eight product quality dimensions as summarized in Figure 10.1.[6] The first, performance on the product attributes acceleration, handling, and comfort, has been the focus of automobiles such as Mercedes-Benz and Porsche. The second, durability, has been associated with Volvo. The third, the conformance to specifications or the absence of defects, has been a characteristic of many Japanese cars. Two more, features and name, will be considered in more detail shortly.

The sixth, reliability, is the consistency of product performance from purchase to purchase and its "uptime," the percent of time that it can

FIGURE 10.1   Quality Dimensions

PRODUCT QUALITY

1. **Performance.** How well does a washing machine clean clothes?
2. **Durability.** How long will a lawnmower last?
3. **Conformance to specifications.** What is the incidence of defects?
4. **Features.** Does an airline flight offer movies and dinner?
5. **The name.** Does the name mean quality? What is the firm's image?
6. **Reliability.** Will each visit to a restaurant result in similar quality?
7. **Serviceability.** Is the service system efficient, competent, and convenient?
8. **Fit and finish.** Does the product look and feel like a quality product?

SERVICE QUALITY

1. **Tangibles.** Appearance of physical facilities, communication materials, equipment, and personnel.
2. **Reliability.** Ability to perform the promised service dependably and accurately.
3. **Responsiveness.** Willingness to help customers and provide prompt service.
4. **Competence.** Knowledge and skill of employees and their ability to convey trust and confidence.
5. **Empathy.** Caring, individualized attention that a firm provides its customers.

---

perform. Tandem Computers developed the concept of several computers working in tandem so that, if one failed, the only impact would be the slowing of low-priority tasks. Its product had substantial value for banks and retailers for which system downtime is particularly undesirable.

Garvin's seventh characteristic, serviceability, reflects the ability to service a product. Caterpillar Tractor has long had a parts and service organization together with a service culture—"24-hour parts service anywhere in the world"—that created a strong point of differentiation. The eighth characteristic, "fit and finish," is illustrated by the impact on perceived quality in the automobile industry of the paint job and fit of the doors, for example.

Service Quality Dimensions

Different dimensions emerge in service businesses. One series of studies of customer perceptions of service quality involving industries such as appliance repair, retail banking, long-distance telephone companies, securities brokerage, and credit cards resulted in the identification of several service dimensions, which included the five listed in Figure 10.1: tangibles, reliability, responsiveness, competence, and empathy.[7]

Certainly a key to McDonald's success in fast foods is the reliability achieved because of its standardization of operations. By making its system as identical as possible in every McDonald's around the world, its goal is to provide the same quality level in every visit. Reliability achieved by standardization is often visible and thus easily understood by customers. In contrast, reliability achieved by a control system behind the scenes may not generate the same quality perception.

Determining Important Dimensions

Customer research can help firms determine how to structure a quality strategy by identifying which dimensions are most important. For example, L. L. Bean, the mail-order purveyor of outdoor apparel and equipment gains insights from regular customer satisfaction surveys and group interviews that track customer perceptions of its quality and that of its competitors' products and services. The company also tracks all customer complaints and asks customers to fill out a short, coded questionnaire to explain their reasons for returning merchandise. Many firms routinely survey customers to determine the relative importance of various quality dimensions, as well as the perceptions and expectations of brands along those dimensions.

Employees, especially those close to the customer, are good sources of information about what quality dimensions are relevant and important to customers. However, several studies have found that manager's impressions can be very wrong. In one case, managers of a financial services firm were unaware of the extent to which customers were concerned about privacy and security in financial service transactions.[8] In another instance, managers were unaware of the customer belief that small appliance repair firms are superior to large ones.

Signals of High Quality

Most of the quality dimensions such as performance, durability, reliability, and serviceability are difficult if not impossible for buyers to evaluate. As a result, consumers tend to look for signals of quality. The "fit-and-finish" dimension can be such a quality signal. Buyers assume that if a business cannot produce good fit-and-finish products, its products probably will not have other more important quality attributes. For example, an electronics firm found that fulfilling commitments regarding information requests affected perceived quality. In pursuing a quality strategy, it is usually critical to understand what drives quality perception and to look to the "small" but visible elements.

Research has shown that in many product classes a key dimension that is visible can be pivotal in affecting perceptions about more "important" dimensions that are difficult if not impossible to judge.[9] For example:

- Stereo speakers. Larger size means better sound.
- Detergents. Suds means cleaning effectiveness.
- Tomato juice. Thickness means quality
- Fruit- flavored children's drinks. Thickness means low quality.
- Cleaners. A lemon scent can signal cleaning power.
- Supermarkets. Produce freshness means overall quality.
- Cars. A solid door-closure sound implies good workmanship and a solid, safe body.
- Orange juice. Fresh is better than refrigerated, which is better than bottled. Bottled is followed by frozen, canned, and finally, dry-product forms.
- Clothes. Higher price means higher quality.

In the service context, the most important attributes, such as the competence of those providing the service, are extremely difficult to evaluate—consider evaluating surgeons, librarians, airline pilots, dentists, or bankers. Customers cope by looking at those dimensions that are

---

Quality at Sheraton

A team of two dozen people developed a service improvement program at Sheraton labeled the Sheraton Guest Satisfaction System.[10] The system involves

- **Employee goals.** To be friendly, acknowledge guests' presence, answer guests' questions, and anticipate guests' problems and needs.
- **Hiring.** Responses to videos of potentially problematic incidents help personnel select a staff that really empathizes with people.
- **Training.** A series of training programs including role playing that help staff cope with difficult situations.
- **Measurement.** Quarterly reports are based on guest questionnaires that rate factors such as bed comfort and lighting, as well as interactions with employees.
- **Ongoing meetings.** Performance is assessed, problems are corrected, and improvement programs are developed.
- **Rewards.** Ten percent of the top performing and most improved hotels each quarter become members of the Sheraton's "Chairman's Club" and become eligible for prizes. In addition, each hotel has its own employee recognition programs.

Sheraton continued its advertising theme, "Little things mean a lot," while the program was taking hold. Only when it feels that the service quality has achieved a sufficient level of performance and reliability, will Sheraton go ahead with plans to announce the "New Sheraton."

---

easily evaluated such as the tangibles—the physical appearance of personnel and a facility. The chairman of one airline was quoted as saying, "Coffee stains on the flip-down trays mean (to the passengers) that we do our engine maintenance wrong."[11] It is thus crucial to understand not only what is important with respect to quality, but also what drives those quality perceptions.

BRAND AWARENESS

Brand awareness is often taken for granted but, in fact, can be a key strategic asset. In some industries where there is product parity, awareness provides a sustainable competitive difference over time. In such cases, awareness, the third most mentioned SCA, in Figure 9.2, serves to differentiate the brands along a recall/familiarity dimension. The extreme case is name dominance, where the brand is the only one recalled. Consider Kleenex tissue, Band-Aid adhesive bandages, Jell-O gelatin,

Crayola crayons, Morton salt, Lionel trains, Philadelphia cream cheese, V-8 vegetable juice, A-1 steak sauce. In each case, how many other brands can you name?

Brand awareness can provide a host of competitive advantages. First, awareness provides the brand with a sense of familiarity, and people like the familiar. Especially for low-involvement products like soap or chewing gum, familiarity can sometimes drive the buying decision. Second, name awareness can be a signal of presence, commitment, and substance, attributes that can be very important even to industrial buyers of big ticket items and consumer buyers of durables. The logic is that if a name is recognized, there must be a reason. Third, the initial step in selecting an advertising agency, a car to test drive, or a computer system is to decide on which brands to consider. Brand recall can be crucial to entering this group.

Brand awareness is an asset that can be remarkably durable and thus sustainable. It can be very difficult to dislodge a brand that has achieved a dominant awareness level. The Datsun name was as strong as that of Nissan four years after its name change.[12] In the mid-1980s, an awareness study on blenders was conducted. In this study people were asked what brand of blender they preferred, and GE was the number two brand even though it had not made blenders for 20 years.[13] Another study of brand name familiarity involved housewives who were asked to name as many brands as they could.[14] On the average, they came up with 28 names each. The age of the brands named was most remarkable—over 85 percent were over 25 years old and 36 percent were over 75 years old.

What are the implications? One is that the establishment of a strong name anchored by high recognition creates an enormous asset. Furthermore, the asset becomes stronger and stronger over the years as the number of exposures and experiences grow. As a result, even a challenging brand with an enormous advertising budget and other points of advantage may find it difficult to enter the memory of the customer.

BRAND ASSOCIATIONS

A key enduring business asset can be the associations that are attached to a firm and its brands.[15] The purchase in the late 1970s of the Weight Watchers business for approximately $120 million by the H. J. Heinz Co. illustrates this point. What was purchased was the strategic potential of the Weight Watchers association with a professional approach to weight control. As O'Reilly, the president of Heinz, noted, "You can say light and you can say very light and you can say extra light and trimline or slimline, but at the end of the day, Weight Watchers has an authority about it" that will win.[16]

The Heinz vision was that the weight control association linked to the Weight Watchers program and customer base would provide the basis for a sustainable competitive advantage not only in the core frozen dinner area but in numerous other extensions as well. During the 1980s, Heinz, in fact, exploited these associations by extending the name relentlessly to new products. By 1989, it was marketing 60 frozen food items and over 150 nonfrozen food items. Each extension not only exploited the Weight Watchers name and its associations, but reinforced them as well. In the 1970s, observers were questioning the wisdom of buying such a mature, unexciting business. In 1989, however, the Weight Watchers area of Heinz had revenues of $1.3 billion and an operating income of over $100 million, close to the total acquisition price of the three companies—all because the potential of a strong association had been reorganized.

A brand association is anything that is directly or indirectly linked in memory to a brand. Thus, McDonald's could be linked to Ronald McDonald, kids, golden arches, having fun, fast service, family outings, or Big Macs. In addition to product attribute and customer benefit associations, brands gain strategic position by association with:

- Use or application (Gatorade is for football games).
- Product user (Miller is for the blue-collar, heavy beer drinker).
- Celebrity (Jell-O means Bill Cosby).
- Life-style and feelings (the Pepsi Generation).
- Product class (Carnation Instant Breakfast is a breakfast food).
- Symbol (the Prudential Rock).

Associations do not appear explicitly in the Figure 9.2 list, although items such as customer service, financial resources, product-line breadth, technical association, and product innovation have an association component. It can be as important to be known as a technically innovative firm as it is to actually be one.

A brand's associations are assets that can provide value in several ways. They can provide an important basis for differentiation. In some product classes such as wines, perfumes, and clothes, most consumers cannot distinguish between various brands. Associations of the brand name can then play a critical role in separating one brand from another. The personality of Cher, for example, provides a point of differentiation for her line of perfumes. Because the personality of Cher is unique, so is the brand that bears her name.

A differentiating association can be a key competitive advantage. If a brand is well positioned with respect to its competitors upon a key attribute in its product class, competitors will find it difficult to attack. Consider the position of Nordstrom's on service or Gatorade in athletics. If a frontal assault is attempted by claiming superiority in such a dimension, a credibility issue may arise. The competitive advantage can be substantial when the association is based on an intangible such as technological leadership, health food, style, or perceived value; any of these are not easily attacked in a shouting match involving tangible attributes.

Many brand associations involve product attributes or customer benefits that provide a specific reason to buy and use a brand. They represent a basis for purchase decisions and brand loyalty. Thus, Crest is a cavity-prevention toothpaste, Colgate provides clean, white teeth, and Close-Up generates fresh breath. "Miller time" provides a reason to buy Miller's beer—a cold Miller can be a well-deserved reward. Bloomingdale's is fun and carries high-fashion merchandise.

Some associations influence purchase decisions by ascribing credibility and confidence to a brand. If a Wimbleton champion uses a certain tennis racket or a professional hair stylist uses a particular hair-coloring product, consumers may feel more comfortable with those brands. An Italian name and accompanying Italian associations may lend credence to a pizza maker.

Some likable associations stimulate positive feelings that are then transferred to a brand. Celebrities like Bill Cosby, symbols such as the Jolly Green Giant, or slogans like "reach out and touch someone" can all, in the right context, be likable and stimulate feelings. Associations and their companion feelings then become linked to a brand. One of the roles of the Charlie Brown characters as spokespersons for Metropolitan Life is to soften the image of an otherwise large, impersonal organization and serious message by linking Metropolitan with Charles Schulz's well-liked characters and the warm, positive feelings they engender.

Some associations create positive feelings during the use experience, serving to transform a product into something different than what it might otherwise be. Advertising, for example, can make the experience of drinking Pepsi seem like more fun and driving a Bronco more adventuresome than without the advertising. For many, opening a Tiffany box and wearing Tiffany jewelry are accompanied by a different set of feelings than if the same jewelry had been presented in a Macy's box.

An association can provide the basis for an extension. The Weight Watchers associations, for example, provided an extension rationale as well as a reason to buy. Honda's experience in small motors makes extensions from motorcycles to outboard motors and lawn mowers plausible. Sunkist has an association with healthy, outdoors activities as well as oranges; this has helped its image in a variety of other products, including fruit bars, soft drinks, and vitamin C tablets.

CUSTOMER ORIENTATION

The second and seventh SCAs listed in Figure 9.2 both suggest customer orientation. A customer focus is something that many organizations profess to have. The problem is to distinguish between lip service and a meaningful culture and set of programs that together represent a meaningful SCA.

Figure 10.2 details a profile of a customer-driven organization. It suggests that more than lip service is involved and sets forth 12 character-

---

FIGURE 10.2   A Profile of a Customer-Driven Organization

A CUSTOMER-DRIVEN ORGANIZATION:

UNDERSTANDS THE CUSTOMER

1. Has contact with the customer. People throughout the business from the top executives to the engineers to the accounting staff all have meaningful first-hand contact with customers.

2. Knows what product or service attributes are important to the customer.

3. Understands what drives customer choice even if it is intangible, such as a retailer's atmosphere or the associations of outdoor life with a beer.

4. Segments. Understands how segments differ and adjusts strategies accordingly.

5. Considers systems' solutions. Recognizes that the customer is interested in solutions to problems rather than buying products, and adjusts its strategy accordingly.

6. Looks to unmet needs, realizing that current offerings may not provide the best response to customer needs.

KNOWS HOW THE CUSTOMER PERCEIVES THE FIRM

7. Knows how the firm is perceived on the basis of solid marketing research.

8. Understands key associations driving perceptions, knows why the business is perceived as it is.

9. Is clearly positioned with a strong set of associations, which could involve the price-quality continuum, a performance attribute, a type of user, a use situation, and an application or product class.

DELIVERS QUALITY/VALUE

10. Quality/value measures drive objectives and compensation. The organization truly cares about what the customer is receiving.

11. Measures customer satisfaction regularly using quantitative survey instruments and qualitative in-depth methods.

12. Is responsive to customer input. Customer suggestions and complaints affect strategy.

---

istics organized around three themes. First, a customer-driven firm should have an in-depth understanding of the customer, based on first-hand contact and marketing research. Second, the firm should have a clear idea about what it wants customer perceptions to be and what they actually are and why. Third, the business should make sure that it is delivering quality or value by measuring customer satisfaction and re-acting to the resulting input.

A study of 140 forest product businesses showed that market orienta-tion is strongly associated with profitability, even after controlling for other factors such as buyer and seller power, size, market growth, and costs.[17] In addition to customer orientation, market orientation includes competitor orientation and the ability of a business to integrate functional areas to provide customer value.

BRAND LOYALTY

A prime enduring asset for some businesses is the loyalty of the installed customer base, listed as item 10 in Figure 9.2. Competitors may often duplicate or surpass a product or service, but they still must face the task of making customers switch brands. Brand loyalty, resistance to switching, can be based on simple habit (there is no motivation to change from the familiar), liking (there is genuine liking of the brand or its symbol, perhaps based on use experiences over a long time period), or switching costs. Switching costs would occur for a software user, for example, when a substantial investment had already been made in train-ing employees to learn a particular software system.

Many firms have taken their customers for granted, only to see them dissipate when competitors attack. MicroPro's Wordstar, which domi-nated the full-featured word processing industry in the early 1980s, lost its position to WordPerfect and others by turning its back on its customer base.[18] Wordstar failed to provide adequate product support to its cus-tomers and, perhaps worse, introduced a new generation product, Wordstar 2000, that was not backward compatible. Thus, customers could switch to WordPerfect as easily as learning Wordstar 2000. As a result, MicroPro's position eroded until its stock was probably worth less than 1 percent of that of the upstart WordPerfect in 1990. Had it only upgraded its basic Wordstar product and offered competitive product support, it might have held its position and WordPerfect may have been a minor player in the software scene.

An existing base of loyal customers provides enormous sustainable competitive advantages. First, it reduces the marketing costs of doing business since existing customers usually are relatively easy to hold—the familiar is comfortable and reassuring. It is often considerably less costly to keep existing customers happy and reduce the reasons to change, than to reach new customers and persuade them to try another brand, especially when they are not dissatisfied. Of course, the higher the loyalty, the easier it is to keep customers happy.

Second, the loyalty of existing customers represents a substantial entry barrier to competitors. Excessive resources are required when entering a market in which existing customers are loyal to or just satisfied with an established brand and must be enticed to switch. The profit potential for the entrant is thus reduced. For the barrier to be effective, however, potential competitors must know about it; they cannot be allowed to entertain the delusion that customers are vulnerable. Therefore, signals of strong customer loyalty, such as advertisements about documented customer loyalty or product quality, can be useful.

Third, brand loyalty provides trade leverage. Strong loyalty toward brands like Nabisco Premium Saltines, Cheerios, or Tide will ensure preferred shelf space because stores know that customers have such brands on their shopping lists. At the extreme, brand loyalty may dominate store choice decisions. Unless a supermarket carries brands like Weight Watchers frozen dinners, Paul Newman's salad dressing, Ashahi Super-Dry beer, or Grey Poupon mustard, for example, some customers will switch stores.

Fourth, a relatively large satisfied customer base provides an image of a brand as an accepted, successful product that will be around and will be able to afford service back-up and product improvements. For example, in 1989, Dell Computer, a mail-order computer firm, advertised an installed base of 100,000 customers, including over 50 percent of the Fortune 500 companies, to reassure prospective customers wary of buying a mail-order computer.

Fifth and finally, brand loyalty provides the time to respond to competitive moves—some breathing room for a firm. If a competitor develops a superior product, a loyal following will allow the firm the time needed to respond by matching or neutralizing. For example, some newly developed high-tech markets have customers who are attracted by the most advanced product of the moment; there is little brand loyalty in this group. In contrast, other markets have loyal, satisfied customers who will not be looking for new products and thus may not learn of an advancement. Furthermore, they will have little incentive to change even if exposed to the new product. With a high level of brand loyalty, a firm can allow itself the luxury of pursuing a less risky follower strategy.

PRODUCT FEATURES—THE AUGMENTED PRODUCT

Levitt points out that product feature differentiation (item 12 in Figure 9.2) is not limited to those product features that the customer expects.[19] Thus, DowBrands changed the house-cleaning market with Spiffits,

---

Brand Equity

A set of brand names can have enormous strategic asset value. Kraft was purchased for nearly $13 billion, more than 600 percent over its book value, because of the value of the brand names it controls. However, because of the pressure of delivering short-term financial results, it is tempting to take actions that can damage brand strength. Promotions may deliver sales, but also can tarnish the image and reduce customer loyalty. Extensions may help establish a new business area while weakening a key association. Advertising can be reduced without noticeable short-term effect but awareness may be eroded.

The need is to explicitly recognize and actively manage brand equity.[20] Brand equity is a set of brand assets and liabilities linked to a brand's name and symbol that add to or subtract from the value provided by a product or service to a firm and/or that firm's customers. The assets and liabilities on which brand equity is based differ from context to context. However, they can be usefully grouped into four categories: brand awareness, brand associations, perceived quality, and brand loyalty. These assets need to be actively managed. It should be recognized that they can require investment in order to be created or maintained. Furthermore, people and systems need to be in place so that programs that will damage them can be identified and resisted.

---

which augments cleaning products by putting them into premoistened towels. A computer firm augmented its basic product to include a diagnostic module that automatically locates failure sources. Such product augmentations may not have been expected by the customer, but they can become the basis for differentiation as long as the customer perceives and appreciates them.

Tom Peters tells the story of the Milliken shop towel (industrial rag) business. Milliken worked with the industrial laundries who were its customers to identify and address their problems, even those unrelated to the towels.[21] Eventually, Milliken was providing computer-based order-entry systems, freight optimization systems, market research assistance, data systems, sales leads, and seminars on telecommunication, selling skills, and production. Milliken became an important resource to these laundries and developed an enormous advantage in retaining the towel business. As a result, it experienced dramatic sales growth and a return in a commodity business that conventional wisdom would say is not a fruitful area for investment.

The idea is to change the nature of a business and its associated key success factors into one in which it is possible to develop SCAs. The problem is to identify augmented product ideas that (1) the customer will value enough to pay for and (2) will represent a sustainable competitive advantage not easily duplicated by competitors.

Milliken addressed both problems by creating customer action teams (CAT). A CAT would typically involve several people from customer firms, as well as an interfunctional team from Milliken. The team would be charged to seek creative solutions to better serve current markets or create new ones. Each year hundreds of such CATs are created. Having the customer on board makes it much more likely that worthwhile problems will be addressed and that any solution will be implemented successfully.

Patent-Protected Features.   A well-conceived patent on a technological innovation can provide the most assurance that a resulting advantage will be sustainable. Howard Head, who revolutionized the ski industry with his metal skis in the 1950s, did the same thing in the tennis racket industry by creating and obtaining a patent for the oversized Prince racket. The relevant patents in each case allowed Prince to control the market for years. For a substantial period, the only competitors were those who licensed the patents from Prince. As a result of Polaroid's patents, Kodak was required to permanently withdraw from the U.S. instant photography market and paid substantial damages as well.

SERVICE FEATURES—THE PERIPHERAL SERVICE

Service firms often can differentiate themselves on the basis of the level and nature of the service features offered. In that regard, it is helpful to distinguish between core and peripheral services.[22] The "core" service involves necessary outputs—a clean hotel room with a comfortable bed, for example. The "peripheral" service may not be needed to supply the core service, but it does improve the overall quality of the service bundle. Thus, a hotel could have an elaborate lobby, garden, or swimming pool.

One way to differentiate a service is by the peripherals offered. A salad bar could be added to a restaurant's offering. An airline could develop a club for its high-volume travelers, or a software house could offer advice on selecting hardware. A peripheral service could involve separate charges or it could be built into the total service package. In any case, it can be used as a device to position and differentiate the offering.

Another way to differentiate the offering is to integrate two or more core services. Luxury hotels operate bars, restaurants, and the core hotel service. The resulting package allows a positioning strategy that is more than the sum of the three operations. Accounting firms have also offered the core service of management consulting. The integration of two core services is most likely to be worthwhile when the combination provides customer value and when the firm's infrastructure supports the two core services.

TECHNICAL SUPERIORITY

Another competitive approach is to maintain technological superiority, the top named SCA in Figure 9.2 for high-tech firms. The question that is often raised is whether technological superiority is sustainable in the face of rapid technological innovation. Certainly, in some cases whoever has the specification advantage at the moment will win. But the more general answer is yes, and it is based on two perspectives.

First, there are many industries in which a firm is consistently ahead of competition year after year—COMPAQ in computers and Intel in microprocessors, for example. The inescapable conclusion is that these firms have developed skills in R&D, manufacturing, and new product introduction that have been maintained over time and provide the base for their success.

Second, there is the concept of intangible associations. Some firms have the image of being technologically advanced—their products over the years have been up-to-date. You don't lose technologically by buying an instrument from Hewlett-Packard, for example. With such an association, a business gets out of the box of playing the specification game. Customers will have a reduced tendency to examine detailed specifications. When such an intangible association as being technologically advanced is established, it is often hard to dislodge—competitors are at a substantial disadvantage.

DISTRIBUTION CHANNELS

Access and/or control of distribution (item 15 in Figure 9.2) can be a key asset. L'eggs Hosiery created a sustainable competitive advantage by introducing its uniquely packaged hosiery (plastic egglike containers with supporting displays) in supermarkets, whereas competitors relied on such conventional channels as department stores.

Access to supermarket shelves can be a sustainable competitive advantage for firms making some categories of packaged consumer products. The access can be due to a track record of new product success, the ability to support the product with promotion and advertising, and an effective sales force. In contrast, a competitor that promises to be the fourth or fifth brand will constantly have difficulty gaining shelf position.

BREADTH OF THE PRODUCT LINE

Another differentiation strategy is to have a broad product line, item 8 in Figure 9.2, so that customers can be provided with a systems solution and can engage in the convenience of "one-stop" shopping. An audio equipment maker possessing a complete line can offer customers total system design and a systems service back-up. There would be no "it's the other firm's component that failed" excuses.

The convenience of one-stop shopping is graphically shown in those retail operations that achieve classification dominance; the product line is so wide and deep that it draws people from large areas. Broad selection allows the firm to dominate its competitors within the product classification. Classification dominance retailers exist in many categories such as records, books, tires, and shoes. Reyers Shoe Store in Sharon, Pennsylvania, for example, draws 1000 to 3000 customers a day and carries an inventory of 125,000 shoes.[23]

A broad product line also creates entry barriers. Studies of market pioneers, those businesses that are first to enter a market, using the PIMS database reveal that their market share strength, even 20 years later, is in part due to their product-line breadth and the associated entry barriers.[24] If a supplier of art supplies, for example, has gaps in its line, a competitor has an opportunity to become a supplier, to have a base from which to expand. Having a full line, even if parts of it make little economic sense when analyzed separately, makes it much more difficult for competitors. In fact, the development of most assets and skills that underlie SCAs involves "overinvestment," in the sense that it might be difficult to justify the expenditures to support assets and skills on the basis of short-term results.

A key issue is the impact of product-line breadth on costs. Product proliferation can potentially increase overhead, manufacturing complexity, and inventory requirements. There is no shortage of examples where adding products undercut costs and resulted in disasters. A PIMS study, however, revealed that, on the average, product-line breadth does not increase manufacturing costs or inventory levels and, in fact, improves profitability by increasing market share and by sharing fixed costs such as a sales force and distribution channel.[24]

SUMMARY

A differentiation strategy is one in which the product offering is different from that of one or more competitors in such a way that is valued by the customers or in some way affects customer choice. Effective strategies need to be valued by the customer and should not be easily copied.

One differentiation strategy is the "quality" strategy, to be the best. PIMS studies show that a quality strategy, on the average, results in larger ROI. Product and service quality is multidimensional. Product quality, for example, includes relatively easy to evaluate dimensions such as "fit and finish" and more difficult ones such as durability and reliability. It is important to manage quality cues so that perceived quality will be high.

Differentiation strategies can also be based on brand awareness, brand associations, a customer orientation, brand loyalty, product features, peripheral services, technical superiority, distribution channels, and product-line breadth.

FOOTNOTES

[1] Drawn in part from David Woodruff, "A New Era for Auto Quality," *Business Week*, October 22, 1990, pp. 84–96; Alex Taylor III, "Why Toyota Keeps Getting Better and Better and Better," *Fortune*, November 19, 1990, pp. 66–79.

[2] Robert D. Buzzell and Bradley T. Gale, *The PIMS Principles*, New York: The Free Press, 1987, p. 7.

[3] Robert Jacobson and David A. Aaker, "The Strategic Role of Product Quality," *Journal of Marketing*, October 1987, pp. 31–44.

[4] John Young, "The Quality Focus at Hewlett-Packard," *The Journal of Business Strategy* 5, Winter 1985, p. 7.

[5] The Schlitz story is described in David A. Aaker, *Managing Brand Equity*, New York: The Free Press, 1991. It draws in part from Jacques Neher, "What Went Wrong?" *Advertising Age*, April 13, 1981, p. 46, and April 20, 1981, p. 49.

[6] David A. Garvin, "What Does 'Product Quality' Really Mean?" *Sloan Management Review*, Fall 1984, pp. 25–43.

[7] Valarie A. Zeithami, Leonard L. Berry, and A. Parasuraman, "Communication and Control Processes in the Delivery of Service Quality," *Journal of Marketing*, April 1988, pp. 35–48; A. Parasuraman, Leonard L. Berry, and Valarie A. Zeithami, "Guidelines for Conducting Service Quality Research," *Marketing Research*, December 1990, pp. 34–44.

[8] Zeithami, Berry, and Parasuraman, "Communication and Control Processes" and Parasuraman, Berry, and Zeithami, "Guidelines."

[9] Zeithami, Berry, and Parasuraman, "Communication and Control Processes" and Parasuraman, Berry, and Zeithami, "Guidelines."

[10] David Walker, "At Sheraton, the Guest Is Always Right," *Adweek's Marketing Week*, October 23, 1989, pp. 20–21.

[11] Tom Peters and Nancy Austin, *A Passion for Excellence*, New York: Random House, 1985, p. 77.

[12] Aaker, *Managing Brand Equity*, p. 57.

[13] "Shoppers Like Wide Variety of Housewares Brands," *Discount Store News*, October 24, 1988, p. 40.

[14] Leo Bogart and Charles Lehman, "What Makes a Brand Name Familiar?" *Journal of Marketing Research*, February 1973, pp. 17–22.

[15] Aaker, *Managing Brand Equity*, Chapter 5.

[16] Anthony O'Reilly, "What's on His Plate?" *Advertising Age*, February 26, 1990, p. 16.

[17] John C. Narver and Stanley F. Slater, "The Effect of a Market Orientation on Business Profitability," *Journal of Marketing,* October 1990, pp. 20–34.

[18] The Wordstar story was drawn in part from Kate Bertrand, "Can MicroPro Catch Its Fallen 'Star'?" *Business Marketing,* May 1989, pp. 55–66, and Aaker, *Managing Brand Equity.*

[19] Theodore Levitt, "Marketing Success Through Differentiation—of Anything," *Harvard Business Review,* January–February 1980, pp. 83–91.

[20] Aaker, *Managing Brand Equity.*

[21] Tom Peters, *Thriving on Chaos,* New York: Knopf, 1987, Chapter C-1.

[22] James M. Carman and Eric Langeard, "Growth Strategies for Service Firms," *Strategic Management Journal,* January–March 1980, pp. 7–22.

[23] "How Reyers Stays a Step Ahead," *Time,* October 15, 1984, p. 93.

[24] Sunder Kekre and Kannan Srinivasan, "Broader Product Line: A Necessity to Achieve Success?" *Management Science,* October 1990, pp. 1216–1231.

11

OBTAINING AN SCA—
LOW COST, FOCUS, AND
THE PREEMPTIVE MOVE

Never follow the crowd.

Bernard M. Baruch

The first man gets the oyster, the second man
gets the shell.

Andrew Carnegie

A strategy can be characterized by its strategic thrust, a combination of functional area strategies and bases of SCAs that represents the essence of the strategy. Five types of strategic thrusts are introduced in Chapter 1 and discussed in Chapter 9: differentiation, low cost, focus, the preemptive move, and synergy. Nearly all these strategies involve differentiation or low cost. The other three types are not so frequently present, but are often pivotal when they are relevant. Other strategic thrusts such as technology, innovation, or marketing could have been identified and discussed.

Differentiation is the subject of the last chapter and synergy is introduced in Chapter 9 and is a recurring theme in the next two chapters. In this chapter, the other three strategic thrusts are covered: low cost, focus, and the preemptive move.

LOW-COST STRATEGIES

The most visible low-cost strategy in the strategic management literature is that based on the experience curve. However, there are other means of obtaining a sustainable cost advantage; they include:

- No-frills product/service
- Low-cost product design
- Raw material cost advantage
- Low-cost distribution
- Labor cost advantage
- Government subsidy
- Location cost advantage
- Production innovation and automation
- Purchasing inexpensive capital equipment
- Reducing overhead
- Scale economies
- The experience curve

No-Frills Product/Service

A direct approach to low cost is simply to remove all frills and extras from a product or service. For example, the membership warehouses such as Price Clubs, Costco, and Sam's all provide warehouse settings usually in low-cost neighborhoods, with amenities like the ability to charge on a credit card and personal service not provided. No-frills airlines, the legal services clinics, discount brokers, and the Hundai automobile company have followed the same general principle. A lower cost is often sustainable because the competition cannot easily stop offering services that their customers expect. Furthermore, their operations and facilities have been designed for such services and are not easily changed.

A firm implementing a no-frills product runs the risk of precipitating matching price moves by desperate competitors. Therefore, the firm considering such a strategy should be sensitive to this risk and should have the financial resources and overall cost structure to survive a possible price war. Arco made a move in the early 1980s to eliminate costly credit card service and substantially reduce its gasoline price. Arco was able to hold the new price difference during a subsequent price war because, in addition to the savings from not handling credit cards, it had a cost advantage in its raw material sources. Interestingly, the elimination of a service made it easier to establish a lower price difference. If Arco's price reduction had not been associated with the elimination of credit card service, competitors then would have had a more difficult time avoiding a price war, because the product would have been so undifferentiated.

Another risk is that competitors will add just a few features and position themselves against a low-frills firm. Motel 6 pioneered the concept of spartan lodging in the early 1960s by giving the world the $6 hotel room with no phone or TV set. The economy lodging industry in the last decade has attracted a host of competitors, most of which aim to offer a bit more than Motel 6 at a comparable or higher price. The result can be feature war.

Low-Cost Product Design

A product's design or composition can create cost advantages. For example, Masonite developed a line of pressed-wood alternatives to wood, alternatives that use sawdust, wood chips, branches, and twigs. The resulting products cost less than half as much as those of their wood competitors.

Japanese competitors have entered several established industries including copiers by designing reliable, simple products involving relatively few readily available (as opposed to customized) parts. A U.S. firm, Fadal, has reversed the tables in the machine tool industry by using the same strategy to retain 20 percent of the metalworking machine market under attack from the Japanese.[1] Fadal produces the Volkswagen Beetle of the industry—a functional, durable machine that is easy to operate and fix. The key is keeping its organization focused on cost and simplicity.

A variant is to augment a product with relatively high-margin accessories or extra features and thus provide a higher perceived value to customers. Several computer firms have achieved a low systems price by including software or printers in a system's price.

Product downsizing is another approach that can be helpful when price pressures inhibit alternatives. It is termed the "Hershey's solution" because Hershey's downsized its chocolate bar when confronted with increases in the price of cocoa.

Raw Material Cost Advantage

A firm's access to raw materials can provide a sustainable cost advantage. For example, a firm might buy undeveloped oil or coal resources, anticipating a time when access would be limited. Fort Howard Paper has achieved a cost advantage by being the only major papermaker to use recycled pulp exclusively.[2] Although not as good as virgin material, recycled pulp provides a key edge in the away-from-home market for toilet paper and other products used in hotels, restaurants, and office buildings.

Low-Cost Distribution

When a major cost component is distribution, the use of a different channel can create substantial cost advantages. In the computer hardware industry, for example, mail-order firms such as Dell, Northgate, Gateway, and Zeos have natural cost advantages because they have none of the fixed costs of a sales force or the expense of compensating retailers. They are especially well-suited for those who know what they want and do not need hand-holding. As the computer industry matures and its products become more user-friendly, the percentage of people who are comfortable with a mail-order alternative increases.

Labor Cost Advantage

In some labor-intensive industries a sustainable cost advantage, at least with respect to some strategic groups, can be based on access to inexpensive labor. The apparel industry, in which labor accounts for about 27 percent of cost, has seen importers make substantial inroads because of their cost advantage, particularly in the area of less fashion-sensitive apparel where a long lead time can be tolerated. A key success factor in many apparel industries is the ability to work with off-shore sources.

Government Subsidy

Some firms receive government subsidies or other special treatment that effectively provides a direct or indirect sustainable cost advantage. For example, steel companies in Europe and Japan are heavily subsidized by their governments. Many national airlines are subsidized and, in addition, they receive help in terms of access to routes. Furthermore, countries like Ireland and states like Virginia can provide substantial incentives to locate there, which can translate into a cost advantage.

Location Cost Advantage

Sometimes the best retail locations are obtained on favorable terms by those who enter early into a market. The competitors are then faced with paying more and perhaps being shut out of some locations. Certainly, one reason for McDonald's success is its long-standing policy of buying real estate. This practice has not only given McDonald's a cost advantage, but it has also contributed significantly to its profits.

Production Innovation and Automation

Innovations in the production process including automation can provide the basis of a sustainable competitive advantage. The problem often is to make them sustainable. One approach is to attempt to keep them a secret by providing plant security and incentives for employees to stay. A second is to keep improving them so that the competitors must match a moving target. The third is to make capacity expansion decisions visible to discourage competitors, like DuPont did in the titanium oxide business when it developed a unique production process.[3]

Purchasing Inexpensive Capital Equipment

Firms sometimes are motivated to divest a business even at a price far below replacement cost or book value. In an industry with significant fixed costs, obtaining low-cost capacity can provide considerable competitive leverage. The opportunity to buy competitors occurs most frequently in mature or declining industries and is discussed in more detail in Chapter 14.

Reducing Overhead

A firm, especially in a mature established industry, can find itself with a bloated work force and excessive overhead that was created over time, perhaps in part during more demanding growth periods. Such a context provides opportunities for cost reductions, especially for a new owner or CEO.

White Industries provides an excellent example of a firm that first acquired low-cost assets, then moved in to reduce overhead and an excess work force. During the late 1960s and 1970s, White bought the appliance brands Franklin (Studebaker), Kelvinator (American Motors), Westinghouse, Philco (Ford), and Frigidaire (GM) from firms who were losing money in the mature appliance industry.[4] As a result, White became one of the major firms in the appliance industry along with Whirlpool, General Electric, and Maytag.

Each of the brands acquired by White had been a division of a large company with heavy overhead that had become a cash trap. White was able to turn each business around within months, in large part because of a very different cost culture and much less overhead. Some overhead was reduced by streamlining the product line and by consolidating production—much of the rest was obtained simply by running an extremely lean operation. The old firms in the face of a strong union presence and established culture were incapable of doing something similar even if they had recognized the need to do so.

Scale Economies

The scale effect reflects the natural efficiencies associated with size. Fixed costs such as advertising, sales force overhead, R&D, staff work, and facilities upkeep can be spread over more units. Furthermore, a larger operation can support specialized assets and activities such as market research, legal staff, and manufacturing-engineering operations dedicated to a firm's needs.

The key is to determine the optimal size beyond which scale economies do not exist. In some industries, such as cereal, for example, it has been shown that only a small market share is required to attain scale economies.

A common mistake is to assume that scale economies will occur even when a firm's volume is based on multiple products or brands. For example, Quaker Oats bought Gaines (Gainesburgers, Cycle, and Gravy Train) to add to its brands (Ken-L-Ration and Kibbles 'n Bits) in order to attain a substantial number two position in the dog food market and a commanding 75 percent share in the semimoist segment.[5] One problem was that the five brand names required their own marketing and production so that there were little resulting scale economies. Furthermore, the larger market presence stimulated a vigorous response by the market leader Ralston—it launched a semimoist entry to undercut what Quaker thought was its cash cow.

The Experience Curve

The experience curve suggests that as a firm accumulates experience in building a product, its costs in real dollars (net of inflation) will decline at a predictable rate. Figure 11.1 shows the experience curve for the Model T Ford as reflected by its price. An 85 percent experience curve means that cost will be reduced by 15 percent each time the cumulated experience doubles. Literally thousands of cost studies by the Boston Consulting Group (BCG) and others provide empirical support. The implication is that the first entry into a market that attains a large market share will have a continuing cost advantage.

The experience curve is distinct from economies of scale and is based on the following.

Learning. The basic idea is that people learn to do tasks faster and more efficiently simply by repetition. Furthermore, over time it becomes worthwhile to improve the task process. Learning has links to the time and motion studies of the early 1900s, the learning curve of the 1930s, and more recently, to quality circles made popular by Japanese firms.

Technological Improvements in Production/Operations. The installation of new machinery, computer/information systems, or other capital equipment to improve production or operations can dramatically affect costs, especially for capital-intensive industries. Furthermore, as experience accumulates, people will learn to use such equipment to its full capability and may even modify it to extend its performance.

Product Redesign. Simplifying products can sharply reduce costs. For example, the number of parts in a door-lock mechanism on a U.S. automobile declined from 17 in 1954 to 4 in 1974.[6] The cost of the mechanism in real dollars fell almost 75 percent during that period. The improvement in cost was credited to as many as 20 individual product improvements, including improvements in metallurgy and casting techniques.

There are several issues that need to be addressed in working with the experience curve concept. First, several products can share a component such as a motor or field service operation, which means that such a component will have the benefit of enhanced volume and will advance along the experience curve faster than other components. Second, the experience curve is not automatic; it must be proactively managed with efficiency improvement goals, quality circles, product design targets, and equipment upgrading. Third, a late entry can access the latest design and will have access to the experience of vendors. Fourth, if the technology or market changes, the experience curve may become obsolete. As Walter Kiechel put it,

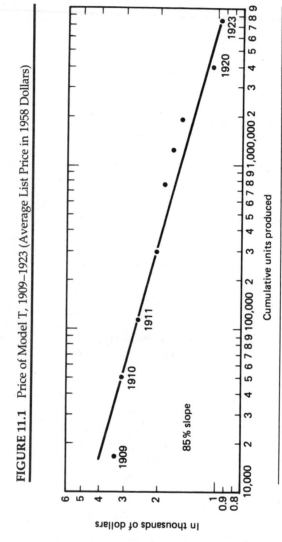

FIGURE 11.1   Price of Model T, 1909–1923 (Average List Price in 1958 Dollars)

SOURCE: William J. Abernathy and Kenneth Wayne, "Limits of the Learning Curve," *Harvard Business Review*, September–October 1974, p. 111.

There you are contentedly making glass bottles for milk, making quite a lot of bottles in fact. You get better at it all the time, producing bottles for less and less per unit, and just rocketing down the old you-know-what. All of a sudden, from out of nowhere, comes some bozo with a wax-paper carton. This character has never even heard of your experience curve, but three years later wax cartons are everywhere and your glass-bottle factory is in cobwebs.[7]

Ford's Model T

The experience of the Ford Motor Company from 1908 to 1923 illustrates how an experience curve strategy can lead a firm to focus obsessively on costs and thus ignore trends, fail to innovate, and end up with an obsolete product.[8] A very well-defined 85-percent experience curve is shown in Figure 11.1. It is worth noting that the steady cost reduction did not just happen. It was caused, in part, by the building of the huge River Rouge plant, a reduction in the management staff from 5 to 2 percent of all employees, extensive vertical integration, and the creation of the integrated, mechanized production process paced by conveyors.

However, in the early 1920s, consumers began to request heavier, closed-body cars that offered more comfort. As Alfred P. Sloan, Jr., the head of General Motors during this time, noted, "Mr. Ford . . . had frozen his policy in the Model T . . . preeminently an open-car design. With its light chassis, it was unsuited to the heavier closed body, and so in less than two years (by 1923) the closed body made the already obsolescent design of the Model T noncompetitive."[9]

As a result, in May of 1927 Henry Ford was forced to shut down operations for nearly a year at a cost of $200 million to retool so that he could compete in the changed marketplace. It seems clear that the very decisions that allowed Ford to march down the experience curve made it difficult for the company to react to the changing times and to competition. The standardized product, extensive vertical integration, and single-minded devotion to production improvements all tended to create an organization that was ill-suited to respond to the changing environment—indeed an organization whose goals and thrust were intimately involved with preserving the status quo, the existing product.

A key to strategy development is recognizing when the experience curve model will apply. In general, it has been most successfully applied in situations characterized by high growth, high levels of value added, continuous-process manufacturing, and capital-intensive industries. When an industry is mature, the experience curve becomes flat, and because it takes so long to double cumulative experience, the experience curve is less useful. If the value added is low, the experience curve will also have little impact. If a purchased raw material such as wheat or sulfur is 80 percent of the cost, there is very little role for experience to play. Some of the most successful applications of the experience curve have been in continuous-process manufacturing contexts such as semi-conductors or capital-intensive heavy industries like steel.

A Low-Cost Culture

A successful low-cost strategy is usually multifaceted, with costs attacked at several fronts and supported by a cost-oriented culture. Thus, the top management, rewards, systems, structure, and culture all stress cost reduction. Heinz, for example, became the low-cost producer in ketchup, frozen French fries, vinegar, and cat food by committing the organization to cost reduction.[10] It held a low-cost operator conference for the firm's top 100 managers, developed new processes to peel potatoes and to reclaim heat from ovens, developed cost- and quality-control teams, shifted Star-Kist production off-shore, and automated soup production in England.

FOCUS STRATEGIES

The focus strategic thrust, whether it involves differentiation, low cost, or both, concentrates on one part of the market or product line. A business that pursues a focus strategy does not attempt to compete across the board in a product market.

One rationale for a focus strategy is that a business simply lacks the resources to compete in a broad product market and must focus in order to generate the impact that is needed to compete effectively. Such a limitation can occur, for example, when an automobile or airplane firm faces heavy product development and tool costs or a consumer products firm cannot afford to support multiple brands.

Another more strategically important rationale is that narrowing the scope of the product line or market served will enhance the match between the strategy and the market, thus creating stronger SCAs and barriers to entry as suggested by Figure 11.2. In most cases, as the product line or market is expanded, compromises will be made in advertising, distribution, manufacturing, and so on, and the SCA and associated entry barriers will be diluted.

Consider the case of Fab 1 Shot. Colgate-Palmolive thought it had a

FIGURE 11.2   Creating Barriers to Entry

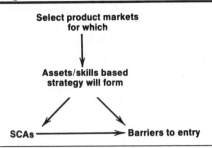

winner when it launched Fab 1 Shot, packets of detergent and fabric softener that would serve a single wash, thus providing convenience to the busy homemaker.[11] Despite a mammoth promotional and advertising effort, the product died, in part because of its high unit cost and a loss of control over the quantity used. In retrospect, the problem was that Fab 1 Shot had attempted to be a mainstream product for a broad market. If the manufacturer had targeted those for whom convenience was extremely important like college students, singles, and apartment dwellers, it might have done well. The customer value analysis would then have been very different and Colgate-Palmolive could have enjoyed a substantial advantage, based in part on a name with a Fab connection and its associated first mover advantage.

A prospective entry will look not only to the difficulty of overcoming barriers formed by skills and assets in place among existing competitors, but also to the potential payoff if the barriers are overcome. If the product-market scope is modest, the payoff will be limited. The concept that competitors will be attracted to the large segments and will ignore the small segment is termed the majority fallacy because appraisals of the large segments overlook the fact that many competitors will be attracted.

The potential of enhancing an SCA by using a focus strategy must be balanced by the fact that it naturally limits the potential business. As a result, profitable sales may be missed. Furthermore, the focused business will often have to compete with larger competitors that will enjoy scale economies. Thus, it is crucial that the focus involves a strategy with meaningful SCAs.

Focusing the Product Line

Focusing on a part of a product line can often enhance the line's technical superiority. In most businesses the key people have expertise or interest in a few products. Those who are the driving force behind a fashion firm

---

The Hernia Hospital

Shouldice Hospital near Toronto specializes in hernia operations.[12] The hospital and staff are thus tailored to the needs of the hernia patient. Patients walk—to watch TV, to eat, and even to and from the operating room. Walking, it turns out, is good therapy. There is thus no need to deliver food to rooms or to have wheelchair facilities. The length of a hospital visit is around half of the norm elsewhere. No general anesthesia is administered because local anesthesia is safer and cheaper for hernia operations. Doctors at Shouldice are exceptionally skillful and productive because they do so many operations. Measured by how often repeated treatment is needed, Shouldice is ten times more effective than other hospitals.

By concentrating on one segment of the medical market, Shouldice has developed a hospital that is proficient, low-cost, and capable of delivering an extraordinary level of patient satisfaction. Ex-patients are so pleased that some 1500 "alumni" came to a reunion.

---

may be interested primarily in women's high fashion. A consumer electronics firm may be founded and run by someone who is very interested in audio quality. When the products of a firm capture the imagination of its key people, the products tend to be exciting, innovative, and of high quality. As the product line broadens, however, the products tend to be me-too products, which do not provide value and detract from the base business. In such a situation the willpower to maintain a focus and resist product expansion may pay off.

A focused product line may also provide a positioning device. The association of a business with a narrow product line can serve to provide a useful image. For example, Neiman-Marcus competes only in the very high-priced end of its industry and appeals to a very narrow segment. Any effort to compete in a broader product market, even if feasible, would risk damaging the exclusive image it has developed for its existing stores. The Raymond Corporation is another firm that is positioned around its limited product line, a line of "narrow-aisle" lift trucks suitable for navigating the narrow spaces in warehouses.

A focus strategy provides the potential to bypass industry key success factors. For example, in the cereal and other packaged foods industries, the ability to establish brand names and distribute branded products is a key success factor. However, firms that focus on private-label manufacture in which cost-control considerations dominate can also do well. These firms insulate themselves from the major manufacturers that would compromise their own brands by producing private labels.

Several software firms have found profitable product niches. One, Spreadsheet Auditor, helps find errors in spreadsheet programs. Another provides an aid for word-processor users whose program lacks a feature or who would like some elements of their program simplified.

Targeting a Segment

Michelin Tires, Calvin Klein clothes, and Portman Hotels all focus on the upper-end segment, those consumers who want the highest quality and are not price-sensitive. Portman will pick up guests at the airport in a Rolls-Royce. An industrial distributor may focus on large-volume users. A clothing retailer might serve only those needing large sizes. A ski manufacturer might serve only competitive skiers. Harley-Davidson focuses on bikers wanting powerful "macho" motorcycles. Armstrong Rubber has performed well over the years by focusing on replacement tires—Sears Roebuck is a major customer.

A Limited Geographic Area

A special type of segmentation variable is geographic location. Geographic segmentation will be effective when it is possible to tailor the product offering and its marketing program to the geographical area served. For example, a regional beer such as the Texas beer, Lone Star, can use local humor and dialects and local promotions such as a rodeo circuit. The resulting local associations can provide SCAs that are not easily overcome by national brands, which are constrained by a national program. A three-store supermarket chain may serve a very limited area with a product and service package suitable for its particular clientele.

Another rationale for geographic segmentation is to obtain cost advantages from operating within a geographic area. For example, businesses such as cement manufacturers, bakeries, and dairies for which transportation costs are substantial may benefit from being regional.

Low-Share Competitors

In many industries there is a dominant firm with substantial scale advantages. A key to competing against such a firm is usually to use some variant of a focus strategy. One approach is to look for a portion of the market in which the dominant firm is making high profits, which may be used to subsidize other parts of its business. Another is to focus on a part of the market that has been neglected and develop an offering and strategy to capture it.

Hamermesh, a Harvard professor and two colleagues, studied low-share firms with good financial performance records and found that a focus strategy was a key to their success.[13] They all tended to (1) compete in a limited number of segments where their strengths were most highly valued, (2) work closely or jointly with customers on R&D, (3) make improvement in manufacturing and operations rather than developing breakthrough products, (4) have strong CEOs, and (5) emphasize profitability rather than growth.

THE PREEMPTIVE MOVE

A preemptive strategic move is an implementation of a strategy new to a business area that, because it is first, generates a skill or asset that competitors are inhibited or prevented from duplicating or countering.[14] The result is a competitive advantage, a first mover advantage, that is sustainable. For example, when a retailer gains access to a set of prime locations, competitors are inhibited from competing because of the resulting location disadvantage.

There is substantial empirical evidence from several studies involving both consumer and industrial businesses that a preemptive move does, on the average, pay off.[15] For example, a study of over 500 mature industrial businesses using the PIMS database showed that pioneer firms average a market share of 29 percent, early followers 21 percent, and late entrants 15 percent. A study of 18 consumer markets showed that the pioneer had a lasting market-share advantage that ranged from 6 market share points (with seven entrants) to 13 (with only two entrants).[16]

A preemptive move with associated sustainable competitive advantages can arise from three sources: technological leadership, preemption of assets, and buyer-switching costs. It can be directed at the supply system, the product, the production system, the customers, or the distribution and service systems as shown in Figure 11.3.

Supply Systems

A business can gain access to the best or least expensive sources of supply of raw material or production equipment. International Nickel and DeBeers based their firms on access to raw materials, nickel and diamonds, respectively. A key advantage of the Red Lobster restaurant chain was its access to the best seafood sources and seafood distribution. Airlines can place large orders for planes, forcing competitors to remain years behind in obtaining the best equipment. Like many preemptive moves, those oriented toward the supply system are risky. If supply commitments are made and business does not materialize or other superior supply sources emerge, such a strategy could backfire.

FIGURE 11.3   Sources of Preemptive Opportunities

SUPPLY SYSTEMS
- Secure access to raw materials.
- Preempt production equipment.
- Dominate supply logistics.

PRODUCT
- Preempt a position.
- Develop a dominant design.
- Secure superior product development personnel.

PRODUCTION SYSTEMS
- Develop production processes.
- Expand capacity.
- Vertically integrate.

CUSTOMER
- Train customers in usage skills—become the familiar brand.
- Get customers to make long-term commitments.
- Gain specialized knowledge about a customer set.

DISTRIBUTION AND SERVICE SYSTEMS
- Occupy prime locations.
- Dominate key distributors or outlets.

Product Opportunities

The first product to be introduced in a market can enjoy substantial advantages. The first competitor has the advantage of occupying a desirable position. Frito-Lay's 99.5-percent service tends to preempt the position of providing the fastest, most reliable service. There simply is not much room for a competitor to exceed 99.5 percent. A competitor is almost forced into another positioning strategy.

The key in some industries is to become the "industry standard." Thus, in the personal computer industry, IBM became the industry standard mainly because of the clout of the IBM name and organization. Furthermore, Microsoft DOS, because of its selection by IBM as the developer of the operating system for its PC, became the industry standard. Competitors with superior products find it almost impossible to compete against an established standard.

A product does not necessarily have to be first to become an industry standard but could have a different design involving a different technology. For example, Matsushita entered the VCR market with the VHS system even though Sony had first established itself with the Beta format. By making the VHS format available to competitors, Matsushita succeeded in ensuring that it was the dominant design.

Production Systems

When a business can pioneer a production process that is effective at reducing cost, enhancing quality, or both, an SCA can be created. Japanese firms have been able to achieve such an SCA in industry after industry. Another approach is to preempt the capacity decision of industry participants by aggressively expanding capacity to discourage competitors from entering the market or competing in undesirable ways. Still another approach is to be the first company to integrate vertically, thereby gaining exclusive access to desirable sources of supply.

Customer Opportunities

A first mover can develop customer loyalty by creating switching costs. There are a variety of ways that switching costs are created:

- **A customer can simply become familiar with the first mover's product or service.**[17] If it is satisfactory, there may be no incentive to try something different, the performance of which is uncertain. The familiarity switching cost is particularly relevant to low-cost convenience products where it is difficult for a customer to justify any search effort.

- **A customer may be enticed or required to make a long-term commitment.** For example, a hospital supply firm made substantial inroads against a dominant, established firm by offering to place computer terminals in hospitals to facilitate ordering emergency products. The terminals ultimately were used to order routine as well as emergency items. Because hospitals needed only one such terminal, the established firm found its belated effort to duplicate the service frustrated— it had been preempted.

- **A customer may invest by learning to use a first mover's product or service.** Switching would require the duplication of this learning investment. Many industrial equipment manufacturers such as Texas Instruments in the area of oil-field instrumentation have generated customers with a knowledge equity in their equipment.

● **A firm may gain specialized knowledge about a customer.** A law firm or advertising agency may become so intimate with a client that it would be disruptive for the client to attempt a new relationship. A computer firm such as NCR may gain such specialized knowledge about a retail chain that it would be risky and expensive for that chain to switch to another computer firm.

Distribution and Service Systems

A retail chain can preempt locations by committing early to an area and selecting prime outlets. The chain will not only have first choice of outlets, but will also discourage competitors by reducing their profit potential. In many industries, distribution channel capacity limits exist. There is only so much shelf space and capacity in a distributor warehouse or sales representative organization. The firm that gets first access to this capacity will receive an investment from the channel member and be hard to dislodge.

Implementing the Preemptive Move

Several threads run through the concept of a preemptive move. First, by definition it involves doing something novel. One does not get there by copying and improving on strategies in place. Innovation is required. Thus, some mechanism must exist to allow ideas for preemptive actions to surface.

Second, the preemptive move often involves the substantial commitment of resources, which implies substantial risk. It is this very commitment, however, that helps make the resulting advantage sustainable, because competitors are reluctant to move against a committed firm. Profit potential for an entrant is always higher if it is likely that existing competitors will exit.

Third, a successful first mover advantage assumes that a competitor will be inhibited or prevented from duplicating or countering. There are cases in which followers actually have an advantage. A follower can:

● Gain access to a product innovation, manufacturing technique, or skilled people at far less cost than the pioneer who developed them.

● Surpass the innovator. P&G saw its share of the disposable diaper market in Japan collapse when a competitor introduced better diapers.

● Select a product-positioning strategy after the pioneer has already committed. Thus, Taster's Choice was a successful follower in a category created by Maxim by positioning along the taste dimensions.

- Wait until uncertainty regarding the appropriate technology or product route is resolved. A first mover like Sony may commit to a technology (Beta) that loses to the competitive technology of a follower.

- Exploit size and marketing clout to overtake an innovator, as IBM did with personal computers and Gallo's Bartles & Jaymes did with wine coolers.

A preemptive move will work best, therefore, when competitors are indeed inhibited from responding. For example, a competitor's "quality/ prestige" brand could be cannibalized and weakened if it introduced a lower-priced brand reacting to a preemptive move at the low end of the market. A competitor might be committed to an existing distribution system or manufacturing process and thus be reluctant to follow a first mover. In deciding to invest in a preemptive move one needs to consider the possible reaction of competitors and, when possible, reduce the likelihood that they will engage in damaging follower strategies.

SUMMARY

Figure 11.4 provides a summary of the five strategic thrusts discussed. Differentiation, the subject of Chapter 10, provides customer value by enhancing a product or service characteristics. Synergy, introduced in Chapter 9, focuses on the advantages created by multiple businesses.

A low-cost thrust involves a sustainable cost advantage, which can be used to invest in the product, support lower prices, or provide high returns. The experience curve, which has been observed in thousands of studies, suggests that value-added costs will decline at a fixed percentage each time cumulative experience doubles, due in part to learning, capital investment, and product redesigns. Among many routes to a cost advantage are the no-frills product, low-cost product designs, low overhead, automation, cost advantages in labor or material, and scale economies.

The focus strategy usually employs either differentiation or low cost, but another important element is the concept of a focus, usually involving a narrowing of either the product line or the market served. A preemptive strategic move is an implementation of a strategy new to a business area that, because it is first, generates a skill or asset, thus inhibiting or preventing competitors from duplicating or countering.

FOOTNOTES

[1] Zachary Schiller, "Fadal's Attractions," *Business Week*, October 22, 1990, pp. 62–66.

[2] Bill Saporito, "Heinz Pushes to Be the Low-Cost Producer," *Fortune*, June 24, 1985, p. 54.

FIGURE 11.4   Alternative Strategic Thrusts—A Summary

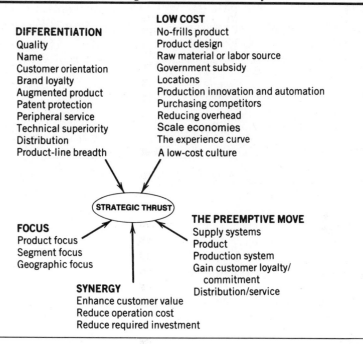

DIFFERENTIATION
Quality
Name
Customer orientation
Brand loyalty
Augmented product
Patent protection
Peripheral service
Technical superiority
Distribution
Product-line breadth

LOW COST
No-frills product
Product design
Raw material or labor source
Government subsidy
Locations
Production innovation and automation
Purchasing competitors
Reducing overhead
Scale economies
The experience curve
A low-cost culture

STRATEGIC THRUST

FOCUS
Product focus
Segment focus
Geographic focus

THE PREEMPTIVE MOVE
Supply systems
Product
Production system
Gain customer loyalty/
  commitment
Distribution/service

SYNERGY
Enhance customer value
Reduce operation cost
Reduce required investment

[3] United States v. E. I. DuPont de Nemours & Company, FTC Docket No. 9108, 1982. Interestingly, DuPont's plan to gain share was challenged by the FTC as being an illegal effort to monopolize. It was held, however, that DuPont's conduct was reasonable, not in violation of the antitrust statutes. DuPont had built excess capacity to respond to market opportunity rather than to deter entry. It did not price below cost, make false announcements of plant expansion, or lock up customers with long-term contracts.

[4] 1981 Annual Report, White Consolidated Industries, Inc.

[5] Bill Saporito, "How Quaker Oats Got Rolled," *Fortune*, October 8, 1990, pp. 129–138.

[6] Walter Kiechel III, "The Decline of the Experience Curve," *Fortune*, October 5, 1981, p. 140.

[7] Kiechel, "The Decline of the Experience Curve," p. 144.

[8] William J. Abernathy and Kenneth Wayne, "Limits of the Learning Curve," *Harvard Business Review*, September–October 1974, pp. 109–119.

[9] Alfred P. Sloan, Jr., *My Years with General Motors*, New York: Doubleday, 1964, pp. 162–163.

[10] Saporito, "Heinz Pushes to Be the Low-Cost Producer," pp. 44–54.

[11] Cara Appelbaum, "Targeting the Wrong Demographic," *Adweek's Marketing Week*, November 5, 1990, p. 20.

[12] William H. Davidow and Bro Utal, "Service Companies: Focus or Falter," *Harvard Business Review*, July–August 1989, pp. 77–85.

[13] R. G. Hamermesh, M. J. Anderson, Jr., and J. E. Harris, "Strategies for Low Market Share Businesses," *Harvard Business Review*, May–June 1978, pp. 95–102.

[14] This section draws on Ian C. MacMillan, "Preemptive Strategies," *Journal of Business Strategy* 4, Fall 1983, pp. 16–26.

[15] William T. Robinson, "Sources of Market Pioneer Advantages: The Case of Industrial Goods Industries," *Journal of Marketing Research*, February 1988, pp. 87–94.

[16] Glen L. Urban and Gurumurthy Kalyanaram, "Dynamic Effect of the Order of Entry on Market Share, Trail Penetration, and Repeat Purchases for Frequently Purchased Consumer Goods," Working Paper, MIT, Cambridge, Mass., January 1991.

[17] Marvin B. Lieberman and David Montgomery, "First-Mover Advantages," *Strategic Management Journal*, Vol. 9, March–April 1988, pp. 41–58.

12

GROWTH STRATEGIES: PENETRATION, PRODUCT-MARKET EXPANSION, AND VERTICAL INTEGRATION

Marketing should focus on market creation, not market sharing.

Regis McKenna

Results are gained by exploiting opportunities, not by solving problems.

Peter Drucker

An objective of most organizations is to grow—in terms of sales, values added, profits, personnel, and resources. Growth introduces vitality to an organization by providing challenges and rewards. In fact, it can be difficult even to survive with a no-growth scenario, because competitors will attack and vulnerable areas will experience declines. With no compensating growth areas, an organization will wither. If a business is reduced below a critical mass and loses needed scale economies, it may no longer be viable. Thus, growth objectives are not only healthy, but they can even be necessary.

A host of different strategies can lead to growth. The mission statement development, discussed in Chapter 2, attempted to specify in a gross way the type of growth strategy that seems most promising for a firm. At this later stage of the planning process, growth strategies need to be considered at a more detailed, specific level. Whereas a mission statement might suggest three or four general growth directions, it is not specific. It is necessary at this stage to identify what types of market or product expansion should be considered and exactly what profit streams should be associated with each type.

Figure 12.1 provides a way to structure alternative growth strategies based, in part, on the product-market matrix introduced in Chapter 2. The first set of growth strategies involves existing product markets. The next two concern product development and market development. The fourth concerns integration strategies and the fifth diversification strategies, which will be covered in Chapter 13. The distinctions between some of these categories may be blurred, but the structure is still helpful in generating strategic options.

GROWTH IN EXISTING PRODUCT MARKETS

Existing product markets are often attractive growth avenues. A firm is established with a base on which to build and momentum that can be exploited. Furthermore, the firm is experienced and knowledgeable so that resources, especially human resources, may already be in place. Growth can be achieved in existing product markets by increasing share through capturing sales held by competitors. Alternatively, product usage among existing customers can be increased.

Increasing Market Share

Perhaps the most obvious way to grow is to improve market share. A share gain can be based on tactical actions such as advertising, trade allowances, promotions, or price reductions. The problem is that share gain by such means can be difficult to maintain. A preferred approach is

FIGURE 12.1   Alternative Growth Strategies

Present products   New products

	I. Growth in existing product markets • Increasing market share • Increasing product usage Increasing the frequency used Increasing the quantity used Find new applications for current users	II. Product development • Add product features, product refinement • Expand the product line • Develop a new generation product • Develop new products for the same market
New markets	III. Market development • Expand geographically • Target new segments	V. Diversification involving new products and new markets • Related • Unrelated

Present markets

Vertical integration

IV. Vertical integration strategies
• Forward integration
• Backward integration

to generate a more permanent share gain by creating an SCA involving enhanced customer value or by overcoming or neutralizing a competitor's SCA. Thus, the need is to create or enhance the assets and skills of the business and neutralize those of competitors. Growth in market share can be based on any of the strategic thrusts detailed in the previous two chapters.

Increasing Product Usage

Attempts to increase market share will very likely affect competitors directly and therefore precipitate competitor responses. The alternative of attempting to increase usage among current customers is usually less threatening to competitors.[1]

When developing programs to increase users, it is useful to begin by asking some fundamental questions about the user and the consumption system in which the product is embedded. Why isn't the product or service used more? What inhibits the usage decision? How does the light user differ from the heavy user in terms of attitudes and habits?

Increased product usage can be precipitated in three ways, as noted in Figure 12.1. First, the frequency of use can be increased. Second, the quantity used in each application can be increased. Finally, new applications can be sought. The first two are detailed in Figure 12.2.

Increasing the Frequency of Use

Reminder Communication.   For some contexts, awareness as reflected in top-of-mind recall of a brand or the use occasion is the driving force. People will know about a brand and its use, but do not think to use it.

Reminder advertising may be what is needed. Steak sauce and other condiment brands conduct reminder advertising campaigns to obtain more frequent usage. A manufacturer of canned spiced ham found that most customers keep the product in their pantry "just in case." The problem was to influence its use in recipes. The strategy used was a reminder advertising and promotion campaign. General Foods conducted a reminder campaign for Jell-O Pudding with Bill Cosby asking, "When was the last time you served pudding, Mom?"

Routine maintenance functions like dental check-ups or car lubrication are easily forgotten and reminders can make a difference. An Arm & Hammer consumer survey revealed that people who use baking soda as a deodorizer in refrigerators thought that they changed the box every four months when actually they did so only every 14 months.[2] An advertising campaign geared to seasonal reminders about replacing the box resulted.

Position for Frequent or Regular Use.   The image of a product can change from that of occasional to frequent usage by a repositioning campaign. For example, the advertising campaigns for Clinique's "twice-a-day" moisturizer and "three glasses of milk per day" both represent efforts to change the perception of the products involved. A related approach is to position for regular use, because a usage habit is the best guarantee that the usage will be maintained. An advertising campaign, for example, might emphasize the need for a floss-after-every-meal habit or to phone a relative once a week.

Make the Use Easier.   Asking why customers do not use a product or service more often can lead to approaches for easier product use. For

FIGURE 12.2   Increasing Usage in Existing Product Markets

Approach	Strategy	Examples
Frequency of use/ consumption	Reminder communication	Jell-O Pudding
	Position for frequent use	Shampoo, car care
	Position for regular use	Flossing teeth after meals
	Make the use easier or more convenient	Dixie-cup dispenser, microwavable
	Provide incentives	Frequent flyer plan
	Reduce undesirable consequences of frequent use	Gentle shampoo
	Use at different occasions	Cereal at snack versus breakfast
	Use at different locations	Radio in shower
Level of use/ consumption	Reminder communication	Increase insurance coverage
	Provide incentives	Special price for accessories
	Influence norms	Use of larger containers
	Reduce undesirable consequences of increased use level	Low-calorie candy
	Develop positive associations with use occasions	Frito-Lay: "Bet you can't just eat one."

example, a Dixie-cup or paper-towel dispenser encourages use by reducing the usage effort. Packages that can be placed directly in a microwave make usage more convenient. A reservation service can help those who must select a hotel or similar service. Frozen waffles and Stove Top stuffing are examples of product modifications that increased consumption by making usage more convenient.

Provide Incentives.   Incentives can be provided to increase consumption frequency. Promotions such as double mileage trips offered by airlines' frequent flyer plans can affect usage. A problem is to structure the incentive so that usage is affected and it does not simply become the vehicle for debilitating price competition. Price incentives such as two for the price of one can be effective, but they also may stimulate price retaliation.

Reduce Undesirable Consequences of Frequent Use.   Sometimes there are good reasons why a customer is inhibited from using a product more frequently. If such reasons can be addressed, usage may increase. For example, some people might believe that frequent hair washing may not be healthy. A product that is designed to be gentle enough for daily use might alleviate this worry and stimulate increased usage. A low-calorie, low-sodium, or low-fat version of a food product may sharply increase the market. The brand that becomes associated with the product change will be in the best position to capitalize on the increased market.

Increasing the Quantity Used

Similar techniques can be employed to increase the quantity used in each use occasion:

- **Reminder communication.** An insurance customer can be reminded to consider increasing the coverage on a house whose replacement value might have increased. A shirt buyer might be reminded to consider a tie or another accessory.

- **Incentives can be used.** A fast-food restaurant, for example, might attempt by pricing or promotion to increase the number of items purchased at a meal. A special price will be available if a drink and fries are ordered with a hamburger.

- **Efforts can be made to affect the usage level norms.** The size of a "normal" serving might change by creating a larger glass or container and influencing its acceptance.

- **The perceived undesirable consequences of heavy consumption might be addressed.** Thus, a light beer or low-calorie salad dressing could remove a reason to restrict the usage level. Life Saver candies have advertised that one piece has fewer calories than people think.

- **Positive associations with use occasion might be developed through advertising.** Thus, a sense of fun and refreshment associated with Pepsi-Cola might encourage heavier usage. Frito-Lay has used the "bet you can't just eat one" tag line to emphasize taste pleasure. A computer equipment firm could associate efficiency with buying a larger system.

New Applications for Existing Product Users

The detection and exploitation of a new functional use for a brand can rejuvenate a business that has been considered a has-been for years. A classic example is Jell-O, which began strictly as a dessert product but found major sources of new sales in applications such as Jell-O salads.

Arm & Hammer baking soda annual sales were around $15 million and stagnating in the early 1970s, when the company started to advertise its product's use as a refrigerator deodorizer.[3] The results stimulated by the initial 14-month advertising campaign were spectacular—the number of households that reported using the product in this application rose from 1 to 57 percent. Later campaigns suggested its use as a sink deodorizer, a freezer deodorizer, a cat-litter deodorant, a dog deodorant, and as a treatment for swimming pools. Within ten years, Arm & Hammer was a $150 million business. By extending its brand further into deodorizer products, dentifrices, and laundry detergent, Arm & Hammer had sales exceeding $400 million by 1990.

Other brands that successfully found growth with new applications are

- Grape-Nuts served over yogurt or ice cream have stimulated sales.

- A chemical process used by oil fields to separate water from oil is used by water plants to eliminate unwanted oil.

- Lipton soup includes recipes for new uses on boxes and in ads that suggest, "Great meals start with Lipton—recipe soup mix—soup." The recipe concept is thus emphasized even in the slogan.

The identification of new uses can best be obtained by market research determining exactly how customers use a brand. From the set of uses that emerge, several can be selected to pursue. For example, users of external analgesics were asked to keep a diary of their uses.[4] A surprising finding was that about one-third of Ben-Gay's usage and over 50 percent of its volume went for arthritis relief instead of muscle aches. A separate marketing strategy was developed for this use featuring dancers (Ann Miller) and football players (John Unitas) who now have arthritis and the brand caught a wave of growth.

Another tact is to look at application areas of competing product forms. The widespread use of raisins prompted Ocean Spray to create dried cranberries. They are used in cookies and in cereal such as Muesli with a "made with real Ocean Spray cranberries" seal on the package. They are also being sold as a snack food tentatively called Ocean Spray Craisins.

Sometimes a large payoff will result for a firm that can provide applications not currently in general use. Thus, surveys of current applications may be inadequate. Firms such as General Mills have sponsored recipe contests, one objective of which is to create new uses for a product by discovering a new "recipe classic." For a product like stick-on labels that can be used in many ways, it might be worthwhile to conduct formal brainstorming sessions or other creative exercises.

If some application area is uncovered that could create substantial sales, it needs to be evaluated. First, a market survey or other forecasting device might be used to estimate the potential level. How many customers could use the product in that way? What level of product purchase would that application support for each customer? Arm & Hammer conducted over 150 market research studies to support its development of new use applications and new products.

Second, the feasibility and costs of exploiting an application area need to be assessed. Some new applications can require substantial marketing programs. Angostura Bitters, a 160-year-old brand used primarily in Manhattans, decided to promote nonalcoholic drinks starting with the Charger.[5] The Charger, a drink that had been sold in bars for decades, consisted of sparkling water, bitters, and lime. Canada Dry was enticed to promote it by putting a packet of bitters with a recipe on the necks of bottles of Canada Dry Seltzer. Tastings were organized at museums and street fairs. Radio ads with a "Charger" theme were run. Other drinks such as the Caribbean, made with cranberry juice, pineapple juice, and bitters, followed.

Third, the possibility that a competitor will take over an application area by product improvement, heavy advertising, or other means, or will engage in price warfare needs to be analyzed. The issue is whether or not a brand can achieve a sustainable advantage in its new application. Ocean Spray is associated with cranberries and this might protect its entry into a cranberry snack, but the firm's name will be of less help in a processed application such as cookies and cereals.

PRODUCT DEVELOPMENT FOR THE EXISTING MARKET

As reflected in Figure 12.1, product development can occur at a variety of levels and it is helpful to distinguish between them. They include the addition of product features, the expansion of a product line, the development of new generation technologies, and the development of new products for an existing market.

Product Feature Addition

Product features can be added. An automobile firm could add a transmission or sunroof option that will improve its penetration of an existing market in which it is competing. For some candy firms, the creation of novel packages provides a key to sales. A clothing firm could add accessories to its line of merchandise. A firm making personal computers could add memory or built-in software. Clearly, such line extensions involve almost total commonality of marketing, operations, and management. Because they represent such visible growth opportunities and are accomplished relatively easily, they can be very enticing. They still absorb resources, however, and should be resisted if the prospective ROI is unsatisfactory.

One type of line extension occurs when high-tech or industrial firms are asked by customers to produce a special-purpose version of a product. The resulting product will have a set of features that may be useful only to a single customer. Such development work can lead to substantial sales and even to new products, but the attraction of a visible customer need can be overly enticing. If this type of development activity is permitted to preempt more ambitious development programs, the long-term health of an organization could suffer.

Product-Line Expansion

A second type of product development activity aimed at existing markets is to expand or broaden a product line. The marketing and distribution effort and perhaps even much of the manufacturing will be common to the product-line extensions. A paint firm may want to add wood stains to its line. A cross-country ski firm could add a racing line for advanced-skier customers who may want to trade up. A book retailer could add children's books and a "how-to" section to its line. The product-line extension will be based on many factors, of course, but will often involve consideration of the following questions:

• **Will customers benefit from a systems capability or service convenience made possible by a broad product line?** The inclusion of a software line and printers with a line of computers provides the potential of offering a more complete system. A customer may want not only systems design but also a firm that provides systems responsibility.

• **Do potential manufacturing, marketing, or distribution cost efficiencies exist from an expanded product line?** To the extent that there are shared costs, the experience and scale effects on costs will be enhanced. The question is whether or not even with this cost advantage, the proposed product-line extension will have a satisfactory ROI.

• **Can assets or skills be applied to a product expansion?** Philip Morris underestimated the difficulty of transferring its marketing magic to the 7Up business and finally gave up.

• **Does a firm have the skill and needed resources in R&D, manufacturing, and marketing to add the various products proposed?** Sometimes an apparently simple line extension like adding wood stains to a line of paints can involve a totally new manufacturing effort, raw materials technology, or marketing effort and, thus, may not fit the capabilities of the firm.

• **Is the new product line compatible with the existing brand?** Maytag needed to expand its line in order to fully support the emerging large retailers that demanded a full line, and bought the brands Magic Chef, Admiral, Norge, and Hoover.[6] These acquisitions gave Maytag its needed full line and presence at the lower end. However, the new lines were not comparable to Maytag in quality, often being at the bottom of *Consumer Reports'* ratings for such appliances, and thus put the Maytag reputation at risk with both dealers and consumers.

Developing New Generation Technologies

Growth can be obtained in an existing market by creating new technology products. Such products can obsolete existing ones, thus providing a source of sales. Compact disks and stereo TV sets were part of the reason that the stagnant home audio market enjoyed a substantial spurt in sales in the late 1980s. The advent of low-fat ice cream such as Dreyer's Grand Light Ice Cream stimulated growth in the ice cream category.

Yamaha Pianos had gained 40 percent of the global piano market, a market that was declining by 10 percent each year and facing competition from Korean firms. Yamaha responded by developing the Disklavier that functions and plays like comparable pianos, except it also included an electronic control system, a modern version of the old player pianos. The system allows a performance to be recorded with great accuracy and stored on a 3.5-in. disk. The new technology can be used by the professional player or composer, the student who learns with a built-in role model or accompanist, and those who would like a great pianist to play in their home. The Disklavier allowed Yamaha to revitalize a business that was buried in a declining market. In addition, they spawned a retrofit subindustry, as well as an industry to support the disks.

The decision to pursue new technologies is particularly tricky for a market leader that has a vested interest in the old technology but faces competitive risks with a strategy of delay and disinterest. The Gillette experience of the early 1960s illustrates this point.[7] Gillette resisted the stainless steel blade technology because its durability meant that people would need far fewer blades and the cost to change the firm's manufacturing and marketing efforts would be high. The company was making in excess of a 40-percent return on investment. As a result, the small British stainless innovator, Wilkinson, and its U.S. rivals, Eversharp and Schick, made major and permanent inroads into Gillette's share and profits. Gillette's share fell from 70 to 55 percent, and its return fell to below

Toward Synergies in Financial Services[8]

During the 1980s a variety of firms developed a broad range of financial services. Sears is the most dramatic example. It brought the real-estate firm Coldwell Banker and the brokerage firm Dean Witter into a firm that already had Allstate Insurance, Allstate S&L, and 25 million active Sears charge-card users. Sears, to exploit the synergy represented by this array of financial services, opened more than 300 financial boutiques in its larger stores, where various combinations of Allstate salespeople, Dean Witter brokers, and Coldwell Banker agents were located. In addition, it introduced the Discovery Card. The final verdict is not in on the Sears effort, but its initial experience illustrates the problems of realizing synergies.

- The concept of leveraging store traffic by locating kiosks in the stores was oversold. The atmosphere and customer types did not lend themselves to Coldwell Banker or Dean Witter. One broker told of attempting to talk to a customer in the toy department with his kids yelling in the background. The profile of a Sears customer is very different from that of the asset-heavy profitable customer of a brokerage firm. Furthermore, the Sears name, which means value and trust in tires and tools, may not have been an asset in securities. By the early 1990s these brokerage units were in only 100 of the largest and most spacious stores.

- The concept of cross-selling is difficult to implement. It is much easier to get an organization behind its own products. In fact, Dean Witter achieved much of its profits from its own mutual funds. However, Dean Witter salespeople in the early 1990s were selling annually around $1 billion of annuities managed by Sears's Allstate Insurance unit.

- Dean Witter suffered damaging losses in its mortgage banking operation after being acquired by Sears. Under Sears, Dean Witter had focused on the retail business and turned its back on mortgage banking. Was this a good strategic move or simply an inevitable result of operating in the Sears culture?

American Express, another financial conglomerate, actively encouraged and managed efforts to exploit synergies such as cross-selling and sharing of office space, data-processing capabilities, and marketing expertise through its "one enterprise" program. Although the company had success in selling life insurance to its cardholders and customers of its stockbrokerage unit, Shearson-Lehman, the experience demonstrated that synergy is elusive. Problems with Fireman's Fund Insurance and Shearson-Lehman have turned the whole venture into something of a disaster.

In contrast, State Farm Insurance has been dramatically successful, becoming one of the largest financial service firms by "sticking to its knitting," avoiding anything but its core insurance business.

30 percent. It is remarkable how rarely the new generation technology comes from the market leader, even when it is investing large amounts in R&D.

New Products for Existing Markets

A classic growth pattern is to exploit a marketing or distribution strength by adding compatible products, products that are not line extensions but are very different even though they share customers with existing products. Synergy is usually obtained at least in part by the commonality in distribution, marketing, and brand name recognition and image. Thus, Arm & Hammer, capitalizing on 97-percent name recognition, successfully introduced a heavy-duty laundry detergent, an oven cleaner, and a liquid detergent.

Lenox, a maker of fine china, exploited its traditional, high-quality image and its distribution system by expanding into the areas of jewelry and giftware.[9] The first jewelry acquisitions included Art-Carved and Keepsake, the leading firms in wedding and engagement rings. Additional synergies are possible because much of Lenox's sales is associated with weddings. H&R Block added legal services to its chain of income tax services, hoping to gain synergy by sharing office space and operations.

Synergies that are expected from product expansion may never materialize. Sometimes they are simply illusory. A food company such as General Foods had little in common with a fast-food restaurant chain that was acquired even though both involved food. More often, the synergy exists, but its benefit is modest and does not overcome the costs and problems associated with a new area. The effort to combine United Airlines, Westin Hotel and Resorts, and Hertz into one organization was aborted, in part, because the potential synergies, mostly involving a common reservation system and cross-selling, were not valued by the stock market.

Anheuser-Busch was disappointed by its efforts to expand into beverages other than beer such as Baybry's Cooler, Dewey Stevens Premium Wine Cooler, Zeltzer Seltzer, and several wines and bottled drinks.[10] Ironically, Anheuser-Busch's greatest weakness was in distribution, an expected strength area. The firm has no problems in the package store where a beer distributor is the key element. However, it is weak in the supermarket where such a distributor is bypassed. By using its beer distribution network, the company had a difficult time keeping prices competitive.

A significant new product risk, of course, is that customer acceptance is not achieved. Clairol, a firm with considerable strength in the personal hair-care market, introduced Small Miracle, a hair conditioner that could be used through several shampoos.[11] It flopped despite a massive marketing effort, in part because customers are more interested in their appearance than the cost or bother of using a hair conditioner frequently, and because they thought the product would build up on their hair if it were not washed off with each use. The Arm & Hammer name also spawned two failures, a spray underarm deodorant, for which the Arm & Hammer name may have the wrong connotations, and a spray disinfectant.

MARKET DEVELOPMENT USING EXISTING PRODUCTS

Market development often involves the virtual duplication of a business operation, perhaps with minor adaptive changes. The market expansion can use the same expertise and technology and sometimes even the same plant and operations facility. Thus, the potential for synergy is large. Of the two basic approaches to market expansion, the first and most obvious is geographical expansion. The second is expansion into different market segments.

Expanding Geographically

Geographic expansion may involve changing from a regional operation to a national operation, moving into another region, or expanding to another country. Rockwell International, after unsuccessful forays into consumer products, decided to focus on expanding sales of its industrial products (which it knows best) outside the United States.[12] The goal was to become a leading supplier of automobile and truck components. Toward that end Rockwell purchased a British auto parts company, planned a joint venture with an Italian firm making truck axles, built a truck brake plant in Germany, and licensed its truck axle technology in Korea.

The key is whether or not the concept that has been proved "at home" can be exported. Federal Express ran into trouble trying to duplicate its concept in Europe.[13] For starters, the firm lacked a first mover advantage in Europe because DHL and others had employed the Federal Express concept years earlier. Setting up a hub-and-spoke system in Europe was inhibited by regulatory roadblocks at every turn. Attempts to short-circuit regulations by acquiring firms with related abilities resulted in something of a hodgepodge—Federal Express owns a barge company, for example. The overuse of English and a decision to impose a pickup deadline of 5 o'clock in Spain (where people work until 8) illustrate just some of the implementation problems.

Expanding into New Market Segments

A firm can also grow by reaching into new market segments. There are, of course, a variety of ways to define target segments and therefore growth directions:

- **Usage.** The nonuser can be an attractive target. An audio electronics firm could target those not owning an audio system.

- **Distribution channel.** A firm can reach new segments by opening up a second or third channel of distribution. A retail sporting goods store could market to schools via a direct sales force. A direct marketer such as Avon could introduce its products under another brand name into department stores.

- **Age.** Johnson & Johnson's baby shampoo was languishing until the company looked toward adults who wash their hair frequently and their need for a mild shampoo—"If it's gentle enough for a baby . . . ." The result was a market-share gain from 3 to 14 percent.

- **Attribute preference.** A firm that has focused on frequency of response in its instrumentation at the sacrifice of accuracy might extend its line to include more accurate equipment to serve the segment that demands more accuracy.

The evaluation of an expansion strategy aimed at new target segments will be much like the evaluation of any prospective market. Its attractiveness in terms of size, growth, and competitive intensity needs to be analyzed. Then a determination is required as to how the firm will compete, focusing on its relative strengths, especially in those areas identified as key success factors.

Evaluating Market Expansion Alternatives

Although synergy can potentially be high, several other considerations are involved in a market expansion:

- First, is the brand operating well in its initial market? There is no point in exporting failure or even mediocrity.

- Second, consider a wide variety of segmentation variables. Sometimes a different way to look at markets will uncover a useful segment.

- Third, identify segments that are not being served well, such as the women's calculator market or the fashion needs of older people.

- Fourth, segments should be sought for which the brand can provide value. Coming into a new market without providing any incremental customer value can be very risky.

● Fifth, make sure that the business can be adapted to the new market. To the extent that conditions differ, is there a convincing plan to adapt the business to the differing conditions? For example, Rheingold Beer, a New York company, failed in an attempt to enter the California market, in part because it tried to use a distribution channel unsuitable for California and in part because a promotion that was effective in New York fell flat in California.

VERTICAL INTEGRATION STRATEGIES

Vertical integration represents another potential growth direction. Forward integration occurs when a firm moves downstream with respect to product flow, a manufacturer buying a retail chain, for example. Backward integration is moving upstream, as when a manufacturer, for instance, invests in a raw material source. A good way to understand when vertical integration should be considered and how it should be evaluated is to consider the possible benefits and costs of a vertical integration strategy:

Benefits	*Costs*
Operating economies	Operating costs
Access to supply or demand	Management of a different business
Control of the product system	Increase in risk
Entry into a profitable business	Reduced flexibility
Enhancing technological innovation	Costs of being "in-grown"

Benefit: Operating Economies

Combining operations can result in better production and related economies:

● **Steps in the production process can be combined, eliminated, or more closely coordinated.** The result can be savings in handling, transportation, and inventory costs. In particular, with uncertainty lessened by the communication and control of the two operations, inventory can often be reduced. Royal Silk distributes its line of silk apparel that it designs and manufactures through a mail order system (sending out 23 million catalogs annually) and over 20 retail stores.[14] The efficiencies of such an integrated operation plus the avoidance of paying to others a huge retail margin allow the firm to sell its product at a low price.

● **Economies of scale are possible.** The combining of two operations can in some cases allow the sharing of warehouses, sales forces, accounting operations, computer facilities, and staff activities such as marketing research. To the extent that a larger operation is more efficient, economies will be observed.

- **Substantial transaction costs are involved in creating a contract between two separate firms.** A search for suppliers by one firm and customers by the other can be expensive. The transaction itself will often involve salespersons, purchasing agents, technical staffs, purchase orders, invoices, and shipping documents. If the two organizations are combined, these transaction costs usually are either eliminated or substantially reduced.

- **Economies related to information gathering are available.** Market research and industry data can be shared by both organizations. Furthermore, the supplier firm should have intimate access to its customer's application and problems.

Benefit: Access to Supply or Demand

Access to Supply. In some contexts a key success factor is access to a supply of raw material, a part, or another input factor; backward integration can reduce the availability risk. A forest products firm may thus acquire timberland. Hewlett Packard lost a key six months to the market with a workstation when a key supplier of chips was six months late, whereas IBM with internal sources did not have that worry. Sometimes suppliers are not capable of or interested in supplying the needed component. For example, when refrigerated boxcars and warehouses were first needed by meat packers, they had to develop them because there was no source.

Access to Demand. Similarly, forward integration could be motivated by a concern about product outlets. Thus, Kemper, an insurance firm, bought regional stockbrokerage firms in order to provide sales outlets in an environment where many of its competitors had merged with brokerage firms.[15] A motivation to gain access to major buyers was behind the investment in car rental firms by major automobile companies—Ford has invested in Hertz and Budget, General Motors in Avis and National, while Chyrsler owns Thrifty and Snappy. These vertical relationships not only provide sales but important exposure to prospective customers of their new models.

Idiosyncratic Products and Services. Whenever only one buyer and one seller exist for highly specialized products and services, there will be an incentive to consider vertical integration. The economist, Oliver

Williamson, terms such products and services "idiosyncratic."[16] When such specialization occurs, the real danger exists that one party or the other may "hold up" the other by taking opportunistic advantage of a change in either its circumstance or the environment. Of course, contractual arrangements can attempt to prevent hold-up problems. In reality, however, it can be very difficult to find a contract that will cover all eventualities in a long-term relationship embedded in a changing environment.

Four types of specializations can be identified:[17]

1. **Brand name.** If one party owns the brand name, the other may develop its equity without controlling the essence of the asset. Thus, in copiers, Ricoh saw the market control and profits controlled by Savin and decided to integrate forward by establishing its own brand name.

2. **Dedicated assets.** When a large asset investment is required, vertical integration may be useful. A can company will have to make a large investment to create a can factory near a beer firm. If their contract was prematurely terminated, the investment would cause excess capacity.

3. **Technological.** A petroleum plant may be designed to use a high-grade ore that is available only from a few sources. If the raw material source was jeopardized, the plant may cease to be viable. The plant could be designed to accept a variety of grades of petroleum. Obtaining such flexibility would, however, require substantially more investment.

4. **Knowledge-based.** A supplier may acquire specialized knowledge and thus become the only practical source for an input factor. For example, a law firm or engineering contractor might become so familiar with the involved product, service, and client firm that for practical purposes no competing suppliers exist, although at the outset of the relationship there were several able competitors. Vertical integration will prevent the supplier from making abnormal profits and perhaps further enhance the degree of knowledge transfer between the two firms.

Benefit: Control of the Product System

It can become necessary to integrate vertically in order to gain sufficient control over the product or service to maintain the integrity of a differentiation strategy. For example, a vital component may need to be made with precision, and outside contractors may be unable to provide it or unwilling to make an investment in the specialized assets needed. Vertical integration may be the only way to ensure that the desired quality is achieved.

Sony has lived with the memory of its superior Beta format being overrun by the VHS consortium of firms. The final nail was hammered in when the movie firms stopped producing films in the Beta format. Sony has become a one-stop shop for entertainment so that, in the future, it can guarantee a supply of software for its hardware products. The Sony 8-mm camera/player system will not be one of the survivors unless software is available. By buying Columbia Pictures, Tri-Star Pictures, Columbia Pictures Television, and CBS Records, Sony has substantial control over such decisions.

Benefit: Enter a Profitable Business Area

A vertical integration decision can simply be motivated by an attractive profit potential. Thus, a chain of retail stores may simply be an attractive business investment, and the fact that it now is an outlet for a firm's product may be a relatively minor consideration. A variant is illustrated by Pentel, a Tokyo maker of pens and art supplies. Pentel developed for its own pen production needs assembly robots designed for small, high-precision jobs. It then exploited this development by selling the product to others.

Benefit: Enhancing Technological Innovation

Vertically integrated firms may have an advantage in achieving technological innovation. First, technical information is more readily shared between business units if they are in the same firm—thus, the R&D effort of an in-house supplier organization can be more focused. This contrasts with the usual inhibitions to the free exchange of information between two firms even if a positive, long-term relationship exists between them. Second, because the scale is larger, the potential is greater for innovation that can impact on several stages of the production process, producing larger returns. Third, vertical integration can facilitate the implementation of new processes or the introduction of new products. When two organizations are involved, a selling job may be required to implement innovations, and many barriers can become established.

Five types of potential benefits associated with vertical integration have been discussed. We now turn to the possible costs and disadvantages.

Cost: Operating Costs

Vertical integration can create potential operating costs that may outweigh the operating economies:[18]

- The added complexity and coordination required will put strains on the management system. There is no guarantee that associated costs will not exceed the transaction costs between two firms.
- The two integrated operations are unlikely to match exactly with respect to the capacity appropriate for efficient operation. As a result, one or the other will probably have excess capacity that will elevate costs.
- Without the discipline of outside price competition, there may be less incentive for cost control. After all, the supplying operation is assured of its customer.
- A transfer price simulating a market price is usually used to cover intrafirm transactions. The danger is that faulty information or organization pressures can cause this transfer price to be either too high or too low. In either case, suboptimal decisions can easily be stimulated. For example, if the transfer price was artificially low, the downstream operation would appear more profitable than it actually was, and thus an unadvisable expansion decision might be precipitated.

Cost: Management of a Different Business

A vertical integration move often involves adding an operation that requires organizational assets and skills which differ markedly from those for a firm's other business areas. As a result, the firm may not be suited to run the integrated operation effectively and competitively. Consider Pillsbury's efforts to manage Burger King successfully. Part of the difficulty was caused by differences in culture, personnel, and operations between fast food and the rest of Pillsbury's operations.

Cost: The Risk of Increased Commitment to a Business

The classic way to reduce risk is to avoid having too many eggs in one basket—to diversify. Vertical integration tends to increase the commitment and investment that are tied to a certain market. If that market is healthy, then integration may enhance profits. On the other hand, if the market turns down, integration may cause profits to be more depressed. Integration also raises exit barriers. If the business becomes weak, the additional investment and commitment created by integration will inhibit consideration of an exit alternative. Furthermore, if one operation becomes dependent on the other, it may be awkward to try to exit from one.

Cost: Reduced Flexibility

Vertical integration usually means that a firm is committed to an in-house supplier or customer.[19] Suppose that technology changes and it is necessary to change suppliers or suffer a substantial competitive disadvantage. The flexibility of changing suppliers may be limited because of a commitment made to an integration partner. Similarly, a decision to integrate into retailing may be regretted if customer preferences dictate that another channel is going to become dominant. There is often a trade-off between flexibility and commitment. Increased commitment provides the potential of higher profits but is associated with a reduction in flexibility, the ability to adapt to changing circumstances.

Costs: Becoming "Ingrown"

The process of actively dealing with suppliers or customers in the marketplace and anticipating supplier technological developments and new customer applications can be extremely healthy. The integrated firm with captive supplier-customer units has a reduced need for that process. Furthermore, there is the previously mentioned reduced pressure on cost control.

Alternatives to Integration

Several alternatives to integration exist. One, using long-term contracts or understandings, can be difficult to maintain as circumstances and power relationships change. Another integration alternative is quasi-integration whereby a relationship is established that lies between a contract and full ownership. Automobile firms that own the special tooling used by their suppliers provide one example.[20] Another example occurs in exclusive dealing agreements that link a manufacturer and a retail chain or distributor providing the needed information transfer and strategy coordination. Another quasi-integration example is a minority equity or debt commitment to another firm, such as Sears frequently does for its suppliers.

Are Integrated Firms More Profitable?

Robert Buzzell of Harvard studied 1649 businesses in the PIMS database to attempt to determine the impact on profitability of vertical integration, defined as value added as a percent of sales.[21]

Figure 12.3 illustrates this relationship. Although net profit as a percent of sales does increase with vertical integration, the return on investment (ROI) does not. The increase in investment that accompanies vertical integration counters the increases in profit. The figure suggests the intriguing concept that the most profitable businesses are at the extremes of the vertical integration spectrum. There is a V-shaped relationship between vertical integration and profitability. Thus, manufacturers should be wary of taking a middle course. The business that puts together systems and farms out component production will tend to minimize investment, seek out low prices, and have maximum flexibility. The heavily integrated firm will maximize the benefits of vertical integration. In the middle ground the benefits of both extremes may be lost.

SUMMARY

One available growth strategy is to grow within an existing product market by increasing market share or product usage. Increased product usage occurs by increasing usage frequency, the quantity used, or by finding new applications. A second growth strategy is to develop new products for an existing market. Product development can be based on adding product features, expanding the product line, developing new generation technologies, or adding different products that are sold to the same market. A third growth direction is market development, expanding the market either geographically or by targeting new market segments. A key consideration in product or market expansion or diversification is determining whether synergy will be created.

Vertical integration represents another growth direction. It can provide operating economies, improved access to supply or demand, im-

FIGURE 12.3   Vertical Integration and Profitability

Vertical Integration— Value Added as Percentage of Sales	Net Profit as Percentage of Sales	Net Profit as Percentage of Investment (ROI)	Number of Businesses
Under 40%	8%	26%	267
40–50%	8	22	341
50–60%	9	20	389
60–70%	10	22	338
Over 70%	12	24	314

SOURCE: Adapted from Robert D. Buzzell, "Is Vertical Integration Profitable?" *Harvard Business Review*, January–February 1983, p. 97.

proved control over supply or demand, an entry into a profitable business area, and a way to enhance the development and implementation of
technological innovations. On the other hand, it can also create operating
costs, problems associated with managing very different businesses,
increased risk, reduced flexibility, and the costs of being excessively
"ingrown." Alternatives to integration include long-term contracts,
quasi-integration, and partial integration. Firms with average levels of
vertical integration achieve somewhat better returns than businesses at
the extremes of the vertical integration spectrum.

FOOTNOTES

[1] This section draws on the excellent paper by Philip E. Hendrix, "Product/Service Consumption: Implications and Opportunities for Marketing strategy," Working Paper, Emory
University, 1986.

[2] Barnaby J. Feder, "Baking Soda Maker Strikes Again," *The New York Times*, June 16, 1990,
p. 17.

[3] Jack J. Honomichl, "The Ongoing Saga of 'Mother Baking Soda,'" *Advertising Age*,
September 20, 1982, pp. M2–M3.

[4] Linden A. Davis, Jr., "Market Positioning Considerations," *Product-Line Strategies*, New
York: The Conference Broad, pp. 37–39.

[5] Robert Hanson, "Angostura's Past Helps Revive Bitters," *Adweek's Marketing Week*, May
23, 1988, pp. 53–55.

[6] Robert L. Rose, "Image to Protect: Maytag's Acquisitions Don't Have the Reputation for
Quality Enjoyed by Its Washers," *Wall Street Journal*, January 31, 1991, p. B-1.

[7] Robert F. Hartley, *Marketing Mistakes*, 3rd ed., New York: Wiley, 1986, pp. 91–105.

[8] "The Peril in Financial Services," *Business Week*, August 20, 1984, pp. 52–56; "Sears
Roebuck's Struggling Financial Empire," *Fortune*, October 14, 1985, pp. 40–43; "Synergy
Works at American Express," *Fortune*, February 16, 1987, pp. 79–80; Michael Siconolfi,
"Dean Witter Proves an Asset to Sears Confounding Pundits," *Wall Street Journal*, March 15,
1991, p. 1–6.

[9] "Lenox: Capitalizing on Its Image to Launch New Luxury Lines," *Business Week*, October
19, 1981, p. 144.

[10] "A-B Set to Can Beverage Unit?" *Adweek's Marketing Week*, December 7, 1987, pp. 1, 6.

[11] *Advertising Age*, August 16, 1982, p. 1.

[12] "Rockwell International: Reaching for the Automotive Market Abroad," *Business Week*,
May 5, 1980, p. 87.

[13] Daniel Pearl, "Federal Express Finds Its Pioneering Formula Falls Flat Overseas," *Wall
Street Journal*, April 15, 1991, pp. A1–A6.

[14] David Kiley and Pak Melwani, "The Prince of Silk Moves into Packaged Goods," *Adweek's Marketing Week*, July 11, 1988, p. 17.

[15] "Kemper: Buying Brokerages to Keep the Competition at Bay," *Business Week*, May 3, 1982, p. 57.

[16] See Oliver E. Williamson, "Comparative Economic Organization," *Administrative Science Quarterly*, September 1991, and Oliver E. Williamson, "Transaction-Cost Economics: The Governance of Contractual Relations," *Journal of Law and Economics* 22, October 1979, pp. 233–261.

[17] David J. Teece, "Markets in Microcosm: Some Efficiency Properties of Vertical Integration," Working Paper, Stanford University, November 1981.

[18] Ajay Bhasin and Louis W. Stern, "Vertical Integration: Considerations of Efficiency, Risk, and Strategy," in Michael G. Harvey and Robert F. Lusch, eds., *Marketing Channels: Domestic and International Perspectives*, Norman: University of Oklahoma Printing Services, 1982.

[19] Michael E. Porter, *Competitive Strategy*, New York: The Free Press, 1980, p. 310.

[20] Williamson, "Comparative Economic Organization."

[21] Robert D. Buzzell, "Is Vertical Integration Profitable?" *Harvard Business Review*, January–February 1983, pp. 92–102.

13

DIVERSIFICATION

Tis the part of a wiseman to keep himself today for tomorrow, and not venture all his eggs in one basket.

Miguel de Cervantes

Put all your eggs in one basket and—WATCH THAT BASKET.

Mark Twain

A tobacco firm buys a frozen-food company, a cola firm enters the wine business, a chemical company goes into swimming pool supplies, or an aerospace firm starts making automobile parts. Such diversification moves represent both opportunities for growth and revitalization and the substantial risk of operating an unfamiliar business in a new context.

Diversification is the art of entering product markets different from those in which a firm is currently engaged. The two growth strategies discussed in Chapter 12, product expansion and market expansion, usually involve entry into new product markets, thus representing diversification. However, diversification can also involve both new products and new markets. A diversification strategy can be implemented by either an acquisition (or merger), or by starting a new business venture.

It is helpful to divide diversification into "related" diversification and "unrelated" diversification. A related diversification is one in which the two involved businesses have meaningful commonalities, which provide the potential to generate economies of scale or synergies based on an exchange of skills or resources. In a related diversification, the resulting combined business should be able to achieve improved ROI because of increased revenues, decreased costs, or reduced investment, which are attributable to the commonalities. As noted in Chapter 9, such commonalities can involve similar:

- Distribution channels
- Image and its impact on the market
- Sales or advertising effort
- Facilities
- Production processes
- R&D effort
- Operating systems
- Staff needs[1]

The product expansion growth strategy normally involves the same market and distribution system so it would qualify as a related diversification. The market expansion growth strategy is usually also a related diversification because it applies the same production technology and often a similar market and distribution system. Vertical integration is seldom a related diversification, however, because typically it lacks an area of commonality.

An important issue in any diversification decision is whether, in fact, there is a real and meaningful area of commonality that will affect the ultimate ROI. If such a meaningful commonality is lacking, the diversification may still be justifiable, but the rationale will need to be different.

Thus, the concept of a related diversification is more than an issue of definition. In the following section we consider the rationale and risks of related diversification and then those of unrelated diversification.

RELATED DIVERSIFICATION

Exchanging Skills and Resources

Related diversification provides the potential to attain synergies by the exchange or sharing of skills or resources. One business unit must have skills or resources that are "exportable" to another company or business unit. Thus, a first condition of successful related diversification is to identify skills or resources that are exportable or that are needed and can be "imported." The second condition is to find a partner or business unit that can either provide or use them. The third is to ascertain whether the organizational integration needed to accomplish such an exchange is feasible. Skills or resources that can be usefully imported or exported can take a variety of forms. In particular, they can be associated with any functional area such as marketing, production, or R&D.

Brand Name

One commonly found resource that is exportable is a strong established brand name like Hershey's, Sunkist, Coke, Puma, BMW, or Campbell Soup. A strong brand name can provide name familiarity that will help in the new-product tasks of acquiring awareness, generating trial purchases, and gaining distribution. It can take $50 to $100 million to establish a brand name for a new consumer brand.[2]

Often more important than name recognition is what the name means, the brand associations. As Figure 13.1 indicates, four types of associations are relevant in making brand extension decisions:[3]

- **An image of high (or low) perceived quality.** If the name IBM, Betty Crocker, or Heineken is attached to a new product, there will be a presumption that it will be a high-quality product, backed by a strong firm.

- **Attribute associations with the brand or product class that are helpful in the new context.** For example, Hiram Walker used the Häagen-Dazs name on one of its liquors to create associations with a product class (premium ice cream), which suggest it is rich and creamy and is used by upscale, discriminating consumers.

- **Attribute associations that would be negative in the new context.** For example, Heineken wine might be expected to taste like beer, Log

FIGURE 13.1   Brand Name Associations—Häagen-Dazs Candy

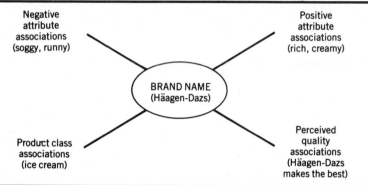

Cabin pancakes would be expected to be soggy, or a McDonald's Theme Park might be perceived as plastic, cheap, and dangerous.

- **Associations with a product class.** For example, to many people, Heineken means beer, whereas Carnation lacks a clear link to any one product class.

Three factors determine what associations will carry over into a new context:

1. **The strength of the attribute or quality associations in the existing context.** If these associations are weak to begin with, they will be weaker in the new context.

2. **The fit of a brand into the new context.** There needs to be a link such as a common use situation (hair care), user type (glamorous, upscale), functional benefits (speedy delivery), or an attribute (salty). Vaurnet sunglasses are associated with skiing and fashion, and thus a skiwear line as a brand extension would make sense, because it would share a common use context and involve the fashion attribute.

3. **Whether or not it is plausible to consider the brand in the new context.** Would the makers of the brand be perceived as having the expertise to make the new product class? Thus, a "fashion-driven firm" like Vaurnet would probably be able to make skiwear, because a fashion touch is the key. A movement by Vaurnet into skis might be stretching it, however. To the extent that the new brand context is implausible, the positive attribute and quality associations will be weak, but negative associations still may emerge.

A brand extension can potentially provide substantial support for a brand name by increasing its awareness level and by reinforcing its associations. For example, the Sunkist associations with oranges, health, and vitality are reinforced by the promotion of Sunkist juice bars and Sunkist vitamin C tablets. However, extensions also have the potential to damage a core brand by creating undesirable attribute associations or weakening those that exist. Thus, the Sunkist health image may be weakened by Sunkist fruit rolls. The strong product class associations of Kleenex and A-1 might be hurt if they were extended.

Perhaps the worst potential result of an extension is a foregone opportunity to create a new brand equity. Consider where P&G would be without Ivory, Camay, Dreft, Tide, Cheer, Joy, Pampers, Crest, Secret, Sure, Folger's, and Pringles and their other 70 or so brands. Suppose instead the firm sold P&G bar soap, P&G laundry detergent, P&G dishwashing detergent, P&G toothpaste, P&G deodorant, P&G coffee, and P&G potato snack.

Marketing Skills

A firm will often either possess or lack a strong skill in marketing for a particular market. Thus, a frequent motive to diversify is to export or import marketing skills. Black & Decker had developed and exploited throughout the 1980s an aggressive new products program (e.g., cordless screwdrivers and HandyChopper), effective consumer marketing (for names like Spacemaker, Dustbuster, and ThunderVolt cordless tools), and intensive customer service and dealer relations.[4] The acquisition of Emhart with its branded door locks, decorative faucets, outdoor lighting, and racks provided Black & Decker with an opportunity to apply its marketing skills and distribution clout to a firm that lacked a marketing culture.

Applying marketing skills is not always as easy as it appears. Philip Morris, having successfully rejuvenated Miller Beer that it had purchased in the early 1970s, attempted to similarly apply its marketing skills when it bought 7UP. The firm started by positioning 7UP as a caffeine-free soft drink, building on the "health" interests of consumers, and it spent hundreds of millions of dollars on such a campaign. Seven years later, in 1986, it gave up and sold the line to Pepsi-Cola. The problems that beset Philip Morris included the reaction of competitors who rushed caffeine-free drinks to the market, the power of existing distributors, and the limited appeal of lemon-lime drinks. Coca-Cola made a similar misjudgment when it created Wine Spectrum and failed in its efforts to overcome Gallo, in part because of Gallo's control over distribution. Coca-Cola eventually gave up, selling out to Seagram's. The experiences of Philip Morris and Coca-Cola illustrate the uncertainty of applying skills even in industries that seem well-suited on the surface.

Distribution Capacity

A firm may have a good product line but lack presence in a key distribution channel. Thus, Black & Decker's distribution strength helped provide a boost to the Emhart lines. The marriage between the drug firms Bristol-Myers and Squibb was motivated in part because Squibb had an established distribution operation in Europe that Bristol-Myers lacked[5] and Bristol-Myers had more presence in Japan and Latin America than did Squibb.

Linking an Innovative Product to a Sales/Service Capacity

A small company can often create or enter a market area and do well with an innovative product. As the market matures, however, the necessity for a strong service organization becomes more important. The smaller firm might then consider joining forces with a larger firm, with a service organization that can be adapted to the product involved. The larger firm would benefit from the innovative product and gain entry into a growth field. The smaller firm would, in turn, gain the needed service and a larger distribution network that was becoming critical to its continued viability.

Linking R&D and Product Development with Marketing

A firm may be highly skilled at R&D and new product development, but it may lack skills in either marketing or production. For example, a joint venture between Rhone-Poulenc, a French chemical giant, and Morton-Norwich was formed with Rhone supplying new ethical drugs in exchange for Morton's marketing skills in the United States.[6] Like many international joint ventures, this one eventually collapsed, with each partner believing that the other was not willing or able to deliver its part of the bargain.

Exploiting Excess Capacity

One type of resource that is often easily exchanged is excess capacity. A sales force may have the capacity to carry more lines, a retailer may have excess shelf space or sites, a factory may go unused during certain periods or have unused space, a computer system and support may be under-utilized, or a trucking firm may have unused space in its trucks. Often an operation needs to be staffed for peak demand only and during other periods excess capacity exists. If some way can be found to use it, a substantial, sustainable cost advantage could ensue. For example, multiple-screen theaters were an innovation that exploited excess capacity.

The Elusive Search for Synergy

The concept of a total communications firm that includes advertising, direct marketing, marketing research, public relations, and sales promotion was intended to generate synergy by effective cross-selling and by providing clients with more consistent coordinated communication efforts.[7] Young & Rubican has the "whole egg," whereas the Ogilvy Group promises a harmonious blend of services with "Ogilvy orchestrations."

Although there are some successes—AT&T business systems has attained a more consistent approach through its communication using "the right choice" theme—the difficulty of achieving hoped-for synergy is all too clear. Less than 10 percent of clients use more than one service and anecdotes about the problems abound. When Bristol-Myers used a Y&R direct marketing unit to help attack a problem with advertising, a competitive conflict between two Y&R units surfaced as each subtly hinted the other was less effective and that the budget should be shifted accordingly. Also, Foote Cone referred a client to a sales promotion unit that did not coordinate or perform well. The client became upset and that ended such referrals, for a time at least. A basic problem is that many organizations added to a communications firm are small, autonomous, not of comparable quality to the lead advertising firm, and do not have a culture of coordination.

An example of synergy based, in part, on exploiting excess capacity is the Los Angeles sports empire of Jerry Buss. Buss owns four sports teams, including the Lakers basketball team and the Kings hockey team, all of which play in his 17,500-seat Forum and appear on his Prime Ticket regional cable channel, which reaches nearly 1.6 million homes.[8] The teams provide a product for the Forum and the cable channel, both of which have excess capacity. Furthermore, the cable channel helps generate interest in the teams and other Forum events such as rock concerts.

The first step in exploiting excess capacity is to identify those assets that have utilization slack. The next step is to determine alternative uses for the excess capacity. Finally, the most promising uses should be evaluated.

Achieving Economies of Scale

Related diversification can sometimes provide economies of scale. Two smaller consumer products firms, for example, may not be able to afford an effective sales force, new product development or testing programs, or warehousing and logistics systems. However, the combination of these firms may be able to operate at an efficient level. Similarly, two firms, when combined, may be able to justify an expensive piece of automated production equipment.

Sometimes a critical mass is needed in order to be effective. For example, a specialized electronics firm may need an R&D effort, but R&D productivity may be low if it is not feasible to have several researchers who can interact.

Risks of Related Diversification

Even related diversification can be risky. There are three major problems.

- **First, relatedness and potential synergy simply do not exist.** Strategists often delude themselves that a synergistic justification exists by manipulating semantics. In 1968, for example, General Foods, frustrated with an FTC antitrust decision ordering it to avoid buying any firms marketing to supermarkets, bought Burger Chef, a chain of 700 fast-food restaurants.[9] The logic was that it was in a fast-growing industry and was "food-related." The fact was that this relatedness was of little value. General Food's efforts to manage Burger Chef were a disaster. In 1972 alone, an $83 million write-off had to be taken, many times the purchase price of $16 million.

- **Second, potential synergy may exist but is never realized because of implementation problems.** This happens when a diversification move involves integrating two organizations that have fundamental differences and/or because one of the two organizations lacks the ability or motivation to undertake programs necessary to make the diversification work. In Chapter 16 the implementation issue is discussed in more detail.

- **Third, possible violations of antitrust laws create an additional risk when an acquisition or merger is involved.** Ironically, as the degree of relatedness and synergy potential increase, so does the possibility of an antitrust problem.

UNRELATED DIVERSIFICATION

Unrelated diversification lacks commonality in markets, distribution channels, production technology, or R&D thrust to provide the opportunity for synergy through the exchange or sharing of assets or skills. The objectives are therefore mainly financial, to generate profit streams that are either larger, less uncertain, or more stable than they would otherwise be. Figure 13.2 summarizes the motivations for both unrelated and related diversification.

FIGURE 13.2   Motivations for Diversifications

RELATED DIVERSIFICATIONS	UNRELATED DIVERSIFICATIONS
• Exchange or share skills or assets, thereby exploiting: brand name marketing skills distribution capacity service operation R&D and new product capability excess capacity economies of scale	• Manage and allocate cash flow. • Obtain high ROI. • Obtain a "bargain" price. • Restructure a firm. • Reduce risk by operating in multiple product markets. • Tax benefits. • Obtaining liquid assets. • Vertical integration reasons. • Defending against a takeover. • Providing executive interest.

Manage and Allocate Cash Flow

Unrelated diversification can balance the cash flows of SBU entities. A firm which has many SBUs that merit investment might buy or merge with a cash cow to provide a source of cash. The acquisition of the cash cow may reduce the need to raise debt or equity over time, although if the cash cow is acquired, resources will need to be expended. ITT, for example, purchased Hartford Insurance in the 1970s in order to provide a source of cash for its many SBUs that had a net need for cash.

Conversely, a firm with a cash cow may enter new areas seeking growth opportunities or simply areas to generate future earnings if its core cash cow eventually falters. The tobacco firms of Philip Morris and Reynold's have used their enormous cash flows to buy a host of firms such as General Foods, Nabisco, and Del Monte. One motivation is to provide alternative core earning areas in case the tobacco cash cow is crippled by effective antismoking programs or by successful damage litigation.

Entering Business Areas with High ROI Prospects

A basic diversification motivation is to improve an ROI by moving into business areas with high growth and ROI prospects. The Heinz purchase of Weight Watchers in the late 1970s, discussed in Chapter 10, illustrates such a motivation.[10] The vision paid off. By 1989 Heinz was selling 210 different products, from salad dressings and yogurt to frozen desserts to pizza, under the Weight Watchers name and was making over $100 million per year (nearly what they paid for the business ten years earlier).

The motivation to enter attractive businesses is understandable when the present core business is declining in the face of adversity. Thus, tobacco companies have moved into the area of packaged goods. Seagram's facing declining liquor sales bought Tropicana Products even though it involved a completely different distribution system and retail environment.[11]

A study of 61 conglomerates showed that firms tended to acquire firms with a higher return, suggesting that a motivation for diversification is to enter business areas that are attractive with respect to growth and profitability.[12] Evidence also indicates that acquired firms tend to be in more R&D-intensive industries, and thus more growth-oriented, than acquiring firms.[13]

Obtaining a "Bargain" Price for a Business

Another way to improve ROI is to acquire a business at a "bargain" price so the investment involved is low and the associated ROI will therefore be high. As Chapter 14 discusses, bargains may indeed be available in declining industries when firms decide to exit at any price. However, there is substantial evidence in finance suggesting that when publicly traded stocks are involved, "bargain prices" are rare because the market is based on relatively detailed and dispersed information. In fact, evidence exists that acquired firms, on the average, sell for a premium of 10 to 50 percent, depending on the year analyzed.[14]

The Potential to Restructure a Firm

An acquisition can provide the basis for a restructuring of the acquired firm, the acquiring firm, or both.[15] The objective would be to change the thrust of a firm from one set of industries to another. Not incidentally, the thrust change may result in investors perceiving the firm to be in more attractive industries, thus causing its stock price to rise. For example, Esmark was dramatically restructured when it sold its oil and gas businesses and its Swift operation and concentrated the resulting assets on its consumer products' businesses.

The key is to identify firms that are undervalued with respect to their potential after a restructuring. One approach suggested by Booz Allen acquisition specialists is to group a firm's businesses into four categories:[15]

1. **Core businesses.** The core business might represent 25 to 60 percent of sales. Strategically, the business core should be strong and have some sustainable competitive advantages on which to build. The core business has probably been used to attempt diversification.

2. **Successful diversifications.** Those would be the firm's stars with strong positions in attractive markets.

3. **Unsuccessful diversifications.** An undervalued firm typically has a substantial proportion of sales in unsuccessful diversifications, which is a major drag on performance.

4. **Nonoperating investments.** These could be stock investments or physical assets carried below realizable market.

Unsuccessful diversifications and their effect on performance may generate associations and perceived risks that cause a firm to be undervalued. The core business, successful diversification, and nonoperating investments may be worth much more than the current firm as a whole, even if the unsuccessful diversifications were liquidated or divested. Another possibility is to spin off the core business, which by itself may be valued relatively highly, and thereby use the successful diversifications as a base to generate a new core business. If the original core business was in an industry that was not highly regarded by the stock market, then the revised core could be valued higher.

Restructuring has become controversial for two reasons. First, restructuring often is stimulated by outside investment interests that finance takeovers by having a firm assume a large debt. The surviving businesses are burdened with this debt and thus capacity to finance growth and change is greatly reduced. For example, Lucky stores went from being a firm with three healthy retail chains and little debt to one engaged only in food retailing with a massive debt load. Second, outside investors who restructure are accused of neglecting long-term business interests as they are driven to improve short-term performance and increase the price of a stock. Their short-run orientation may cause them to liquidate or milk portions of a business that are potential long-run assets. The takeover of a timber company, for example, resulted in a dramatic increase in tree cutting, which sharply enhanced profits at the expense, in some people's view, of the long-term value of the firm.

Reducing Risk

The reduction of risk can be another motivation for unrelated diversification. Heavy reliance on a single product line can stimulate a diversification move. Hershey's was almost totally dependent on the candy and confectionery business, a business that was vulnerable to an increased interest in health and health foods.[16] Thus, Hershey's purchased Friendly Ice Cream, a $200 million-a-year chain of family restaurants based in Massachusetts, and the Skinner Macaroni Company with the goal of making nonconfection revenues about 30 percent of sales. Of course, there is the real risk that the new business areas may be money-draining headaches, such as Mobil found out when it acquired Montgomery Ward.

Reducing risk can also lead to entering businesses that will counter or reduce the cyclical nature of existing earnings. Thus, Blount, a general contractor and farm equipment maker, purchased a specialty steel concern in an effort to develop three different business areas, each associated with a different business cycle.[17]

Stockholder Risk Versus Management Risk

Diversification may reduce the market risk facing a firm and thus protect the firm's employees, customers, and managers. Managers, in particular, face the loss of a job and reputation from a downturn in their business over which they may have no control, and thus may be motivated to diversify. However, risk reduction obtained from unrelated diversification is of no value to stockholders who are free to diversify by holding a portfolio of stocks. Based on the premise that stockholders are the only relevant stakeholders of a business, it can be argued that the reduction of risk is not a legitimate objective.

Even stockholders cannot diversify from "systematic risk," that portion of variation correlated with general economic conditions and measured by the beta of a business. Thus, a diversification that would reduce a firm's systematic risk would be of value to stockholders.

Tax Implications

Tax considerations can stimulate mergers or acquisitions of unrelated firms. Firms can accumulate large tax-loss carryovers, which they cannot exploit. Thus, Docutel, with a large series of losses from its automatic teller machines, purchased a profitable sweater manufacturer that could utilize these losses to reduce taxes.[18] Mergers have also been motivated by firms that have under-utilized tax incentives to make capital investments.

Obtaining Liquid Assets

A firm can become an attractive acquisition candidate because of substantial liquid assets that can be readily deployed or because of a low debt-to-equity ratio that provides the potential to support debt financing. Stevens compared 40 acquired firms with 40 comparably sized firms and found that the only statistically significant difference between the two groups was that the acquired firms had lower leverage ratios and higher liquidity than the other firms.[19]

Vertical Integration Motivations

A vertical integration is usually an unrelated diversification. In Chapter 12, some of the motivations that apply to vertical integration are discussed, such as obtaining operating economies, gaining access to or control of supply or demand, and enhancing technological innovation.

Defending Against a Takeover

The threat of an unfriendly takeover can lead to an acquisition. One firm bought a small banana company to generate an antitrust obstacle to a takeover by United Fruit. Martin Marietta responded to a takeover move by Bendix by attempting to buy Bendix with the help of a third firm, United Technologies. The complex and expensive maneuvering ended with a fourth company, Allied Corporation, buying Bendix, while Martin Marietta remained independent.

Providing Executive Interest

For the executives making the decision, diversification can be stimulating. It can also lead to the prestige of a larger organization. Wayne I. Boucher interviewed in depth 14 experts on mergers as to the motivations involved.[20] One conclusion was that enhancement of personal power as measured by the sales volume controlled by a chief executive may be a moderately important motivation in merger decisions. Another related conclusion is that the merger decisions are ultimately made by one person, the CEO.

An analysis in *Fortune* of Beatrice Foods suggested that a stock buyback was definitely indicated, because the firm's earnings were at 14.4 percent of its stock price.[21] However, Beatrice, a sprawling conglomerate with over 400 profit centers and 9000 products, continued instead to buy diverse firms. In early 1982, for example, Beatrice bought Northwest Industries, which owned the Coca-Cola Bottling Company of Los Angeles, for $580 million, which was 22 times its earnings. The fact that diversification activity is more stimulating and interesting than stock buybacks may account for the Beatrice moves.

Risks of Unrelated Diversification

The very concept of an unrelated business, where by definition there is no possibility to improve that business through synergy, suggests risk and difficulty. Many knowledgeable people have made blanket statements warning against unrelated diversification. Peter Drucker claims that all successful diversification requires a common core or unity represented by common markets, technology, or production processes.[22] He states that without such a unity core, diversification never works; financial ties alone are insufficient. Among the major risks are:

- Attention is diverted from the core business.
- Managing the new business is difficult.
- The new business is overvalued.

Unrelated diversification, if unsuccessful, may actually damage the original core business by diverting attention and resources from it. Quaker Oats embarked on an aggressive acquisition program in the early 1970s, going into toys and theme restaurants.[23] In the process, however, the company allowed its core business areas to deteriorate—the new product effort suffered and the share and shelf facings fell as a result.

A firm's potential for difficulties in managing a diversification is magnified when an unrelated business is involved. Numerous firms have found they could not manage a diversification, especially when an acquired firm is involved. The new business may require assets, skills, and an organizational culture that differs from that of the core business. Furthermore, a skilled, valued management team in an acquired company might leave and be difficult to replace.

A business area might be incorrectly evaluated. For example, environmental threats may be overlooked or misjudged. If an acquisition is involved, its strategic liabilities, weaknesses, and problems may be undiscovered or miscalculated. American Can in 1978 purchased Sam Goody Inc., a record store chain, after extensive financial analysis, only to be stunned two years later when top Goody officials were indicted for dealing in counterfeit records and tapes.[24] General Host, a food store and baked goods firm, acquired Cudahy, the meat-packing firm, just before its plant and methods were made virtually obsolete by new packers with highly automated plants.[25] National Intergroup, with steel and oil as its core businesses, bought a drug wholesaler, only to find a price war was starting and that a project to sell computer services to druggists and the Ben Franklin chain was a disaster.[26]

In an interesting study reported in *Fortune*, the 10 largest mergers of 1971 were evaluated 10 years later.[27] With respect to estimated 1981 earnings per share, half of the firms would have been better off without the acquisitions. Furthermore, only three of the acquisitions had returns on investment exceeding 10 percent, as compared with the 13.8-percent median return for the Fortune 500 companies. An interesting observation was that the acquiring firms were, on the whole, bad investments during the same period. Half actually had a negative return. This performance may reflect the quality of management decisions, or it may simply reflect unfavorable conditions that the acquisitions were designed to alleviate.

Performance of Diversified Firms

Although it is surely true that individual efforts to expand into new product markets that appear attractive have been successful, the aggregate "on average" record, according to dozens of studies, is somewhat discouraging especially with respect to a return on asset measures. In an influential study, Richard Rumelt, a policy professor at UCLA, attempted to compare related diversification strategies with less related and unrelated diversification.[28] He categorized a sample of Fortune 500 firms as to whether each firm was

- "related-constrained," all of its component businesses are related through a common skill or asset (e.g., General Foods)
- "related-linked," where only one-to-one relationships are required between businesses (e.g., General Electric)
- "unrelated"

Rumelt found that the level of diversification among the Fortune 500 companies was high, around two-thirds. He also showed that the related-constrained strategy was the highest in performance, followed by the related-linked, and finally by the unrelated. Another study showed that 50 related diversifications in the 1975 to 1984 period had a significantly higher ROA than 20 unrelated diversified firms.[29]

Michael Porter examined 2021 acquisitions made in new industries by 33 large diversified U.S. companies from 1950 to 1980 and found that over half were divested by 1986.[30] Furthermore, of the 931 acquisitions that were unrelated 74 percent were divested.

ENTRY STRATEGIES

When the decision is made to enter a new product market, the entry strategy becomes critical.[31] Figure 13.3 summarizes seven alternative strategies with their advantages and disadvantages.

The most common entry routes are internal development and acquisition. Developing a new business internally means that a concept, strategy, and team can be created without the limitations, liabilities, or acquisition cost represented by an existing acquired business. An internal venture is a variant in which a separate entity with the existing firm is established, so that the new business will not be constrained by existing organizational culture, systems, and structure. IBM's PC venture, in which the IBM PC was developed and marketed in a separate organizational entity in a remarkably short time, is a visible example.

The acquisition route saves calendar time. By one estimate, the average time for a start-up business to break even is eight years.[32] An acquisition can mean that a firm becomes an established player in a matter of

FIGURE 13.3 Entry Strategies

Entry Strategy	Major Advantages	Major Disadvantages
Internal development	Uses existing resources Avoids acquisition cost especially if unfamiliar with product/market	Time lag Uncertain prospects
Internal ventures	Use existing resources May keep talented entrepreneurs	Mixed success record Can create internal stresses
Acquisitions	Saves calendar time Overcomes entry barriers Problem of integrating two organizations	Costly—usually Buy redundant assets
Joint ventures or alliances	Technological/marketing unions can exploit small/large firm synergies Distribute risk	Potential for conflict in operations between firms Danger of value of one firm reduced over time
Licensing from others	Rapid access to technology Reduced financial risk	Will lack proprietary technology and technological skills Will be dependent on licensor
Educational acquisitions	Provide window and initial staff	Risk of departure of entrepreneurs
Venture capital and nurturing	Can provide window on new technology or market	Unlikely alone to be a major stimulus of firm growth
Licensing to others	Rapid access to a market Low cost/risk	Will lack knowledge/ control of market Will be dependent on licensee

Source: Adapted from Edward B. Roberts and Charles A. Berry, "Entering New Businesses: Selecting Strategies for Success," *Sloan Management Review*, Spring 1985, pp. 3–17.

weeks. Perhaps more important, it means that substantial entry barriers such as distribution or brand name recognition are overcome. A variant is an educational acquisition in which a small firm is acquired that is not established as a major force, but will provide a window into the technology or market that will provide knowledge, experience, and a base from which to grow. For example, Procter & Gamble indicated that its acquisition of the Tender Leaf Tea brand is "an initial learning opportunity in a growing category of the beverage business."[33]

The other options shown in Figure 13.3 represent reduced risk and commitment, as well as a reduced chance that the route will lead to an established business supported by SCAs. A joint venture will share the risk with others and provide one or more missing and needed assets and skills. For example, a small firm with technology could enter into a joint venture with a larger firm with financial resources and access to distribution. Licensing a technology provides a fast way to overcome one entry barrier, but will make it difficult to gain control of that same technology in the future. Both of these entry options are important in international business contexts and are discussed in detail in Chapter 15. An alternative to a joint venture is an alliance in which the parties share assets to attack a market. Sony, for example, has cooperative technology-sharing arrangements with a host of small high-tech firms that serve to keep Sony on the cutting edge of technology and provide the small firms with access to Sony's production, engineering, and marketing assets.

The lowest involvement options are to license a technology to others to make and market or to enter into a business as a venture capital investor. General Electric and Union Carbide are among firms that have made minority investments in young and growing high-tech enterprises in order to secure some relationship to a new technology. Both licensing and becoming a venture capital investor offer the potential to increase involvement over time if the business does well and, in the meantime, to control any risk.

Selecting the Right Entry Strategy

Roberts and Berry suggest that the selection of the right entry strategy depends on the level of a firm's familiarity with the product market to be entered.[34] They define familiarity along two dimensions: (1) market and (2) technology or service embodied in the product.

With respect to market factors, three levels of familiarity are defined:

● **Base.** Existing products are sold within this market.

● **New/familiar.** The company is familiar with the market because of extensive research, the presence of experienced staff, or by having links with the market as a customer.

- **New/unfamiliar.** Knowledge of and experience with the market are lacking.

An analogous set of three levels of familiarity with the technologies or services embodied in the product is set forth:

- **Base.** The technology or service is embodied within existing products.

- **New/familiar.** The company is familiar with the technology because of work in related technologies, an established R&D effort in the technology, or extensive focused research in the technology.

- **New/unfamiliar.** Knowledge of and experience with the technology are lacking.

The basic suggestion is that as the level of familiarity on these two dimensions declines, the commitment level should be reduced. Fig-

FIGURE 13.4 Optimal Entry Strategies

Market factors			
New unfamiliar	Joint ventures	Venture capital or educational acquisitions	Venture capital or educational acquisitions
New familiar	Internal market developments or acquisitions (or joint ventures)	Internal ventures or acquisitions or licensing	Venture capital or educational acquisitions
Base	Internal base developments (or acquisitions)	Internal product developments or acquisitions or licensing	Joint ventures
	Base	New familiar	New unfamiliar

Technologies or services embodied in the product

SOURCE: Adapted from Edward B. Roberts and Charles A. Berry, "Entering New Businesses: Selecting Strategies for Success," *Sloan Management Review*, Spring 1985, pp. 3–17.

ure 13.4 shows the baseline entry strategy recommendations that follow from a familiarity assessment. Of course, there will be contexts in which a high-commitment approach in the unfamiliar/unfamiliar cell will make sense; Roberts and Berry suggest, on the basis of experience and theory, that substantial risk is associated with such an approach and the option of gaining familiarity should be seriously considered.

SUMMARY

Related diversification involves the potential to attain synergies by the exchange or sharing of skills or resources, whereas such potential is largely lacking in unrelated diversification. Figure 13.2 summarizes the motivation of both diversification routes. The major risks of related diversification are (1) that implementation difficulties will prevent the synergies from being realized and (2) the synergies do not exist in the first place. The management problems and potential for mistakes are magnified when an unrelated business is involved. Studies have found that firms engaged in unrelated diversification tend, on the average, to underperform other firms.

Figure 13.3 illustrates a variety of ways to enter a market besides acquisition and internal development. When the market and technology are unfamiliar, it is especially risky to attempt an entry requiring a large commitment.

FOOTNOTES

[1] In an empirical study of related versus unrelated diversification, Richard P. Rumelt suggested that a related diversification would involve similar markets and distribution systems, production processes, or science-based R&D. Richard P. Rumelt, *Strategy, Structure, and Economic Performance*, Boston: Division of Research, Harvard Business School, 1974.

[2] "New? Improved?" *Business Week*, October 21, 1985, p. 108.

[3] David A. Aaker, *Managing Brand Equity*, New York: The Free Press, 1991, Chapter 9.

[4] Michael J. McDermott, "The House That Nolan's Building," *Adweek's Marketing Week*, August 14, 1989, pp. 20–22.

[5] "Marriage Becomes Bristol-Myers Squibb," *Business Week*, December 3, 1990, p. 138.

[6] "Morton-Norwich: Pouring Cash into Chemicals and Household Goods," *Business Week*, May 3, 1982, p. 56.

[7] Drawn, in part, from Joanne Lipam, "Ad Firms Falter on One-Stop Shopping," *Wall Street Journal*, December 1, 1988, p. B1.

[8] "Who's the Biggest Sport in L.A.? Jerry Buss," *Business Week*, March 16, 1987, pp. 72–76.

[9] Robert F. Hartley, *Marketing Mistakes*, 3rd ed., Columbus: Grid Publishing, 1986, pp. 155–171.

[10] Aaker, *Managing Brand Equity*, Chapter 5.

[11] Nancy Youman, "So Far, So Good for Seagram's Beverage Shot," *Adweek's Marketing Week*, June 3, 1990, pp. 54–55.

[12] R. M. Melicher and D. F. Rush, "Evidence on the Acquisition-Related Performance of Conglomerate Firms," *Journal of Finance* 29, March 1974, pp. 1941–1949.

[13] M. Gort, "An Economic Disturbance Theory of Mergers," *Quarterly Journal of Economics* 83, November 1969, pp. 624–642; J. J. McGowan, "International Comparisons of Merger Activity," *Journal of Law and Economics* 14, April 1971, pp. 233–250.

[14] James W. Bradley and Donald H. Korn, "The Changing Role of Acquisitions," *The Journal of Business Strategy* 2, Spring 1982, pp. 30–42.

[15] Michael G. Allen, Alexander R. Oliver, and Edward H. Schwallie, "The Key to Successful Acquisitions," *Journal of Business Strategy* 2, Fall 1981, pp. 14–24.

[16] "Hershey: Joining with Friendly to Diversify Away from Chocolate," *Business Week*, January 29, 1979, p. 188.

[17] "Blount: Building More Than Buildings to Broaden Its Base," *Business Week*, August 6, 1979, p. 68.

[18] Docutel Corporation, a case appearing in Derek F. Abell and John S. Hammond, *Strategic Market Planning*, Englewood Cliffs, N.J.: Prentice-Hall, 1979, pp. 65–102.

[19] D. L. Stevens, "Financial Characteristics of Merged Firms: A Multivariate Analysis," *Journal of Financial and Quantitative Analysis* 8, March 1973, pp. 149–158.

[20] Wayne I. Boucher, "The Process of Conglomerate Merger," prepared for the Bureau of Competition, Federal Trade Commission, June 1980.

[21] Geoffrey Colvin, "The Bigness Cult's Grip on Beatrice Foods," *Fortune*, September 20, 1982, pp. 120–129.

[22] Peter Drucker, "The Five Rules of Successful Acquisition," *The Wall Street Journal*, October 15, 1981, p. 16.

[23] "Quaker Oats Retreats to Its Food Lines," *Business Week*, February 25, 1980, p. 153.

[24] "American Can: Diversification Brings Sobering Second Thoughts," *Business Week*, March 24, 1980, p. 130.

[25] Arthur M. Louis, "The Bottom Line on Ten Big Mergers," *Fortune*, May 3, 1982, pp. 84–89.

[26] Gregory L. Miles, "National Intergroup: How Pete Love Went Wrong," *Business Week*, March 6, 1989, pp. 56–64.

[27] Louis, "The Bottom Line."

[28] Richard Rumelt, "Diversity, Strategy and Profitability," *Strategic Management Journal* 3, 1982, pp. 359–369.

[29] Paul G. Simmonds, "The Combined Diversification Breadth and Mode Dimensions and the Performance of Large Diversified Firms," *Strategic Management Journal*, Vol. 11, No. 6, 1990, pp. 399–410.

[30] Michael E. Porter, "From Competitive Advantage to Corporate Strategy," *Harvard Business Review*, May–June, 1987, pp. 43–59.

[31] Edward B. Roberts and Charles A. Berry, "Entering New Businesses: Selecting Strategies for Success," *Sloan Management Review*, Spring 1985, pp. 3–17.

[32] Ralph Biggadike, "The Risky Business of Diversification," *Harvard Business Review*, May–June 1979, pp. 102–111.

[33] Procter & Gamble Company, 1983 Annual Report, Cincinnati, Ohio, 1984, p. 5.

[34] Roberts and Berry, "Entering New Businesses."

14

STRATEGIES IN DECLINING AND MATURE MARKETS

Anyone can hold the helm when the sea is calm.

Pubilius Syrus

Where there is no wind, row.

Portuguese proverb

Strategic planning is often associated with a search for healthy growing markets and the development of strategies to penetrate those markets. However, as the discussion in Chapter 5 makes clear, there is a variety of risks in high-growth contexts, including the possibility that a market can be crowded with competitors, each trying to find a niche. On the other hand, declining markets as well as mature markets can represent real opportunities for a business following the right strategy, in part because they are not as attractive to competitors. Thus, declining markets are not always to be avoided.

Of course, a competitor in a declining market will attempt to obtain SCAs and compete successfully. In a market characterized by zero or negative growth, however, the options of milking and even exiting often should be considered. The portfolio models may put them forth as baseline alternatives. Thus, it is important to understand these options as well.

In this chapter several strategic alternatives especially relevant to declining markets are considered:

1. Create a growth context by revitalizing the industry so that it becomes a growth industry or by focusing on a growth submarket.
2. Be the profitable survivor in the industry by dominating the market, thus encouraging others to exit.
3. Invest only to maintain position and look to other business areas for growth.
4. Milk or harvest—withdrawing resources so that they can be invested elsewhere.
5. Exit or liquidate, salvaging existing assets.

CREATING GROWTH IN DECLINING INDUSTRIES

An implicit assumption surrounding situations without apparent growth prospects is that the existing industry participants have fully exploited the market potential. If that assumption is untrue, a dramatic opportunity exists for a business that participates in revitalizing the industry and assumes a commanding position in a new growth context. As suggested by Figure 14.1, industry revitalization can be created by new markets, new products, new applications, revitalized marketing, government-stimulated growth, and the exploitation of growth submarkets.[1]

New Markets

An obvious way to generate growth is to move into a new market area with the potential for new growth. The market may not have been ready

FIGURE 14.1   Revitalizing a Stagnant Market

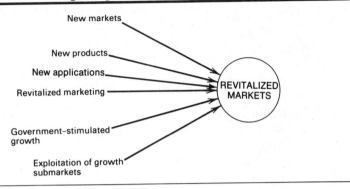

New markets

New products

New applications

Revitalized marketing

REVITALIZED MARKETS

Government-stimulated growth

Exploitation of growth submarkets

for a product; or its price may have not been appropriate for the market; or perhaps no firm considered the market. In any case, it represents untapped sales potential for the industry.

Some industries have seen international expansion fuel growth. Barbie, for example, has multiplied its overseas business nearly sevenfold to $700 million during the 1980s.[2] It found substantial growth in Europe and is looking to Eastern Europe for more. Some consumer products such as appliances, farm equipment, or consumer electronics evolve naturally from the most developed countries to the least developed countries.

A firm can look to new segments. Texas Instruments designed a calculator for women, a neglected market in a mature product category, despite the fact that 60 percent of buyers are women.[3] The new calculator, termed the Nuance, looked like a compact with a latch-key cover in either purple or soft beige. Its rubber keys were contoured for comfort and staggered so that long nails would not create double strokes. The result was a spurt of growth.

New Products

Sometimes a dormant industry can be revitalized by a product that makes obsolete the existing installed base and accelerates the replacement cycle. Such a rebirth occurred in the home audio market in the early 1980s, after it had been stagnant for a decade.[4] Compact disks were perhaps the major factor. By providing the ability to upgrade the sound of an audio system, they not only generated sales but also stimulated users to upgrade their speakers and receivers as well. The advent of stereo TV sets was also a factor. U.S. stereo sales moved to a growth rate of around 10 percent in the mid–1980s.

New Applications

A new application for a product can stimulate new industry growth. In Chapter 12, the graphic example of baking soda and its use as a deodorizer is given. The cranberry industry has created new growth by finding new recipes for its product and encouraging its use outside holiday meals. The small refrigerator opened up new sources of sales in the office or student dormitory.

The task is to find and exploit new applications. The concept of lead user discussed in Chapter 3 can be helpful. Find out how customers, especially those customers who have concerns that reflect emerging trends, are using the product.

Revitalized Marketing

A product class may be revived by a fresh marketing approach, changing the distribution channel by using hardware stores or direct selling, selling the product to firms to use as a giveaway promotion item, changing the pricing structure, or perhaps by changing the advertising. A new advertising campaign caused the sale of a dormant headache product to suddenly start growing at an annual double-digit pace.[5] The stimulus was a marketing effort focusing on the blue-collar Southeast. The original packaging and bitter taste were restored after efforts to improve it did not affect sales. The key, however, was advertising that featured testimonials from workers with thick southern accents and associations with events such as bass-fishing tournaments and minor league baseball.

Government-Stimulated Growth

There is an old adage, "If all else fails, change the rules of the game." Strategically, the idea is to change the environment so that industry sales will be enhanced. A government body can provide incentives for change such as providing tax incentives for installing home insulation or refurbishing low-income housing. Or a government might dictate that air bags shall be installed in cars or gasoline engines restricted, thus stimulating new industries.

In the 1970s, recycling plants designed to solve the waste management problem failed for a variety of reasons, some of which were technological. More recently, however, a technologically old approach of converting refuse into energy by burning it has become a growth area, in large part because of government regulation of landfill sites and tax incentives provided to those with alternatives to dumping trash.[6]

Look to Growth Submarkets

Some firms have been successful in declining or mature industries because they have been able to focus on growth subareas, pockets of demand that are healthy and perhaps even growing nicely. The superdry, nonalcoholic, and microbrewery brands are all growing nicely in the mature beer market. Convertibles are again growth segments in the automobile industry.

Firms facing a declining market or extreme price competition can sometimes exploit their installed customer base to create a stable or growth service or support business. Westinghouse Electric Power Systems Company, faced with a decline of the electrical power industry, compensated by expanding its service and replacement parts business, developing an "on-location" repair capability that provided a stable business base.[7]

Sometimes a growth submarket has the same visibility and risks of any growth market, but it also can be neglected because its identity is subtle or because it is small and emerging. The neglected growth submarkets are attractive because they are likely to receive less competitive attention.

BE THE PROFITABLE SURVIVOR[8]

The conventional advice is to avoid investing in declining markets, to milk or exit businesses that are trapped in a declining situation. However, an aggressive alternative in a declining industry is to invest in order to obtain or strengthen a leadership position. The concept is that a strong survivor may be profitable, in part because of competition that is milking its business and in part because the investment might be relatively low. The cornerstone of this strategy is to encourage competitors to exit. Toward that end a firm can:

- Be visible about its commitment to be the surviving leader in the industry.

- Raise the costs of competing by price reductions or increased promotion.

- Introduce new products and cover new segments, thus making it more difficult for a competitor to find a profitable niche. Thus, General Foods, the maker of Maxwell House, Sanka, and Brim, introduced a line of international coffees, including Orange Cappuccino and Café Vienna, to serve a small specialized segment.

- Reduce competitors' exit barriers by assuming long-term contracts, supplying spare parts and servicing their products in the field, or by supplying them with products. An example of the latter would be a retailer that was doing its own baking. A regional bakery could supply private-label products to the retailer, thus enabling it to exit.

- Create a national, dominant brand in a declining industry that is fragmented. Chesebrough-Ponds, for example, bought Ragu Packing, a regional spaghetti-sauce maker, in 1969.[9] Making the brand national moved Ragu from $20 million in sales in 1969 to more than $200 million in 1979, which represented a 62.8 percent market share. This was accomplished in the context of a food market that was growing 2 percent annually.

- Purchase a competitor's market share and/or its production capacity. This is the ultimate removal of a competitor's exit barriers. It further removes the possibility that a tired competitor will be taken over by a more vigorous organization.

Purchasing Competitors

The purchase of a competitor in a mature or declining industry can have a significant benefit, if the competitor can be purchased at an attractive price. Often a competitor who has decided to divest will be motivated or have no option but to sell at a price based on the book or market value of its assets, which may be a small fraction of what the typical investment levels have been for the industry. The result can be a very attractive return on investment.

Kunz, a maker of passbooks for financial institutions, operated in a declining industry caused by the growth of electronic banking, which had made its product superfluous.[10] Kunz was able to buy competitor assets under book value, and the payback period was sometimes measured in months. Because the asset value was so low and because the expertise to run the business was in place, the return on investment turned out to be extremely high. In the late 1980s, Kunz was having record years in a business area others had written off as all but dead decades earlier.

White Industries, as noted in Chapter 11, has become the third largest appliance manufacturer by buying such names as Kelvinator, Westinghouse, Philco, and Frigidaire from firms that were strongly motivated to exit. As a result, White bought them at very low cost. After quickly streamlining the product lines and applying proven cost-reduction techniques, White turned around each money-losing operation in a matter of months.

HOLD OR MAINTAIN POSITION

There are several alternatives to investing aggressively in a declining situation in order to become dominant and to encourage others to exit. An extreme alternative is to exit the business at any cost. Another is to milk the business by minimizing investment not absolutely needed to maintain operations and to maximize cash flow out of the business.

Still another alternative is to allow enough investment to hold or maintain the position of a firm but to avoid growth-motivated investment. A hold strategy involves an adequate level of investment and operating support to maintain product quality, production facilities, and customer loyalty. In terms of the BCG matrix, a distinction might be made between weak and strong cash cows. A strong cash cow probably would warrant a hold strategy rather than a milk strategy. A variant is a selective hold strategy, whereby a hold strategy is employed in some portion of the business while other portions are milked or allowed to grow.

A hold strategy is appropriate when an industry is declining in an orderly way, pockets of enduring demand exist, price pressures are not extreme, a firm has exploitable assets or skills, and a business contributes by its presence to other business units in the firm. A hold strategy would be preferable to an invest strategy when an industry lacks growth opportunities and a strategy of increasing share would risk triggering competitive retaliation. The hold strategy can be a long-term strategy to manage a cash cow or an interim strategy employed until the uncertainties of an industry are resolved.

A problem with the hold strategy is that if conditions change, reluctance or slowness to reinvest may result in lost market share. The failure of the two largest can manufacturers, American and Continental, to invest in the two-piece can process when it was developed caused them to lose substantial market share. They were engaged in diversification efforts and were attempting to avoid investments in their "cash cow" can business.

Hayes and Garvin, cited in Chapter 8, suggest that a national decline in reinvestment as measured by R&D spending, the book value of plant and equipment, and other measures is caused by a bias toward disinvestment policies.[11] They believe the bias is the result of artificially high hurdle rates, undue pessimism about long-term prospects, a failure to account for the residual values of investments, and a failure to realize the extent to which existing capital stock is deteriorating. The net result of this bias against reinvestment can turn a hold strategy into an unintentional milking strategy.

MILK OR HARVESTING

A milk or harvest strategy aims to recover cash quickly. Investment and operating expenses are reduced in order to enhance cash flow. It differs from a hold strategy in that a reduction in sales and market share is acceptable, even if it ultimately means that a business will fail. The underlying assumptions are that the firm has better uses for the funds, that the involved business is not crucial to the firm either financially or synergistically, and that milking is feasible because sales will decline in an orderly way.

It is useful to distinguish between a fast and a slow milking plan. Fast milking involves sharp reductions in operating expenditures and per-haps price increases to maximize short-term cash flow, and to minimize the possibility that any additional money be invested in the business. A fast milking strategy will accept the risk of a sharp sales decline precipi-tating a market exit. Slow milking involves sharply reducing a long-term investment in plant, equipment, and R&D, but only gradually reducing expenditures in operating areas such as marketing and service. Slow milking attempts to maximize the flow of cash over time by prolonging and slowing the decline.

A classic example of a slow milking strategy was that of Chase & Sanborn coffee.[12] In 1879, Chase & Sanborn became the first American company to pack roasted coffee in sealed cans. In 1929, it combined with Royal Baking Powder and Fleischmann to form a company called Stan-dard Brands. During the 1920s and 1930s, Chase & Sanborn advertised heavily and dominated the coffee industry. "The Chase & Sanborn hour," starring Edgar Bergen and Charlie McCarthy, was one the most popular radio shows of its time. After World War II, instant coffee and General Foods' Maxwell House both appeared. Instead of fighting the heavy advertising of Maxwell House, Chase & Sanborn chose a milking strategy. Over the years, advertising support for the brand was reduced until, finally, advertising was stopped entirely. In 1981, Standard Brands merged with Nabisco, which then sold off the coffee business for about $15 million to a small Miami firm, General Coffee. Standard Brands also followed the slow milking strategy with Royal Pudding when that prod-uct was faced with another General Foods brand, Jell-O.

Conditions Favoring a Milking Strategy.   Several situation-related charac-teristics can lead to a milking strategy rather than a hold or exit strategy:

1. If the decline rate is pronounced and unlikely to change but not excessively steep. If there are pockets of enduring demand that will ensure that the decline rate will not suddenly become precipitous.

2. The price structure will be stable at a level that allows profits to be made among the efficient firms.

3. The business position is weak but has enough customer loyalty, perhaps in a limited part of the market, to generate sales and profits in a milking mode. The risk of losing relative position with a milking strategy is low.

4. The business is not central to the current mission of the firm.

5. A milking strategy can be successfully managed.

Implementation Problems.   The implementation of a milking strategy can be difficult. One of the most serious problems is that a suspicion by employees and customers that a milking strategy is being employed can create a momentum of its own, which may upset the whole strategy. In fact, the line between a milking strategy and abandonment is sometimes very thin. Customers may lose confidence in a firm's product and employee morale may suffer. Competitors may attack more vigorously. All these possibilities can create a sharper-than-anticipated decline. To minimize such effects, it is helpful to keep a milking strategy as inconspicuous as possible.

Another serious problem is the difficulty with placing and motivating a manager in a milking situation. Most SBU managers do not have the orientation, the background, or the skills to engage in a successful milking strategy. Adjusting performance measures and rewards appropriately can be difficult for both an organization and the managers involved. A reasonable solution, to use a milking specialist, is often not feasible simply because such manager types are rare. Most firms rotate managers through different types of situations, and the career paths simply are not geared to creating specialists in executing milking strategies.

When the Premises Are Wrong.   Another concern is that the premises on which a milking strategy is based turn out to be wrong. The information regarding market prospects, a competitor move, a cost projection, or another relevant factor could have been erroneous.

A resurgence in product classes that were seemingly dead or in terminal decline gives pause. Oatmeal, for example, has experienced a sharp increase in sales because of its cost and associations with naturalness and health. In men's apparel, suspenders and pocket watches are appearing more frequently. Fountain pens, invented in 1884, were virtually killed by the appearance in 1939 of the ballpoint which became the disposable accessory of a disposable-minded society.[13] However, the combination of a desire for prestige and nostalgia provided a major comeback for the high-end fountain pen. In the late 1980s, Cartier was selling more fountain pens than ballpoints and industry sales have seen years in which sales doubled. One advantage of milking rather than divesting is that it may be possible to detect such a resurgence and change strategies.

DIVESTMENT OR LIQUIDATION

As Figure 14.2 suggests, when a business environment and business position are both unfavorable, then the final alternative, divestment or liquidation, is precipitated. Among the conditions that would suggest an exit decision rather than a milking decision are the following:

1. If the decline rate is rapid and accelerating and there are no pockets of enduring demand that are accessible to the business.

2. The price pressures are anticipated to be extreme, caused by determined competitors with high exit barriers and by the lack of brand loyalty and product differentiation; thus, a milking strategy is unlikely to be profitable for anyone.

3. The business position is weak; there exists one or more dominant competitors that have achieved irreversible advantage. The business is now losing money and future prospects are dim.

4. The firm's mission changes as the role of the business becomes superfluous or even unwanted.

5. Exit barriers can be overcome.

A set of exit barriers can inhibit an exit decision. In particular:

FIGURE 14.2   Strategies for Declining or Stagnant Industries

		Business position in key segments	
		Strong	Weak
Industry environment Rate of decline Pockets of demand Price pressure	Favorable	Invest or hold	Milk or exit
	Unfavorable	Milk or exit	Exit

Source: Adapted from Kathryn Rudie Harrigan and Michael E. Porter, "End-Game Strategies for Declining Industries," *Harvard Business Review*, July–August 1987, p. 119.

- Specialized assets such as plant and equipment that have little use to others.

- Long-term contracts with suppliers and with labor groups, which are expensive to break.

- Commitments to provide spare parts and service backup to retailers and customers. For example, in the 1960s, many vacuum-tube manufacturers such as RCA also made TV sets that used specialized tubes.[14] The customers' assumption that RCA would supply parts provided a substantial exit barrier for the RCA vacuum-tube business.

- An exit decision may affect the reputation and operation of other firm businesses. Thus, RCA in the 1960s was also concerned with the impact that a decision to back away from supporting its TV sets would have on future TV business and dealer networks.

Government restrictions can effectively prohibit an exit decision. Railroads have long been required to operate declining, money-losing routes.

Managerial pride may be a factor. Professional managers often view themselves as problem-solvers and are reluctant to admit defeat. Several anecdotes describe firms that have sent a series of executives to close down a subsidiary, each of whom after arriving convinced him- or herself that the subsidiary could be saved and then failed at such an effort. Furthermore, there is the emotional attachment to a business that has perhaps been in the "family" for many years and may even have been the original business on which the rest of a firm was created. It is difficult to turn your back on such a valued friend.

SELECTING THE RIGHT STRATEGY FOR THE DECLINING ENVIRONMENT

The spectrum of investment alternatives ranges from invest to hold to milk to exit. The choice of the optimal alternative depends on five types of analyses. The questions presented in Figure 14.3 serve to summarize the main issues.

Market Prospects

A basic consideration is the rate, pattern, and predictability of decline. A precipitous decline should be distinguished from a slow, steady decline. One determining factor is the existence of pockets of enduring demand, segments that are capable of supporting a core demand level. The cigar industry has experienced a slow, steady decline, in part, because the

FIGURE 14.3   The Investment Decision in a Declining Industry

---

SOME STRATEGIC QUESTIONS

Market Prospects

1. Is the rate of decline orderly and predictable?
2. Are there pockets of enduring demand?
3. What are the reasons for the decline—is it temporary?

Competitive Intensity

4. Are there dominant competitors with unique skills or assets?
5. Are there many competitors unwilling to exit or contract gracefully?
6. Are customers brand-loyal? Is there product differentiation?
7. Are there price pressures?

Performance/Position

8. Is the business profitable? What are its future prospects?
9. What is the market-share position and trend?
10. Does the business have some SCAs with respect to key segments?
11. Can the business manage costs in the face of declining sales?

Interrelationship with Other Businesses

12. Is there synergy with other businesses?
13. Is the business compatible with the firm's current strategic thrust?
14. Can the firm support the cash needs of the business?

Implementation Barriers

15. What are the exit barriers?
16. Can the organization manage all the investment options?

---

premium segment is stable and loyal. The vacuum-tube industry has had replacement demand even after vacuum tubes had all but disappeared from new products. In the leather industry, leather upholstery is still a healthy market.

Another factor affecting the decline rate, particularly in dynamic industries, is product obsolescence. When disposable diapers were introduced, the sale of rubber panties for babies dramatically declined.

A related consideration is the predictability of a pattern. If the pattern is based on demographics such as the size of the teen population, then it may be predictable. In contrast, predicting a fashion or technology is riskier, and a slow decline may turn suddenly into a steep decline. Another risk is that a declining market could be revived. For example, the natural food trend has revived oatmeal, and an inflation-stimulated price sensitivity at one point gave Kool-Aid a resurgence.

Competitive Intensity

A second consideration is the level of competitive intensity created by the industry structure. Are there one or more dominant competitors that have substantial shares and a set of unique assets and skills that form formidable sustainable competitive advantages? Is there a relatively large set of competitors that is not disposed either to exit or to contract gracefully? If the answer to either of these questions is yes, the profit prospects for others may be dismal. One consideration is whether or not competitors agree about the decline of an industry. The competitors in the baby food industry in the 1960 to 1978 period simply did not believe that the rate would decline as much as it did (42 percent) or for as long as it did (20 years).[15] As a result, there was overcapacity in the industry and substantial price pressures.

Another perspective comes from customers. A key to making a profit in a declining industry is price stability. Are customers relatively price-insensitive, such as buyers of premium cigars or replacement vacuum tubes? Is there a relatively high level of product differentiation and brand loyalty? Or has the product become a commodity? Are there costs involved in switching from one brand to another?

Business Position Appraisal

An appraisal of a business position should focus on an analysis of the business strengths and capabilities, as well as current performance. Sources of firm strength in a declining environment are usually quite different from those in other contexts. The strengths reflect the reality that there are fewer products to make and fewer customers to serve. Thus, sources of strength such as economies of scale, vertical integration, and technological leadership may actually be liabilities. What is helpful in a declining industry are:

● Established strong relationships with profitable customers, especially those in the pockets of enduring demand.

● A strong brand name. At this stage it will be difficult for competitors to alter their images significantly. Thus, the nature of an established image can be most important.

● The ability to operate profitably with under-utilized assets.

● The ability to reduce costs as business shrinks.

- Flexibility in applying assets and resources.
- A large market share if economies of scale are present.

An analysis of current profitability is important to the assessment of future position, but care is needed, especially if an exit decision is involved. Book assets, for example, may be overstated, because their market value could be small or even negative if they have associated obligations. Some overhead items that would have to be shifted to other businesses under an exit alternative might be properly omitted from some analyses.

Interdependencies

An investment decision can be affected by interdependencies with other businesses. A business may support other firm businesses by providing part of a system, by supporting a distribution channel, or by using excess plant capacity or a by-product of another production process. If the firm is vertically integrated, the other components might be affected by a decision to leave a particular business.

A visible closing down of a business may generate a credibility problem for the parent corporation, especially if a large write-off is involved. Closing down could affect access to financial markets as well as the opinion of dealers, suppliers, and customers about the firm's other operations. When Texas Instruments (in 1981) closed its digital watch and magnetic bubble memory groups, areas TI had pioneered, shock waves were undoubtedly felt among customers, supplies, and other stakeholders.

An exit decision can also be precipitated for reasons that have nothing to do with a business or its environment. A firm, for example, may face a liquidity problem and simply require cash. Or a strategic decision at the firm level may be to refocus resources into an unrelated core business, and the subsequent restructuring dictates the sale of a business independent of its position or prospects.

Implementation Barriers

Finally, there may be a set of implementation problems associated with each option. The exit barriers affect the exit option. The milk option presents difficult management problems in that both the managers and customers involved will have to accept a disinvest context. The hold option is also a delicate issue, because a passive investment strategy can inadvertently lead to a loss of position.

SUMMARY

One strategic option in a declining or stagnant industry is to create a growth context by revitalizing an industry. Such efforts can involve new markets, technologies to obsolete existing products, new applications, revitalized marketing, government-stimulated demand, and growth submarkets. A second option is to be the profitable survivor by strengthening a leadership position and encouraging others to exit, perhaps by buying their assets.

A decision to hold position involves investing only enough to maintain product quality, facilities, and customer loyalty. A milk strategy also involves a reduction in investment but differs from a hold strategy in that a loss of share is acceptable, even if it ultimately means that a business will fail. The exit alternative is usually inhibited by exit barriers such as commitments to customers and specialized assets.

The investment decision in declining markets should rely on an analysis of market prospects, competitive intensity, business position, interdependencies with other businesses in the firm, and implementation barriers. The strategic questions in Figure 14.3 summarize.

FOOTNOTES

[1] A good discussion of ways to grow mature products can be found in the provocative book by Jagdish N. Sheth, *Winning Back Your Market*, New York: Wiley, 1986.

[2] Gretchen Morgenson, "Barbie Does Budapest," *Forbes*, January 7, 1991, pp. 66–68.

[3] Aimee Stern, "TI Liberates the Calculator," *Adweek's Marketing Week*, August 22, 1988, p. 3.

[4] "High-Tech Music Has the Audio Market Rocking," *Business Week*, June 2, 1986, p. 100.

[5] Ronald Alsop, "Folksy Ads Help in Reviving Old-Time Headache Powder," *The Wall Street Journal*, January 20, 1987, p. 18.

[6] Colin Leinster, "The Sweet Smell of Profits from Trash," *Fortune*, April 1, 1985, pp. 150–154.

[7] "More Manufacturers Are Selling Services to Increase Returns and Smooth Cycles," *The Wall Street Journal*, December 26, 1978, p. 2.

[8] Some excellent research has been done on strategy development in declining industries, on which the balance of this chapter draws. It has been reported in Michael E. Porter, *Competitive Strategy*, New York: The Free Press, 1980, Chapter 8; Kathryn Rudie Harrigan, *Strategies for Declining Businesses*, Lexington, Mass.: Lexington Books, 1980; and Kathryn Rudie Harrigan and Michael E. Porter, "End-Game Strategies for Declining Industries," *Harvard Business Review*, July–August 1983, pp. 111–120.

[9] "Chesebrough: Finding Strong Brands to Revitalize Mature Markets," *Business Week*, November 10, 1980, p. 73.

[10] J. B. Kunz, Corporation (A), Case 9-577-115, Intercollegiate Case Clearing House, Soldiers Field, Boston, Mass., 1977.

[11] Robert H. Hayes and David A. Garvin, "Managing as if Tomorrow Mattered," *Harvard Business Review*, May–June 1982, pp. 70–79.

[12] Milton Moskowitz, "Last Days of Chase & Sanborn," *San Francisco Chronicle*, February, 22, 1982, p. 56.

[13] Erik Colonius, "Mightier Than the Ballpoint," *Newsweek*, July 3, 1989, p. 65.

[14] Kathryn Rudie Harrigan, *Strategies for Declining Businesses*, Lexington, Mass.: Lexington Books, 1980, Chapter 4.

[15] Harrigan, "Strategies," p. 153.

15

GLOBAL STRATEGIES

Most managers are nearsighted. Even though today's competitive landscape often stretches to a global horizon, they see best what they know best: the customers geographically closest to home.

Kenichi Ohmae

A powerful force drives the world toward a converging commonality, and that force is technology. . . . The result is a new commercial reality—the emergence of global markets for standardized consumer products on a previously unimagined scale of magnitude.

Theodore Levitt

My ventures are not in one bottom trusted, nor to one place.

William Shakespeare, The Merchant of Venice

Many firms find it necessary to develop global strategies to compete effectively. A global strategy can be contrasted with a multidomestic or multinational strategy in which separate strategies are developed for different countries and are implemented autonomously.[1] Thus, a retailer might develop different store groups in different countries that are not linked but operate autonomously. A multidomestic operation is usually best managed as a portfolio of independent businesses where independent investment decisions are made for each country.

A global strategy, in contrast, is conceived and implemented in a worldwide setting. Scale economies may therefore depend not on local market share but on worldwide volume. Furthermore, some of the components and the assembly involved might be located throughout the world in a search for cost advantages. Plant location decisions might be made to gain access to markets by bypassing trade barriers.

A global strategy can result in strategic advantage or the neutralization of competitors' strategies. For example, product development in one market might create product performance levels that will represent an SCA in another. Or a cost advantage may be generated from the scale economies generated by the global market. Operating in various countries can lead to enhanced flexibility as well as meaningful SCAs. Investment and operations can be shifted to respond to trends and developments emerging throughout the world or to counter competitors that are similarly structured.

Even if a global strategy is not appropriate for a business, making the external analysis global may still be useful. Competitors, markets, and trends from other countries may lead to the identification of important opportunities, threats, and strategic questions. A global external analysis is more difficult, of course, because of the different cultures, political risks, and economic systems involved.

The motivations for global strategies, presented next, is followed by discussions of the standardization versus customization issue, the risks of foreign investment, joint ventures, exporting and licensing, and the conditions under which a global strategy is appropriate.

MOTIVATIONS UNDERLYING GLOBAL STRATEGIES

A global strategy can involve one or more motivations in addition to simply wanting to invest in attractive foreign markets. The diagram of these motivations, shown in Figure 15.1, provides an understanding of the scope and character of global strategies.

FIGURE 15.1   Motivations for Global Strategies

Obtaining Scale Economies

An analysis of three British industries in the 1970s showed the power of scale economies resulting from a global perspective.[2] The British firms— British Leyland in automobiles, ICL in computers, and Ferranti in semiconductors—all had dominant positions in the British market, at times about twice that of their U.S. competitors—Ford, IBM, and Texas Instruments. The U.S. firms operated globally, however, and, unlike the British firms, had only a small percentage of their sales in England and had substantially larger shares in Europe. As a result, the U.S. firms far exceeded their British competitors in terms of performance as measured by ROI.

Scale economies can occur from product standardization. The Ford world car concept, for example, allows product design, tooling, parts production, and product testing to be spread over a much larger sales base. However, the standardization of the development and execution of a marketing program can also be an important source of scale economies. Consider Coca-Cola that, since the 1950s, has employed a marketing strategy—the brand name, concentrate formula, positioning, and advertising theme—that has been virtually the same throughout the world.[3] Only the artificial sweetener and packaging differ across countries. McCann-Erickson claims to have saved $90 million in advertising production costs over 20 years by producing worldwide Coca-Cola commercials.

Several influential observers have suggested that the SCAs emerging from worldwide scale economies are becoming more important, and in many industries they are becoming a necessary aspect of competition. Theodore Levitt, in a visible article on the globalization of markets, posits that worldwide communications have stimulated demand and fashion patterns to be similar across countries even in less developed countries.[4] Kenichi Ohmae, longtime head of McKinsey in Japan, cites a litany of products that are virtually identical in Japan, Europe, and the United States, including Nike, Pampers, Band-Aids, Cheer, Nestlé coffee, Kodak film, Revlon, and Contac.[5] He notes that people from different countries, from youths to businesspersons, wear the same fashions.

Ohmae also suggests that the long-accepted waterfall model of international trade is now obsolete.[6] In the waterfall model a firm first establishes itself in a domestic market. It then penetrates the markets of other advanced countries before moving into underdeveloped countries. The experience of Honda in motorcyles is representative. After creating a dominant position in Japan with considerable scale economies, it entered the U.S. market by convincing people that it was "fun" to ride its small, simple motorcycle and by investing in a 2000-dealer network. With its scale economies thus increased, Honda expanded its line to include larger cycles and then moved into the European market.

The new model, according to Ohmae, is that of a "sprinkler," where a product is exposed all over the globe at once. He points to products such as the Sony Walkman, Canon's AE-1, and the Minolta A-7000, which exploded worldwide in a matter of months. The Walkman actually took off first in California. Under the sprinkler model, the strategy needs to be radically different. A firm introducing a new product doesn't have time to develop a presence and distribution channel in a foreign market. Rather, it must form a consortium involving other firms that have established distribution in other countries, so that a new product can go global immediately.

Desirable Global Brand Associations

Brand names linked to global strategies can have useful associations. Just the concept of being global can symbolize the ability to generate competitive products in addition to strength and staying power. Such an image can be particularly important with pricey industrial products or consumer durables like cars or computers where there are customer risks—the product may be unreliable or technologically surpassed by a competitor. Japanese firms such as Yamaha, Sony, Canon, and Honda operate in markets where technology and product quality are important and have benefited from a global brand association.

Access to Low-Cost Labor or Materials

Another motivation of a global strategy can be to use the resulting access to many countries to reduce costs. There can be substantial cost differences with respect to raw materials, R&D talent, assembly labor, and component supply. Thus, a computer manufacturer may purchase components from Korea and Singapore, obtain raw materials from South America, and could assemble the final products in six countries throughout the world in order to reduce labor and transportation costs. Access to low-cost labor and material can be an SCA, especially when it is accompanied by the skill and flexibility to change when one supply is threatened or a more attractive alternative emerges.

Access National Investment Incentives

Another way to obtain a cost advantage is to access national investment incentives, which provide ways for countries to achieve economic objectives focused on target industries or depressed areas. Unlike other means to achieve changes in trade such as tariffs and quotas, incentives are much less visible and objectionable to trading partners.

Among the available incentives are outright grants, rent-free land and buildings, tax holidays, accelerated depreciation, low-interest loans, subsidized energy or transportation, and free employee training.[7] The British government offered Nissan $282 million to locate a plant in Britain, provided at least 60 percent of the value added of the cars was sourced in Britain. Sony received a $6.7 million grant to locate a television tube factory in a high-unemployment area of Wales. South Korea, Israel, Taiwan, and Brazil have provided special arrangements for more than 40 percent of the U.S. companies investing there.

Cross-Subsidization

A global presence allows a firm to cross-subsidize, to use the resources accumulated in one part of the world to fight a competitive battle in another.[8] Consider the following: One competitor uses the cash flow generated in its home market to attack a domestically oriented competitor. For example, Michelin in the early 1970s used its European profit base to attack Goodyear's U.S. market. The defensive competitor (i.e., Goodyear) could reduce prices or increase advertising in the United States to counter, but by doing so, it would sacrifice margins in its largest markets. An alternative is to attack the aggressor in its home market where it has the most to lose. Thus, Goodyear carried the fight to Europe to put a dent in Michelin's profit base.

The cross-subsidization concept leads to two strategic considerations:[9]

● To influence an existing or potential foreign competitor, it will be useful to maintain a presence in its country. The presence should be large enough to make the threat of retaliation meaningful. If the share is only 2 percent or so, the competitor may be willing to ignore it.

● A home market may be vulnerable even if a firm apparently controls it with a large market share. A high market share, especially if it is used to support high prices and profits, can attract foreign firms that realize the domestic firm has little freedom for retaliation. A major reason for the demise of the U.S. consumer electronics industry was the fact that the firms involved restricted themselves to U.S. marketing, which placed them at a substantial disadvantage to their global competitors that had the option to cross-subsidize.

Dodge Trade Barriers

Locating component and assembly plants can help gain access to markets by penetrating trade barriers and fostering goodwill. Peugeot, for example, has plants in 26 countries from Argentina to Zimbabwe. The importance of this motivation was shown by a survey of 108 U.S.-based multinational firms.[10] As Figure 15.2 indicates, two of the primary reasons offered for foreign investment were to overcome tariff barriers (28 percent of respondents) and to respond to government pressures to produce locally (19 percent).

Locating final assembly plants in a host country is a good way to achieve favorable trade treatment and goodwill, because it will usually provide a visible presence and generate savings in transportation and

FIGURE 15.2   Reasons for Foreign Investment—108 U.S. Multinational Firms

Reasons	Percent
Overcome tariff barriers	27.6
Gain economies of scale	26.7
Take advantage of government incentives	21.0
Follow customers	20.0
Respond to government pressures to produce locally	19.0
Lower wage rates	13.3

Source: Marie E. Wicks-Kelly and George C. Philippatos, "Comparative Analysis of the Foreign Investment Evaluation Practices by U.S.-Based Manufacturing Multinational Companies," *Journal of Business Strategy*, Winter 1982, pp. 19–42.

storage of the final product. Thus, Caterpillar operates assembly plants in each of its major markets, including Europe, Japan, Brazil, and Australia, in part to bypass trade barriers.[11] Japanese auto and TV firms have located assembly plants in the United States and elsewhere and have made sure that the plants are well publicized.

Political objectives can also be achieved by locating component plants in foreign countries. For example, Siemens sources components for its circuit breakers in Brazil and effectively swaps the components made in Brazil for finished products manufactured elsewhere.[12] Sometimes sourcing decisions can directly affect a sale. Italy's state-controlled airline, Alitalia, ordered McDonnell jets only after McDonnell agreed to place substantial orders for subcontracting work with Italian companies.

Sometimes, however, a major commitment is required. Mexico, for example, had a 60 percent local content requirement for automobile production in the early 1980s, and Brazil 85 percent.[13] Because these two countries accounted for well over half of automobile demand in Latin America, their positions on imports were significant.

Access to Strategically Important Markets

Some markets are strategically important because of their market size or potential or because of their raw material supply, labor cost structure, or technology. It can be important to have a presence in these markets even if such a presence is not profitable. Because of its size, the U.S. market, for example, is critical to those in industries in which scale economies are important, such as automobiles or consumer electronics.

Sometimes a country is important because it is the locus of new trends and developments in an industry. A firm in the fashion industry may benefit from a presence in countries that historically lead the way in fashion. Or a high-tech firm may want to have operations in a country that is in the forefront of the relevant field. Sometimes adequate information can be obtained by observers, but those with design and manufacturing groups on location will tend to have a more intimate knowledge of trends and events.

STANDARDIZATION VERSUS CUSTOMIZATION

A key issue in the development of a global strategy is the extent to which the strategy, particularly the marketing strategy, will be standardized across countries. The more standardization, the more potential there is for scale economies. The vision of a single product sharing not only R&D and manufacturing but also a common name, position, package, and advertising drives some people's version of the ultimate global strategy;

Parker Pen: A Global Strategy That Failed

In 1985, Parker Pen launched a global business strategy to combat Cross from above and the Japanese from below.[14] The centerpiece of the strategy was a rolled-ball pen called the Victor to be priced throughout the world at a low (for Parker) $2.98, which was to be made at a new automated production facility for $0.29. The common advertising campaign used the theme, "It's wrought from pure silver and writes like pure silk," and the slogan "Make your mark with a Parker." The effort was a disaster—it was so bad in many of its 150 markets, local units resisted pressures to adapt the product. A Parker executive was quoted as shouting at a meeting at the London agency branch, "Yours is not to reason why, yours is to implement."

The common pricing was a problem especially for some countries that had established a position either above or below that reflected by the new price. The selected name did not have the greatest associations in all countries. The advertising and resulting associations were judged by many to be bland and ineffective. Furthermore, there were manufacturing problems affecting Parker's ability to deliver its product.

Among the casualties of the global branding strategy were some effective local branding efforts. For example, the offbeat agency of the highly profitable Parker unit in England, one of 40 agencies used by Parker prior to globalization, had developed a particularly successful campaign. It associated the brand with people with the elan to deliver a well-crafted insult written with a Parker. One such insult was a note to an airline reading, "You had delusions of adequacy?" The campaign's humor was very British and would not have worked elsewhere.

---

the assumption is that it will lead to decisive efficiencies and scale economies.

Two strong motivations for a standardized global brand and position are the media spillover and cross-country customer travel, which can be extensive, especially in Europe. Brand awareness, in particular, can benefit from the exposure of a brand in a different country when customers travel between countries. When media coverage overlaps regions, a global brand can buy exposures much more efficiently. In particular, as the European common market matures, there is likely to be more and more media overlap and customer crossover and thus more payoff to a global brand strategy.

A third rationale for a standardized global marketing strategy is the associations that can result. The image of being a global player achieved by firms like IBM, Ford, and Canon can provide prestige and reassurance to customers. In other contexts, a "home" country association can be the essence of a brand's positioning. For example, Levi's are U.S. jeans, Chanel is French perfume, Dewar's is Scotch whiskey, Kikkoman is

Japanese soy sauce, and Bertolli is Italian olive oil. In each case, the brand is established in its home country and the country itself is central to the image of the brand. In such a context, a standardized strategy may pay off. Figure 15.3 summarizes.

However, the reality is that a standardized global product and marketing effort is not always desirable or even possible. In general, each element of a marketing program needs to be analyzed to determine whether or not the advantages of standardization outweigh the gains in effectiveness amassed in tailoring the program to local markets. It is very much like deciding whether or not to market the same soup in Texas and New York. There are times in which standardization is not the answer and it makes sense to tailor the product and marketing program to a particular country.

The Customization Option

To achieve standardization for some aspects of a strategy can be difficult in the face of the differences between countries and involve little potential for scale economies. For example, Kentucky Fried Chicken has been successful in Japan, but only after the firm realized the U.S. model of free-standing units would not work in land-scarce Japanese cities, when it changed its menu (fries replaced mashed potatoes and slaw became less sweet), and when it adopted Japanese training methods. Insisting on a U.S. clone in Japan would have saved little money and guaranteed failure.

Distribution and personal selling are two elements that usually need to be adapted to the realities of a country. One study involving seven

FIGURE 15.3   Marketing Strategy—Customization Versus Standardization

Standardization Provides	Customization Provides
Scale economies in the development of advertising, packaging, promotion, etc.	Names, associations, and advertising that can be developed locally tailored to local market
Exploitation of media overlap exposure to customers who travel	selected without the constraints of standardization
Associations of a global presence of the "home" country	Reduced risk from "buy local" sentiments

major Japanese firms and 46 different product categories conducted by Japan's Hiro Takeuchi and Harvard's Michael Porter revealed that distribution and selling organizations tend not to be standardized—there are simply few economies of scale involved and there is often a substantial fit problem.[15]

However, if firms are willing to make the investment and commitment to a different distribution/selling system in Japan, it can result in attacking or creating competitive barriers. For example, Coca-Cola developed an in-house delivery system that has become an important advantage, leading to its domination in the Japanese soft-drink market. Xerox exported the U.S. system of extensive personal sales/service to Japan in the 1960s and is often regarded as a model of how to succeed in Japan. Kodak in 1985 broke the Fuji lock on the Japanese market only when it built its own distribution network. The Kodak approach not only gave the firm access to a market but also direct contact with its customers, providing better information on customer needs.

The Takeuchi and Porter study of Japanese firms found that a brand name and advertising theme are likely to be standardized across countries. The use of a common name for some Japanese firms like Canon, Yamaha, and Honda can work, but for other firms the constraint that the name be the same in all countries is very confining and can result in the use of bland choices and are neither memorable or meaningful. Most names, especially names with useful associations, will have a damaging meaning (or will be preempted) in some countries. For example, P&G's Pert Plus, the very successful combination shampoo and conditioner, is sold as Rejoy in Japan, Rejoice in much of the Far East, and

---

Indicators That Strategies Should Be Global

- Major competitors in important markets are not domestic and have a presence in several countries.
- Standardardization of some elements of the product or marketing strategy provide opportunities for scale economies.
- Costs can be reduced and effectiveness increased by locating value-added activities in different countries.
- Competitors have the potential to use the volume and profits from one market to subsidize gaining a position in another.
- Trade barriers are important barriers to worthwhile markets.
- A global name can be an advantage.
- When local markets do not require products or service for which a local operation would have an advantage.

Vidal Sassoon in the United Kingdom because the Pert Plus name (or something similar) was preempted. The Budweiser name is not available to Anheuser-Busch in most of Europe because it is owned by a small Czechoslovakian brewery.

A local brand can benefit from distinct associations that can be useful—even pivotal. Is there any tendency to "buy home-grown" or any positive feeling toward local traditions or characteristics that can be integrated into a brand's positioning strategy? Or does the global brand have negative associations locally because it has an undesirable meaning in some countries or is tied to a country's politics and thus is subject to the ups and downs of international events?

A worldwide advertising theme may simply not be appropriate in some countries because of the competitive context. A British Airways globalization effort involved the centralization of advertising, which resulted in "the world's favorite airline" theme. It featured a 90-second commercial that showed the Manhattan skyline rotating slowly though the sky. Even in the United States, where the campaign originated, managers wondered if the replaced campaign (which emphasized traditional British values with the theme "we'll take good care of you") was not more effective. In countries where British Air was an also-ran, the claim did not make much sense. Furthermore, there were operational problems. For example, 90-second ads could not be used in South Africa.

A decentralized approach to the development of marketing programs can generate a product or advertising campaign that can be used globally. Levi Strauss got its successful Dockers pants from a product development effort in its Brazilian operation. When Polaroid was repositioning from a "party camera" platform to a more serious, utilitarian one, a campaign developed in Switzerland was the most effective.[16] It promoted the functional use of instant photography as a way to communicate with family and friends—the "learn to speak Polaroid" campaign. If local units had not been free to generate their own campaigns, this superior campaign would not have surfaced.

The Costs of Creating a "Global Brand"

When a new product is developed, most firms will attempt to make it a global product with a common name and position. The pressure for standardization is particularly strong in Europe, where there is now considerable media overlap and fewer distinct distribution systems. However, a more difficult issue is whether or not to create a global brand when regional brands are in place.

When a brand is established in a country, for example, it has an equity based on its awareness level and a set of associations that are often very valuable. Changing the name and/or position simply in order to conform to a standardized global brand may be extremely costly. The effort to change the Datsun name to the global brand Nissan in the United States in the early 1980s probably cost over $1 billion.[17] As part of the effort, the effective "Datsun, we are driven" campaign was replaced with the expensive but punchless one, "the name is Nissan." Five years after the name change, the Datsun name was still as strong as the Nissan name.

A new name also kills any associations that the old name might have developed. The VW Rabbit attempted to recapture some of the funkiness and magic of the manufacturer's earlier Beetle using imagery associated with the rabbit symbol. Although for many reasons the Rabbit was a poor substitute for the Beetle, it did develop some positive associations. It was later replaced with the global brand name, Golf, which was worse with respect to associations. Heinz is one firm that does not put its name on the products it acquires outside the United States because it wants to retain their associations.

If an existing name has weak associations, of course, it has little to lose by changing. In the late 1980s in the U.S. market, Mars successfully changed the name of its Kal Kan dog food to "Pedigree" and its Kal Kan cat food to "Whiskas" to create a worldwide name.[18] In contrast to Kal Kan, which mainly was associated with cans, the name Pedigree was associated with a quality, expensive pet that would only be served the best food and the name Whiskas was feline-sounding and likable.

Some brands are positioned quite differently in different countries. For example, Heinz baby food and Levi's jeans both have a strong value position in the United States and a premium position in other markets. Clearly, it would be foolish to force a common position on such brands in order to achieve a standardized global brand.

The rush to standardized global branding is somewhat ironic as there is a strong move to regional marketing in the United States. Firms like P&G, Campbell Soup, and others are giving local marketing units responsibility for sales promotions and advertising that had previously been centralized.

Creating a Standardized Offering—The Lead Country

When standardization seems to provide worthwhile benefits, an implementation question arises. How is the standardization strategy developed? One approach is to develop a global product. Canon, for example, developed a copier with the constraint that a common design be used throughout the world in order to maximize production economies. As a result, the copier could not use the standard paper size in Japan, creating a substantial customer inconvenience. The problem with a truly global standardization objective is the risk that the result will be a compromise; a product and marketing program that almost fits most markets will not be exactly what is needed anywhere. Such a result is a recipe for failure or mediocrity.

Another strategy is to identify a lead country, a country with a market that is attractive because it is large or growing or because the brand has a natural advantage there. A product is then tailored to that market so its chances of success in that country are maximized. It is then "exported" to other markets, perhaps with minor modifications or refinements. A firm may have several lead countries, each with its own product. The resulting stable of global brands will each have its own home.

Nissan cars, for example, are designed for the United States, Japan, or Europe, as opposed to designing world cars.[19] Thus, the firm developed a corporate fleet car for the United Kingdom, and a sporty "Z" model and a four-wheel drive family vehicle for the United States. Once the lead country model is developed, it can then be offered to managers in other countries. Thus, the Z model may be offered to Japan because it appeals to a small segment there. In fact, Nissan sells monthly about 5000 Z models in the United States, as compared with 500 in Japan.

Implementing Global Strategies Involving Standardization

Implementing global strategies can be especially difficult when they focus on the standardization of some element of a product line or marketing program. Inevitably, foreign operations then lose autonomy—have decisions and programs imposed on them. Two problems emerge. First, the ability of foreign managers to fine-tune strategies to their country is reduced. Second, a motivation problem will arise. A French advertising manager, who is talented and creative, will not enjoy becoming essentially the translator of a home-office advertising campaign, nor will a local business strategist readily accept a strategy developed elsewhere. A variety of approaches to deal with these problems have been tried.

Centralizing Decision Making.   One approach is simply to centralize decision making and forcefully require standardization. One risk is the resulting incentive to avoid change or deviations in order to preserve scale economies. The case of Lego Toys illustrates this problem.[20] A Japanese competitor, Tyco, successfully started selling its toys in plastic buckets that could be used for storage after play. A suggestion by its U.S. management that a similar package be sold by Lego was rejected, in part because the bucket did not seem compatible with the Lego image but also because it was a departure from the worldwide standardization policy that had been so successful. The Danish headquarters changed its mind two years later, but only after severe damage had been done to the U.S. market.

Selective Standardization. Another approach is to centralize some elements of a strategy but leave others under the control of country managers—those that are most skillful in tailoring the strategy to local conditions. Timken believed that a reinforcement of its technology position was going to be critical in the emerging global market.[21] Thus, it integrated its international research effort but left manufacturing and other functions to originate geographically. Similarly, Corning centralized the pricing function for its TV tube but left other strategy elements to foreign managers.

Using Communication and Persuasion. The least disruptive way to create a change toward global thinking is by communication and persuasion.[22] Nestlé, a firm with a tradition of active, autonomous subsidiaries, publishes a quarterly marketing newsletter that reports innovations in marketing programs and the results of new product introductions. Johnson's Wax holds periodic meetings of all marketing directors twice a year to encourage global thinking and the sharing of ideas. Systematically transferring people from line to staff positions can also help build a global thrust. Unilever employs high-caliber advertising and marketing staffs that become involved in subsidiaries' marketing programs by reviewing strategies, coaching managers, and making substantive suggestions. They frequently visit the field to discuss new concepts and deal with local problems.

Team Management. Procter & Gamble, in attempting to move away from highly autonomous subsidiaries, launched the "Pampers experiment," in which a European manager developed a Pampers strategy for the whole continent.[23] The approach, designed to eliminate the diversity in brand strategy, failed because it ignored local knowledge, underutilized subsidiary strengths, and demotivated country managers to the point where they felt no sales responsibility. The replacement strategy was the creation of "Eurobrand" teams, management teams of product people from each country headed by a person from the "lead subsidiary," the one with the highest level of success and creativity with respect to the brand. The team approach, which successfully launched Vizier, a new liquid detergent, provided motivation, communication, and coordination.

STRATEGIC ALLIANCES

Strategic alliances play an important role in global strategies because it is common for a competitor to lack a key success factor for some market. It may be distribution, a brand name, a selling organization, the technology, R&D capability, or manufacturing capability. To remedy this deficiency internally would often require excessive time and money. When the uncertainties of operating in other countries are considered, a strategic alliance is a natural alternative to reducing investment and the accompanying inflexibility and risk.

For example, IBM, which has relatively few alliances in the United States, has teamed up with just about everyone possible in Japan.[24] It has links with Ricoh for distribution of low-end computers, with Nippon Steel in systems integration, with Fuji Bank in financial systems marketing, with OMRON in CIM, and with NTT in value-added networks. There is even a book in Japanese entitled *IBM's Alliance Strategy in Japan.* As a result, IBM is considered a major "insider" in the Japanese market that competes across the board in all segments and applications.

Strategic alliance is thus becoming a key part of global competition. In fact, Kenichi Ohmae has said that:

> Globalization mandates alliances, makes them absolutely essential to strategy. Uncomfortable, perhaps—but that's the way it is. Like it or not, the simultaneous developments that go under the name of globalization make alliances—entente—necessary.[25]

A strategic alliance is a long-term collaboration leveraging the strengths of two or more organizations to achieve strategic goals. Thus, there is a long-term commitment involved. It is not simply a tactical device to provide a short-term fix for a problem—to outsource a component for which a temporary manufacturing problem has surfaced, for example. Furthermore, it implies that the involved organizations contribute and adapt a needed asset or skill to the collaboration and that this asset or skill will be maintained over time. The results of a collaboration should have strategic value and contribute to a viable venture that can withstand competitive attack and environmental change.

A strategic alliance provides the potential of accomplishing a strategic objective or task—such as obtaining distribution in Italy—fast, inexpensively, and with a relatively high prospect for success. Contrast a strategic alliance in which existing assets and skills can be combined with the problem of creating assets or skills internally.

Forms of Strategic Alliances

A strategic alliance can take many forms from a loose informal agreement to a formal joint venture. The most informal arrangement might envision simply trying to work together (selling our products through your channel, for example) and allowing systems and organization forms to emerge as an alliance develops. The more informal the arrangement, the faster it can be implemented and the more flexible it will be. As conditions and people change, the alliance can be adjusted. The problem is usually commitment. With low exit barriers and commitment, there may be a low level of strategic importance and a temptation to back away or to disengage when difficulties arise.

A formal joint venture (40 percent of alliances formed during the 1970s)[26] involving equity and a comprehensive legal document, on the other hand, has very different risks. When equity-sharing is involved, there is often worry about control, return on investment, and achieving a fair percentage of the venture. A major concern is whether or not such a permanent arrangement will be equitable in the face of uncertainty about the relative contributions of the partners and the eventual success of the venture. One result of the commitment risk is that firms involved tend to drag their heels and the venture may lose a window of opportunity. Another is that equity positions and an accompanying understanding of the limits of each partner's contribution can result in a lack of needed flexibility as conditions change. Furthermore, the parties involved may have an excessive reliance on legal documents to preserve the health of an alliance.

Motivations for Strategic Alliances

Strategic alliances can be motivated by achieving some of the benefits of a global strategy outlined in Figure 15.1. For example, a strategic alliance can:

- **Generate scale economies.** The fixed investment that Toyota made in designing a car and its production system will be spread over more units because of a joint venture with GM in California.

- **Gain access to strategic markets.** A Japanese firm like JVC can provide a VCR design and manufacturing capability but needs a relationship with Thomson to obtain help in accessing the fragmented European market.

- **Overcome trade barriers.** Inland Steel and Nippon Steel are jointly building an advanced cold steel mill in Indiana. Nippon is supplying the technology, capital, and access to Japanese auto plants in the

United States. Nippon gains local knowledge and, importantly, the ability to get around import quotas.

Perhaps more commonly, a strategic alliance is needed to compensate for the absence of or weakness in any needed asset or skill. Thus, a strategic asset can:

- **Fill out a product line to serve market niches.** Ford, for example, has relied on alliances to provide key components of its product line.[27] Its long-time relationship with Mazda has provided many Ford models in addition to access to some Far East markets. More recently, when Mazda decided not to build a minivan, Ford turned to Nissan for help. One firm simply cannot provide the breadth of models that are viable in a major market such as the United States.

- **Gain access to a needed technology.** While JVC gained access to the European market, its European partner accessed a competitive VCR source.

- **Use excess capacity.** The GM/Toyota joint venture used an idle GM California plant.

- **Access a name or customer relationship.** NGK bought an interest in a GE subsidiary whose product line had become obsolete in order to access the GE name and reputation in the U.S. electrical equipment market. A U.S. injection molder joined with Mitsui in order to help access Japanese manufacturing operations in the United States that preferred to do business with Japanese suppliers.[28]

- **Reduce the investment required.** In some cases, a firm's contribution to a joint venture can be technology, with no financial resources required.

The Key—Maintaining Strategic Value for Collaborators

Some obvious difficulties and disadvantages are associated with strategic alliances. A commitment made to a partner may become inappropriate or undesirable when conditions change. A study of 1100 pre–1967 joint ventures between U.S. companies and partners in other developed countries indicated that the majority proved unstable because of organizational or strategic changes made by one of the partners.[29] A more recent study found that 70 percent broke up. A change in a product-market mission for one partner can make a once attractive and synergetic joint venture become a nuisance or even a liability.

A major problem with strategic alliances occurs when the contribution becomes unbalanced over time and one partner no longer has any proprietary assets and skills to contribute. Reich and Mankin argue that in most of the joint ventures involving U.S. and Japanese firms, the U.S. firm contributes a marketing system and perhaps the initial technology and the final assembly function.[30] In fact, in more than two-thirds of 33 consumer electronics joint ventures studied, the U.S. partner only sold and distributed a Japanese product. The Japanese firms thus retain the key business components: product refinement, plant design, and production systems. Over time the most important assets and skills of the joint venture are thus in the hands of the Japanese firm, as is much of the value added. The U.S. partner loses the ability to participate independently in the industry because it lacks the necessary production skills to generate competitive products. Reich and Mankin conclude that, in the aggregate, the United States forfeits whole industries by turning to Japan for low-cost, quality products.

Hammel et al. studied 15 strategic alliances and offered suggestions as to how a firm might protect its assets and skills from its alliance partner.[31] One approach is to structure the situation so that learning takes place and access to missing skills and assets occurs. Compare, for example, the joint Toyota/GM manufacturing facility where GM was involved in the manufacturing process and its refinements with Chrysler's effort to sell a Mitsubishi car designed and manufactured in Japan. In the latter case, Mitsubishi eventually developed its own name and dealer network and now sells its car directly. When the motivation for an alliance is to avoid investment and acheive attractive short-term returns instead of developing assets and skills, that is exactly what will happen.

Another approach is to protect assets from a partner by controlling access. One approach used by many Japanese firms is to have a coordinator of information transfer. Such a position avoids uncoordinated, inappropriate information flow. Another is to clearly limit access to a part of the product line or a part of the design. Motorola, for example, releases its microchip technology to its partner, Toshiba, only as Toshiba delivers on its promise to increase Motorola's penetration in the Japanese market. Still another approach is to keep improving the asset involved so that the partner's dependence continues. The problem of protecting assets, of course, is most difficult when the asset can be communicated by a drawing. It is a bit easier when a complex system is involved—when, for example, the asset is manufacturing excellence.

Making Strategic Alliances Work

Even if an alliance is strategically sound, there are a host of operational problems that can arise. One study of 37 joint ventures uncovered a variety of management problems.[32] In one case, the partners differed in terms of priorities of short-term versus long-term objectives. In another, a British firm could not understand a U.S. partner's obsession with numbers and analysis. In still another, a sensitive decision about the location of a new plant became political.

Basically there are usually two sets of systems, people, cultures, and structures that need to be reconciled. In addition, there are the country-specific cultures and environment to consider. Japanese, for example, tend to use a consensus-building decision process and rely on small group activity for much of its energy; this approach is very different from that of managers in the United States and Europe. Furthermore, the interests of each partner may not always seem to be in step. Many alliances have failed because the partners simply had styles and objectives that ended up to be fundamentally incompatible and killed an otherwise well-conceived alliance.

There are several keys to making a collaboration work. Perhaps the most important is that it be well conceived so that there is ongoing mutual benefit. Partners really have assets and skills that combine to provide strategic advantage. And these assets and skills should continue to be relevant to the venture and be maintained by the partners. If there is a significant ongoing strategic motivation reinforced by success, the problems are more likely to be manageable.

Another key is that there be commitment not only by the firms but by the managers involved. Champions need to exist who will carry the ball during difficult times. Without the people committed to making this happen, it will not happen.

Still another key is that an alliance have or develop methods to resolve problems and to change over time. It is unrealistic to expect any strategy, organization, and implementation to exist without evolving and changing. Partners and the organization thus need to be flexible enough to allow change to occur.

SUMMARY

A global strategy considers and exploits interdependencies between operations in different countries. One of the driving forces toward globalization is obtaining scale economies derived from standardization made possible by commonalities in culture and demand across countries. Other motivations include a desire to access low-cost labor or materials, to access national incentives, to cross-subsidize, to dodge trade barriers, to access strategic markets, and to create global associations.

A key issue is what elements of the strategy should be common across countries. In general, there will often be a trade-off between the scale economies created by standardization and the impact of a custom-

---

Enhancing the Chances of a Successful Alliance

1. Both sides must gain—now and in the future. Make sure that your partner continues to benefit even when it means that you have to give up something.

2. Protect and enhance the assets and skills being contributed—don't let a partner take over the assets and skills being contributed.

3. Be a learner, particularly if the alliance is with a competitor or potential competitor—it is risky to be motivated solely by a desire to avoid investment.

4. Deal with the differences in organizations—people, cultures, structures, and systems—and in country cultures.

5. Recognize that circumstances and markets change—build in some flexibility and change capability.

6. If there is a separate organization involved, give it space. If not, invest in working together as a team.

7. Be clear about expectations and contributions. When possible, have an agreement that covers eventual disagreements or disappointments that could be awkward—but don't rely on legal documents to handle all disagreements and conflicts.

---

ized strategy. A common brand name and position work well when a prestige brand is being marketed, when the position is based on the country involved, and when the technology drives the product. Significant management problems exist in attempting to impose a standardized policy in different countries, in part because of natural rebellion against a "headquarters knows best" attitude.

In global competition, competitors often lack a key success factor such as distribution or manufacturing expertise. A severe liability can sometimes be remedied quickly by a strategic alliance, a long-term collaboration leveraging the strengths of two or more organizations to achieve strategic goals. An alliance can be a formal joint venture or an informal agreement to work together to achieve a strategic end. Key to long-term success is that each partner contribute assets and skills over time and obtain strategic advantage. Toward that end, it is important that each partner make sure that its assets and skills are maintained and protected.

FOOTNOTES

[1] Michael E. Porter makes the distinction between multidomestic industries where multidomestic strategies are appropriate and global industries where global strategies are needed. See Michael E. Porter, "Changing Patterns of International Competition," *California Management Review* 28, Winter 1986, pp. 9–40.

[2] James Leontiades, "Market Share and Corporate Strategy in International Industries," *Journal of Business Strategy*, Summer 1984, pp. 30–37.

[3] John A. Quelch and Edward J. Hoff, "Customizing Global Marketing," *Harvard Business Review*, May–June 1986, pp. 59–68.

[4] Theodore Levitt, "The Globalization of Markets," *Harvard Business Review*, May–June 1983.

[5] Kenichi Ohmae, "The Triad World View," *The Journal of Business Strategy*, Spring 1987, pp. 8–16.

[6] Ohmae, "The Triad."

[7] Robert Weigand, "International Investments: Weighing the Incentives," *Harvard Business Review*, July–August 1983, pp. 146–152.

[8] Garz Hamel and C. K. Prahalad, "Do You Really Have a Global Strategy?" *Harvard Business Review*, July–August 1985, pp. 139–148.

[9] Hamel and Prahalad, "Do You Really."

[10] Marie E. Wicks-Kelly and George C. Philippatos, "Comparative Analysis of the Foreign Investment Evaluation Practices by U.S. Based Manufacturing Multinational Companies," *Journal of Business Strategy*, Winter 1982, pp. 19–42.

[11] Thomas Hout, Michael E. Porter, and Eileen Rudden, "How Global Companies Win Out," *Harvard Business Review*, September–October 1982, p. 103.

[12] Hout, Porter, and Rudden, "How Global Companies," p. 106.

[13] Harry Jupiter, "AMC Chief Urges 'Global Approach,' " *San Francisco Chronicle*, March 25, 1983, p. 50.

[14] Joseph M. Winski and Laurel Wentz, "Parker Pen: What Went Wrong?" *Advertising Age*, June 2, 1986, pp. 1, 60, 61, 71.

[15] Hirotaka Takeuchi and Michael E. Porter, "Three Roles of International Marketing in Global Strategy," in Michael E. Porter, ed., *Competition in Global Industries*, Boston, Mass.: Harvard Business School Press, 1986.

[16] Kamran Kashani, "Beware the Pitfalls of Global Marketing," *Harvard Business Review*, September–October 1989, pp. 91–97.

[17] David A. Aaker, *Managing Brand Equity*, New York: The Free Press, 1991, Chapter 3.

[18] David Kalish, "Cat Fight," *Marketing & Media Decisions*, April 1989, pp. 42–48.

[19] Kenichi Ohmae, "Managing in a Borderless World," *Harvard Business Review*, May–June 1989, pp. 152–161.

[20] Kashani, "Beware the Pitfalls of Global Marketing."

[21] Christopher A. Bartlett, "MNCs: Get Off the Reorganization Merry-Go-Round," *Harvard Business Review*, March–April 1983, pp. 138–146.

[22] Quelch and Hoff, "Customizing Global Marketing."

[23] Christopher A. Bartlett and Summantra Ghoshal, "Tap Your Subsidiaries for Global Reach," *Harvard Business Review*, November–December 1986, pp. 87–94.

[24] Kenichi Ohmae, "The Global Logic of Strategic Alliances," *Harvard Business Review*, March–April, 1989, pp. 143–154.

[25] Ohmae, "The Global Logic of Strategic Alliances."

[26] P. Ghemawat, Michael E. Porter, and R. A. Rawlinson, "Patterns of International Coalition Activity," in Michael E. Porter, ed., *Competition in Global Industries*, Boston, Mass.: Harvard Business School Press, 1986, 345–566.

[27] Louis Kraar, "Your Rivals Can Be Your Allies," *Fortune*, March 27, 1989, pp. 66–76.

[28] Tyzoon T. Tyebjee, "A Topology of Joint Ventures: Japanese Strategies in the United States," *California Management Review*, Fall 1988, pp. 75–86.

[29] L. G. Franko, *Joint Venture Survival in Multinational Corporations*, New York: Praeger, 1971. A later McKinsey and Coopers & Lybrand study reported that 70 percent of joint ventures broke up. See "Corporate Odd Couples," *Business Week*, July 1986, pp. 100–105.

[30] Robert B. Reich and Eric D. Mankin, "Joint Ventures with Japan Give Away Our Future," *Harvard Business Review*, March–April 1986, pp. 78–86.

[31] Gary Hamel, Yves L. Doz, and C. K. Prahalad, "Collaborate with Your Competitors— and Win," *Harvard Business Review*, January–February 1989, pp. 133–139.

[32] J. Peter Killing, "How to Make a Global Joint Venture Work," *Harvard Business Review*, March–April 1986, pp. 78–86.

PART FIVE

IMPLEMENTATION AND THE PLANNING PROCESS

16

IMPLEMENTING THE STRATEGY

The basic philosophy, spirit and drive of an organization have far more to do with its relative achievements than do technological or economic resources, organizational structure, innovation and timing.

Thomas Watson, Jr., IBM

Structure follows strategy.

Alfred D. Chandler, Jr.

Never acquire a business you don't know how to run.

Robert Johnson,
Johnson & Johnson

Korvette's, which started as a luggage and appliance discounter selling from a second-floor loft in Manhattan, became by 1962 a profitable discount chain with a dozen stores.[1] Its initial success prompted an aggressive growth strategy, which turned out to be a disaster. The firm expanded dramatically both the number of stores and the number of cities served, expanded its product line by adding fashion goods, furniture, and grocery products, and added more store amenities.

This growth strategy, which had many similarities to that of other successful discounters like K mart, was defensible. The problem was its implementation. The strategy was not supported by the right people, structure, systems, or culture. Korvette's personnel lacked the depth to staff the new stores and the expertise to handle the new product areas. The centralized structure did not allow for needed adaptation to multiple cities and product lines. The management systems were not sophisticated enough to handle the added complexity. The culture of casual management with low prices as the driving force was not replaced with another strong culture that would be appropriate to the new business areas. As a result, in 1966 the firm was near death, a condition from which it never recovered.

The Korvette story graphically illustrates the importance of strategy implementation. The assessment of any strategy should include a careful assessment of organizational risks and a judgment about the nature of any required organizational changes and their associated costs and feasibility. Toward that end, this chapter first develops a conceptual framework that will help in the analysis of an organization.

A CONCEPTUAL FRAMEWORK

The conceptual framework shown in Figure 16.1 is useful in identifying and positioning organizational components and their interactions.[2] The heart of the framework is a set of four key constructs that describe the organization: structure, systems, people, and culture. The figure includes strategy, which must successfully interact with the four organizational components and organizational performance. It also includes external analysis and self-analysis, which provide a link to Figure 2.1 and the strategy-development process. Recall that a strategy involves the product-market investment decision, the selection of functional area strategies, and the bases for sustainable competitive advantage.

The consideration of each organizational component makes it more feasible to identify actual and potential implementation problems, as well as to determine how an organization would adapt to a new strategy. Each of the four central components and their link to strategy is discussed. The need for achieving a fit or congruence among these four organizational

FIGURE 16.1   A Framework for Analyzing Organizations

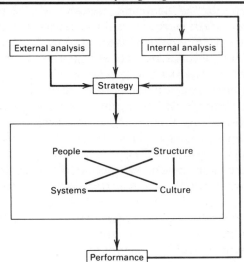

components is then considered. Finally, ways by which an organization can become more innovative and responsive to change are suggested.

STRUCTURE

Organizational structure defines lines of authority and communication and specifies the mechanism by which organizational tasks and programs are accomplished.

Centralization Versus Decentralization

One key structural dimension is the degree of centralization. At one extreme is the centralized functional organization consisting of specialized groups in marketing, sales, production, engineering, R&D, personnel, and administration. It is most appropriate when there is a limited number of closely related product lines and specialization produces benefits and economies. A centralized organization can have coordination and communication problems, especially lower down in the organization, which are only partially addressed by the use of committees or meetings. Centralization becomes less effective as the product lines diffuse, coordination becomes important, and specialization does not represent an important asset.

In contrast, a divisional structure emphasizes a decentralized organization based on product or market groupings. Each division has its own functional resources. An extension is the holding-company structure in which each business unit stands alone as a separate business. The divisional form is more flexible in a growth context where innovation is important. A new division can have a different set of people, systems, and culture, for example, than the parent organization. Attempting to support different cultures, systems, and sets of personnel comes at a cost, however. It strains the organization, increases communication problems, and makes it less likely that any positive organizational synergy will result.

There are, of course, variants on these two models. Functional units such as advertising or production can be organized by product or market. A division might share a sales force with another division. A matrix organization is one in which a manager, such as a product advertising manager, might report both to a functional advertising manager and a division manager responsible for the product line.

An important issue is determining how a strategy, such as a move into a new product market, will fit into the existing organizational structure. Will it fit into an existing product group or will a new group be required? In either circumstance, will it suffer from a lack of attention and interest? Will expected synergies emerge? What adjustments or major changes will have to be made? Can it use one of the existing sales forces or must it have its own dedicated sales team?

Ad Hoc Task Forces or Project Teams

Another organizational form that often is used to accomplish a critical task is the ad hoc task force. A team of manufacturing, marketing, and engineering people might be established to develop a new product. Or a team involving people from manufacturing, marketing, R&D, and public relations could be formed to deal with a disaster, such as the tampering with Tylenol packages. Another example would be a team that is formed to examine a technological threat or opportunity and to recommend a response. Still another would be the quality circle concept, made popular by Japanese firms, whereby groups work to improve productivity or service.

After observing the effective use of task forces in many firms, Tom Peters offers some guidelines.[3] First, he suggests that team members be assigned 100 percent to a team and be evaluated by the team leader—the goal is to breed total commitment. Second, give team members authority to commit resources from their function to the product so it doesn't become starved. Third, have the group live together, "off-site" if possible, to provide focus and a team spirit for accomplishing "mission impossible." Fourth, allow outsiders such as vendors, distributors, and lead customers in on the project. Fifth, have well-defined goals and deadlines.

Informal Communication

A study of 43 firms judged successful over a 20-year period was conducted by McKinsey and reported in the best-selling book, *In Search of Excellence*, by Peters and Waterman.[4] One observation of the McKinsey study was that successful firms tended to have a high, even intense level of informal communication. The open-door policy at IBM, the MBWA (management by walking around) philosophy at United Airlines and other firms, the ad hoc meetings that included customers at 3M, the campus atmosphere and beer parties at Hewlett Packard, and the informal top management meetings at Caterpillar illustrate some of the mechanisms used to foster informal communication.

Xerox during the 1970s had a dismal new product record that was a major factor causing it to lose its dominant position to Kodak, Savin, Canon, and others. During that period, Xerox failed to draw on two key assets. One was an innovative computer group called PARC (Palo Alto Research Center) that was a leader in the key microprocessor technology that was to be the heart of most machines in the 1980s. The other was Fuji Xerox of Japan that had the capability of building small copiers. The lack of communication and coordination with these assets turned out to be tragic for Xerox and illustrates the strategic importance of organizational structure and the communication system that it fosters.

SYSTEMS

Several management systems are strategically relevant. Among them are the planning system (which is discussed in the following chapter), the budgeting system, the accounting system, the information system, and the measurement and reward system.

Budgeting System

The best strategies can fail because needed investment does not materialize. An examination of the budgeting system can uncover budgeting risks facing a new strategy, especially one that does not fit a familiar pattern within a firm and that is a short-term cash drain. The short-term profit pressures "win" too often.

Another problem is that too many resources go into fading businesses. A partial solution is zero-based budgeting, whereby a business needs to justify investment on an absolute basis instead of relative to the past year or to current earnings.

Accounting and Information Systems

Key elements in any management system are the accounting and information systems. The risk that the systems cannot be adapted to the needs of a new strategy can be very real. An accounting system that is well conceived and contains valuable historical data can be seriously damaged by reorganizations caused by new strategies. Or a system that worked well for an electronics instruments firm may generate deceptive information when applied to a new service business. A growth context puts added strain on the accounting and information system.

Measurement and Reward System

The measurement and reward system over time influences behavior and thus strategy implementation. It is important to ensure that it fosters behavior that will lead to the strategy objectives. A key aspect of the strategy of a large consulting firm with over 20 offices was to obtain firmwide synergy, efficiency, and consistency.[5] Thus, despite the fact that each office had a good deal of autonomy, performance measures such as overhead control, productivity, and revenue were made at the firm level.

A concern in designing measurement and reward systems is to balance the short-term and long-term perspectives. An orientation that is too short run will doom many strategies. One approach is to tailor the performance measurement to the nature of the business.[6] A high-growth SBU, for example, could be measured on the basis of market share and on the development of an asset, such as a service system or quality performance. A survey of owners' problems during the first 90 days of ownership could play a key role. Measures such as ROA and cash flow would not be central. In contrast, a low-growth SBU might be exclusively evaluated on ROA and cash flow.

PEOPLE

A strategy is generally based on an organizational skill that, in turn, is based on people. Thus, strategies require certain types of people. Depending on the strategy, it is important to know the number and quality of the people with respect to their experience, depth, and skill in:

● A functional area such as marketing, heavy manufacturing, assembly, finance

- A product or market area
- New product programs
- Managing particular types of people
- Managing a particular type of operation
- Managing growth and change

Make, Buy, or Convert

If a strategy requires capabilities not now available in the business, it will be necessary to obtain them. The "make" approach, developing a broad managerial or technical base by hiring and grooming workers, ensures that people will fit the organization, but this approach can take a long time.

The "convert" approach, converting the existing work force to the new strategy, takes less time. AT&T is an example of a firm that attempted to change its orientation from that of service to marketing largely by retraining existing staff. There are a host of strategies, particularly those precipitated by acquisitions, in which the faulty assumption that the "old" staff could adapt to the new context caused a strategy to fail. A supermarket buying team, for example, could not be adapted to the needs of a discount drugstore, mainly because a discount orientation and background was missing.

The "buy" approach, bringing in experienced people from the outside, is the immediate solution when a dramatic change in strategy needs to be implemented quickly but it involves the risk of bringing in people who are accustomed to different systems and culture.

Motivation

In addition to the type and quality of the people, the level and nature of their motivation affect strategy implementation. There are, of course, a variety of ways to motivate people, including the fear of losing a job, financial incentives, self-fulfillment goals, and the development of goals for the organization or groups within the organization such as teams or quality circles.

The McKinsey study concluded that the successful firms studied tended to treat employees as important in many tangible and intangible ways that affected motivation. In particular, people were trusted and given the control and opportunity to make things happen. Furthermore, the individual's status was enhanced by titles like "hosts" (Disney), "crew members" (McDonald's), and "associate" (J. C. Penney), and there was wide use of celebration, sometimes corny, but usually oriented to recognizing individuals.

CULTURE

An organizational culture as suggested by Figure 16.2 involves three elements:

- A set of "shared values" or "dominant beliefs" that defines an organization's priorities
- A set of norms of behavior
- Symbols and symbolic activities used to develop and nurture those shared values and norms

Shared Values

The concept of shared values or dominant beliefs underlies a culture by specifying what is important. The values need to be shared by everyone in the organization so that they are reinforced and widely accepted. Virtually all in the organization should be able to identify the shared value and describe its rationale.

The shared value can have a variety of foci. It can involve, for example:

- A key asset or skill that is the essence of competition. We will be the most creative advertising agency.
- An operational focus. SAS focused on on-time performance.
- An organizational output. We will deliver zero defects or 100 percent customer satisfaction.
- An emphasis on a functional area. Black & Decker transformed itself from a firm with a manufacturing focus to one with an almost manic, market-driven approach.
- A management style. This is an informal flat organization that fosters communication and encourages odd-balls to do their thing.

FIGURE 16.2 Organizational Culture

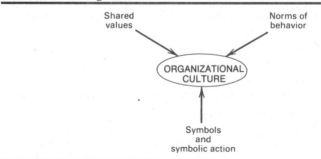

Values at Levi Strauss

Levi Strauss has a well-defined set of values that serves as the basis for a strong culture.[7] The values have two primary dimensions.

The first is a commitment to social values. The firm aspires to be a company that "our people are proud of and committed to," that values a diverse work force, and that epitomizes high standards of ethical behavior. This commitment is seen in the firm's approach to tough issues ranging from plant closings to AIDS in the workplace.

The second is a commitment to the people in its organization. Levi's explicitly sets out to provide employees with an opportunity to contribute, learn, grow, and advance on merit. It also wants its people to "feel respected, treated fairly, listened to, and involved" and to attain satisfaction from accomplishments, friendships, and balanced personal and professional lives. This commitment to its employees involves recognition of accomplishments, clear communication about individual goals and performance, and empowerment. Empowerment, which is a central concept, means that people have the authority and resources (including access to information) to act.

- A belief in the importance of people as individuals.
- A general objective. A belief in being the "best" or comparable to the best. Komatsu set out to beat Caterpillar. Samsung strove to be a major player in microwave ovens. Sharp wants to be one of the most innovative in the area in which it competes.

Norms

To make a real difference, the culture must be strong enough to develop norms of behavior or informal rules that influence decisions and actions throughout an organization. They guide people's behavior, suggesting what is appropriate and what is not. Charles O'Reilly of the University of California at Berkeley talks of culture being a social control system with norms being behavior guides.[8] The fact is that strong norms can generate much more effective control over what is actually done or not done in an organization than a very specific set of objectives, measures, and sanctions. People can always get around rules. The concept of norms is that people will not attempt to avoid them because they will be accompanied by a commitment to shared values.

O'Reilly suggests that norms can vary on two dimensions: the intensity or amount of approval/disapproval attached to an expectation and the degree of consensus or consistency with which a norm is shared.[9] It is only when both intensity and consensus exist that strong cultures emerge.

Norms affect behavior consistent with the shared values. Thus, in a "quality service" culture, an extraordinary effort by an employee, such as renting a helicopter to fix a communication component (a Federal Express legend), should not seem out of line and risky, but something that most in that culture would have done under similar circumstances. Furthermore, sloppy work affecting quality would be informally policed by fellow workers, without reliance on a formal system. One production firm uses no quality-control inspectors or janitors. Each production-line person is responsible for the quality of his or her output and for keeping the work area clean. Such a policy would not work without being supported by a strong culture.

Symbols and Symbolic Action

Corporate cultures are largely developed and maintained by the use of persistent, consistent, and visible symbols and symbolic action. In fact, the more obvious methods of affecting behavior, to change systems or structure, for example, are often much less effective than seemingly trivial symbolic actions.

A host of symbols and symbolic actions are available. A few of the more useful are discussed.

The Founder and Original Mission.   A corporation's unique "roots," including the personal style and experience of its founder, can provide extremely potent symbols. The strong culture of the Shaklee Corporation is due largely to the founder's involvement in holistic medicine, his contributions to vitamin development and use, and his ability to arouse enthusiasm in groups. The concept of entertainment developed by Walt Disney, the customer-oriented philosophy of J. C. Penney, and the product and advertising traditions started by the founders of Procter & Gamble continue to influence the cultures of their firms generations later.

Modern Role Models.   Modern heroes and role models help communicate, personalize, and legitimize values and norms. Archie McGill, the former IBM executive whose mission was to change the AT&T culture to one focusing on marketing, became a symbol of the new culture. Other examples are the several managers at 3M who tenaciously pursued an idea despite setbacks until they succeeded in building a major division, and the Frito-Lay service people who have maintained customer service in the face of natural disasters.

Activities.   The executive's use of time can be a symbolic action affecting the culture. An airline executive who spends two weeks a month obtaining a firsthand look at customer service sends a strong signal to the organization. Patterns of consistent reinforcement can represent another important symbolic activity. For example, a firm that regularly recognizes cost-saving accomplishments in a meaningful way with the visible support of top management can, over time, affect the culture.

Questions Asked.   A. W. Clausen of the Bank of America reportedly shifted concern from revenue to profit by continually asking about profit implications. Eventually, when a type of question is continually asked by top executives and made a central part of meeting agendas and report formats, it will influence the shared values of an organization.

Rituals.   Rituals of work life from hiring to eating lunches to retirement dinners help define a culture. Tandem's extensive interview process for new employees, the fact that people must accept the job before salary is discussed, the orientation sessions involving senior executives, and its regular Friday afternoon beer bust are all rituals that contribute to the culture.

Organizational Structure as a Symbol.   Pfeffer argues that organizational redesign can be primarily a symbolic, attention-focusing process.[10] Thus, the creation of departments of consumer affairs, service, product development, or the emphasis on a particular market may focus the attention of those within and outside an organization on an effort to change or reinforce existing values.

Corporate Culture and Strategy

Organizational culture provides the key to strategy implementation because it is such a powerful force in providing focus, motivation, and norms. Many strategies involve a focus on an organizational asset or skill such as product quality level, service system, or customer support, or a functional area like manufacturing or sales. The culture, when compatible, can provide support. If it is not compatible, on the other hand, the culture can generate a set of motivations and norms that may cripple the strategy.

A new strategy's fit with an organization's culture is of greater concern than the strategy's fit to the other organizational components because culture is so difficult to change. An oil company CEO developed elaborate diversification plans that failed because they were incompatible with the firm's oil business culture.[11] The difficulties experienced by AT&T during the 1970s in its efforts to change from what was a service/production/internal focus to a marketing/external orientation illustrate the power of the culture and how difficult it is to change. AT&T very visibly changed its strategy and even the associated structure and systems (introducing product/market organizations and sales incentives), but was inhibited by the culture. When AT&T hired different types of personnel—MBAs and marketing people—it found inconsistencies between the new people and the change-resistant culture.

When a new strategy is proposed, it is important to understand the relationship of that strategy to the shared values and norms of the organization. Is it compatible? Will the culture have to be modified? If so, what impact will that have on the organization? Often the worst case develops when a strong positive culture is sacrificed to accommodate a new strategy and the result is an absence of any positive culture. The Korvette case illustrates.

Some empirical evidence suggests an association between successful strategies and strong cultures. The McKinsey study described by Peters and Waterman concludes that the successful firms in their sample tended to be value-driven. In fact, they indicated that the best all-purpose advice emerging from their study was to "figure out your value system . . . what your company stands for . . . what gives everyone the most pride."[12]

OBTAINING ORGANIZATIONAL CONGRUENCE

It is critical that a strategy match the culture. However, each organizational component needs to fit, to be congruent with each other as well as compatible with the strategy. If an inconsistency exists, there is potential that the implementation of the strategy will be affected. Figure 16.3 lists a set of questions that provide a basis for analyzing an organization and its relationship to a proposed strategy.

The congruence concept suggests that interactions between organizational components should be considered, such as:

- Do the systems fit the structure? Does the compensation system emphasize teamwork rather than individual performance when teamwork and cooperation are required?

- Do the people fit the culture? Is there sufficient consensus in the organization about the "rules of the game" to enable the organization to achieve its goals? For example, can a rapidly growing organization be sure that new people will understand and accept a totally informal communications system?

- Do the people fit the structure? Can they operate within the organizational groups and integrate mechanisms to complete the task? For example, creative or entrepreneurial managers may be uncomfortable in a highly structured organization.

FIGURE 16.3   Obtaining Information About Organizational Components

---

STRUCTURE

• What is the organization's structure? How decentralized is it?
• What are the lines of authority and communication?
• What is the role of task forces, committees, or similar mechanisms?

SYSTEMS

• How are budgets set?
• What is the nature of the planning system?
• What are the key measures used to evaluate performance?
• How does the accounting system work?
• How do product and information flow?

PEOPLE

• What are the skills, knowledge, and experience of the firm's employees?
• What is their depth and quality?
• What are the employees' expectations?
• What are their attitudes toward the firm and their jobs?

CULTURE

• Are there shared values that are visible and accepted?
• What are these shared values and how are they communicated?
• What are the norms of behavior?
• What are the significant symbols and symbolic activities?
• What is the dominant management style?
• How is conflict resolved?

STRATEGY

• Where would the new strategy fit into the organization?
• Would the new strategy fit into the strategic plan and be adequately funded?
• Would the systems and culture support the new strategy?
• What organizational changes would be required for the new strategy to succeed?
• What impact would these changes have? Are they feasible?

• Does the structure fit the culture? Does the structure complement the values or norms of the organization? For example, a top management group accustomed to controlling dedicated resources may be less effective in a matrix organization where persuasion and coordination are more important.

Pascale and Athos observed that ITT during the 1960s and 1970s under Harold Geneen seemed to be effective because all of the elements of the organization fit together well.[13] Geneen obtained information from product area managers, as well as from lengthy formal meetings with line managers. With this information and a focus on key performance measures, he exerted a high level of personal control over a wide variety of business activities. His approach worked, in part because the culture, people, systems, and structure all fit together and supported the strategies. For example, the people hired were tested to ensure that they would adapt to the Geneen approach and then they were provided with both financial and nonfinancial incentives to adapt.

Hit-Industry Topology[14]

The concept of needed congruence between strategy and organizational components can be illustrated by the three very different types of firms that compete in "hit industries." A hit industry is one in which the goal is to obtain, produce, and exploit a hit product, which will have a relatively short product life cycle. Examples of such industries include movies, books, records, fashions, publishing, video games, computer software, venture capital (especially in high-tech areas), and oil. Industries with short life cycles are interesting because many of their organizational problems are more intense and graphic in that context.

Figure 16.4 presents a simple model of a hit industry. It suggests three rather different functions that need to be performed. The model conceptualizes the functions as being performed by different organizations, although often two or more coexist within the same organization. An oil industry analogy provides a conceptual framework.

The first organizational type is termed "drillers." They are the wildcatters who find oil fields and drill wells, the talent scouts and artists of the record industry, the producers and writers in the movie industry, and the editors and authors in the publishing industry. A key success factor is to find and keep the key people with the talent and background to locate or create the new wells, properties, or projects. An ultimate goal, in the record business, for example, would be to get a lock on performing talent and keep them so happy they would not consider leaving. Key people tend to be creative, high-energy, decisive risk-takers. They thrive in a flat organization with little structure and with high bottom-line incentives.

The second organization type is termed "pumpers." They are the well operators and refiners of the oil business, the record pressers, the movie directors, and the printers in publishing. The key success factors in a pumping organization are operations, production engineering, and

FIGURE 16.4   A Model of Hit Industries

Strategy	Drillers	Pumpers	Distributors
Structure	Flat, loose Amorphous	Centralized Tight control	Decentralized Loose control
Bottom-line performance incentives	High	None	Low
People	Product development	Production control	Marketing and distribution
Culture	Stay loose Move fast Take risks	Disciplined Cost-oriented Avoid risks	Promotion-oriented Controlled risks
Key success factors	Finding and keeping key people Idea source Get products to market quickly	Exploit the experience curve Operations Production Engineering	Distribution channels Inventory Promotion Positioning Pricing

an ability to exploit the experience curve. The key people are disciplined, cost- and production-oriented, in production and control jobs, and risk-avoiders. A centralized organization with tight controls provides an appropriate context.

The third type specializes in distribution. These distributors are the pipeline operators and retailers in the oil industry and the distributors and retailers in the record, film, and publishing industries. The key success factors in the distribution business usually include having access or even control over distribution channels, inventory control, physical distribution, and promotion. The key people are in marketing and distribution. A decentralized structure with loose controls and some bottom-line incentives is often effective.

The hit-industry organizational topology exposes some problems. Typically, an organization starts as a drilling company. After establishing some products and experiencing rapid growth, a desperate need emerges to control production costs, to develop a secure, effective distribution channel, and to professionalize the marketing effort. As a result, pumper and distribution people are brought in. The organization will take the form of either a pumper or a distributor, depending on which function is most critical or which type of person becomes the CEO. In any case, the system, structure, and culture of the organization change and the drillers who started the business become uncomfortable and leave, perhaps to start a competing business. When the existing wells dry up or are damaged by competition, no one in the organization is available to create new ones.

One challenge in any business is to keep access to drillers. One approach is to keep the drillers satisfied by financial incentives and organizational mechanisms, such as ad hoc groups with extraordinary freedom and autonomy. However, special incentives create inequities and disincentives for others. If "entrepreneurial" engineers are becoming millionaires, whereas those charged with maintaining existing products are on a salary, tensions are bound to mount. Furthermore, the entrepreneurial groups may need to have access to facilities and the expertise of the pumpers and distributors, and providing that access may compromise their "separateness."

Another way to approach the fit problem is to restrict the organization to one function—to allow other organizations to perform the other functions. Venture capital firms restrict themselves to being drillers and do not become involved in the other functions. Publishers are largely distribution companies; their production is farmed out. The drillers are actually the authors, who are not part of the organization. Without in-house drillers, however, access to new ventures becomes limited. Other firms may successfully contract with the best independent drillers. Or the price for the proven drillers may become so high that profits are limited and the risk high.

Another problem arises when pumpers and distributors share an organization. If one of the two clearly dominates, the problem is minimized. If each is equally significant, however, there could easily be a fit problem.

ORGANIZING FOR INNOVATION

Although the achievement of high congruence among organizational components and strategy leads to organizational effectiveness in the short to medium term, it can also inhibit desirable and even necessary change. An organization can become so integrated and the culture so strong that only compatible changes are tolerated. For example, when faced with a technological threat, firms often respond with even greater reliance on the obsolete familiar technology.

The challenge is twofold. First, it is necessary to create an organization that can successfully operate a strategy congruent with the organization and still have the ability to detect the need for fundamental change. If a significant change in strategy is needed, a major organizational change undoubtedly will be required as well. Second, there is a need to be innovative in the context of an ongoing strategy that is congruent with the organization, to have the ability to create new or improved products or processes and enter new markets. There follows a discussion of how each of the organizational components can be adjusted to help the organization enhance its ability to innovate and detect the need to change.[15] The key is to create an effective learning system with the ability to acquire and process information about customers, competitors, and technology.

Structure

Effective internal linking mechanisms that connect disparate functions encourage problem solving throughout the organization. Teams, committees, or task forces can bring together individuals to work on issues created by trends, threats, or opportunities. At Xerox, for example, an innovation board brings a diverse group of marketing, production, and R&D executives together to discuss and evaluate new corporate ventures. Formal meetings, perhaps associated with the planning process, can provide a setting for individuals throughout the organization to share ideas. NCR has "show-and-tell" meetings in which R&D, marketing, and manufacturing people discuss their plans and problems.

Another approach to innovation is to create numerous joint ventures and alliances especially with small, upstart, and overseas firms.[16] Hewlett-Packard is involved in hundreds of joint ventures and alliances that put it in contact with firms having unique access to customers, foreign markets, technologies, and software systems. Fuji Xerox is among the many Japanese firms that have alliances with suppliers in order to bring expertise to bear on needed innovation.

Alliances and joint ventures aid innovation by:

- Transferring knowledge about product and process improvements.
- Providing the stimulation of the problems and perspectives of another organization.
- Providing missing technologies that are roadblocks to innovation.
- Reducing the time required to implement innovation, thus making them more attractive.

Major new business ventures may require separate entrepreneurial units, small autonomous groups of people representing all the important functions that join together to create a product or a business and nurse it through the early stages of life. Used by 3M, IBM, Xerox, and many others, such a group is usually autonomous enough that it can bypass the decision process and resist pressures to conform to existing formal and informal constraints. When such a group is set off by itself, often off-site, it is called a "skunkworks." A key to entrepreneurial units is to have a business "champion" committed to the concept. Texas Instruments reviewed 50 new product introductions and found that every failure lacked a voluntary product champion.[17]

Operating on a bit larger scale is the new venture group, a self-contained group that is charged with generating totally new business start-ups. Though popular in the early 1980s, many firms lost patience with such groups.[18] The problem is that the commitment to the new areas comes from the venture team rather than the firm. Almost by definition, the new business will represent a diversification that is not within the basic vision of the firm. As a result, unless the new venture hits quickly, the support often fades.

Simple Structures with Lean Staffs.   Several studies have suggested that innovation and change are easier when the organization is relatively small and flat. The large vertical organization with seven or eight levels usually inhibits innovation. For example, in the McKinsey study the successful firms resisted dealing with increased size by resorting to complex organizational forms and large staffs.[19] In particular, none viewed themselves as having a formal matrix structure. Instead, a basic organization structure was based on a single dimension, usually the product division. These firms maintained flexibility by reorganizing frequently, by using task forces and project centers, and by supporting small, autonomous divisions that usually had control of functional activities. For example, Johnson & Johnson breaks its $5 billion company into 150 independent divisions and 3M forms a division whenever a new product line reaches $20 million. Another study of innovative firms found an effort to keep operating divisions and total technical units small, below 400 people, to avoid bureaucracies.[20]

People

Most innovations—from product or process refinements to more radical changes—occur when two disparate concepts or disciplines are merged. Thus, one approach is to attempt to have people with different experiences and backgrounds. Someone who knows how it was done in another firm or industry can contribute a different perspective. Hewlett Packard and other high-tech firms brought in consumer product marketers to help stimulate innovation. Another approach is to rotate employees through an organization. An engineer who is on the firing line as a service manager may have ideas for improvement that would not occur to someone who had become accustomed to the chronic problems.

Several informal roles are critical to the innovation process, and it is helpful for the organization to locate and encourage people to fill these roles. In addition to the venture champion, there are idea generators who continually ask, "Why not?", sponsors, senior managers who provide support and resources for embryonic ideas, and gatekeepers who have access to external information sources.

One approach is to hire "renegades," those who have professionally demonstrated the ability to innovate. Tom Peters tells of once selecting a person who had made a one-ton cookie as an undergraduate—his point is that someone who has done something so unusual and intriguing will probably do so again.[21] Sony reportedly once hired some people who excelled in off-beat areas—one was an opera singer. Peters also indicates that renegades need to be protected from bureaucrats who are frequently irritated by those who do not conform. Furthermore, there should be a horizontal "project" career path so that a productive renegade does not have to move into a different role in order to succeed in the organization.

Reward Systems

Incentives and rewards play a major role in stimulating innovation. Bonuses, stock options, and promotions can be based on innovation-related accomplishments. The key is to develop measures of an area in which innovation is needed and performance targets. For example, targets that would stimulate innovation could be set with respect to:

- The elapsed time for new product development
- Quality improvement
- Cost reduction
- Performance specification
- Size or weight of a product
- Speed of delivering service

Innovation prizes at 3M, Canon, and Hewlett-Packard provided special status to innovative individuals and teams. Another tack is to reduce the risk of being a member of a new venture team that failed. At 3M, for example, team members are assured of receiving comparable jobs if a venture does not work out.

Culture

Some firms develop an innovation culture. A key shared value is either innovation or something closely related that fosters change. Firms such as Intel, Hewlett-Packard, Cray Research, 3M, Sharp, Kao Soap, and Sony overtly attempt to foster a culture in which innovation is a shared value and the norms and symbols support it.

A study attempted to identify norms that would help promote the generation of new ideas and the implementation of new approaches.[22] Over 500 managers from diverse industrial and consumer firms were asked to identify such norms. The answers, which were remarkably similar across industries, are shown in Figure 16.5. Note that the norms all serve to facilitate the process of introducing new ways of doing things and to help people implement them.

SUMMARY

An analysis of an organization can help estimate the cost and feasibility of implementing particular strategies. The analysis is best structured by looking at organizational components such as structure, systems, people, and culture.

Organizational structure defines the lines of authority and communication and can vary with respect to degree of decentralization, the informal communication channels, the use of task forces and alliances, and how flat and lean it is. The management systems such as the planning system, the budgeting system, the accounting systems, the information system, and the measurement and reward systems all can influence strategy implementation. Types of people and their motivations are often the basis of the skills needed to support SCAs. Because organizational culture, which involves shared values, norms of behavior, and symbols and symbolic activities, is so difficult to change, the fit of a new strategy to the culture is particularly important.

These organizational components must fit with each other as well as with the strategy. The "congruence" principle is illustrated by the hit-industry topology, which contrasts the functions of "drillers" who de-

---

FIGURE 16.5   Norms That Promote Innovation[23]

A. NORMS TO PROMOTE CREATIVITY	B. NORMS TO PROMOTE IMPLEMENTATION
1. **Risk-Taking**	1. **Common Goals**
• freedom to try things and fail	• sense of pride in the organization
• acceptance of mistakes	• teamwork
• allow discussion of "dumb" ideas	• willingness to share the credit
• no punishments for failure	• flexibility in jobs and budgets

A. NORMS TO PROMOTE CREATIVITY

- challenge the status quo
- forget the past
- willingness *not* to focus on the short term
- expectation that innovation is part of your job
- positive attitudes about change
- drive to improve

2. Rewards for Change

- ideas are valued
- respect for beginning ideas
- build into the structure:
  budgets   opportunities
  resources   tools
  time   promotions
- top management attention and support
- celebration of accomplishments
- suggestions implemented
- encouragement

3. Openness

- open communication and sharing of information
- listen better
- open access
- bright people, strong egos
- scanning, broad thinking
- force exposure outside the company
- move workers around
- encourage lateral thinking
- adopt the customer's perspective
- accept criticism
- don't be too sensitive
- continuous training
- intellectual honesty
- expect and accept conflict
- willingness to consult others

B. NORMS TO PROMOTE IMPLEMENTATION

- sense of ownership
- eliminate mixed messages
- manage interdependencies
- shared visions and a common direction
- build consensus
- mutual respect and trust
- concern for the whole organization

2. Autonomy

- decision-making responsibility at lower levels
- decentralized prodecures
- freedom to act
- expectation of action
- belief that *you* can have an impact
- delegation
- quick, flexible decision making
- minimize the bureaucracy

3. Belief in Action

- don't be obsessed with precision
- emphasis on results
- meet your commitments
- anxiety about timeliness
- value accomplishing things
- hard work is expected and appreciated
- empower people
- emphasis on quality
- eagerness to get things done
- cut through the bureaucracy

velop products, "pumpers" who focus on production, and "distributors" who specialize in marketing and distribution.

A challenge is to create an organization with structure, systems, people, and a culture to stimulate and accommodate innovation. Toward this end, the culture and reward system can support innovation and the organization can encourage different perspectives to interact so that ideas are generated. Alliances and task forces can also play a role. Finally, innovative workers can be obtained and protected.

FOOTNOTES

[1] Robert F. Hartley, *Marketing Mistakes*, 4th ed., New York: Wiley, 1989, Chapter 8.

[2] Many such frameworks have been advanced by behavioral scientists and management consulting firms. The McKinsey firm, for example, developed what it calls the 7-S framework, which includes strategy, structure, systems, skills, staff, style (of management), and shared values.

[3] Tom Peters, "Part Two: Get Innovative or Get Dead," *California Management Review*, Winter 1991, pp. 22–23.

[4] Thomas J. Peters and Robert H. Waterman, Jr., *In Search of Excellence: Lessons from America's Best-Run Companies*, New York: Harper & Row, 1982.

[5] Paul J. Stonich, ed., *Implementing Strategy*, Cambridge, Mass.: Balenger, 1982, p. 133.

[6] Stonich, *Implementing Strategy*, p. 135.

[7] Robert Howard, "Values Make the Company: An Interview with Robert Haas," *Harvard Business Review*, September–October 1990, pp. 133–144.

[8] Charles O'Reilly, "Corporations, Culture, and Commitment: Motivation and Social Control in Organizations," *California Management Review*, Summer 1989, pp. 9–25.

[9] O'Reilly, "Corporations, Culture," p. 13.

[10] Jeffrey Pfeffer, "Management as Symbolic Action," *Research in Organizational Behavior* 3, 1981, p. 1.

[11] Howard Schwartz and Stanley M. Davis, "Matching Corporate Culture and Business Strategy," *Organizational Dynamics*, Summer 1981, p. 18.

[12] Peters and Waterman, *In Search of Excellence*, p. 279.

[13] Richard Tanner Pascale and Anthony G. Athos, *The Art of Japanese Management*, New York: Warner Books, 1981, Chapter 3.

[14] The hit-industry topology was developed in discussions with Dr. Norman Smothers.

[15] See Michael Tushman and David Nadler, "Organizing for Innovation," *California Management Review* 3, Spring 1986, pp. 74–92. Several of the examples that follow were suggested by this excellent article.

[16] Tom Peters, "Part One: Get Innovative or Get Dead," *California Management Review*, Fall 1990, pp. 22–23.

[17] Peters and Waterman, *In Search of Excellence*, p. 203.

[18] Aimee L. Stern, "The Ventures that Failed," *Adweek's Marketing Week*, January 30, 1989, pp. 37–38.

[19] Peters and Waterman, *In Search of Excellence*, Chapter 11.

[20] James Brian Quinn, "Managing Innovation: Controlled Chaos," *Harvard Business Review*, May–June, 1985, pp. 73–84.

[21] Peters, "Part Two: Get Innovative," pp. 9–23.

[22] O'Reilly, "Corporations, Culture."

[23] O'Reilly, "Corporations, Culture."

17

FORMAL PLANNING SYSTEMS

Chaotic action is preferable to orderly inaction.

Karl Weick

Those that implement the plans must make the plans.

Patrick Hagerty,
Texas Instruments

Strategy development requires systematic and structured information-gathering, a willingness to consider new directions, managerial insight, and an ability to think strategically. Given that the effort, the will, and the talent all exist, the question addressed in this chapter still arises: How does one begin and sustain the process of developing, refining, and changing strategies? The reader may want to review the first two chapters, which provide an overview of the book and the concepts and methods that need to be captured in the strategy-development process.

THE FORMAL PLANNING SYSTEM

The need is to plan the planning process by specifying what needs to be accomplished when. A well-defined calendar specifying what tasks need to be accomplished by what dates will help provide structure and discipline. Planning forms and agendas for key meetings will flesh out the structure, providing detail and clarifying the tasks to be accomplished. In the appendix a set of illustrative planning forms is presented.

The planning process can be a focused effort done in a one- to two-week period. The discussion agenda shown in Figure 17.1 can structure the effort (it includes a condensed version of the sets of questions that appeared in the external analysis chapters). However, spreading out the planning process over a longer period allows time to expand the information base, to conduct analyses, and to conceive and to consider more strategic alternatives. Sometimes, for example, the identification of a key strategic question or issue cannot be anticipated but emerges during the process.

The following outline provides a four-step process that can be scheduled over a one- to four-month time period.

1. **External/self-analysis workshop**   1–2 days
   - Address the questions in Figure 17.1 covering external and self-analyses.
   - Specify scenarios and identify strategic opportunities, threats, questions, strengths, weaknesses, and problems.
2. **Strategy development workshop**   1–2 days
   - Address Figure 17.1 the questions in covering strategy development.
   - Reduce the strategy choices to a limited number of strategies and growth directions. Attempt to prioritize them.
3. **Strategy presentation**   1–2 days
   - Present the selected strategy or two or three strategies from which one is to be selected.

FIGURE 17.1   Strategy Development: A Discussion Agenda

CUSTOMER ANALYSIS

- What are the major segments?
- What are their motivations and unmet needs?

COMPETITOR ANALYSIS

- Who are the existing and potential competitors? What strategic groups can be identified?
- What are their levels of sales, share growth, and profits?
- What are their strengths, weaknesses, and strategies?

MARKET ANALYSIS

- How attractive is the market or industry and its submarkets? What are the forces reducing profitability in the market, entry and exit barriers, growth projections, cost structures, and profitability prospects?
- What are the alternative distribution channels and their relative strengths?
- What industry trends are significant to strategy?
- What are the current and future key success factors?

ENVIRONMENTAL ANALYSIS

- What environmental threats, opportunities, and trends exist?
- What major environmental scenarios can be conceived?
- What are the major strategic questions and information-need areas?

SELF-ANALYSIS

- What are our strategy, performance, costs, point of differentiation, strengths, weaknesses, strategic problems, and culture?
- What is our existing business portfolio? What has been our level of investment in our various product markets?

STRATEGY DEVELOPMENT

- How can our offering be differentiated? How can we add customer value by doing something better or differently than competitors? How can perceived quality be enhanced?
- Can a cost advantage be gained by offering a no-frills product or by reducing product costs?
- Can synergy, focus, or a preemptive move be employed to gain advantage?
- What is the strategic vision? What are the key assets and skills to be maintained or developed?
- What alternative growth directions should be considered? How should they be pursued?
- What investment level is most appropriate for each market—withdrawal, milking, maintaining, or growing?
- What are the alternative functional area strategies?
- What strategies best fit our strengths, our objectives, and our organization?

- Project key performance measures such as investment, sales, and profits through the planning horizon.
- Develop objectives, including one-year objectives to guide implementation.

4. **The annual plan**   1–2 days

- Present a refined, selected strategy.
- Present the programs that will support the strategy implementation.
- Present a detailed financial plan for the coming year.

General Electric, one of the most experienced users of formal planning systems, spreads the process out over much of the year and explicitly deals with the need to communicate vertically within the organization. Its system, summarized in Figure 17.2, involves the following steps:[1]

1. **January.** A corporate-level environmental review identifies issues of corporate-level concern, such as energy prices or supply. An issue analysis, perhaps using scenario analysis, is conducted. Corporate-level guidelines indicating the firm's major priorities and goals are given to the SBUs.

2. **February–June.** Each SBU updates its five-year strategic plan, focusing on how to enhance its long-range competitive position. In addition, the SBU determines its response to corporate guidelines.

3. **July–September.** The top management committee evaluates the SBU plans, assesses risks, and decides on resource allocation priorities. The emphasis is on objectives and resource requirements rather than the specific SBU strategies proposed to achieve objectives.

4. **October–December.** Each SBU develops detailed operating programs and budgets for the coming year.

5. **December.** SBU budgets receive final approval at the corporate level.

Of course, there are numerous variations of formal planning systems. In some, managers develop and get approval for statements of objectives and broad strategic directions before they develop specific strategies or operating plans. In others, the SBU managers completely develop plans and their only contact with corporate management, if there is one at all, might be a final review.

Planning Forms

Standardized forms can help specify the content of presentations. When strategies are being tracked over time, the use of similar planning forms

FIGURE 17.2 General Electric's Corporate Strategic Planning Cycle

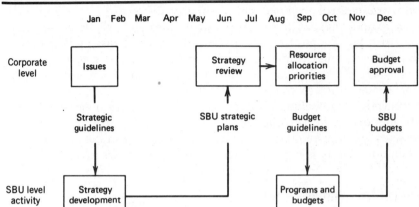

SOURCE: Dale J. Hedhuis, "Commentary" in Dan E. Schendel and Charles W. Hofer, eds., *Strategic Management,* Boston. Little, Brown, 1979, p. 243.

from year to year makes relevant comparisons much more feasible. In an organization containing multiple businesses, planning forms can encourage a common format and content so that cross-business comparisons will be easier.

The most useful and appropriate forms will depend on context. In general, they will vary for different industries and even different firms within an industry. The appendix provides a set of illustrative forms that should be viewed as a starting point in form development.

Advantages of a Formal Planning System

Scott Armstrong of Wharton reviewed 15 efforts to compare the performance of firms using formal planning systems with comparable firms not using formal planning systems.[2] Improved performance was found in 10 of the studies, in 3 there was no difference, and in 2 performance was inferior. Thus, the results are consistent with a belief that planning is useful.

Another perspective comes from a study of nearly 1100 strategic decisions made by 129 Fortune 500 firms during the mid–1980s.[3] Each was scaled on whether or not its formal planning systems were critical to making the decision (5 on a 5-point scale), or whether or not the decision was made outside the planning system (1 on a 5-point scale). About one-third of the decisions received a score of four or five—the average was 3.1. The formal planning system tended to be more influential when the decisions were important, risky, global, or involved a divestment.

Perhaps the most important benefit of a formal planning system with well-defined responsibilities is that it forces executives and managers to take time out to consider strategic questions. Without that impetus, artificial though it may sometimes be, routine tasks will generally absorb their available time. A formal planning system can also help make feasible the tasks of responding to a dynamic environment and of managing strategically a complex organization with limited resources. Armstrong also analyzed relevant behavioral science experiments and concluded that formal planning systems are more useful when large changes are occurring either in the environment or in the organization, when uncertainty is high, and when complex tasks are involved.

Role of the Planning Staff

Perhaps the most accepted fact about strategy development is that the function of a planning staff is not to create strategies. That function needs to be a line activity. A possible exception is when an acquisition or divestiture is to be considered.

In general, the proper role of a planning staff is to support the planning process. First, it can plan and coordinate the planning process itself. Second, it can conduct research and gather information on issues relevant to strategy development. Third, it can assist the line people in strategy development by helping them generate and evaluate alternative strategies.

Top-Down Versus Bottom-Up Systems

Planning systems can be top-down or bottom-up or some combination of the two. In a top-down system, the top management creates the strategy. An advantage is that the strategy-creation process can more easily be pursued across existing SBUs. Without a top-down orientation, resource allocation, synergy development, and strategy coordination across SBUs are more difficult. Also, top management may be more comfortable with strategy development and long-range perspectives than operating managers.

In a bottom-up system, the process is driven by those at the lowest levels at which a business management responsibility exists. An SBU manager should be closer and more responsive to the immediate environment than top management and thus more capable of generating effective strategies. Furthermore, an SBU manager's authority to develop strategies should enhance his or her motivation to implement the strategy. The most appropriate system will depend, in part, on the level of decentralization that exists in a firm. A high level of decentralization is most compatible with a bottom-up planning system.

PITFALLS OF A FORMAL PLANNING SYSTEM

There have been several efforts to identify systematically the pitfalls and difficulties of operating an effective planning system. Studies by Gray of 300 executives, Ringbakk of 268 firms, Steiner of over 200 planning directors, Henry of 50 large firms, and Kumar of 26 firms all focused on the major difficulties encountered in operating planning systems.[4] Some of the recurring problems of planning systems can be identified from these studies, numerous individual commentaries, and the experience of applying the ideas in this book.

The Spreadsheet-Driven Process

One all-too-common version of planning is dominated by spreadsheet logic. The idea is to generate income statements and balance sheets for years into the future using nifty, powerful spreadsheet programs. The focus is on projecting past financial data into the future and features elegant accounting. There is a strong bias toward making next year's strategy an extension of last year's strategy. As a result, a firm's plan is internally oriented and there is little likelihood that any strategy change will be considered. To the extent that spreadsheets support such a process, they can be a real handicap.

In contrast, an effective process will be externally oriented, focusing on environmental threats and opportunities. The aim will be to develop new strategic options rather than to extrapolate last year's strategy. Thus, devices that are helpful in identifying new options, such as scenario analysis, portfolio analysis, and growth direction analysis, will be used. The identification of potential strategies, even if not pursued, can help an organization become more sensitive to change and more adaptable. The process can stimulate the development of assets and skills so that options not now available to the firm would become feasible.

Dominance of Short-Run Financial Objectives

Most businesses set goals that involve short-term financial measures such as sales, profit, ROI, or market share. If other goals exist, they are often vague and become dominated by these quantitative ones, which then influence strategy development and choice. A bias toward milking a business and under-investing in the production process to improve the short-term financial performance is often introduced. Hayes observes that too many manufacturing companies have starved the production area in order to generate short-term cash.[5] He also suggests that financial goals may have encouraged firms to make unwise acquisitions in an effort to achieve growth.

The more appropriate focus should be the nurturing and development of assets and skills that will form the basis of SCAs in the future. What assets and skills will be needed to maintain an SCA or to develop new strategic directions? What objectives and programs will be responsive? A key question is which type of goal drives the planning system.

Planning Is Restricted to the Annual Cycle

One danger is that managers never have the time to think strategically. The annual planning cycle ensures that at least once per year the day-to-day problems will be set aside and a strategic review will occur. The problem is that all too often managers finish a plan with a sigh of relief, feeling their reward is being able to set aside the difficult issues for yet another year. However, threats, opportunities, and strategic windows do not always coincide with a planning cycle. Thus, the system must allow for information to be received and analyzed and decisions made outside of the planning cycle.

Plans That Are Too Rigid and Detailed

A strategic plan with the blessings of top management can become a straitjacket to those implementing it—a device that inhibits reactions by stimulating the "It's not in the plan" response to proposals for change. Jack Welch, the CEO at GE, noted that, "Once written, the strategic document can take on a life of its own, and it may not lend itself to flexibility. . . . An organization can begin to focus on form rather than substance."[6] William Bricker, CEO of Diamond Shamrock, has a similar concern: "Why has our vision been narrowed? To my mind there is one central reason our strategies have become too rigid . . . . A detailed strategy is like a road map . . . telling us every turn we must take to get to our goal . . . . The entrepreneur, on the other hand, views strategic planning not as a road map but as a compass . . . and is always looking for the new road."[7]

The process should help a business sense and adapt to change rather than inhibit it, in part by supporting the stimulation of strategic thinking and decisions outside of an annual planning cycle. Among the devices that can help are:

- An ongoing analysis of information-need areas. The identification of strategic questions and associated information-need areas should lead to information-gathering and analyses that will detect emerging threats and opportunities and stimulate a review of strategy.

- A consideration of flexibility in making strategic decisions, especially those that involve substantial commitments or affect assets and skills.

- The use of contingency plans. A contingency plan is an alternative strategy or set of actions that will be triggered by a particular event, such as a strike, the loss of a key raw material source, the loss of a major customer, or a technological shift.

Lack of Commitment to the Process Outputs

The other extreme is the all too familiar story of a set of plans with gold-embossed covers lying on the shelf, unused. The plans may be too vague, with little relevance to actual operations, or, more likely, they are not influential because they have not been integrated into the management system. There may be no set of objectives or interim decision points being monitored by top management. The link to the operating plan may not be clear and effective. The operating plan and its associated short-term success measures may dominate the managerial system. This lack of commitment is often reflected in an over-reliance on a planning staff to generate strategies and a lack of time spent by top management on the process.

MODIFYING A PLANNING SYSTEM—A CASE STUDY

The Dutch multinational firm, SHV, provides an instructive example of a firm that modified its planning system when it was deemed to be ineffective at its key objective, formulating strategy.[8] SHV is a $5-billion company, consisting of about 100 operating businesses organized into 14 industry-oriented groups covering a wide range of activities from shipping to retailing in 20 countries. Its planning system had deteriorated into rather sterile and repetitive annual rituals, which rarely resulted in creative alternative strategies. Among the problems were excessive reporting requirements, undue emphasis on operating plans, and ineffective use of the time of both top management and the planning staff. In an effort to rejuvenate the planning activity, the firm made the following changes in their system.

Streamlining Reports

Over the years, the quantity of information required by the system, especially financial data, had grown enormously. The need for much of this data was not obvious to those preparing it. New reporting requirements called for a small number of key financial measures to be supported by insightful analyses and explanations. For example, why was a measure below plan? In addition, a small number of nonfinancial parameters, carefully tailored to the individual businesses, were emphasized. These parameters tended to reflect the following:

● "Early warnings" of changes in business performance.

● Progress toward the (not more than four) key, active programs that are supporting the strategy.

● Changes in key trends or events involving customer segments, competitors, or environmental factors that are deemed to affect the basic assumptions underlying each strategy.

The net effect of these changes was to increase the proportion of nonfinancial data being reported and to tailor the information to the business involved.

Strategy Review Levels

Each SBU had generated a strategic plan that was reviewed by top management. One problem was that each SBU absorbed comparable time on the part of top management, regardless of its strategic importance. The new system provides for three levels of analysis and review as portrayed by Figure 17.3.

FIGURE 17.3   Guidelines for Depth of Strategy Review

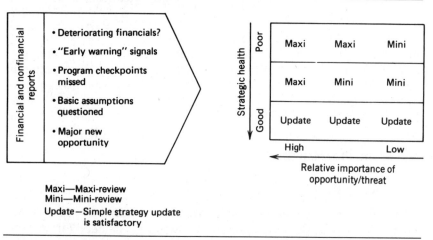

SOURCE: Adapted from Arie J. Rijvhis and Graham J. Sharman, "New Life for Formal Planning Systems," *Journal of Business Strategy* 2, Spring 1982, p. 103.

The first, termed a maxi-review, applies to businesses clearly in trouble financially and strategically or facing a major opportunity or threat that could transform the character of the business. A maxi-review represents a complete reappraisal of the business strategy and can take four or five months of planning effort. The second, a mini-review, applies to businesses meeting their financial targets but facing one or more important opportunities or threats. The mini-review involves one or two months of planning effort, focusing on the validity of the existing strategy or a major decision. The third level is a simple strategy update in which progress is reported but no decision is addressed.

Flexible Scheduling

The scheduling of the maxi- and mini-reviews under the new system is not tied to a planning cycle, but is flexible. Reviews can start at any time of the year and can take whatever time is needed. In practice, strategy reviews have taken from two months to two years. Thus, the reviews can be pursued when they are needed and timely. Although they are not tied to a planning cycle, they are part of a planning system so reviews do tend to be precipitated when they are needed. Furthermore, the SBU managers may choose whatever planning horizon is most appropriate—as few as three years for some SBUs and as many as seven years for others.

Top-Down Strategizing

The prior system of bottom-up planning tended to be constrained by the existing organizational units. In the new system, the executives heading the 14 business groups have primary responsibility for generating strategies, whereas operating-level managers provide input and develop the operating plans. The new system recognizes that major strategy changes can require the restructuring of an organization. Thus, SHV's strategic plans now consider implications for organizational structure and management resources, as well as financial implications.

Role of the Planning Staff

Under the old system, the planning staff had been inundated annually with a vast quantity of material, to the point where they had time only to attempt to detect shortcomings and inconsistencies and to organize the paper flow. Under the new system, the planning staff has a more constructive role. It consults with group management prior to the strategy reviews and also during the reviews, prior to the presentations. Furthermore, line managers are cycled through the planning staff so that greater understanding exists between the staff and line people.

Results

These changes have had two major consequences. First, the enhanced flexibility of the planning process allows the process to be adapted to the needs of the individual businesses. Second, the new system reinforces the responsibility of group management for the development of strategy.

GETTING STARTED

When a firm or SBU wants to develop and consider strategies and is not blessed (or burdened) with a formal planning system, the appropriate focus should be on developing strategies rather than a planning system. The approach is to follow the structured process outlined in Chapter 2. An external analysis should aim to identify strategic threats, opportunities, and questions. The companion self-analysis should identify strategic strengths, weaknesses, problems, and constraints. The consideration of alternative missions and strategies should follow. The evaluation phase can then involve cycling back to strategic questions raised in the prior analysis and perhaps gathering more information.

The format of generating information and conducting analyses can vary. However, it is usually helpful to bring the involved people to an off-site retreat for two to five days in order to guarantee uninterrupted time. The group, perhaps aided by prior research, can systematically cycle through the elements of the external analysis, self-analysis, and strategy development. The Figure 17.1 agenda provides a series of questions that can help structure discussion. The use of a focused discussion at a retreat ensures that the strategy-development process at least gets started. It also provides a setting for the development of objectives and policies, the interchange of information, and the testing of strategic assumptions and alternatives.

SUMMARY

The planning process can be structured by four phases: an external self-analysis workshop, a strategy-development workshop, a strategy presentation, and the annual plan presentation. GE spreads the process over a year and provides for vertical communication of issue analyses and strategic priorities and goals.

A formal planning system, which can be either top-down or bottom-up, forces attention to the process and provides mechanisms to handle the associated complexity. Among the pitfalls of a formal system are:

- The spreadsheet orientation of projecting accounting measures.
- The dominance of short-run financial objectives.
- Plans that are too rigid and detailed.
- A lack of commitment to the process outputs.

One effort to improve a formal planning process streamlined the reports, created levels of strategy reviews, provided flexibility in terms of scheduling, and moved to more of a top-down planning system. When a strategy review is initiated for the first time, the emphasis should be on strategy development guided by external analysis and self-analysis rather than on the development of a planning system.

FOOTNOTES

[1] Dale J. Hedhuis, "Commentary," in Dan E. Schendel and Charles W. Hofer, eds., *Strategic Management*, Boston: Little, Brown, 1979, p. 243.

[2] J. Scott Armstrong, "The Value of Formal Planning for Strategic Decisions: Review of Empirical Research," *Strategic Management Journal* 3, July–September 1982, pp. 197–212.

[3] Deepak K. Sinha, "The Contribution of Formal Planning to Decisions," *Strategic Management Journal*, October 1990, pp. 479–492.

[4] Daniel H. Gray, "Uses and Misuses of Strategic Planning," *Harvard Business Review*, January–February 1986, pp. 89–97; Kjell A. Ringbakk, "Why Planning Fails," *European Business*, Spring 1971, pp. 15–27; George A. Steiner, *Strategic Planning*, New York: The Free Press, 1979, pp. 287–298; Harold W. Henry, "Formal Planning in Major U.S. Corporations," *Long-Range Planning*, October 1977, pp. 40–45; P. Kumar, "Long-Range Planning Practices by U.S. Companies," *Managerial Planning* 26, no. 4, 1978, pp. 31–38.

[5] Robert H. Hayes, "Strategic Planning—Forward in Reverse?" *Harvard Business Review*, November–December 1985, pp. 111–119.

[6] Jack Welch, "Managing Change," keynote address, dedication convocation, Fuqua School of Business, Duke University, April 21, 1983.

[7] William Bricker, "Entrepreneurs Needed," *Oil and Gas Digest*, November 15, 1982.

[8] Arie J. Rijvnis and Graham J. Sharman, "New Life for Formal Planning Systems," *Journal of Business Strategy* 2, Spring 1982, p. 103.

APPENDIX: PLANNING FORMS

A set of standard forms can be helpful in presenting strategy recommendations and supporting analyses. They can encourage the useful consistency of the presentation over time and across businesses within an organization. They can also provide a checklist of areas to consider in strategy development and make communication easier. The following sample forms are intended to provide a point of departure in designing forms for a specific context. The external analysis in the example is drawn from the express delivery industry.[1] The forms are for illustration purposes only.

Planning forms need to be adapted to the context involved: the industry, the firm, and the planning context. They may well be different and shorter or longer given a particular context. Forms for use with other product types, an industrial product, for example, could be modified to include information such as current and potential applications or key existing or potential customers.

The Express Delivery Industry

Section 1. Customer Analysis

A. Segments

Segment	Market Size	Comments
Front door	*Large*	*Secretaries, staff, wants advice from carrier*
Back door	*Large*	*Nonretail shippers; very knowledgeable*
Freight forwarders	*Medium*	*Shipping companies; very knowledgeable*
Individuals	*Medium*	*Infrequent users*

B. Customer Motivation

Segment	Motivation
Front door	*Services provided, brand-awareness, image, price, delivery time**
Back door	*Convenience, delivery time, price, reliability, tracking services*
Freight forwarders	*Geographic coverage, price, reliability, tracking services*
Individuals	*Brand name, services provided, price, convenience, time of day delivered, delivery time*

*Note: Delivery time refers to time of day of delivery.

C. Unmet Needs

- Expanded international coverage
- Overnight international service
- Automated shipping, billing, etc.—link user's computer to shipper's
- Expanded domestic coverage

Section 2. Competitor Analysis

A. Competitor Identification

● Most directly competitive: Federal Express, UPS, Airborne Express, U.S. Postal Service

● Less directly competitive: passenger airlines, DHL, TNT, smaller courier services

● Substitute products: facsimile machines, electronic mail, computer-to-computer links, regular U.S. mail, nonexpress delivery services

B. Strategic Groups

Strategic Groups	Major Competitors	Share
1. *Fully integrated, international*	*Federal Express*	43%
	UPS	25%
2. *U.S.-based, expanding internationally*	*Airborne Express*	11.9%
	U.S. Postal Service	11.2%
	Consolidated Freight	6.9%
3. *Foreign-focused, expanding in United States*	*DHL*	*
	TNT	*
4. *Limited-service couriers/freight forwarders*	*Various regional companies*	*
5. *Passenger airlines*	*United*	*
	American	*
	Delta	*
	and many others	

* Market-share data included only the major players in the domestic market. DHL and TNT share the remaining 2 percent of the domestic market, along with the passenger airlines, freight forwarders, and couriers.

Strategic Groups	Characteristics and Strategies	Strengths	Weaknesses
1. *Fully integrated, international*	• *Broad product offering* • *Worldwide service* • *Emphasis on building customer loyalty* • *Aggressive advertising* • *Heavy investment in technology and aircraft*	• *Financial muscle* • *High brand awareness* • *Control of complete delivery chain* • *Economies of scale*	• *High fixed costs*

Strategic Groups	Characteristics and Strategies	Strengths	Weaknesses
2. U.S.-based, expanding internationally	• Broadening international product line and services through third parties and joint ventures • Strong in domestic market • Targeting niches for domestic expansion	• More flexible cost structure than Group 1	• Lack of control over delivery chain • Lack of brand awareness • Trying to catch up to Group 1
3. Foreign-focused, expanding in United States	• Established international presence • Attempting to strengthen U.S. position • Diversity of services	• Experts in customs	• Still not well-known in United States
4. Limited-service couriers/freight forwarders	• Regionally based • Acquisition candidates	• Low overhead • Low fixed costs • Flexibility	• Service quality variable • Lack of brand awareness
5. Passenger airlines	• Delivery services secondary to passenger carrier business	• Low marginal cost • Brand awareness	• Reliance on delivery couriers • Reliability variable

C. Major Competitors

Competitor	Share	Characteristics and Strategies	Strengths	Weaknesses
Federal Express (Group 1)	43%	• Differentiation through innovation and use of technology • International and product line expansion under way; purchase of Tiger International cargo airline	• Highest brand awareness • Best tracking and reliability reputation • Entrepreneurial culture	• High prices • Potential financial vulnerability due to costly international expansion

Competitor	Share	Characteristics and Strategies	Strengths	Weaknesses
UPS *(Group 1)*	25%	• *Late entry into express delivery market* • *Significant increase in advertising and technology investment* • *International expansion via acquisitions* • *Goal of making international coverage equal to domestic promise of "delivery to every address"*	• *Ground delivery fleet and distribution centers* • *Low costs* • *Financial strength; little debt and huge assets*	• *Service quality and tracking perceived to be lower than FedEx* • *Tight culture slow to respond to changing market*
Airborne Express *(Group 2)*	11.9%	• *No marketing budget* • *Emphasis on relationships with major clients* • *Fastest growing company over past five years* • *Targeting niche markets such as medical samples*	• *Own airport* • *Flexible costs and pricing for international services* • *Experience in joint ventures* • *Use of EDI links to major customers*	• *Little control over international delivery chain* • *Lack of brand awareness*
TNT Skypack *(Group 3)*		• *Australia-based* • *Owns part of Airborne Express, which it tried to buy* • *World's largest transportation organization*	• *Diversity of services tailored to customer needs* • *Financial strength*	• *Weak U.S. presence*
Harper, Robinson *(Group 4)*		• *Does not own planes, boats, or trucks* • *Works with couriers and airlines in coordination role*	• *Sophisticated customs and tracking systems* • *Flexible costs and pricing* • *Strong ties to major customers,*	• *Little commitment to express delivery segment* • *Control over delivery chain* • *Could be driven out by fully*

Competitor	Share	Characteristics and Strategies	Strengths	Weaknesses
		as freight forwarder	*including IBM and 3M* • *Strong international presence being expanded through acquisitions*	*integrated companies*
United Airlines Small Package Service (Group 5)		• *Will carry package on next flight*	• *Can provide same-day service* • *Very low marginal cost*	• *Customer must pay extra for pic up or drop off* • *Little commitme to express delive segment* • *High rates* • *Reliability varia*

D. Competitor Strength Grid

| | | Competitor Strength Grid | |
| | | Express Delivery Services | |
Assets and Skills	Weakness		Strength
Service quality	PA	DHL,C TNT AE,UPS	FX
Use of emerging technologies	C,PA USPS CF	DHL,TNT AE,UPS	FX
Name recognition	C	TNT,DHL CF,PA,AE USPS,UPS	FX
Strong culture	C,PA USPS CF	DHL TNT,AE	UPS,FX
Entrepreneurial thrust	USPS PA CF,DHL	UPS TNT AE C	FX
Ability to generate strong advertising	AE,C,PA CF	TNT,USPS DHL UPS	FX
Customer ties	CF PA DHL	TNT USPS,UPS AE,C	FX
Breadth of product line	PA C	TNT,DHL CF FX,AE	UPS,USPS
Geographical coverage			
United States	PA,C DHL,TNT	AE,CF,FX	UPS,USPS
International	AE,C PA,USPS	CF DHL,TNT	FX
Hub warehousing	C,USPS,DHL CF,TNT	UPS AE UPS,PA	FX
Financial resources	C DHL	AE FX PA,TNT,USPS	CF,UPS
Cost structure	CF FX DHL,TNT	USPS,PA C AE	UPS
Ownership of planes			
United States	C TNT,DHL	USPS	CF,AE,FX,UPS,PA
International	C,AE USPS	CF UPS	DHL,FX,TNT,PA

Key:
AE: Airborne Express
C: Couriers/freight forwarders
CF: Consolidated Freightways/Emery
DHL: DHL
FX: Federal Express
PA: Passenger airlines
TNT: TNT Skypack
UPS: UPS
USPS: U.S. Postal Service

Section 3. Market Analysis

A. Market Identification: Express Delivery Market—United States and Worldwide

B. Actual and Potential Market Size and Growth

	1989	Projected 1990	Growth Rate
Domestic	11.0 billion	12.1 billion	11%
International	6.5 billion	8.1 billion	25%

Factors Affecting Sales Levels

● Improved technology for package routing
● Development of international markets
● Success of alternative technologies—electronic mail, facsimile

Segments with high unrealized potential

● Geographic segments—some routes both domestic and international are untapped
● Peripheral services—assistance with shipping function, cost analysis
● Just-in-time inventory segment
● Medical shipments—lab tests, etc.

C. Market Profitability Analysis

Barriers to Entry

● International
      entrenched overseas rivals
      cumbersome foreign regulations
      foreign business restrictions, route awards
● Domestic
      intense competition
      large capital investment in equipment, technology

Potential Entrants

● Local, national delivery services not supplying overnight shipment services
● Airlines

Threat of Substitute Products

- Electronic mail
- Facsimile

Bargaining Power of Suppliers

- Most players vertically integrated
- Many suppliers—little power

Bargaining Power of Customers

- Large corporate accounts (IBM) have power to demand large volume discounts.
- With the exception of large corporate accounts, individual customers are diffuse so they historically have had little power.
- Customers' opportunity to switch providers has increased over the years, with increased numbers of market participants.

D. Cost Structure

- Cost to own/maintain fleet: trucks cheaper than planes
- Union versus nonunion labor
- Firms that rely on other carriers will fare better in a recession because of lower fixed costs

E. Distribution Systems

Major Channels

- Customer dropoff at drop box/company-operated storefront
- Company pickup on regular route
- Company pickup on customer demand

Observations/Major Trends

- Convenience (pickup on demand) is important segment of the express delivery market
- Proliferation of drop boxes

F. Market Trends and Developments

- Morning delivery is becoming industry standard, increasing cost structure

- Sophisticated information systems to track packages and maintain delivery schedules increasingly important
- Ability to link customers directly to company for automated shipping and billing
- International capabilities desirable for growth

G. Market Key Success Factors

Present

- Guaranteed overnight delivery
- Pickup on demand
- Volume discounts

Future

- Faster delivery times than competitors (which could be difficult since some competitors are likely to be instantaneous)
- International capability
- Provide broad range of delivery services

Section 4. Environmental Analysis

A. Trends and Potential Events

Source	Description	Strategic Implications	Time Frame	Importar
Technological	*Improved technology and increased popularity of fax machines and electronic mail*	*Substitute for express delivery*	*Now*	*High*
	Internal systems development	*Enables companies to differentiate products and compete on a nonprice basis*	*Now*	*Med.-Hi*
	Automated customer linkage systems	*Automated shipping and billing linkages increase switching costs for companies and increase loyalty to specific express delivery companies*	*Now*	*High*

Source	Description	Strategic Implications	Time Frame	Importance
Economic	*Recession or depression*	*Decreased revenues cause cost control to become a bigger issue; increased concern about ability to finance projects with debt as interest rates rise*	*Now*	*High*
	Increased fuel prices	*Should affect all competitors equally; those with fuel-efficient aircraft and large ground networks should fare best*	*Now*	*Low*
	Global sourcing	*Creates a need for competitors to have the ability to serve markets worldwide*	*Now*	*High*
	JIT production methods	*Creates need for express delivery industry to deliver parts and supplies quickly*	*1990s*	*Med.-High*
	Hub warehousing	*Creates a new market for express delivery*	*Now*	*Low*
Governmental	*Domestic industry regulation*	*Undermines the competitive nature of the industry; probability of occurrence is low, but companies will need to proactively fight it*	*1–5 Years*	*Low*
	Landing slot restrictions	*Limits areas of operations for industry competitors*	*Now*	*Medium*
	Foreign regulations	*Affects expansion opportunities for competitors; makes companies unable to compete in certain markets; important for companies to create foothold in Europe before 1992*	*Now*	*Low-Med.*

Source	Description	Strategic Implications	Time Frame	Importa
Cultural	*Fast-paced life-style*	*Creates opportunity for market for individuals to exist; not a high priority because this is a small segment of the market; also, this trend is not as strong outside the United States*	*1980s*	*Medium*
Demographic	*Increased income*	*Profitable companies and individuals with increased incomes are less cost-conscious and can afford the luxury of express delivery*	*1980s*	*Medium*

B. Scenario Analysis

Scenario I: Pessimistic

The world economy stagnates, in part because of protectionist pressures. Electronic mail experiences greater acceptance and fax machines gain penetration. Europe resists U.S. competition, in part because of regulations and in part because of vigorous efforts by DHL and TNT to compete. Fuel becomes a problem.

Scenario II: Optimistic

The world economy is fueled, in part because of stimulation from the common market and Eastern Europe. Alternatives to express delivery grow but not dramatically. Applications for express mail expand. The fuel problem is manageable.

C. Key Strategic Questions

● How severe will the recession/depression be, and how will it ultimately affect the express delivery industry?

● How much more will fuel prices rise, and how long will they remain high?

● Will facsimile machines, electronic mail, and other new technologies make the express delivery of documents obsolete?

- Will the government decide to regulate the industry? If so, what types of regulation are likely to be implemented, and what will be their effect on the industry?
- Will new passenger fees at domestic airports (intended to build a fund for airport improvements) result in better facilities and ease congestion at airports? Will it be easier for express delivery companies to secure landing slots at restricted airports?
- Will people and companies decide that express delivery is an unnecessary luxury and reduce usage of the service?
- Will global sourcing and JIT production methods proliferate, increasing the need for express delivery services?
- Will international competitors enter the U.S. market, and will the access of U.S. companies to foreign markets be restricted?
- In the future, will competition be based on service rather than price?

Section 5. Self-Analysis

A. Peformance Analysis

Objective Area	Objective	Status and Comment
1. *Sales*		
2. *Profits*		
3. *Quality/service*		
4. *Cost*		
5. *New products*		
6. *Customer satisfaction*		
7. *People*		
8. *Other*		

B. Summary of Past Strategy

C. Strategic Problems

Problem	Possible Action

D. Characteristics of Internal Organization

Component*	Description—Fit with Current/Proposed Strategy

* Structure, systems, culture, people.

E. Portfolio Analysis

B, Our own business
C1, Competitor 1
C2, Competitor 2
C3, Competitor 3
etc.

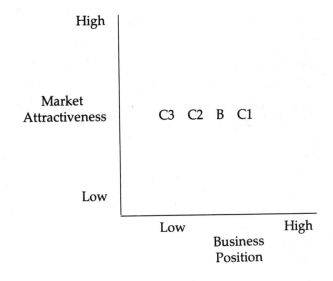

NOTE: The analysis can be repeated by market segment. Each segment can be distinguished by dots, circles, squares, triangles, etc.

F. Analysis of Strengths and Weaknesses

Reference Strategic Group	Skills/Skill Deficiencies, Assets/Liabilities, Strengths/Weaknesses with Respect to Strategic Groups

G. Financial Projections Based on Existing Strategy

	Past	Present	Projected
Operating Statement			
Market share			
Sales			
Cost of goods sold			
Gross margin			
R&D			
Selling/advertising			
Product G&A			
Div. & corp. G&A			
Operating profit			
Balance Sheet			
Cash/AR/inventory			
AP			
Net current assets			
Fixed assets at cost			
Accumulated depreciation			
Net fixed assets			
Total assets—book value			
Estimated market value of assets			
ROA (base–book value)			
ROA (base–market value)			
Uses of Funds			
Net current assets			
Fixed assets			
Operating profit			
Depreciation			
Other			

Resources Required

_____

_____

_____

NOTE: Resources required could be workers with particular skills or backgrounds, or certain physical facilities. A negative use of funds (i.e., profit) is a source of funds. Projected numbers could be for several relevant years (i.e., 19__, 19__, 19__, and 19__).

Section 6. Summary of Proposed Strategy

A. Statement of Mission/Vision

B. Strategy Description

● Investment Objective
Withdraw
Milk
Maintain
Grow in market share
Market expansion
Product expansion
Vertical integration

● Strategy Thrusts
Differentiation
Low cost
Focus
Synergy
Preemptive move

C. Assets and Skills Providing SCAs

D. Key Strategy Initiatives

E. Financial Projections Based on Proposed Strategy

	Past	Present	Projected
Operating Statement			
Market share			
Sales			
Cost of goods sold			
Gross margin			
R&D			
Selling/advertising			
Product G&A			
Div. & corp. G&A			
Operating profit			
Balance Sheet			
Cash/AR/inventory			
AP			
Net current assets			
Fixed assets at cost			
Accumulated depreciation			
Net fixed assets			
Total assets—book value			
Estimated market value of assets			
ROA (base–book value)			
ROA (base–market value)			
Uses of Funds			
Net current assets			
Fixed assets			
Operating profit			
Depreciation			
Other			

Resources Required

FOOTNOTE

[1] This example is drawn, in part, from a research paper by Juliane Babcock, Amy Louis, Jenifer Randall Turnbull, and Susan Underberg, 1991.

INDEX